HENRY WILLIAMSON

AND THE
FIRST WORLD WAR

ANNE WILLIAMSON

SUTTON PUBLISHING

This book was first published in 1998

This paperback edition first published in 2004 by
Sutton Publishing Limited · Phoenix Mill
Thrupp · Stroud · Gloucestershire · GL5 2BU

British Library Cataloguing in Publication Data
A catalogue record for this book is available from the British Library

ISBN 0 7509 3552 9

Typeset in 10.5/12pt Joanna.
Typesetting and origination by
Sutton Publishing Limited.
Printed and bound in Great Britain by
J.H. Haynes & Co. Ltd, Sparkford.

Contents

Acknowledgements   vii
Preface   xi
    Key dates in the Life of Henry Williamson   xv
    The Henry Williamson Society   xvii
'To An Unknown Soldier', page from manuscript   xviii

1	A Dreaming Youth	1
2	Private 9689 and the London Rifle Brigade	7
3	In the Trenches – Christmas 1914	33
4	Promotion	57
5	Transport Officer at the Front	84
6	With the Bedfordshires	165
7	Beyond Reality: Henry Williamson's fictional writings on the First World War	188

Appendix: Maps of the Western Front   213
Notes   217
Bibliography   244
Index   247

Dedicated to all who took part in the First World War

Lost for ever in Ancient Sunlight, which arises again as Truth
(Henry Williamson, The Wet Flanders Plain, 'The Valley of the Ancre')

Henry Williamson never forgot.

'We will remember'

Acknowledgements

I am indebted to the efforts of Brian Dolan of the Henry Williamson Society, who undertook the arduous task of being my research assistant, almost involuntarily, as the original question I referred to him grew into what he must often have felt to be an unending and at times turbulent stream.

Brian has worked patiently through the many obscure and difficult points I have thrown at him, not only diligently but also with the greatest of good humour, which has frequently saved my sanity — if not literally then certainly metaphorically! His letters full of amusing 'asides' have been highlights in the difficult task of putting this book together and I am grateful to him beyond measure. I certainly would not have been able to finish the work within the publisher's deadline without the input of his expertise and time and there are many details that would not have been clarified. A great deal of research never shows in the final product: only the tip of the iceberg is seen, but to see this small percentage an enormous amount of legwork has to be done.

I have drawn also on the work of other members of the Henry Williamson Society already published in the Society *Journal* which is acknowledged *in situ*. However, I am further indebted to Peter Cole who sent me his manuscript notes made some years ago at the Newspaper Library on items relevant to Williamson's life during the First World War.

Major Tim Morley, another Society member, provided me with notes on the structure of the Army hierarchy which gave me something to cling onto within the plethora of 'brigades' and 'battalions' etc. I am likewise grateful to David Filsell who very kindly provided me with copies from his own typescript to further clarify the composition of the infantry divisions of the First World War.

The frontispiece illustration of a drawing by the well-known war artist C.R.W. Nevinson, which is possibly the original sketch for his oil painting 'A Group of Soldiers, 1917' and was given to Henry Williamson by the artist himself, is reproduced by permission of his niece, Mrs Anne Patterson, holder of the Copyright of Nevinson's estate. I would also like to express my gratitude to the courtesy and helpfulness extended by the staff at the Imperial War Museum, London, particularly Jan Bourne, Documentation Manager, who provided me with background information on C.R.W. Nevinson. A short article on this background can be found in HWSJ, no. 34, September 1998.

The Trustees of the Liddell Hart Centre for Military Archives, the depository for the text of the letter from Henry Williamson to Captain Sir Basil Liddell Hart, have kindly given permission for its use in this work (the letter itself is Copyright of the Henry Williamson Literary Estate). This letter was drawn to my attention by John Glanfield, who came across it when engaged on research at the centre.

In his later writing about the First World War Henry Williamson relied extensively for reference purposes on The History of the Great War Based on Official Documents – Military Operations, Belgium and France 1914–18, compiled mainly by James E. Edmunds and published by Macmillan over several years. (All the volumes in Williamson's archive were published by Macmillan, although they inform me other publishers were involved with some volumes.) Thus by necessity I have also made great use of these volumes. All specific references are in situ but I would like to pay particular tribute here to what is not only a most remarkable work but also surprisingly easy and interesting to read.

Quotations from Henri Barbusse, Under Fire (Le Feu) are from J.M. Dent's Everyman Library edition, No. 798 (reprint 1969), translated by W. Fitzwater Wray, introduction by Brian Rhys. Dent's have kindly given permission for their use in this work.

Librarians and archivists are very patient with obscure queries and try hard to find the answers to difficult questions. I am particularly indebted to Jamie Campbell of the North Devon Reference Library at Barnstaple, to the reference librarians at Manchester and Cambridge and the archivists at the Essex Record Office and Hertfordshire Record Office.

Finally, I add to the list my husband, Richard Williamson, for his support in general and, in particular, for photographing the artefacts from Henry's archive.

All quotations from Henry Williamson's previously unpublished archive material and from his published work are Copyright of the Henry Williamson Literary Estate.

ACKNOWLEDGEMENTS

Please note that grammar and spelling contained in Henry's letters home have been kept as they are in the original holograph documents. These letters were written in pencil under the stress and difficulties at the Front; they reflect his hopes and his fears and are a remarkable witness of that era — and became an *aide-mémoire* to his later writings.

ACKNOWLEDGEMENTS

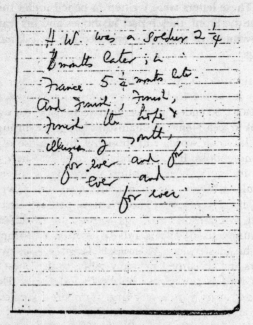

*H.W. was a soldier 2¼ months later; in France 5¼ months later.
And Finish, Finish, Finish the hope and illusion of youth,
for ever and for ever and for ever.*

*(Written in later life at the end of Henry Williamson's childhood 'Nature
Diary' which ended with his first visit to Georgeham, North Devon, in
May 1914.)*

Preface

On the day that the First World War ended, 11 November 1918, Henry Williamson recorded in his diary: 'Armistice signed at 5.30 this morning. PEACE !' So ended just over four years of hellish warfare.

This book traces Henry Williamson's progress through that war virtually in his own words and thoughts, by the use of his diaries, letters and notebooks. It must surely be special to have a first-hand account of its everyday happenings published some eighty years later, partiularly when the man concerned was a writer of vast output and literary renown. Though now perhaps best known for *Tarka the Otter*, Williamson's writings on the First World War itself run to many hundreds of thousands of words, encompassing five volumes of his masterpiece *A Chronicle of Ancient Sunlight*,[1] written in his mature years and acclaimed by many critics as the finest writings on the war, as well as the earlier books *The Wet Flanders Plain*[2] and *The Patriot's Progress*,[3] apart from a very large number of articles written for newspapers and magazines on the subject.

The First World War had a profound effect on all who took part in it and certainly on the very sensitive young Henry Williamson. He came from an ordinary middle-class adolescence and was plunged into the confusion of a bloody and terrible catastrophe, of which he was to write so truly in the future. His experiences in the First World War were a crucible that marked everything that he did, felt, and wrote during the rest of his life. When the war began he was a raw naïve youth as is so evident in his diary writings; by the time it was over he was set towards his life's driving purpose to show the world the 'Truth' as he saw it. His main objective, having endured those four years of war, crystallized in his resolve to do his utmost to show the futility of war, the stupidity of its causes, and to try to explain and educate the world, through the medium of writing, and finally to ensure that such a catastrophe would never happen again.

This is epitomized in a letter from Henry Williamson to Captain Sir Basil Liddell Hart written from his Norfolk Farm on 9 July 1939, immediately before the outbreak of the Second World War.

Williamson, referring to their mutual friendship with T.E. Lawrence as an introduction, wrote to invite Liddell Hart to a meeting to take place on the evening of Sunday 16 July at the Earls Court Exhibition Hall. This letter (which has only very recently been drawn to my attention) contains the clearest statement in existence that Williamson's belief and only intent was purely and solely to maintain peace and to prevent another war:

> . . . It may be that I suffer from illusions; but every experience in the Great War, every thought and feeling I have had since, every word I have struggled to write, finds its meaning and aspiration in the ideas and hopes (still in the pioneer stage) of British Union; and I cannot help believing that in the course of time it will be the means of bringing the truth to our land and people and Empire. At present it is like Cairo to TEL in 1916; and cannot be proved. An Idea.
>
> Please forgive this intrusion if you are busy, or disinclined; but the way to a peaceful Europe is so different from the usual conception, which seems to be leading direct to war.
>
> Yours faithfully, Henry Williamson.
>
> P.S. T.E.S. would have come to this way of seeing things, I believe, had he lived.[4]

Liddell Hart replied on 22 July apologizing for the delay in replying as he had been away. He stated that he himself doubted the value of 'mass movements of any kind' and suggested that they met for lunch later on in the autumn to discuss such matters. Events overtook them and the meeting never took place.

The son of a bank clerk and of a typical Victorian middle-class background, Henry Williamson was an extremely sensitive child, nervous and highly strung; he was always frightened of doing the wrong thing and getting into trouble, yet it seems quite wilfully committed those misdemeanours that would earn him a beating. He was frightened of his father, William Leopold Williamson, who, by all accounts, was what we understand to be a typically stern and withdrawn Victorian man.[5] He was jealous of his two sisters, between whom he was sandwiched, who although they annoyed their father continuously as they grew up, as children enjoyed the softer approach afforded to young girls. Henry Williamson also became increasingly irritated by his mother as he grew into adolescence; he felt that she should have stood up more to what he saw then as his hectoring father, although later in life he saw the situation more from his father's viewpoint and offered a sympathetic rendering of his feelings in his books.

In gaining knowledge for the background events leading up to the First World War, and in the events of the war itself, I have drawn extensively on Henry Williamson's own collection of books, both reference and first-hand accounts by others, particularly the *Official History*.[6] There has been no intention of writing a history of the war, which has been done thoroughly and ably by many others, but I felt that it was necessary to give at least a simple commentary and background of events to show how Williamson's own experience and his fictional writings fit into the total scenario.

In recent years we have gained a far better insight of what the First World War was like, as anniversaries have given rise to television documentaries using archive film which enables us to understand its full horror. In looking at that war, we must not forget the overall view of which the British contribution was only a part: the valiant defence by the French and Belgians of their own countries, and the role of other Allies. Massive losses were sustained by the Indian troops who were involved from the earliest stages; many countries, like Portugal and Algeria, outside the conflict contributed, while the overwhelming participation of the Russians on the Eastern Front until late 1917 kept a large part of the German Army occupied and inflicted enormous losses on them, thus dividing their strength. Henry Williamson pointed out in a letter home to his mother in 1917 just how much more dreadful it could have been if the whole of the German Army had fought on the Western Front from the beginning.

It has been fashionable to vilify the generals of the First World War, in particular Field Marshal Sir Douglas Haig. Although in the years immediately after the war Henry Williamson also blamed the generals, in later years he supported Haig (always the scapegoat) and was unstinting in his praise, particularly in his essay 'Reflections on the Death of a Field Marshal'.[7] It has been easy in hindsight to criticize the decisions that were made during the height of the battle and to point to the huge losses of British men. But careful reading of the *Official History* of the First World War reveals no such criticism. Rather it shows that politics played a large part in all the decisions that were taken and Haig had not only to deal with the politicians but also to constantly adjust his plans (often against his will) to that of the French generals who were in overall charge. He also had to struggle against a very imperfect system of communications and was on occasion deliberately given misleading information. It can be seen from official records that British losses were no larger in proportion to the number of troops involved than any of the other countries, frequently they were less in proportion. This does not make them any less appalling, of course, but war is a bloody business. Death and destruction are inevitable. Mistakes are made. Recently it would seem that the tide has turned although some commentators still persist in this rather bigoted view. However, most modern commentators recognize that much of the criticism has been merely an over-reactive 'wiseness after the event'.

It has also been fashionable for certain sections of the media to vilify Henry Williamson: to put labels onto him that he did not truly deserve because they made easy eye-catching headlines. Apart from concentrating on his later political stance (largely exaggerated and frequently misinterpreted – the letter quoted earlier shows clearly what HW was trying to achieve), some critics have had a most peculiar attitude to his war writings, confusing the fact that his writing was fictional, however much or little it was based on his real life. Instead of criticizing, as some have, the fact that Williamson did not take part in many of the battles that his alter ego Phillip Maddison does in the novels, and thus branding him a liar, the war volumes of *A Chronicle of Ancient Sunlight* should be seen as an overview – a statement about the total war. In fact the work in its entirety is an overview of life in the first half of the twentieth century, a social history encompassing events that happened within that era.

Percipient critics have called Henry Williamson 'the English Proust' for his writings recall in vivid detail time now lost. This present volume reveals the backbone that all his subsequent writings on the First World War are built on.

It also reveals what life was like for one ordinary British patriot. Henry Williamson, like the hero of his book *The Patriot's Progress*, was himself a 'John Bullock', an 'Everyman' of the First World War. His war was not particularly distinguished. He was not a hero. He won no medals, other than the general handouts for being present. He was constantly afraid. This book reveals him in all his vulnerability. There is no deliberate sense of the dramatic, just the everyday happenings of a man caught up in a horrible war. Henry Williamson fought for his country; he endured; above all, he was a patriot.

KEY DATES IN THE LIFE OF HENRY WILLIAMSON

1895	Born 1 December, at 66 Braxfield Road, Brockley, London. Parents were William and Gertrude Williamson.
1900	Family moved to 11 (now 21) Eastern Road, Brockley.
1907–13	Attended Colfe's Grammar School, Lewisham.
1913–14	Clerk with Sun Fire Insurance Office in the City. In January 1914 HW joined the London Rifle Brigade as a Territorial.
1914	On 5 August was mobilized as a private in The London Rifle Brigade.
1914–18	War Service, serving in France on the Western Front.
1919–20	After demobilization returned to family home. Became reporter on *Weekly Despatch*, Fleet Street. First articles published in several leading periodicals. Found living at home too restrictive.
1921	In March left home, riding on his Norton motorcycle to Georgeham in North Devon where he rented a cottage next to the church. First book *The Beautiful Years* (vol. 1 of *The Flax of Dream*) published in October. Other volumes of *Flax* followed and further nature books.
1925	While working on a book about an otter, he met Ida Loetitia Hibbert, daughter of a local gentleman and official of the Cheriton Otter Hunt. They were married on 6 May 1925. First son born February 1926.
1927	*Tarka the Otter* published in the autumn to great acclaim. This won the prestigious Hawthornden Prize for Literature the following year. Prize presented by John Galsworthy (to whom he was unknowingly related).[8] With the prize money he bought a field at Ox's Cross above Georgeham where he built himself a Writing Hut.
1929	The family moved to Shallowford near South Molton, Devon, where over the next few years thirteen more books were published, including *Salar the Salmon* (1935). Four further children born.
1937–45	Bought and moved into Old Hall Farm, Stiffkey, Norfolk. In addition to reclaiming the derelict farm, HW wrote a further eight books and wrote hundreds of articles. Sixth child born in 1945.

1945   In October, exhausted, he sold the farm. The family
            moved to Suffolk but the marriage was virtually over
            and HW returned to Devon the following year alone
            and later was divorced.

1949   Married Christine Duffield, a teacher. Son born 1950.
            Later divorced.

1951–69   His major work, the semi-autobiographical novel
            sequence collectively entitled *A Chronicle of Ancient
            Sunlight* written and published in fifteen volumes. The
            writer and critic John Middleton Murry said, 'This
            will be one of the most remarkable English novels of
            our time.'

1972   Published his final book *The Scandaroon*, tale of a racing
            pigeon, the writing as fresh as the first book he ever
            wrote. (Total *oeuvre* over fifty books – see Anne
            Williamson, *Henry Williamson* for complete list or apply
            to the HWS, see opposite.)

1974–5   Worked on script for the film of *Tarka*, but health was
            failing and task too much. Filming went ahead
            unknown to him.

1977   HW died at Twyford Abbey Nursing Home in London
            on 13 August 1977. He was buried in Georgeham
            Churchyard in North Devon, next to his first home. A
            Memorial Service was held on his birthday, 1
            December, at St Martin-in-the-Fields, London. Address
            given by Ted Hughes (Poet Laureate).

THE HENRY WILLIAMSON SOCIETY

President: Richard Williamson
Patrons: The Countess of Arran, Lord Buxton KCVO MC DL

In 1980 the Henry Williamson Society was formed. Its stated aim is:

to encourage interest in and a deeper
understanding of
the life and work of Henry Williamson

Two meetings are held each year, one in the spring and the other in the autumn, and the Society publish a substantial Journal (edited by Anne Williamson) and also a Newsletter.

Readers interested in joining the Society should contact the Secretary:

Sue Cumming, 7 Monmouth Road, Dorchester, Dorset, DT1 2DE

The Society maintains a comprehensive website at:
www.henrywilliamson.org

The Henry Williamson Society Journal 34 (September 1998) entitled 'Reality in War Literature' contains material which is referred to in the present text, including facsimile reproduction of Henry Williamson's own copy of The Orders for the Attack on the Hindenburg Line, May 1917.

This and other Journals and books published by the HWS can be obtained on application to the Publications Manager:

John Gregory, 14 Nether Grove, Longstanton,
Cambridge, CB4 5EL

'To An Unknown Soldier of the Great War, from one who survived'
(September, 1932)

The page of manuscript reproduced above is from a talk Henry Williamson prepared in 1932 for broadcasting on Armistice Day that year. But the BBC did not find it suitable and it was not used. It was printed with some amendments in *Goodbye West Country* (1937) where Henry shows his sadness that: 'no one has spoken to you, or for you, Soldier, . . . the lack is most sad.'

The manuscript version opens more powerfully than the printed one (which had to change 'voice' to 'words' and lost 'etheric waves'), giving an immediate vision of contact with that mass of dead men waiting in eternity:

> It may be that the etheric waves will carry this voice, or the thoughts behind it, to its destination. The unknown soldier and those with him who did not return, may be waiting, curiously and a little sadly, this address to the living. Therefore the voice must strive to say what is true. . . .

I

A Dreaming Youth

In the summer of 1914 Henry Williamson, at 18½ years of age was, as he wrote in 1964 in an essay published to commemorate the fiftieth anniversary of the outbreak of the First World War, 'a dreaming youth'.[1]

I was a dreaming youth who had said goodbye to freedom and happiness; soon I must leave school and be enclosed in a sunless office. My dream lay in the countryside of north-west Kent which began four miles from London Bridge. Here partridges were still to be seen on the Seven Fields of Shrofften. There were roach in the little cattle-drinking ponds, each inhabited by its pair of moorhens. Below the Seven Fields, which sloped to the grey Bromley road, there were trout in the watercress beds by Perry's Mill. Then came Southend Pond. Thence towards London the River Ravensbourne was dying. . . .

My own woods, or preserves as I thought of them, were safe. They lay up to a dozen miles away. I was the fortunate holder of a card signed 'Constance Derby', giving me permission to study wild birds in Holwood Park at Keston. Squire Norman had also given me leave to roam his woods and coverts at The Rookery, and Shooting Common. Likewise I was allowed to roam the estate called High Elms near Downe, owned by Lord Avebury. My farthest 'preserves' were at Dunstall Priory, near Sevenoaks, and Squerryes Park at Westerham. Not that I belonged to such places. I had written formal letters, as instructed in a book of etiquette studied in the public library, to the owners, and in every case had received a gracious reply.

The Williamson family (Henry's parents, William Leopold and Gertrude, his two sisters, the slightly older Kathleen and Doris, a little younger, and Henry himself) lived at 11 Eastern Road opposite the Hilly Fields in Lewisham in south-east London. Henry Williamson had been educated at the local grammar school, Colfe's, which was run on the public school principle.[2] Although he had won an entrance scholarship in 1907 and it is obvious that he was interested in writing from an early age, he was not to prove a scholar. His energies during his school days were devoted mainly to outdoor pursuits. He took a full part in various sports, particularly being a keen cross-country runner and becoming Captain of Harriers in his last year. He was a keen member of his local scout troop, at that time still a very new and exciting movement for boys. It is particularly significant that he was a member of the school rifle team and took part in shooting competitions at Bisley, where he usually took a very high score. Above all he loved to be out in the countryside, cycling around the lanes of Kent looking for birds' nests and collecting eggs, sometimes with his especial school friends Terence Tetley, Rupert Bryers, Victor Yeates, Hose, and 'Bony' Watson (whose christian names are never mentioned) but, as his 1913 Lett's School Boy's diary shows, he was at his happiest when alone.

Henry's entries in his diary show the thoughts of a typical seventeen-year-old youth; the first stirrings of curiosity about sex, the squabbles and intrigues among the cliques and gangs at school, and their pastimes both at school and at home. Particularly noticeable are frequent visits to the local Hippodrome usually with Terence Tetley and Victor Yeates, but mainly the entries refer to 'birding' expeditions.

This diary was supplemented by fuller nature notes in an exercise book, now coverless and much stained, entitled rather pompously in the self-conscious way of adolescence, and in a rounded juvenile handwriting, 'Official diary of observations made in 1913, as supplementary to pocket diary'. These notes were to be used in his writing in later years, first in the early book *Dandelion Days*[3] as a nature diary that the boy-hero Willie Maddison kept and then directly as 'A Boy's Nature Diary' added into a revised edition of *The Lone Swallows* published in 1933.[4] Here is a direct example of Henry's intense early interest in natural history and it is evident that, like Wordsworth, 'fair seed-time' had his soul.[5] Apart from the tiniest of amendments here and there (a very few commas and semi-colons added, some full names taken out, and a few paragraphs deleted) the published version was exactly as it was written in 1913 and shows his early ability for writing and a marked tenacity for sticking to his self-allotted task over several months, which was to be one of the strengths of the adult writer, but was perhaps unusual in a schoolboy. Already the obsession for writing was apparent.

Henry Williamson left school at the end of May 1913. Unfitted for and uninterested in university entry (although he had passed the Cambridge matriculation examination that March, admittedly with only 3rd class Honours) his last months at school had been spent in the 'Commercial Class' – which according to his later novels was known as the 'Special Slackers' by the boys and some of the staff. Here he learnt book-keeping and other clerical skills, and certainly practised shorthand as there are several 'coded' messages in his 1913 diary. At the beginning of August 1913 he started work as a clerk with the Sun Fire Insurance Company in an office in the City; a fairly mundane prospect and the first step on the ladder of middle-class mediocrity. But the events of 1914 changed the lives of many, and Henry Williamson in particular.

The summer of 1914 was idyllic for the young Henry. He was ostensibly a young man working in the City and, however humbly, earning his own living (from his diary entries it appears that he was paid £5 every two months supplemented by extra earned from working overtime). Yet he was still little more than a child in his emotional make-up, in his inner psyche. He spent Easter 1914 at the home of his cousins Charlie and Marjorie Boon[6] at Aspley Guise near Woburn Abbey in Bedfordshire, where as usual they roamed around the countryside, including the Woburn Estate, looking for birds' nests. His pocket diary notes that he 'saw swallows, martin, chiffchaffs, warblers etc' and found a kestrel's nest in a nearby field 'in an old magpie's nest (in oak tree). Saw birds hovering near, and female flew off nest (one egg, fresh). Just laid today. I don't think birds will desert.'

Then in May 1914 he went by train to Devon, having been invited to spend his annual two weeks' holiday with his father's sister, his Aunt Mary Leopoldina, who rented (seemingly on a long lease) a cottage in the village of Georgeham,[7] a couple of miles inland from the north Devon coast near Braunton. Apart from his pocket diary he also wrote up notes in the previous year's 'Eggs Collected' exercise book, so precise details of this holiday are known. He spent his time roaming the Devon countryside, climbing the steep hill north out of Georgeham to the confluence of lanes at the top of the hill known as Ox's Cross, passing the gate that led to the field that he was in future years to buy. No doubt he leaned over the gate to catch his wind after the steep climb and so saw for the first time beyond the empty field that great breath-catching view across the intervening countryside to the estuary of the rivers Taw and Torridge. He continued down the other side into the woods at the tiny hamlet of Spraecombe. On other days he found his way to the huge sand-dune complex at Braunton Burrows at the end of the estuary, and favourite of all, walking out along the cliff path that led to the wild black craggy clifftop known as Baggy Point. This remote and romantic landscape instantly struck into his inner being and became his soul's home. In later years he would look back at this time as 'The Last Summer'. In that anniversary essay of 1964 Henry Williamson describes that first journey down to Devon.

With bag and rod, and wearing a new pair of grey flannel trousers and Donegal tweed jacket costing 3s. 6d. and 12s. 6d. respectively, I bought a return excursion ticket at Waterloo for 9s. 6d. This left a credit of 8s. 3d. in my Post Office Savings book.

Everything seen during the long journey to the West Country from my carriage window was fresh. . . . Rambler roses grew on all the platforms we stopped at, with beds of wallflower, sweet william, and pansy. Porters wearing red ties, for emergency signalling, spoke in burring voices that made the words unintelligible. Faintly from afar came the cries of sheep, heard during long stops. Enormous glass globes bulged inside the frames of lamp-posts. I wanted the journey to continue for ever. Now we were thundering over iron bridges; below swirled greenish water. An angler with a two-handed salmon rod stood on one bank holding the butt well forward to keep pressure on the fish, which leapt — a salmon! If only they would stop the train.

The valley widened under hills leafy with oaks. Seven buzzards were soaring, tier over tier, in the evening air. Seven! A bird seen hitherto only in photographs in the fortnightly parts of British Birds, by Richard and Cherry Kearton. If only I might find a nest, and take back a buzzard to be tamed, and then set free upon the Hill, where my father and other men flew large kites, in tiers of two and three, some of them almost of man-lifting size and held on winches with steel wire. My buzzard would outsoar them all.

At last, nearly twelve hours after leaving Waterloo Station, we stopped at my destination, a village of thatched cottages and orchards; across the road ran a trout stream. I had been told by my aunt that a jingle would be waiting for me. This turned out to be a small tubby twowheeled affair like a governess cart. A fat Exmoor pony seemed to be asleep in the shafts. The driver had a big brown moustache and said he was Arty who had come for me. We went up a steep hill so slowly that I got out and walked to help the pony which then stopped. I pushed the jingle to keep it from running back . . .

The days were wide and shining, the sands bore only prints of gull and shore-rat and my own wandering tracks. Sky and sea were fused in a candent blue. I walked all day and every day and in the mystic night of dew on rising corn and the voice of the crake in the later milky mists of moonlight. The white owl floated over the hedge and down the lane. Heather was nearly in bell, and the paler blossoms of ling were appearing among the stunted furze bushes of the moor. Twelve, fifteen, once nearly thirty miles in one day, to Exmoor and back, my face dark brown, my bony limbs all sinew. I fished in the brook, using a dark hawthorn fly, and caught my first trout.

His true 1914 diary was more prosaic and he recorded:

Saturday 16 May
Sparrowhawk and 2 missle [sic] thrushes in field. Barn owl in cottage roof. 'Cob'. Nightjars 'reeling'. Cuckoos on gate. Stonechats; hopeless watch for nests.

Sunday 17 May
Spraecombe – deserted tin mines (?silver) works & cottages (wagtail, owl etc). Caves. Cuckoo flying. Cole-tits nest with young. Buzzard hawk & raven (?crow). Barking cry of buzzard & crows shriek when they saw him.

Tuesday 19 May
Found crows nest in coombe at Georgeham – 4 eggs, nearly fresh. There were 4 other crows nests there, all new looking, but empty. Took the eggs.

Wednesday 20 May
Got a fresh willow-wren's egg. In quarry near coombe, saw Kestrel fly out. Looking for nest in cleft on rocks & saw female sparrow-hawk fly out of ledge at base of furze-bush. One egg. Saw magpies building near.
Mist over sea. 'Saunton Marshes' (= Braunton Burrows)

Saturday 23 May
Spraecombe. Yellow bunting. Chiffchaff.

Sunday 24 May
Saunton sands. Ringed plover.

Tuesday 26 May
Goldcrest. 3 nests. Seagulls down cliff.

Saturday 30 May
Spraecombe. Buzzard in fir-tree. Aerie. Many years nests. 3 eggs. Nearly hatched. Luck.

The actual diary note about the buzzard's nest was expanded just a little more in the 'Eggs Collected' exercise book:

May 30
Buzzard, Common (very rare). In wood near mansion at Spraecombe. Wood was sloping on side of hill, composed of ash, fir, oak, and beech. Nest a huge aerie where, keeper said, buzzards have nested for many years. Difficult climb, as nest was situated thus; [a little sketch accompanies this] on horizontal branches. Three large eggs, set hard. One was slightly cracked. Another was scarcely marked at all. The old birds settled at some distance, and uttered plaintive crys: like a large kestrel. There are several pairs about here: they can often be seen soaring over the hills. The nest was I believe, several nests of different years.

Sunday 31 May
Saunton. Plovers (Ringed) Curlews. Saw wild goose.
Whit-Monday 1 June
Home. Baggy point for farewell. Gulls on nest. Cormorant.

'The Last Summer' essay fills this briefest of final notes out for the reader:

And on the last day visited my near and familiar sands and headland and to all I said Goodbye, I shall return, speaking to tree, cliff, raven, stonechat and the sky as though they were human like myself. And at last, the black bag packed and the walk up and down hills until the last descent from Noman's Land, a waste-plot where, of old, suicides were buried, with its views over sandhills to the estuary and far away the blue risen humps of Dartmoor. It was over, but the magic remained as I sat still with nine others all through the night and into the dawn, and Waterloo at six in the morning which, to my relief, was as fresh as the mornings in Devon.

After this break in Devon there were no more entries, only the poignant words that were added on the last page of his 'Nature Diary' in later years that show what this simple holiday was to mean to him for the rest of his life:

H.W. was a soldier 2¼ months later;
in France 5¼ months later
And Finish, Finish, Finish,
the hope and illusion of youth,
for ever and for ever and for ever.

2

Private 9689 and the London Rifle Brigade

Once Henry Williamson had settled down to his new adult life as a clerk in the Sun Fire Insurance Office in the City he quickly became aware of the existence of the Territorial Rifle Brigade. There was in fact, with the official knowledge of the great probability of war, an active recruitment campaign in progress to increase the numbers. Several people from the office already belonged as did various friends around his home. Henry Williamson actually enlisted in the Territorial Force, the 5th Battalion City of London Regiment, the London Rifle Brigade on 22 January 1914,[1] enrolment No. 9689. His diary entry for 9 January states: 'Territorial grant £4, Clayton (Tailor) 10/-' and a further entry on 12 January, 'Paid Tailor £2'. (He later wrote that he joined because he wanted a new suit. Here is the proof.) Strangely these dates precede the official one by ten days. He was expected to attend three drills a month and no doubt his experience at rifle shooting while at Colfe's Grammar School stood him in good stead. Henry Williamson gives a good description of the School of Arms in *How Dear Is Life*,[2] which is borne out by and enlarges on the factual description given by K.W. Mitchinson in *Gentlemen and Officers*.[3] Attendance was also obligatory at the summer training camp, and this was looked forward to with great excitement. Mitchinson also verifies that the London Rifle Brigade did pay a subscription and were the butt of various jokes because of this, being regarded by the regulars and most of the other Volunteer units as a 'smart lot of cranks'.[4]

The London Rifle Brigade, known as the LRB, was formerly the 1st London Volunteer Rifle Corps of the City of London Rifle Volunteer Brigade.[5] The Rifle Volunteer Force was created originally as a result of fear of a threat from an invasion of the French army in the mid-nineteenth century. At that time France had begun to modernize its navy and the British Government became increasingly uneasy. In 1859, in order to create a defensive force should an invasion actually occur, it was decided that each county should raise its own 'Volunteer corps' which would be linked to the growing national interest in rifle shooting (with attendant clubs) and the Lord-Lieutenants were instructed to begin recruiting. The first unit raised by the City of London came into being on 23 July 1859 at a meeting convened by the Lord Mayor and was called 'The London Rifle Volunteers' taking as its motto Primus in Urbe.[6]

Recruiting was particularly successful, eighteen hundred signed up within the first week, and so two battalions were formed, thus giving the status of Brigade, and in 1860 HRH the Duke of Cambridge was appointed Honorary Colonel. He apparently never missed an annual inspection until his death in 1904.[7] He created the regimental toast which reveals the over-riding social make-up of the battalion : 'Gentlemen and Officers, of the LRB'. The original headquarters were at No. 8 Great Winchester Street but in 1893 the Regiment moved to new and fine premises situated in Bunhill Row designed by Lieutenant Colonel Boyes and erected entirely from regimental funds.

In 1908, when the possibility of a new national crisis was perceived, the 'Territorial Force' (despite much opposition) was formed by Lord Haldane. The Rifle Volunteer Forces, including of course the LRB, were taken under the new command. From that time the Bunhill Road headquarters were shared with the Post Office Rifles; 130 Bunhill Row, situated just north-west of Liverpool Street station, was the largest drill hall in London and when not in use for parades was fully equipped as a gym and boxing ring. It possessed an excellent billiards room, which was run along the lines of a fairly exclusive club with subscription fees being paid by its members.

On becoming part of the Territorial Force the battalion was reduced from sixteen to eight companies, namely : A, D, E, G, H, O, P, and Q. The LRB attracted the young, middle-class patriot, mainly young men from the southern suburbs who travelled into the City to work as clerks. Bunhill Row was close by and so it was easy for the men to call in after work for the evening drills, or to use the sports facilities, or simply to have a drink. 'Bohemian Concerts' and suppers in London restaurants were held when the men all wore dress uniform. Another feature was a strong athletics team which competed with other Territorial battalions, especially in the annual march of a 13 mile half-marathon course completed in full marching order, which in 1913 was won by Captain Husey and the London Rifle Brigade team.[8]

There was also a London to Brighton march, probably created

deliberately as an opportunity for publicity and recruiting. In 1911 the LRB did the march in eighteen hours but the London Scottish won the next two years. Then in April 1914 the LRB team, under Captain Ralph Husey, established a new record by completing the 52½ mile march in fourteen hours twenty-three minutes.[9]

Kevin Mitchinson, describing the LRB on the eve of war sums up the situation thus: 'Somewhat understrength, but a unit which through its social composition had developed a particular brand of esprit, and one which had through its marching, shooting and drill, reached a good standard of proficiency.'[10] Official figures show that by July 1914 the total number of non-commisssioned men with fully paid up subscriptions according to the company records was 603. Once war was declared a further 350 men were admitted very quickly to bring the Brigade up to full strength.[11] There was no lack of volunteers and the list had to be temporarily closed, until a Second Battalion was organized in September. It was considered by the men of the LRB that should an emergency arise the battalion would be on home defence duties around London as guard duty for bridges, railways and power stations, or at the most used as a deterrent force against possible invasion of the east or south coasts of England.

So the summer passed and the longed-for annual two-week camp to be held on the coast at Eastbourne approached. The battalion was split into two contingents; the first was to leave on 1 August for two weeks, followed by a second wave later. Henry Williamson was in the second contingent. But he was destined never to go on the camp. The first contingent of men set off by train from Waterloo on 1 August, the Saturday of that fateful Bank Holiday weekend, but the camp was cancelled on hearing of Germany's declaration of war; they were abruptly returned to London the very next day and were dismissed at Waterloo. The second contingent never set off.

In Williamson's novel How Dear Is Life,[12] the headlines read out by Richard Maddison (after reminding his family of their German heritage), from the special Sunday edition of The Trident, were in fact those of the Daily Mail for Sunday 2 August. Headlines and sub-headlines reflect the concern and confusion which was compounded by a disclaimer: 'We print all news under reserve. The Government censorship all over the continent is exceedingly strict.' The newspaper hinted that much news was held back and that it might even have been tampered with at source 'to give a false impression' of the situation in what were now enemy countries.

ALL EUROPE ARMING – PRECAUTIONARY MEASURES – RUSSIA'S PARTIAL MOBILISATION – BRITISH FLEET PUTS TO SEA – MR. ASQUITH ON THE CRISIS – EXTREME GRAVITY – FINANCIAL STRAIN – FOREIGN BOURSES DEMORALISED

FIGHTING NEAR BELGRADE – BRIDGE BLOWN-UP – AUSTRIAN CAPTURE OF AMMUNITION

HOPES OF PEACE – HIGHEST INFLUENCES AT WORK – RELIANCE ON GREAT BRITAIN

GERMANY BEGINS WAR – HER TROOPS IN LUXEMBURG – BREACH OF NEUTRAL STATE – CONTROL OF LINE TO INVADE FRANCE – GERMAN DECLARATION OF WAR ON RUSSIA – FIRST SHOTS

INVASION OF LUXEMBURG – GERMAN ADVANCE – GOVERNMENT OFFICES SEIZED – FATE OF BELGIUM – GERMAN REFUSAL OF PLEDGE – FRENCH PLEDGE – THE IMPORTANCE OF LUXEMBURG – GERMANY'S BREACH OF EUROPEAN LAW

FRANCE'S CLAIM ON BRITAIN – GERMANY THE AGGRESSOR – 'TO BE ABLE TO CLAIM BRITISH SUPPORT'

TODAY'S CABINET – LAST EFFORTS TO LIMIT WAR – THE NAVY READY – GREAT BRITAIN'S POSITION

THE KAISER'S ORDER – MOBILISE OUR ENTIRE FORCE – SAFEGUARDING THE EMPIRE

WAR FEVER IN BERLIN – SPEECHES BY KAISER AND CHANCELLOR

HOW FRANCE MOBILISED – UNCANNY CALM – SCENE IN PARIS – THE LAST WORDS OF THE GERMAN AMBASSADOR

THE DECLARATION OF WAR BY GERMANY – EMBASSY STAFF LEAVE ST PETERSBURG

'The Austrian declaration of war against Servia appears to have been followed by action . . . But the hostilities, actual or rumoured, between Austria and Servia, shrink into insignificance before the military preparations and movements now reported, apparently with substantial basis, to be in progress in every part of Europe.'[13]

By Wednesday 5 August the same paper recorded another set of headlines and text:

GREAT BRITAIN DECLARES WAR ON GERMANY – SUMMARY REJECTION OF BRITISH ULTIMATUM – ALL EYES ON THE NORTH SEA – INVASION OF BELGIUM

HOME FLEETS — SUPREME COMMAND — SIR JOHN JELLICOE K.C.B. — THE KING'S MESSAGE TO THE FLEET

FIRE AND SWORD IN BELGIUM — GREAT GERMAN ADVANCE — BATTLE NEAR LIEGE — TOWNS ABLAZE — LIEGE FIGHTING — GERMANS IN GREAT FORCE — ATTACK ALL ALONG THE FRONTIER

WILL ENGLAND DELAY — KING ALBERT'S SUPREME APPEAL TO THE EMPIRE

30 GERMANS DROWNED — TORPEDOE BOAT SUNK

BOMBS FROM THE AIR — GERMAN AIRMAN OVER FRENCH FRONTIER TOWNS

THE NATION CALLS FOR LORD KITCHENER — IS LORD HALDANE DELAYING WAR PREPARATION? — WHAT IS HE DOING AT THE WAR OFFICE?[14]

The military machine swung into action. The actual arrangements for procedure in the event of war had been laid down three years previously so when the order for mobilization was signed by King George V, this was activated into a detailed but precise routine. The descriptions Williamson later wrote in his novels of mobilization, training and early war were based on his own experiences in the London Rifle Brigade.

> Headquarters was all faces, movement, equipment, rifles, grey kit-bags. The drill hall was portioned off into eight sections, one for each company. Letters on the wall denoted the company areas, 'A' on the left to 'H' at the far end. He went to 'B' Company and was told to draw rifle and bayonet from the Armoury downstairs.
>
> Hundreds of men in all sorts of suits, morning coats, tweed coats, blue serge, carters' jackets, were waiting to join up....
>
> Later in the morning, his bayonet was collected, without its sheath, and taken away with many others in a wheel-barrow. They were, said Lance-Corporal Mortimore, to be sharpened on the grindstone....
>
> After some drill by sections, they paraded outside in the street for a route march. They were in drill order, wearing webbing belts with bayonets only. Rolled greatcoats, water-bottles, entrenching tools, ammunition in side-pouches were left in line on the floor of the company area.
>
> As they marched off, rifles at the slope, angles varying considerably, some people on the pavement cheered. Phillip felt proud to be taken for a real soldier defending England. Led by Captain Forbes who had led the famous, record-breaking London-Brighton march — they entered a park ... the man next to him, with whom he had exchanged names, Baldwin, told him that they were in Hyde Park....[15]

At the end of Hyde Park some of the beautifully polished carriages were stopped by soldiers. "They're commandeering horses for regimental transport," said Lance-Corporal Mortimore.[16]

When 'B' Company got back, they piled arms in the drill hall, and before being dismissed, were told to find their own lunches, and to be back at 2 o'clock. They would be paid 2s. a day in lieu of rations for the time being; and £5 10s. for equipment money — shirts, socks, towel, razor and case, table-knife, spoon, fork, comb, clasp knife with tin-opener, tooth brush, shaving brush, and housewife fitted with needles, threads, buttons, etc. Five pounds ten shillings! Plus salary, plus overtime! If the war ended soon, he would buy that wild-fowling gun!

How Dear Is Life, Chapter 11, 'Military Ardour'

For the first few days the men returned to their own homes at night, but it was decided this was very inefficient and potentially hazardous to organization should an emergency arise, and a decision was made to keep the men together. The London Rifle Brigade then spent a few days at the Central Foundation School, Merchant Taylors, in Cowper Street, before going on to Charterhouse School. (The schools were away for the summer vacation.) By 24 August they were encamped at Bisley, a scene familiar from Henry's schooldays, but which must have had a frightening unfamiliarity about it because of the very changed circumstances in which he now found himself. In the middle of September the Brigade moved on to the main training camp in Ashdown Forest near Crowborough, Sussex.

So the war began for Henry Williamson, aged 18 years and 8 months, No. 9689, a private in P Company of the London Rifle Brigade: a very emotionally young and raw youth in a wild flux of alternating excitement and trepidation. At this point, separated from his family for the first time, he began to write letters home, mainly to his mother. These, when read in conjunction with the added details from his 'photographic memory' that can be found in How Dear is Life, provide an accurate and vivid picture of his life at this time.

Most of these letters are written in pencil and some are very difficult to read. Spelling, punctuation and grammar have been kept exactly as the original holographs. It is noticeable that only the first one is addressed to 'Hildersheim', the name given to their home in Eastern Road. One feels that his father urgently instructed Gertrude to point out to their son that he had removed the German nameplate from the gate on hearing that the two countries were at war, and that the house was only to be known by its number from then on.

Some of the letters show intense irritation with his mother, which must have been very hard for her to bear at such an emotional time, but this can surely be seen as a expression of his own inner fear of the situation. Of greatest interest are his thoughts on the probable outcome of the war. These were no doubt formed from conversation with his fellow men and officers, and from reading the newspapers, and they show that even at this early stage he had a good grasp of what the war was to entail. Readers familiar with Williamson's novel *How Dear Is Life* will recognize how the author used some of these letters, albeit changed about a little, in the chapter entitled 'War Correspondence'.

Postcard
To: Mrs Williamson, Hildersheim, Brockley, S.E.   12.8.14
From: Central Foundation School, Cowper Street, City Road, E.6
May move off (anywhere) at a moments notice so we are billetted here for a bit (may be 1 hour, or a week). Love to all, HWW. Will write when we are stationed.

Lettercard
To: Mrs Williamson, 11 Eastern Rd, Brockley.   18.8.14
From: Charterhouse School.
Dear Mother, Will you please send by return of post that Railway ticket for camp at Eastbourne. I think it is either in the first long drawer or the second in my room. Please send it now, or I shall have to pay for losing it. Last night the Colonel asked us to volunteer for foreign service; 90% of the men did. I have volunteered. I am afraid it means training for several months, then Belgium if the war continues. Don't forget the ticket. I may not see you all again. Give my love to Father and the girls + Grandfather. Your loving son.

                                        [Added at top] Write to me often

To: Mrs Williamson, 11 Eastern Road, Brockley.   24.8.14
From: P Company, London Rifle Brigade, Bisley Camp.
Dear Mother, We are in this camp now. We sleep 12 in a tent like sardines, and have an awful time all day with marching in full kit, on Sat we marched 13 miles with full kit, 70lbs in the hot sun and dust, marching from 7.30 − 1.30. It's a great pity, but apparently my kit-bag was lost in transit, so I am still with these

thin boots and same dirty old shirt and vest. I hope it will turn up soon, or I will kick up a row. Please write to me – all the other boys have them except me. Please send me quarter pound three nuns, one small air cushion (not a rubber one, but a sort of canvas, about 1 foot by 9 inches, about 1/6. Gamages or Boots sell them). Love to all. I sometimes wish I hadn't joined. Tell everyone to write to me. HWW. Love to all. I should like you to make me a woolen head cap.

[Added at top] Write soon. I am not going to volunteer now until later.

Dear Mother, to continue my letter of this morning. Will you please send me as a gift, two one-ounce packets of three nuns a *week* as I can't get it in this hole. The hardships of this life are awful. It takes a lot to exhaust me, as it does father, but after a 20 mile (or 8 hour) march without food & full kit & rifle in the brazen sun, one flops down and gasps for water and breath. Marching here, we (the LRB) passed literally hundreds of chaps, grown men and youths, lying still on the roadside, overcome with sunstroke and exhaustion. I am afraid that poor old Terence who at present has not very good enduring powers would have gone red in the face, then stumbled and collapsed. Many of the boys of the LRB cried with the pain of blistered feet (which were blisters the length of their soles, and generally blood blistered) but not one fell out!! The pace is about 2½ mph as we have the wagons and horses to consider, and there are many blockages in traffic. We sleep like pigs in our tents, and with unwashed hands, feet and body. Thank God the food is plentiful and good, though coarse and badly cooked generally. Will you make me a blue woolen cap to sleep in, covering the ears and head thus. [Small sketch here] Tell Terence to write to me ocasionally when he can spare a moment, and if he wants to. It is one of the few pleasures of this life of continual discomfort, hardship and self-sacrifice to receive a letter occasionally. The general opinion here is that we shall be away for *at least* one year. If this is so, we shall be changed into hogs by the way we feed. Don't forget a small air cushion to sleep my head on. About 12 ins by 9. Not made of rubber, but a kind of thin brown shiny canvas. Boots sell them for 1/6. Please don't pay anymore than this. I may have a days leave in a month or so's time when I will come home for a few days escape from this place. I am further worried by the fact that my kit bag has apparently been lost, thus I am filthy and unable to change. Give my love to Grandpa, and all at 12, not forgetting the Tetleys all my friends and B [his sister Biddy] and father and yourself. We shall be asked to volunteer in 6 months time, but I shan't go as it's too awful (the life I mean) unless we are in great trouble. Love to all. HWW. Don't show this letter to anyone except family & Tetleys & No 12.

On headed paper of the London Central YMCA Marquee. Territorial Camp.
From: P Company, London Rifle Brigade, Bisley, Surrey.   29.8.14
Dear Mother, Thanks very much for the things you sent me. The cap is very nice at night. There is a big YMCA Marquee erected here, and writing materials and tables etc where one can write letters and sit for free. I have got my kit bag tonight, and I now have four pairs of socks, so don't trouble to send me a lot, except one thick pair made by your self, which I shall treasure highly. The LRB has volunteered as a Battalion for foreign service. We are having hard training tonight, but I am quite fit and am not troubled 'physiquilly' [this was probably a family joke] at all. I can bear the hard work now without any trouble. We had entrenching-tool work today, where each man has to dig a mound for himself as cover when under fire. Of course, I see all the papers, as it is like a small town in Bisley Camp. We are all to be vacinated soon, a nasty and unhealthy business. An airship sailed over the camp last night and lighted it up with a searchlight. Great excitement, and we nearly shelled it, but an officer rushed up in time, and pointed out that it was an english type, in fact the 'Beta'. A narrow escape for the ship, as we were loading and an aeroplane gun was finding the range. Please don't join the Ladies Rifle Club, as the kick and recoil would hurt you. It is possible for you to get a pass to see me one day, but I expect I shall have leave soon, so don't bother to come. How is father liking the Rifle Club and special police work? It is all rot about those Russians landing in Scotland. It has been officially denied, besides, they may as well go via the North Pole. I wonder how Robt Sheppard is? [Robert Sheppard, a Colfe's pupil at the same time as HW, was at this time a midshipman in the Royal Navy] I expect his mother is anxious. You must not mind my going abroad. It is not probable that we shall relieve regulars at Malta etc, because the Colonel said we should, if needed (when trained) go to Belgium to guard the lines of communication etc. It is probable

that if LRB does go (and we shall be needed against those never ending masses) abroad, that about one fifth will return alive. The others will join their comrades in the deep, deep sleep. Still, I must not alarm you: I have volunteered because I know you want me to help the allies in my best manner. I had a nice letter from Terence. Do not forget to ask everyone to write occasionally, as it is nice for we poor devils to receive a letter when the others do. I hope Grandpa is well and all right. Give my love to father, and dear Biddy and Kathie. It is very hard to leave home and friends and have only the memory of them left. I wonder if I shall ever see Holwood Park again, and play tennis on the Hill? And tame jackdaws and owls? I wonder, but it is in Higher Hands than mine. I must close now, with great love to yourself and all the others. Your loving son. Harry.

YMCA *headed paper*
From: As Before, Bisley.   31.8.14
Dear Mother, thanks for your letter. I was in hospital today — influenza. Give my old rat (if you don't want him) to Terence Tetley (if he wants it) in remembrance of me. Four deserters (not LRB men) were brought in today. We have three other filthy battalions here — comprising a brigade with us. Give my love to father and the others, and tell him to buy a pull-through with wire gauge on it, to keep the barrel clean. One of the battalions here has scarlet fever — cause, the unsanitary conditions in the lavatories. We have our own run now, properly constructed. "Post goes in three minutes" so I must close. Love from Harry. HWW. I have my kit bag.

YMCA *headed paper*   2.9.14
Dear Mother, Thanks very much for the socks. But really, I have four pairs, and I daren't wear the pair you sent me for marching, because the seams in them would blister my feet terribly. But I shall sleep in the last pair, but please don't trouble to make anymore — five pairs are really enough. Can you send me my woollen sweater when you can, I am very cold at night. My throat is very raw, I shall see the Doctor tomorrow, but military hospital is to be avoided when possible — they are neither as tender or considerate as civilian hospitals. A rumour is current that we are off to Egypt soon, but we are fed up with similar rumours, and don't believe. We caught a

mouse today – had it for dinner. (Liar). How and where is R. Sheppard? Has Tetley his bike yet? How much money has father of mine now? I should like to know where I stand. Hose was discharged yesterday. He is glad & sorry. [Horace Hose, HW's friend from Colfe's, had joined the LRB as a Private but was discharged through ill-health.] By the way, no-one under 19 on Sept. 1st 1914 can go abroad. Therefore I shall probably stay at home with a lousy lot of swines in other rotten regiments, all mixed up together. Please don't send news like this "Manur has fallen" "English eating hartily on dead Germans" etc. I see all the papers as there is a small town here. However, I welcome local news such as Thildonck etc, and what the territorials are doing. Does the Hilly fields seem desolate of fellows? Has slacker Burkit joined yet? I don't like the photo you sent me: it is the worst you have ever taken. The hat is like a flower garden. Send me a nice one, as for instance the one taken at Aspley. I don't like to think that you send me only a badly taken photo, so please send me one of the family group that I took in the sitting room with the old Brownie – a time exposure. Tell Charlie [Boon] that L.E. Hammond, his friend's brother, has rejoined the LRB. Do arrange that I have a shoal of letters from all kinds and classes of people. I should like at least a half dozen each post. This war is a nasty one – the Colonel says that the result is by no means to be forecast – the Russians are so slow, and not quick enough. Before long, Paris will be beseiged and the allied armies will need enormous reinforcements to drive the Germans back. I wonder if Robt will any fight? Don't forget the sweater and letters. Ask father to write. Give my love to Grandpa and Uncle Hughie, and all at No. 12 and all the naybers (much shorter) and to father and Bids and Kath and to yourself and all. Love from your affectionate son, Harry. Don't forget to nail up and repair the birds nest boxes before Jan or Feb. Ever see the hawks now? Tell me if so or not. HWW

From: Bisley. LRB.   5.9.14

Dear Mother, thanks for the Jersey. I really don't know what to say. I may have leave for 24 hours next weekend. Can you ring up and say an excuse? Or write – father dangerously ill – or sister dying etc. Then I will apply to Colonel. Still, don't do it if you don't think it's right. Are we cold here? In the daytime it's as hot as Hades. We don't notice the heat though. In the night the mists creep up, and saturate everything. With one small blanket, and often sleeping on

the ground miles from camp, often with no blanket in the sand, with only an overcoat (this is part of the training scheme) one gets cold as the north pole. I can tell you, you won't recognise me when I return. My hands are horny. I can march miles with full kit without any notice of the heat etc, and my face is dark mahogany. I am what is known as a hard-bitten, silent, cursing tommy! (French foreign legion kind). Tell Terry I would eat Burkit and him now. I was vaccinated today. I have written to Old Bird, Duncan, Bryers.[17] We are being innoculated for typhoid soon. Tell father to look after my bike for me. Don't touch my eggs or my diaries – they are both sacred to me as remenisences of happy days. We rise at six. One hours Swedish. 8 – Breakfast – "Tea" (green water with grease, but drinkable to we "sojers") Bread, fat, "jam" (turnips). Drill, scurmishing 8.30 to 1. 1 Dinner ("skilly", meat, potatoes, bread in a stew – good stuff). 2-4 Drill +c. 4 "Tea" Bread, jam. Muck about till 9.15. Same monotonous stuff everyday. Don't mind it. "Scrap" nearly every day. Will you send me my new pipe – first or second long drawer – "Civic" this shape. [Rough sketch drawing here] No 27 Civic, I think. Salary cheque Sept 29 or thereabouts. £6.5/ – + £1.11.6. (roughly overtime). We must send every available man to France. We shall want 3 million there, perhaps more. When we barter for terms in Berlin, we shall be backed up by an enormous force to enforce our terms. We shall loose millions before this happens. We shall win in the end. But the cost!! It will mean nearly death for England. Let Father write his opinion in length. I will keep it. Love to all. Don't forget pipe: and message to Terry to see me on his bike one day here – I will send him a pass when he lets me know the date. Will you come and see me here if I cant get leave. I will write when. Love to all dear. Harry. *Keep this.*
[On back of this sheet is a cartoon drawing of himself showing the weight of gear etc., see plate 3.]

YMCA headed paper. 'With HM Forces on Active Service.'
9689 HW Williamson, P company, London Rifle Brigade, Bisley,

6 September 1914

Dear Mother, Today is Sunday. I have just wandered up to the 'Middlesex' Club where the LRB men are entertaining their visitors to lunch. Nearly everybody has someone to see him on Sunday. I have nobody. I am as an orphan, an outcast. Still, the journey is long, the days are hot, the travelling irksome, so perhaps I am too unreasonable to expect a visitor. Even the poor boys here — those who in times of peace are carters and the like — are visited by parents and relations, even who perhaps, can ill afford the Railway fare from London. However, it is no use my speaking, because we may go away at any minute. We may go anywhere. Perhaps I shall not see you again in this life — one never knows, and any opportunity there was is now gone for ever. Love to all. HWWilliamson.

YMCA headed paper, and the same day   6 Sep. 14
Dear Mother, I have just remembered that I asked you not to come down so don't take any notice of the letter complaining. If I can't get leave next Sunday, I will write. I shall only know Sat. morning, so will wire if I get it. You can only come in by the pass which I have to procure. Love to all, Yrs affec. son, Harry.
Send old brown boots. Those ones Father gave me. As soon as poss. Keep enclosed letter

[The following sheet is unheaded and undated, but is fairly certainly the letter referred to above.]

I write often, don't I? I wish you would write neatly in ink, I don't like a scribbled letter. Don't forget a nice small photo of the lot of you. Ask Father to send his opinions about the Germans. Mine is this (keep this letter) 'The Germans will crush the Allied Forces abroad. We shall send all our available men — thousands and thousands. They will go in an unceasing stream, but each time Germany will, by force of numbers, decimate us. This will go on for months. We shall lose the flower of our youth. But there will come a time when the Germans will have to subside. But meantime our Expeditionary Force will be no more. More will go abroad — they will likewise go, until about 9 months. Then we shall be able to take the offensive. Russia will be no good in the offensive. She will not reach Berlin, and be not much good to us. Germany will send a force over very soon. It will be swamped almost immediately. Now it will come to this. *Every available man* except those needed for home defence, will be sent on the continent, *millions and millions!!! We shall lose an appalling amount. We must* have an enormous army there when peace is signed, to enforce our terms. England will not be a scene of fighting, except a little, but she will be drained of her youth. France will be crippled for hundreds of years, she will be a vast waste. Russia will not be much spoilt. Her forces will be scattered, and repulsed. Germany will gasp for breath for centuries. England will be exhausted for years but will otherwise be intact. Our fleet will preserve shipping etc, but our men will disappear for 50 years or so. Belgium will be a desert. Austria will be broken. This is my opinion. Please send me Fathers. Keep this letter as a 'curio'.

Picture postcard: 'Queen's Park, Reigate'. Date-stamp is faint – 10 SEP[?]
To: Mrs Williamson, Hildersheim, Brockley, SE
Here today (Weds) marching towards Dover. Writing soon, important news. Love. HWW

To: Mrs. Williamson, etc.   16 Sep. 14
On road. Off for Camp Hill Camp, nr. Tunbridge Wells. Send Mrs. Chapman's address. Writing later. Love to all. Address letters as above. HWW

<u>Please forward</u> 'P' Company, LRB, 130 Bunhill Row, EC
Undated
([the above is] My postal address) East Grinstead. Leave the eggs where they are
Dear Mum and Father, I hope you are all well. I aint received the parcel yet. You see, we are in billets now, and have no kit bags so cant carry any luggage, so big parcels are not given out yet. But small parcels reach me, but don't send clothing in small parcels as I have only a small haversack. Little parcels of about 2 inches by 4 can be had though. We are moving on Tuesday – to Crowborough perhaps, or anywhere. Anyhow if we go to Tunbridge Wells, send Mrs. Chapman's address as I will call for some food etc. So send it as soon as possible. *And do up parcels* well and tight or I shall only get fragments. I haven't had father's letter yet. He isn't very keen to write is he? I can't write to everyone at home, but my letters are addressed to you all. The important news is this. Our Brigadier General (Regular) has taken command of a Regt in France. Before he left he sent us a message to the effect that he is pleased with our training and fitness and hopes that we shall very shortly take our place in the firing line. Very complimetary, but rather disquieting, eh? I enclose letters to be read & kept for me. Show

Terry & Efford those letters from Bird & Duncan. Please send me a 10/ – note as I have lost some money. We are enjoying ourselves now – are fit & 20 miles march is nothing. Good food. Write soon. Love to Grandpa. Yours affec. Harry.

Letter to Henry Williamson from Frank Lucas, Headmaster of Colfe Grammar School

[School Crest embossed]

Colfe Grammar School
Lewisham Hill, S.E.
7. 9.1914

My dear Williamson,

Many thanks for your most interesting letter. The hardships will not be without their use & when you get fit, – why, glorious. I speak having suffered in many a weary walk & climb & ride. Tasks of fatigue are wisely taken at intervals. I regularly take them now. This mention to cheer you in your trial with thoughts of the ultimate gain & the pleasant memories.

Very many old Colfeians have taken the post of honour. We hope to make a roll of all such for undying memory. Never was there a more righteous war – civilisation against despotism. None of us can survive with honour unless there is victory.

It is quite probable the war may be short. What sort of soldiers are made by scurging & spitting in the face. There can be no ideals. The cry of 'Fatherland' has no inspiration for men thus treated.

You & all Colfeians will bravely face your destiny, as we must all. And we must hope & trust though all the strings of our lyre be broken.

Please remember me most kindly to all the fellows & to them & to you my kindest wishes. And when you lie in the field amid all the panoply of war, seeking memories of the past ere sleep falls upon you, think that my thoughts will be with you nightly in my solitary walk between 10 & 11 p.m. with regrets that I cannot be with you to share your fighting & hardships.

Kindest wishes. Very truly yours, F. W. Lucas

Letter to Henry Williamson from Leland Duncan

[School Crest]

SOLI DEO HONOR ET GLORIA

Abraham Colfe Club
Rosslair
Lingards Road
Lewisham
7 Sept. 1914

My dear Harry,

I was very pleased to get your letter & to be in your remembrance – it is very satisfactory to hear of so many O.C's who are 'out' against the enemy. Of those in the L.R.B. Denny is in the Machine Gun Section & I think Cotter & Westmoreland are also in the Regt. I do not know yet of any others. Ask Denny if you see him. He is President of this Club for the present year. [i.e. The Old Colfeian Ass.] Costello is in the H.A.C. Rackham, Lungley & Hickisson are in the 2nd Co of London Yeo/Westminster Dragoons. They are at Pirbright. Norman Gibbs in the 21st Co. of London Rgt at St. Albans. In the 20th Co. of London are 2 Moffatts, Murphy, Moorcock, Rapson, C. Hoys, Burdick, Bailey, W.W. Green, L.Piper, M.Piper, Burrell, P. Wood, 2 Allports, Crossman & Jones – perhaps others. I want to compile a complete list if I can. A Roll of Honour surely. Jack Glaisher is [in] the 7th R. Fusiliers at Colchester. I wish you were all in one Corps – but still it is as well for the Army to have Colfe backbone spread!

I shall be interested to hear how you all get on – my warmest wishes go to you all – everyone of you & I hope I shan't forget you in remembrance before Him, who, as you say, will decide the final end – Let us all look forward to a great triumph & a reunion of O.Cs to celebrate it later on.

Curious you should be in the same old spot. You are rather fortunate to be at such a pleasant place as Bisley. I'll give your messages to Bennett etc. Glad you wrote to the 'old man'.

If you get an opportunity I shall always be glad of a card & report any O.C. you run against, for my list. I am doing 12 hours a day & fear the next No. of the Mag. must be postponed a bit.

All good fortune – *Vivent les Colfes!*

Ever & always yours, Leland L. Duncan.

[A copy of the old Colfeians Roll of Honour, 1914–1918, marked by HW himself with those of his own friends, can be found in HWSJ 39, September 2003, p.28]

YMCA headed postcard
To: Mrs Williamson.   17 Sept. 14
From: Pte. HW Williamson, P Coy. London Rifle Brigade, Camp Hill
                                            Camp, Crowborough.
Thanks for parcel & contents. Would you please send me my
naturalists telescope with the strap securely packed to me. Don't
send any clothes yet, till I advise you. Arrived here (Ashdown
Forest) at 1 am Weds last. No tent pegs available except a few, &
tent collapsed in night (Gale with pouring rain all night) Slept
around camp fire in wood. Soaked. Have you sent 10/ – yet? Will
write a letter when time available. Trench digging here, & houses
being blown up to clear way for artillery for 10 miles.

YMCA headed paper   19. Sept. 14
9689 Pte. Williamson, P Coy. LRB CampHill Camp, Crowborough.
Dear Father, Thanks very much for the decent letter and the 10/-.
You are evidently a 'hot shot'. Six bulls out of 7 on the miniature
is very good.

I wanted the money more for reserve than to spend. It arrived in
time. The other money I had quickly went when we were billetted,
in meals and decent food. Boots being soled, new clothing, brandy
bottle, baths etc. We get a good meal out whenever possible. I will
now tell you why the money was a godsend. We arrived here in the
bleak, cold, windy spot (we are camped on the heights of Ashdown
forest, the highest part of Sussex on weds. Wind continual, with a
fine gritty dust. We arrived at 3pm and ate our 'emergency ration'
¼lb bread and cheese. Rain. Wet through and thoroughly hungry,
we slept all night on the damp ground under the stars. Breakfast –
undrinkable 'tea' (no milk or sugar) and one slice bread. For dinner,
merely uncooked boiled mutton. ½ the chaps couldn't eat it but I
wolfed 2 lbs of it. For tea, no milk or sugar, and 3 Huntley and
Palmers lunch biscuits. Result today – several men high temperatures
and delirious – pneumonia. No drinkable tea today – and 3 loaves
per 12 men for all day. Starvation, slow and terrible. A little meat
(uncooked) & vegetables at 2 o'clock. We can't get enough bread for
the 12,000 men near here. Luckily I can apparently stand it, and
damp and hunger and hardship do not affect me as the others. Still,
its pretty awful. And the life here is hell itself. Work all day, and
nothing at night except sit in damp dark tents & shiver. A pipe is the
only consolation, but baccy is low – no canteen to get more. The

YMCA marquee is a real blessing but only benches to write on. I really believe that if I ever come back I shall be changed evermore – all the chaps are already hardbitten and slowly soured. Enough of this – I can stand these conditions. My vaccinated arm came up in 5 days to marks this size [drawing, pea size] and then didn't fester but healed up and there are now healthy scars. My feet are like horn and I am very hard and fit. Don't let mother send any more food as we may shift any minute, night or day. Navvies at Newhaven are digging trenches and blowing up houses and trees to clear the way for mounting guns. An invasion is shortly expected we hear. The Terriers are for relieving regulars, but the LRB and a few 'crack' regiments will fight in France. We expect to march on London soon, & get new kit, and 2 days leave, so when I send a telegram get the house full of food and tell Terence to stand by. The London Scottish (Barnes[18] is in it) is in Paris. Phil Woods regiment will not go, as they are the usual lot.

The Artists, HAC, LRB, and Westminster may go together, If they go before I am 19, I shan't be allowed to go, so I will be drafted into the extra Home Defence LRB regiment now being recruited.

I bought cake and chocolate from pedlars with some of the 10/ – and also for the starving chums in our tent who are broke. When I come home after the war (how long will it last? I hope Germany will go broke soon, it is costing her £3,000,000 a day) we will have a good time, tennis etc, and we will spend a holiday at Watergate Bay.

Will you, on a Sunday, if you have time, put my bike in preserve. Those gulls eggs in the cupboard which are not blown must be burnt, but please don't burn the Buzzards eggs if by any chance they are there. The gulls eggs are some of them blown, with a hole in them, so lock them in my drawer. I want some of them to remind me of my lovely holiday in Glorious Devon with Auntie Mary. By the way, are the taxes up? If you are hard up, dont forget you can use my salary in the common pool of the family. Spend it if necessary, I shant expect it back at all, and am really not earning it. So if you are pressed at home, spend my £50 a year on Mother & yourself & the girls as a present. I am afraid this war will mean the ruin (financially & otherwise) and break-up of many English families. Be sure that if I go abroad, I will fight like a devil and a Williamson against these barbarians who are doing the Fiends own hellish work in wrecking the peace of Europe, and causing grief and anquish in millions of homes. A chap here who lost his son in the war cursed them, and it was terrible to hear. I feel the same at times, and if there ever is a bayonet charge I will be one of the first to stab and thrust at them. Time is getting short, so I must now end this. When I come home for leave, get a good dinner at 7pm with Terence and only our family to celebrate it. A banquet rather, and a hot bath. Could you ask mother to send me 2 ozs of 3 nuns and 2 ounces of Players Navy Cut medium as soon as poss, as the pipe is a great comfort. Put up the bird boxes in Feb for the tomtits. Now I must close, Love to all, Your affectionate son, Harry.

France – soon Berlin – about 3 months. Watergate Bay Next June!!

[And the following note is written at the top of one of the pages]

On Sept. 28 you ought to receive £6. 5/ – and about £1.11.6 overtime. Don't write a letter of acknowledgement but just pay cheque in.

YMCA headed postcard: date-stamped: 25 SP '14
To: Mrs Williamson.
Just a line to let you know I am OK. New cook sargeant good food. Enjoying myself. 'Leave' possibly for weekend during Oct. Thank father for tobacco. No time to write. Received cake (last parcel received). All grub mutually shared out. Send clothes (washed ones) and homemade cakes etc etc please. All grub is divided among tent – 12 boys. [and added on front] Send washed clothes. Any parcel sent after cake? Not received here yet (Thurs evening). May have leave in 10 days time. Love.

Camp Hill Camp, Crowborough, Sunday.   [*Undated*]
Dear Mother, Father & Sisters, Please excuse my not having written before, but this week we have been full up with work both night and day. We have now a cook sargeant who is a Regular, so the grub is very good, and he is a decent chap.[19] Thankyou for the tobacco (Father) Did you send a parcel after the one that contained the cake? For I have not received any after that, except the tobacco. I should like the shirt and would be glad of two more

pairs of knitted sox, as the pair you made me are good. Auntie Mary sent me from the Stores some Belgium chocolate, the sort we got at Wespelaer. Also could you get some black or dark brown blanket, and make a sleeping bag for the legs only (too large otherwise) make them like this [here a sketch]

flaps that can be buttoned up

You need not slit the bag to make 2 separate legs, but just strongly sew it in the middle, & make the legs very baggy, but see that the whole is not too heavy or big. (I want it to go in my kitbag plus the other clothes, I have bought a large kitbag.) So I should like sox, one army shirt (2/6 each down Lewisham) bag, And now & then a parcel of cakes (home made if you like) and goodies (Don't send any jam). We are now quite used to the hardships, and are enjoying ourselves. The Bishop of London goes back today; his sermons have been excellent. I will send you a little book he gave us. I have applied for leave next weekend but its a doubtful case. It may be any weekend now as I am applying every week till I get it. What do you think of the position now? The germans appear to be holding good positions, and I think that it will take a long time, and a great waste of men to dislodge them; even then they will retire to still better positions. I expect I shall be away round about here somewhere on my birthday, who knows? This war looks as if it will be a long one. Do you read Blatchford in the Weekly Despatch? He is very good this week on 'The danger of the Submarine' and warns us again. I now have 24/ – in hand. We draw 7/ – a week pay. Jack Bryant is with the Royal Flying Corps. He joined about a year ago. Don't forget those things will you. And send my old water bottle in 'the servants bedroom' with the straps. Most of the bottles here are busted, and we can't get any more. Now I must close, with anxious expectation of clothes etc. Yours affec. Harry.

YMCA headed postcard: date-stamped 30 Sp 14
To: Mrs Williamson, etc.   Camp Hill Camp.
Writing. In all prob. will be coming home this weekend. Will send telegram. (Will only know on Sat. morning) Send clothes (in parcel) as quick as poss. love HWW. However its only a doubt about coming. May not get leave.

YMCA headed paper   1. Oct. 1914

as before (Crowboro) (The address on the envelope is swank)
Dear Mother, Thanks very much for the blanket: it will do very
well; also the shirt. We were inoculated yesterday (Weds) at 5
o'clock, and at 7 I was in a low fever and headache, and couldn't
keep from positively rattling with ague. My left arm (where the
serum was injected) is practically paralysed, and it feels as if I had
all the arm festered. Perhaps I shall be better by tomorrow; as it
goes off soon. I am normal now (Thurs) except for arm and
general weakness.

About this leave. If I get it (and only 6 are allowed each week
from the Company – 112 men) I shall know on Saturday
morning; and perhaps I shant have time to let you know by
telegraph. But perhaps I had better send a telegram if I don't come
to stop any preparation. I shall catch the 4.55 from Crowboro' and
get home abt. 7.30. I shall get in L'ndon Bdge at 6.30. I shall go to
Brockley Stn and home by bus. Even if I fail this time, I may
succeed in the following weekends.

No, the LRB hasn't gone to Malta. There are many millions of
rumours going about – witness Penrose's version of our trip to
Egypt some time ago. However, the London Scottish (with them
Barnes) is in Paris.

I am writing this to catch the post, so it must of necessity be
short. I shall catch the 6.45 train back from L'ndon Bdge to
Crowboro: however you might enquire about all trains, as I would
be imprisoned if late back. I hope to come home. Let's go for a
walk on Sunday morning. Must end now. Yours loving son, Harry.

Ask Terence if I come. Would he like to book us two a seat at
Lewisham Hippo for 2nd house Sat? As of old, in circle. Ask him.
HWW. Love to all

YMCA headed paper   Camp Hill Camp. 8. Oct. 14
Dear Mother, Thanks very much for ['cake' crossed out] clothes &
bottle. Don't show Grandpa this letter, because I am sorry that the
sox are too small and too thin for the feet but thank him very
much for remembering me. When you next write could you buy
from Benelfincks or Gamages that small 1/ – Scouts tent lamp
(oil). The water bottle you sent will do very nicely, thankyou. I
have about 9 pairs sox so really dont want any more, except that
pair you are making for me. Don't send any more food yet; we are

full up now. Would you please send me my black dress-belt and sword scabbard they are in my second long drawer. Dont forget my lamp either as I need it badly. As we are getting the new short rifle soon, I expect it will be very soon when we go off, probably where the Scottish are. If we move off abroad soon, we shall come to London first, I suppose, so there will be plenty of time for Father & you to see me off. Has the overtime come yet? You had better take the money I owe you about £2.5. — isnt it? How much have I now, about £9, eh?

I don't know what you mean about my photo. I didn't know it had been taken. I suppose Kathie saw a group with Peroly in it & inferred that I was likewise in a group. We had a group of the tent taken, but I was the only one absent by a fluke. Still if Kathie has actually seen me, I should like to see the photo. I am in a hurry so must now say goodbye. Give my love to all. We went to Tun. Wells yesterday for a swim in the Baths. 11 miles there, 11 back, in full marching order!! Good bye Harry.

YMCA headed paper   Crowboro' 11 Oct 1914

Dear Mother, Just a few lines to let you know that I am all right, and have not gone abroad yet. However, the call may come any minute now. We are busy all the time now so letters will of necessity be not so frequent as before. What do you think of the fall of Antwerp? The place that 'could hold out for months'! Heaven help London if the Germans bombarded it. As we are having & have had a long hard training, one might assume that we are destined for the front. On the other hand, now that 'the pistol pointed at England head' is in the hands of the Germans, we may stop in England for home defence.

It is known from private information here that the Germans are attempting a raid. Their plan, I think, is this. All the aircraft they can get, all the fleet, & all the transports, to strike at one part of our coast suddenly. Naturally all our battleships cant be at the same time at once. Tell Father the Huns haven't started to run yet. If he reads the September 'National Review' he will be surprised at the warning of the writer against the Cabinet. It is well worth reading. It says that in the Black Week, Haldane didn't want any interference of England: Asquith didn't want any Expeditionary Force and Churchill saved the situation in ordering Fleet Mobilization 'on his own' before the war. Also, the Territorials at the event of war are untrained: we have no army really: all are practically recruits now in England.

I arrived safely last week, and in time. The train stopped at New X at 6.50 so I started about 1 hr too soon. If we start for unknown destination, I don't think I shall ask you to see me off, at, say, Southampton or Dover, because it would perhaps unsettle things for you all. Tell Terence to tell me when he's coming down here. Why dont you come one Sunday? Must close now, Love to all, Harry.

Postcard: Crowboro, date-stamped 15 Oct. '14
To: Mrs Williamson
We may move off anywhere any second now, so I wouldn't trouble to come on Sunday, as you might find me gone. But if I am not, I should like you to come down on Sunday 25th. Write me if you can. Please hurry up and send the lamp, whether fragile or not, as it is badly needed. Otherwise it will be too late to use it. I should like a pair of boots from Grandpa – 10½ size – marching. love HWW

YMCA headed paper   *[no address, no date]*
Please come on Sunday as arranged. Write me what time train arrives. Who is coming? What facilities will you make for lunch. Will you have lunch with me at the Crest Hotel here (2/6)? Write and tell me. You cant come any weekday as we may be out all day & night anytime. So come on sunday. Of course I may be on fatigue & then I shant be able to meet you at the station. Fatigue means duty that keeps one to the camp. So then if I am not there to meet you, will you come on to the Camp? Camp Hill Camp, 2nd. London Brigade. But most prob I will be at the Station. Thanks for scarf etc. & socks. Has Terence his bike yet? Love Harry. No pass is now necessary.

Picture postcard: 2nd Brigade 1st London Division, Camp Hill, Crowborough [see plate 5], date-stamp is unclear – [?] Oct 14
To: Miss K. Williamson, 11 Eastern Road, Brockley, S.E.
This is a little bit of our camp. There are about 80,000 men near here within a days march of the coast. Love HWW

YMCA headed paper

P Coy. Camp Hill Camp Crowboro.   18th. Oct 1914

Dear Mother, we have been very busy lately so you haven't received so many letters as perhaps you would like to. Terence didn't turn up today. Has he his bike yet? Of course, as we are under 3 hours notice to move off at any time, I couldn't possibly come home with him, as it is too great a risk without a pass. About that lamp. As we burn candles (which we have to buy ourselves) in the tent, any little oil lamp would be a blessing. Some have electric lights in the other tents, & others hurricane lamps. We have to burn candles, so a little oil lamp would be a blessing. Still, as you are uninclined to get one as I particularly asked you, perhaps I had better write to other people for it. So please don't trouble any more about it. I will arrange for it & any other little necessities of life that help to improve the existence here. If there are any little debts owing to you from me, please deduct from the sum that you have. Also do you think it advisable to get rid of my suits and saleable things at home? In all probability I shall never have need of them again. So if you want the room, get rid of the contents. There is some talk of going away at dawn tomorrow. I believe we are to fill up the gaps in the Kings Royal Rifles, that were sadly decimated at the Battle of the Aisne. If that is so, then it is goodbye for most of the chaps for ever. So if you hear of our departure you musnt mind at all. I am glad that Efford has not forgotten me. I hope that Father is enjoying his rifle practice. Tell him the German church at Forest Hill was raided, & found to be full of ammunition and machine guns etc. in the crypts and vaults. I expect there are many similar about. Heaven help us if by any chance the Germans manage to land a raiding force. We shall then know what it is to be betrayed, as Antwerp has learnt. We have a German officer as an officer in the LRB, naturalized it is true, but nevertheless a German. Incidentally, he spends two months every year in the Fatherland. I wonder? By the way, dont you think that the situation in France is serious? The Germans are very near our coasts now. The nights are very cold here. In fact, terribly bleak. But we now have three blankets, and sometimes 4, apiece. I dont think you need trouble Grandpa to remember me as regards any little present. How is Kathie getting on? Is she doing well at the Prue, or does she still owe money to a few Tailors? I hope she is earning a large income now. How is Biddy? Has she left school yet? Has Lieut. Williams called yet? If so, how did he shape? I must close now, as I must prepare my equipment. Hoping that you are all well and comfortable, I remain, Your affectionate son, Harry.

PS D.Milo sent me a p.c. saying she was coming to Crowborough today, but I did not see her. Please send Tom Efford's gift as soon as possible. PS. I suppose that you are coming down next Sunday? Write and tell me the time of the arrival of the train, and I will meet you if poss. Mind you tell me who is coming & get Kath & Bid to come. Ask Terence to always give me long notice when he is coming to avoid disappointment on both sides. Please dont forget to tell him. Has he got his bike?

YMCA headed postcard: date-stamped 23 Oct. 14
To: Mrs Williamson, etc
8 o'clock Weds morning. Order just arrived 'Battalion will embark on Saturday' (destin. unknown) may therefore be in London any time before Saturday. Dont come to Crowboro. Will wire if we are coming to town. Or if we entrain anywhere. May be go to S. Africa. Love HWW

Lettercard: date-stamped 29 Oct. 14
To: Mrs Williamson, etc.
Camp Hill Camp.
Dear Mother, Come on Friday with Father – in time for tea (4pm) at the Camp here. The LRB is one of several regiments (Territor) for the Front in France. No leave will be obtained at all. Southampton probably on Sat. at noon. If Father & you dont come on Friday, the last chance will have departed. Bring some money for me, a brandy flask (small for pocket) Dont fail. Wire reply. Love HWW

Postcard: post-marked Chichester 4.45 PM 4 Nov. 14
To: Mrs Williamson, etc.
In the train LBSc Ry, Weds 4 o'clock. Just passed Shoreham. We have trained to Southampton now. May go to France tonight (we are for France official) Goodbye, good luck, no time for more. Love Harry.

Postcard: date-stamped Crowboro 5 Nov. 14
To: H.W. Williamson, Esq. Hildersheim, Brockley, SE
Camp Hill. Wednesday. [Written in another's hand]
Just off. Quite well – HWW per W Blelarks
Williamson wished me to send the above message. He seemed
well & happy.

The troopship *Chyebassa*, formerly of the British India Steam
Navigation Company took them to Le Havre, 4 November 1914.[20]
Mitchinson described the scene thus: 'Companies were allocated
particular areas, "P" for example being crammed in a hold with
rudder chains clanking below and horses stamping above. Once
under way the men were allowed to move about the ship. The
Chyebassa was one of fourteen transports being shepherded across by
three destroyers on a calm sea and the troops disembarked at Le
Havre early the next morning.'[21]

In the Trenches – Christmas 1914

When the *Chyebassa* decanted about 850 men, including thirty officers,[1] of the London Rifle Brigade at Le Havre on the morning of 5 November 1914, the war had already passed its first phase. The initial German advance across Belgium had been catastrophic, meeting little opposition from the poorly equipped and ill-organized Belgian army, despite their valiant attempts at defence. (As a neutral state Belgium had not been actively preparing for war, however apprehensive their leaders may have been.)

The first wave of the British Expeditionary Force (BEF) under Field Marshal Sir John French had landed in France on 16 August: four infantry divisions formed into two army corps commanded respectively by General Sir Douglas Haig and General Sir Horace Smith-Dorrien, plus a Cavalry Division under Major General Allenby. They hastened to the scene of the fighting and two days later were at Le Cateau, where Sir John French set up his General Headquarters, and shortly advancing on Mons. A map in the *Official History* giving the disposition of troops shows the odds against them; a weighty and solid line of the First to Seventh German Armies against a much smaller and scattered First to Fifth French Armies along their own border, with one small Belgian Army in the middle of Belgium (Liège had already fallen as the first casualty of the war) and finally the equally small contingent of the BEF between Le Cateau and Mons.[2]

By 21 August Brussels had fallen and the Belgian king and government retired to Antwerp. On 22 August the French Armies and the BEF were facing the German Armies just north of the French/Belgian Border and on Sunday 23 August the BEF contingent of 36,000 men met the German Army at Le Condé Canal near Mons. Fighting was fierce. The first lesson the British learnt was that their 13 pounder guns did not have as good a range as the new 'heavy' guns of the Germans but equally that their own rifle power was superior. But the German thrust was too much for them and by 24 August the Battle of Mons was over; the British troops were in full retreat against the German advance, whose goal at this point was to take Paris. By the time they reached Le Cateau General Smith-Dorrien decided the men were too exhausted to continue and therefore that he would stand and fight. A fierce battle ensued with severe losses and the men had eventually to give way, but this gained time for the main body of troops to make an orderly retreat rather than the virtual rout previously.[3] General Joffre, Commander-in-Chief of the French army, became a rock of strength despite the fact that his men were suffering traumatic defeats (due to their own basic weakness against the better organized and equipped Germans).[4]

At the beginning of September the Germans were advancing on all fronts and certainly had the upper hand. Their goals were being achieved and they must have been assuming victory was in sight.[5] The Allied retreat and the German advance continued and by 4 September the Germans had crossed the River Marne (which joins the Seine just west of Paris). Now the French and British armies were facing the Germans in a long line which stretched across to the German/French border in the east and curved up on its western end to the north-east of Paris, the BEF being situated in a vital position at the heel of the curve just 10 to 15 miles to the south-east of Paris, with the Sixth French Army on their left to the north and the Fifth French Army to their right to the east.[6] General Joffre saw this line-up as a great chance to turn the tide. A battle plan was drawn up. On 5 September the Sixth French Army under General Maunoury situated to the north-east of Paris, facing the First German Army under General von Kluck, went into action.

The Battle of the Marne had commenced. Due to a confusion of orders the French Fifth commanded by D'Esperey and facing the Eastern flank of von Kluck's German First, and the French Ninth under Foch facing von Bülow and the Second German Army, did not take action until the following day, with the French Fourth, Third and Second Armies spread out to their right against the German Fourth, Fifth and Sixth. The BEF, further back and facing von Kluck, were even slower to start but gradually made sure progress. This time the Allies took the advantage. The Germans were gradually forced back until by 12 September von Kluck's army was once again on the north side of the River Aisne with the other German Armies just south of it and curved down to the eastern border, an Allied gain of nearly 40 miles. But the British and the French had difficulty crossing the Aisne quickly. This delay gave the Germans the opportunity to gain the higher ground, to get reinforcements to the area and to entrench themselves. This was the beginning of the stalemate. It was now six weeks since the opening offensive by the Germans so the Schlieffen Plan (see Note 4, p. 222) was not working exactly to order. The first phase of the war was over.

The German/French front now turned almost directly north and, each trying to outflank the other, gradually worked towards Lille (and therefore Dunkerque and the other Channel ports) as clearly shown in the *Official History*.[7] The British remained with the French Fifth Army to defend the original line north of the Aisne against the German Seventh Army. But at the end of September it was decided to withdraw them from this position which isolated them (particularly the Commanding Officers) from BEF reinforcements now landing in the north and, in order to confuse the enemy, this commenced secretly at night at the beginning of October. They were to return to their original positions and objectives and together with the reinforcements to guard the Channel ports against the Germans and assist Belgium and France against the enemy threat there.

Meanwhile a brigade of Royal Marine Infantry troops had landed at Dunkerque on 20 September, with overall orders to harry the enemy communication lines and to give the impression of being the advance of a larger body of troops. A small force of these were then sent forward to help the grave situation at Antwerp, on which German troops were advancing, but they were too small in number to be of real use. Antwerp, under threat of imminent attack, was evacuated on 8 October amid much confusion. The Marine troops helped cover the retreat. King Albert and his government moved to Ostend. The civilians of Antwerp and elsewhere in Belgium had to pay a terrible price under enemy occupation.

Further BEF troops were sent over and Field Marshal Sir John French and his original troops arrived from the Aisne. General Headquarters were set up at St-Omer. General Joffre and Sir John French drew up fresh plans. It was decided that the British Force should assist the French Tenth Army which was now facing the German Sixth (already joined by large reinforcements) in this northern area. By 15 October all had concentrated and were dug in in the area from Arras northwards to Ypres – the area to be known to us all simply as the Flanders Plain.

The First Battle of Ypres commenced directly and continued until 17 November, with a crisis point on 30/31 October. It is then that one finds the first mention of the 14th County of London Battalion, the London Regiment – known as the London Scottish – and it is of considerable interest to compare the actual train of events with Henry Williamson's fictional account of the 'London Highlanders' in How Dear Is Life. The London Scottish had arrived in France on 16 September[8] and the route of the 'Highlanders' as described in the novel is confirmed in their regimental history.[9] They arrived at Ypres on the night of 30 October and their participation in the battle that followed is recorded in the Official History: 'The London Scottish 750 strong, under Lieut-Col. G.A. Malcolm, the first Territorial Force battalion to go into action, had been sent up to Ypres to the I Corps near Hooge on 30 October.' On arrival they met with some confusion and were shunted around from place to place, eventually being sent to St Eloi but again orders were changed and General Haig sent them back to Ypres to 'proceed by motor-buses' to assist the hard-pressed Cavalry Corps, under the command of Lieut.-Gen. Allenby, who were trying to hold the Messines Ridge. They went into action on the morning of 31 October, occupying trenches and subjected to heavy artillery and machine-gun fire. Another contingent was sent to oppose the Germans threatening Wytschaete where the men met heavy fire with little cover. Their losses at this battle were 321 men.[10] They were considered to have fought with great bravery. The regiment was sent a telegram of congratulations and thanks from Sir John French and a letter of approbation from General Allenby. Henry Williamson shows Phillip to have a defective rifle at this point in How Dear Is Life. Official records confirm that fifty per cent of the London Scottish rifles were defective. Apart from the official histories, Henry Williamson made use of Field Marshal French's personal account of the fighting as a source for material.[11] Henry's copy has several marginal notes marking dates and times against the descriptive text[12] and here the text of the letter from Allenby and French's own telegram are given in full.[13]

The London Rifle Brigade arrived at Le Havre on the morning of 5 November. The Short History of the LRB relates that disembarkation was 'a tedious business, and the progress through the town to the rest camp at the top of the hill was one of the worst forms of route march the Battalion had ever experienced. Frequent checks but no halts, taught the true weight of packs and kit; and a perfunctory inspection on arrival at the camp completed the exhaustion.'[14] Colonel Bates [only Capt. at the time] particularized the chaos by giving as example the fact that they only learnt on landing 'quite by accident' that officers no longer wore Sam Browne belts or carried swords, engendering 'a frantic rush at the last minute to procure web equipment' while 'swords and belts were left at the base'. The complaints of the men were no doubt somewhat more basic!

The march taken to the rest camp at the top of the hill by the 'London Highlanders' in *How Dear Is Life* is that taken by Henry Williamson and the LRB.[15] Reaching the camp they found it a dirty and ill-organized place. There were not enough tents, and the men had to sleep in the open air. The following day was equally chaotic. Colonel Bates noted (in restrained tones that obviously belie his real feelings) in his *Short History of the LRB*:

> There was much to learn about entrainment in France. . . . An advance party had been sent forward some two hours earlier, and the rest of the Battalion and the transport were at the station by 4 p.m. The train was not due to leave until 9p.m. French trains and the French railway system became familiar later on in all their ramifications but at first Hommes 40 Chevaux (en long) 8 aroused suspicions that were only too well justified in the next 21½ hours before the train reached its destination. The experience was not a unique one.[16]

Henry Williamson's first letter home from France was written, in pencil, sometime during that first day, although not posted until 11 November.

Date-stamped Army Post Office [APO] 39, A, 11 Nov. 14. Passed by Censor 1113
To: Mrs Williamson, Hildersheim, Eastern Rd, Brockley, S.E., L'Angleterre.
From: [Address heavily scored out]   6 November 1914
Dear Mother, I am quite well. I am not allowed to state where I am or any clue whatever to my whereabouts as all letters are read (those written by us) before being sent abroad. However we are now in a 'Rest Camp' at a place where wounded soldiers are 'rested' after having been hit by the Germans. Did you get my postcard sent from the train? [Here a sentence has been scored out] We don't know what our job is but I expect it will not be very exciting at first. I hope you are all well at home. The address at the head of this letter will reach me all right. (see my post

script) We haven't seen any signs of war yet. We are allowed two ounces of tobacco a week. Write as often as you like, and number each letter as it is sent. Then I will know if any are lost. The bread here is very nice and the rolls resemble those at Brussels. Send an English newspaper (not the Daily Mail as we have it here) occasionally. We are forbidden to send picture postcards now. I am in a hurry to catch the mail, so I must close. Give my love to Terence & to all at home. Goodbye, & dont expect a letter too often, your loving son Harry. PS Since writing this letter we have had to cross out the name of our battalion & also the general address. However if you like address letters to me as before C/o GPO. You had better mention that we are not the home service one. Also I have scratched out several sentences that perhaps the Censor would not pass. HWW. PS I was not seasick.
[Countersigned at bottom and on envelope by J.R. Somers-Smith][17]

When the Battalion arrived at St-Omer on 7 November[18] they found they were not expected, and therefore no arrangements had been made for accommodating them, and so they had to wait in the train for a further three hours. Eventually the first night was spent in 'some old artillery barracks . . . about as dismal and dirty as can be imagined'.[19]

The following day they marched 3½ miles south-west to a 'large unfurnished and unfinished convent . . . There was no water laid on, no light, no method of heating or of drying clothes, no furniture, and no possibility of supplementing rations. . . . Training, which consisted chiefly of trench digging and artillery formation, was carried out daily regardless of weather.'[20] Against this paragraph HW has noted: 'Wisques. First heard the guns here at night.'

The Battalion stayed at the Convent at Wisques for a week. Mitchinson fills out the above terse description, confirming that it rained every day and that the men were not allowed to wear their greatcoats so were continuously wet and miserably cold. Apart from digging, they practised loading and firing their rifles which 'had been converted to take the new ammunition, unlike those used by the London Scottish on Messines Ridge a few days earlier.' According to Mitchinson some of the men were nervous of guard duty in the convent crypt where the shrouded coffins of long dead nuns loomed out of the darkness as they patrolled.[21]

Date-stamped APO, B, 42 : Nov. 17, 14 : Censor 1113

To: Mrs. Williamson, etc.   November 11

Dear Mother, This letter cant tell you much for the authorities are very strict about us writing. However, since landing at —, we travelled 36 hours in the train and arrived at the town of —. We stopped the night in barracks, & the next day (Sunday) we marched to a convent where we are now staying. We [this sentence is scored out but is, with difficulty, readable: 'heard the Germans afar attacking all day & can see their flashes at night.'] We are having a hard time but its use will be seen & appreciated when we take our turn in the trenches. You must not worry about me at all, & if I should be the one to be struck, then you will know that I have at least done my duty. I saw Barnes [of the London Scottish] in hospital at —,[22] & he wants get back at the Germans & we are all keen to rival the Scottish in the firing line.

13.11.14 The enclosed letter has been soaked through with rain as all day Friday we were digging trenches in the pouring rain. Please send plenty of chocolate at once, as very shortly we may be thrashing Germans & then it is much needed when cramped & cold. Write and tell Auntie Mary that I received her letter which was much welcomed, & I am afraid I shant have much time to write back. I have a fearful cough thro the rain & wind. Tell Auntie Mary that she is quite right about where we are. I don't think I shall meet Captn Parry Jones of the Welch Fusiliers, as they are at the actual firing line & we are not. I must close now, with love – Harry. PS Please send chocolate well packed & 2 pairs thick *best* socks at once. Enclose addressed envelope with every letter.

[Countersigned on letter and envelope 'G.E.S. Fursdon'][23]

During 15–22 November the British line was reorganized. In his summing up in the *Official History* at this point, Brigadier General Edmonds stated that 'The [First] Battle of Ypres formed the last phase of open fighting, before the belligerents settled down to undiluted trench warfare.'[24] This then was the situation that Henry Williamson and his fellow soldiers of the London Rifle Brigade were about to enter.

On 15 November orders were received for the Battalion of the London Rifle Brigade to proceed to the front. The *Official History* states that the '5th City of London Battalion, The London Regiment (London Rifle Brigade) arrived in France 5th November 1914 [and went] To 11th Brigade, 4th Division, 19th November 1914.' The

11th Infantry Brigade was composed of the 1st Somerset Light Infantry, 1st East Lancashire Regiment, 1st Hampshire Regiment and The Rifle Brigade (The Prince Consort's Own) (a totally separate Regiment and not to be confused with the London Rifle Brigade).

On 16 November the men marched from the convent at Wisques to Hazebrouck: 'The distance was 17½ miles, and the roads pavée almost the whole way. There was also some rain. . . . However not a single man fell out of the column.'[25] The following day they marched a further 11 miles to Bailleul where they spent two nights in billets, and where they found the Artists' Rifles and Honourable Artillery Company also billeted. Colonel Bates remarked that 'while on the march it had been possible, for the first time, to see aeroplanes being shelled'. On 19 November they 'moved one stage nearer to the firing line in a snow-storm'. Henry has written in the margin 'Romarin'.[26]

Date-stamped APO 11, B, 24.11.14 : Censor 1113
To: Mrs Williamson, etc.   November 19th 1914
Dear Mother, I received several letters from you lately. We have moved about a lot since last writing, and we are now in a little village in the country we visited two years ago with Uncle Percy & Grandfather. You remember?[27] As I explained last time we have to give no information in letters, as, if they fell into wrong hands it might be useful to our enemies. All day & most of the night huge detonations shake the air around us, and the sounds are rather awe-inspiring at first. You remember Barnes? Well he has returned all right from the trenches, after several days of firing. I saw him the other day, and he does look gaunt and hard-bitten. You may not hear from me by letter (but you will by the printed regulation postcard) because we shall have no time to for reasons that you may possibly guess. So don't worry if you dont hear from me except by card for several weeks perhaps. We saw Taube aeroplanes being shelled by the British the other day, one was brought down, I believe. We also saw several ugly dirigibles, hovering over the battle, trying to get ranges etc. It is rather exciting out here. You know ['father's', crossed out] Granfather W's regiment?[28] Well they are out here. They have been in action only once, & that while digging reserve trenches, a long time ago. I expect you read of it in the 'Daily Mail'. They are rather tired of doing nothing. I have obtained another identity disc. Goodbye now, & love to all & mind you dont worry, your loving son, Harry.

[Countersigned on letter and envelope 'G.E.S. Fursdon']

On 20 November they were visited by the Commanding Officer of the 11th Infantry Brigade, Brigadier General Hunter-Weston (according to a note by Williamson, known as 'Hunter-Bunter')[29] who addressed the officers and explained how the Battalion would gradually be assimilated into the Front Line. At this point the Battalion was reorganized from eight companies into four. This 'doubling up' had already been carried out by the regular troops. Colonel Bates states that for some unknown reason the LRB had not been allowed to carry this out previously.[30] Henry's Company 'P' together with 'G' became No. 3 Company under Major Burnell. At dusk that evening half the Battalion proceeded via Ploegsteert to the trenches on the eastern side of Ploegsteert Wood. The Companies were on trench duties on a rotational basis and when not at the Front were billeted in 'Plugstreet' village and at a nearby farm. Colonel Bates states that when the men were not actually in the line as 'support' troops, the whole day was invariably taken up with 'fatigues' of all kinds. This earned them the nickname 'Fatigue Fifth'. The main tasks were building dug-outs and the remaking of support lines in the wood, one of which in particular they named 'Bunhill Row' after their luxurious (as it then must have seemed to them) London headquarters. These roads were called 'corduroy' paths, as Henry notes in an irritated margin note in the *Official History* where they are referred to as 'duck boards'.[31] They consisted of thin wooden poles from tree branches 'corded' together and laid down to form a solid route.

A postcard, labelled 'Correspondence militaire' [not the official printed type]
Date-stamped APO 11, B : Censor 1113 : 8.12.14

To: Mrs Williamson, etc.   6 December
Quite well but rather seedy: just returned after 3 days in trenches [then crossed out but readable] – flooded out by rain. Rotten time this time: continually shelled and maxims and rifle fire. Thank Auntie B. & Mary & Effie for parcels & Granpa. Have got fur coat. Send chocs: sweets, cake, sardines, milk etc., Love Harry.

Henry Williamson does not mention in this postcard the visit of His Majesty King George V who paid his first visit to the Army accompanied by HRH The Prince of Wales between 30 November and 5 December, seeing all the troops except those in the trenches,[32] where Henry would have been at that time. But he heard all about it from his comrades, and the opening paragraphs of *A Fox Under My Cloak* describe the occasion as the London Highlanders stood to attention 'silent, staring ahead, depersonalized' for the inspection.[33]

Date-stamped APO 12, B, 16 Dec. 14: Censor 1675
To: Mrs Williamson, etc.
I am in No. III Company now.   Sunday December 13
Dear Mother, As I write, I am sitting by the stove of a little cottage in the Belgium village of —. Last night we returned from the trenches (for the third time) and we thanked God that we had a decent place to go to. It has been awful in the trenches. For two days and nights we have been in nearly 36 inches of mud & water. Can you picture us, sleeping standing up, cold and wet half way up to our thighs, and covered in mud. As we crept into the trenches at dead of night over 1 foot of mud, the Germans sent up magnesium flare, and we had to crouch flat while scores of bullets spat amongst us. The people at home cannot imagine the terrible hardships we go through. Think of us in the River Ravensbourne at home in the mud & water for 50 hours on end! When I returned my overcoat weighed 24 lbs! My feet now are twice their normal size, and I have such rheumatism in my right leg that it is agony to move. I have received the compass a long time ago. I dont understand what you mean by saying that you will refund the extra postage if I had to pay any. The last letter you wrote is a very funny one, and appears to be more of a business letter than one to a son at the front. Also I received the cake, plum pudding, sardines, choc, braces etc. & newspaper. When you send again would you send the choc. as the blue tinned stuff is, as loose choc gets fearfully wet & slimy over here. Also the tinned cafe au lait is just the thing and I would like some with every parcel, also small tins of sardines (i.e. one tin can then be opened at a time & will do for each meal) also the oxo is welcome. Send also a box (tin box if poss) of matches & a fat (thick) candle with each parcel. Also the cake & plum pudding are very good. Certainly keep my eggs if you would treasure them. I have the cross you gave me, and treasure it much. Send a stout addressed envelope in each letter with paper, for a reply. I cant often write letters but when I sign myself 'Harry' on the Field post cards, you will know that I am in the trenches, & when 'HWWilliamson' I am resting behind them. Do you understand? It must interest you hear where we

went. We landed at Havre & went for 2 days 'cattle truck' journey to St. Omer (where we lived in a convent) & we are now fighting, where I may not say, but you can guess the district if you get a map and read the papers. I have a feeling that I will return safe. We all think the war will end soon, thank God when it does. The only danger in the trenches is the awful shells and snipers. It must please Father to know that a Corporal & I waited 1 hour for a sniper, & I had the pleasure to shoot him in the end. Otherwise we practically never see a German. Altho' we are entrenched within 100 yards of their trenches. You see if you send tinned things they are watertight & can be carried so easily and compactly. Send a shirt once in 6 weeks, will you? We have had about 30 casualties so far. I think, mainly snipers & shell fire which latter is hell. The destruction is awful here. Farmhouses and church shelled and burned, cows and sheep bayonetted, & shell holes everywhere. I expect you have seen a lot about us in the papers. [Next sentence heavily scored out] I will write a separate account by different letter now. Tell Terence that I think it rather callous of him to have forgotten me, especially as we are such pals. Efford has written often. Give the dear old boy my love & thanks, will you. His letters are very cheering to poor chaps such as us. Believe me, night and day, we pray for peace. You and the others are always in my thoughts. Send sox occasionally & also 100 State Express cigarettes in *waterproof* tin (for active service) or rather pocket case. Now I must close. Love to girls & dad & Granpa etc etc, your poor lad, Sonny. Tell Father to let Mr. Hooton know what I am doing.

[Countersigned 'G.E.S. Fursdon']

Date-stamped APO, 12, B: DE.21.'14. Censor 1675
To: W.L. Williamson, etc.   17 December 1914
Dear Father, I am now resting from work in flooded muddy trenches (3 feet nearly of water) in a French cottage about [scored out, but it is readable – '2 miles'] behind the British 'wall of steel'. After coming from the depths, my feet swelled to such an enormous size and were so numbed that I am now under the care of the Doctor. I daresay you might like to hear of the doings of the Exped Force here, so here we are. We have been sitting tight in our present positions for the last 2 months. The Germans (& Austrians with them) have attacked very occasionally, & when they do, we

mow them down, & they return decimated. The trenches at present are in an awful condition, full of water, and awfully cold. Owing to the wet we cant light our usual *coke fires*, & therefore no cooking. We get into the trenches by communication trenches, but we have to creep up thro' mud & water to 50 yds exposed (we only go in at night). Generally we get in without any mishap. At intervals during the night the Germans send up brilliant white lights, to see if we are creeping up to attack. ['Intermittent' crossed out] A little rifle fire is kept up the whole time by the Germans. Their snipers in day time pick off a man now & then, as they are mostly crack shots. Now & then, as we sit or stand about in our dug-outs – thics [thus]

[a small sketch inserted here]

we hear 'thang' preceded by a noise like an engine letting off steam in London Bdge Stn & we all dive into our dugouts to avoid shrapnel bullets and splinters. Another time we hear a terrific whistling, and a big percussion shell will blow a hole about five feet deep and 12 feet across in the earth away from the trenches (if we are lucky) or in the trenches (if we are not). When the latter case, the results can only be imagined. Five of our men were wounded by the splinters from one shell the other day. We are very glad when the night comes when we are relieved. We get out of the trenches amid a few bullets but we arent seen, so its only a fluke if one is hit. I saw through a loop hole an Hun sniping, so a Corporal and I watched. I fixed my rifle on him & when the Corporal saw his head 'up' I loosed off & we believe we got him for good. I hope so. We are all absolutely knocked up when we return. Our rifles are a stick of mud & our coats are an awful weight – 20 lbs at least. Our artillery gives them hell sometimes, when the guns blow their trenches to bits, & they have to nip out & run for their 2nd. line of trenches. Believe me, our artillery now (but not at first as, say [two words scored out] from Mons, when we were driven 210 miles in 9 days) is much better & stronger than the Germans. While in cottages resting yesterday, we had several small shells burst within eight yards of our cottages. Blowing great holes in the earth. The people here were terrified but we get used to such things. The Germans appear to make great efforts to destroy all the churches here; the one here is absolutely ruined. The Taubes are greatly afraid of our aeroplanes and also our guns, which are very accurate. Will you call & see Mr.

Hooton & tell him how I am getting on? I havent time to write to the chaps at M.L. [Mincing Lane, i.e. Sun Fire Insurance office] Also give my love to Mr. Brett & Mr. Phipps there. I must end now, as the time is short. Love to all, I am, yr affec son, Harry.

[Countersigned 'G.E.S. Fursdon']

On 19 December the 11th Infantry Brigade was part of an attack which had begun on 17 December. Sir John French's Army operation Order for that day stated: 'It is the intention of the Commander-in-Chief to attack vigorously all along the Front tomorrow'.[34] Mitchinson states that the purpose of this attack was to convince the Germans that the pause after the Battle of Ypres was only temporary, and to thus relieve pressure on the troops on the Eastern Front.[35] Colonel Bates in the *Short History of the LRB* recorded the action thus:

> The object of the attack by the 11th Infantry Brigade in front of Ploegsteert Wood on this date was to clear its edges, including German House, and, if possible, establish a line in front in the part afterwards known as the 'birdcage'.
>
> The Somerset Light Infantry and Rifle Brigade attacked. The London Rifle Brigade was in support. The weather could not have been worse, and the ground was impossible. The result was that the wood was cleared, and German House remained in No Man's Land.
>
> The London Rifle Brigade was not called upon to continue the attack. This was the first experience the Battalion had of anything like heavy artillery fire, and also of the difficulty of consolidating at night in an unknown bit of ground. Two half-companies were engaged in assisting with this work, while the rest of the Battalion spent a miserable night in the marshes in the wood.[36]

A tape made by Henry Williamson in his later years for the Imperial War Museum describes his terror and that of his friend Baldwin 'with ashen face' as they waited in the trenches, and that his abiding memory afterwards of the wounded being brought in was of one man singing 'Oh for the wings of a dove' as he was carried back through the wood.[37]

This whole attack is described in the opening chapters of *A Fox Under My Cloak*. The volume opens with the London Highlanders in billets and expecting to remain there for Christmas; they decide to organize a football tournament but are suddenly ordered to return back to their billets as 'the battalion had orders to move immediately'. This is all corroborated in the official records of the London Scottish and is a very good example of Henry Williamson's skill at weaving together reality and fiction. For example, we read of Phillip building a fire at night to boil his mess tin for some Nestlé's café-au-lait which of course was actually sent to Henry by his mother in her parcels. Another interesting detail concerns the goat-skin coats issued to the soldiers. 'Some speculation . . . arose in the platoon when knee-length goat's-skin coats were issued. . . . The jerkins had broad tapes which cross-bound the white and yellow hairy skins against the chest and round the waist.'[38] (Henry mentions in one of his letters that he 'had his fur coat'.[39]) On 19 December, immediately after this description in the novel, comes the order to attack. In real life this was Williamson's first full experience of battle. After this skirmish his platoon had a rest turn in billets and he wrote to his mother on 21 December:

Date-stamped APO, B, 11 ; 24 DE '14 : Censor 1675
To: Mrs Williamson   21 December 1914. Same place in Belgium.
Dear Mother, how are you all at home? I expect that by the time you get this you will have had Xmas. I wish you would send me the Daily Mail every other day, & also magazines (Pearsons etc) would be immensely appreciated. I see by a paper of the 18th that Whitby and Scarborough have been bombarded. The photographs in it are similar to sights very common here. The church here is smashed to bits and also many houses. Behind where we are billetted, we have several batteries of heavy field howitzers and the Germans, after we have given them 'what-for' with the Cannon, drop shells where they think our guns are in the hope of putting them out of action. We have had several shells burst within 40 yds of the house, but we dont mind at all. I shall have some tales to tell you when I get home — tales that you never read in the papers, or soldiers letters. Tales of [several words heavily scored out — possibly 'the London Rifle Brigade'] and how good luck has always been its lot when the odds seem overwhelming. The other night (we are about 2 miles from trenches) we heard suddenly the plock plock of rifle fire, and it gradually swelled in sound till it became a roar, mingled with the pop,pop,pop, of maxim guns. Blinding white rockets lit up the sky, and field guns suddenly

flashed and boom! and shriek a shell speed on its errand of death. Then boom, boom, boom, continual & awful sounds our cannon spoke in the night. We then knew that our men were attacking. In the morning we heard that several German trenches had been taken. You perhaps will read in the official communique 'In the district of — we have made slight progress, & have taken several German trenches.' We are winning here, slowly but surely. We have progressed here perhaps 200 yds in 2 months. But the Germans cant stop us. I daresay when our new troops come out, which I hope will be soon, we shall drive them back as sleet before a nor'easter. Love from Harry. I have received a parcel containing choc & sweets from the CSSA which I presume is from Father. So thanks very much. Also a parcel containing [letter ends here – any further page missing]

[Countersigned 'H L Johnston']

But he was back in the trenches over Christmas as we read in his next letter written in pencil and with a small Union Jack pinned to the top of the page. This letter relates the phenomena of the 1914 Christmas Truce.

Date-stamped APO, B, 12:28 DE 14: Censor 1675

To: Mrs Williamson, etc   Dec 26 1914. Trenches

Dear Mother, I am writing from the trenches. It is 11 o'clock in the morning. Beside me is a coke fire, opposite me a 'dug-out' (wet) with straw in it. The ground is sloppy in the actual trench, but frozen elsewhere. In my mouth is a pipe presented by Princess Mary. In the pipe is tobacco. Of course, you say. But wait. In the pipe is German tobacco. Ha Ha, you say, from a prisoner or found in a captured trench. Oh, dear, no! From a German soldier. Yes a live German soldier from his own trench. Yesterday the British & Germans met & shook hands in the Ground between the trenches, & exchanged souvenirs, & shook hands. Yes, all day Xmas day, & as I write. Marvellous, isn't it? Yes. This is only for about a mile or two on either side of us (so far as we know). It happened thiswise. On Xmas eve both armies sang carols and cheered & there was very little firing. The Germans (in some places 80 yds away) called to our men to come & fetch a cigar & our men told them to come to us. This went on for some time, neither fully trusting the other, until, after much promising to 'play the game' a bold Tommy crept out & stood between the trenches, & immediately a Saxon came to meet him. They shook hands & laughed & then 16 Germans came out. Thus the ice was broken. Our men are speaking to them now. They are landsturmers or landwehr, I think, & Saxons & Bavarians (no Prussians). Many are gentle looking men in goatee beards & spectacles, and some are very big and arrogant looking. I have some cigarettes which I shall keep, & a cigar I have smoked. We had a burial service in the afternoon, over the dead Germans who perished in the 'last attack that was repulsed' against us. The Germans put 'For Fatherland & Freedom' on the cross. They obviously think their cause is a ['— thing one', scored out but initialled HWW] just one. If you get a Daily Mail of Dec 23 & turn to the letter page you will see an article entitled 'Snapshots from the Front' & in the second snapshot an account is given of what we, with others, have done, and the identical apparatus is mentioned. When you find a sentence or word 'blacked out' & not initialled by me, it is the work of the censor. Many of the Germans here are, or were, waiters. [i.e. in England before the war.] Thank Efford for his chocolate. Auntie Belle for the cigarettes. I have had an awful time with swollen feet and my toes are frostbitten now. But it is all in the days work, as is working all night at digging or etc & sleeping in wet and mud. Where we are billetted (8 of us in a cottage in a town which is shelled now and again) we have a good time. There is a family of Belgians here whose house has been destroyed, and the old mother, about 56 yrs old, is very jolly and resourceful, as well as comical.

[Any further pages are missing — although the tiny flag is pinned through all that is there.]

Unknown to Henry, his father arranged to have this letter printed in the Daily Express, and the cutting still exists in his literary archive. Apart from the pipe presented by Princess Mary that Henry mentioned there was also the gift of a tin of tobacco which still exists, together with some of the original tobacco and its wrapper, a wrapper from a packet of cigarettes, and Christmas card and photograph sent by Princess Mary to all the troops at the Front (see plates 8 and 9a).

Mitchinson relates that the fraternization was reported back to England in many letters, and that several of these appeared in the newspapers. He also states that, 'the sources agree that the initial stages of the truce began with the Germans erecting Christmas trees on their parapets and asking the troops opposite to exchange songs during the night of 24–25 December.'[40] as Henry Williamson relates in *A Fox Under My Cloak*.

The *Official History* also refers to the incident but in restrained tones: 'During Christmas Day there was an informal suspension of arms during daylight on a few parts of the Front, and a certain amount of fraternization. Where there had been recent fighting both sides took the opportunity of burying their dead lying in No Man's Land, and in some places there was an exchange of small gifts and a little talk, the Germans expressing themselves confident of early victory. Before returning to their trenches both parties sang Christmas carols and soldier songs, each in its own language, ending up with 'Auld Lang syne' in which all contingents joined.'[41]

The fraternization over Christmas 1914 made a deep and lasting impression on Henry Williamson. A moving and compelling description of it can be found in 'Heilige Nacht', the third chapter of *A Fox Under My Cloak*, which includes a scene of the Germans digging a grave for a dead comrade: 'The Germans had made a cross from ration-box wood, marked in indelible pencil: *HIER RUHT IN GOTT EIN UNBEKANNTE DEUTSCHER HELD* (Here rests in God an unknown German hero).' He could never forget what he learned that day – that the German soldiers thought as deeply and sincerely as the English that they were fighting for God and their country. He was to realise also that he had German blood in his own veins, and that he had in effect fought his own 'cousins' (as his Aunt Maude, his father's sister, pointed out to him in a letter some years later). As time passed his thoughts about the causes of the war deepened and hardened. He saw that war was created by greed, misplaced zeal and bigotry and that this was an underlying political *raison d'être*. All these factors affected him deeply and came to determine his life's purpose; to show the world, through his writing, that truth and peace lay solely in beauty and the open air, and that this was the only way to avoid a repetition of war.

After a few days the truce ended and the fighting recommenced. There are conflicting official accounts of its length – from two days to a week. It was not approved of officially, although there is the suggestion that it was condoned because it allowed a certain amount of essential repair work to take place. Certainly it was not allowed to happen again: the next time the Germans called a similar truce, they were fired upon.

Henry's next letter home reveals that he had been unwell for some time.

Postcard: *APO, B, 11, 8 JA 15: Censor 1675*
To: Mrs Williamson
Still a bit sick, but hope to be all right in a day or two. Awfully wet here; the trenches are often knee deep in water here, in spite of bailers & pumps. Hope you are well. Have just recd parcel dated 17 Dec & Effords cake.
Love HWW
   [Countersigned 'H L Johnston']

Date-stamped APO, B, 11: 10 JA 15 : Censor 1675
To: Mrs Williamson   9 January 1915 Belgium
Dear Mother, I am writing a little letter to you now quite personal. By the same post I am sending another of general interest. I see that my letter of Xmas day has appeared in the Daily Express. Perhaps you would like to send it to the same paper but I think that the Daily Mail is a better paper. I have received your parcel containing Efford's cake & another apricots etc. The latter arrived late, eh? I suppose you know that if you send a parcel to me under 11 lbs in wt. via Military Forwd. Officer, it wont find me? About the waders, I think that they would be too fragile for trench work, but jack boots would be fine for the mud when doing fatigue work in the mud. Good stout boots up to knee (not rubber boots) and water-tight up to knee, would be the very thing. If you get them with lacings up the middle they will leak. I am sure that you could get some somewhere in London. The Germans have fine boots, like this – [sketch of a boot to knee] (all leather) – But 'for heavens sake' dont send seamens or sewermens boots, about 20lbs in weight. They must be comparatively light. I take 10 or 10½ size boots. Also a Bryant & Mays 'Service' Match box. I have a present for you when I return. A beautiful filigree-work cross in silver. All shell fragments, German helmet spike etc etc Love to all Harry.
   [Countersigned 'H L Johnston']

Date-stamped APO, 47, B: 19 JA 15 : Censor 1994
To: W.L. Williamson, The National Bank Ltd., 13 Broad Street,
London, EC – crossed out & forwarded to 11, Eastern Road.

10 January 1915, Belgium

Dear Father, I received your most welcome letter last night, for
which many thanks. If I were you, I should chuck the official
constable work. It must be very fatiguing, especially as you are so
busy in the City. Also, the Defence Force you mention (composed
of elderly men, I presume?) may be very nice as a sort of hobby,
but, believe me, in case of invasion (by invasion I mean an army
landing) they would be of no use whatsoever, unless under the
control of the Army Authorities.

Suppose an hostile army managed to establish itself in this
country. It would perhaps, advance on London. It is possible, for
the sake of argument, that it would defeat a division or two of our
men (preceding the army) sent hurriedly against it. It might get
to, say, Romford. The streets of London would perhaps swarm
with patriotic men armed with rifles and bandoliers eager to repel
the Hun. The Huns have met our army at Romford, and the armed
citizens are in reserve, waiting. Suddenly a most awful
bombardment would begin. No sign of an enemy, yet huge shells
would hurtle out of the heavens and with a terrific 'womp' would
explode. Houses would crumple up, huge holes would appear in
the roadways, factories and warehouses burn furiously. We will
suppose that our army at Romford is overcome: and reserves are
coming up from the Midlands and South-west. Meanwhile the
bombardment would continue, London (or any other town)
would be a smoking heap of ruins, dead women and civilians
bestrewing the streets. Where would the patriotic but wholly
useless men be, who are not in the regular army? Perhaps a day
later the Germans would appear armed with field guns and
maxims and another fearful carnage would ensue. A few may be
killed by the citizens, but then no mercy would be shown to the
rest, and an awful state would result.

Of course it is very hard to imagine what would happen in case
of hostile columns marching on London, because London is an
unfortified (to all intents and purposes) town from the inside. But
a smaller town, in Belgium or France, of strategical importance
would perhaps be protected by a ring of forts: the houses near
would be blown up to clear the way for gunfire, and rings of

earthworks and trenches strongly fortified with barb wire entanglements and other encumbrances would be prepared. The Germans, aided by their colossal siege-artillery, would have no difficulty in reducing the forts by simply 'blowing them to hell' as we say out here. Then the lines of trenches would be subjected to a terrific shrapnel-fire, the invaders would deploy, or extend and aided by reserves and supports, would advance under our rifle fire and perhaps shrapnel fire from field artillery. After fierce attacking, they might perhaps take the first-line trenches with the bayonet, and we would retire to the second-line & then attack would again press forward. Perhaps it would be successful, and the Germans would gain access to the town. Now would be the chance of the armed civilians to show their mettle. Supposing they have withstood the awful bombardment, the flames, the falling buildings, they would 'snipe' the invaders. Result – all civilians ruthlessly slaughtered. Again they would, preceeding this, to have no chance to fire. The retreating army, the defenders, would explode mines to wreck the streets, and obstruct the streets, in fact, do everything to hinder the advance of the invaders. Believe me, if (IF) the germans can land a force sufficiently strong (three army corps at least) to make any attacks or advance on London possible, then the Defence Leaguers would not be the slightest good at all, unless taken over by the military to man trenches in the fields, or positions that surround London.

Now about the war here. We go up to the trenches as usual to relieve other Companies. We pump there as usual, we get wet, cold and miserable there as usual. We hold the same trenches as we held (i.e. the Allies) ten weeks ago. So do the Germans. Generally speaking the position has not changed here. We lose a small percentage of men owing to shell fire and sniping – so do our enemies. We see by this, that, if the war is to end by our military superiority over the Germans, it is going to take a long time to drive them across Belgium. Our only hope is that, when the floods and ooze have subsided somewhat, we can, by superior numbers, drive their flanks right back and so force their whole line to withdraw. I see the French are doing splendidly in Alsace. I will, in another letter, sent simultaneously with this one, endeavour to tell you what this war looks like, and the battlefield to the observer. You might, if you think that its general interest warrants it, send it on to the Mail, as you did the other letter to the Express (rotten paper).

I must close now. The paraffin in the peasants lamp here is costly, and I hear his sabots clopping as he comes to tell me that the straw is laid in his best room for us to repose. My muddy blanket is warm, and my fur coat looks inviting, so I must now go to bed. With a final drink of cafe, and a last cigarette, I close this letter. Love to all at home, your affectionate son, Harry.

[Countersigned H Y Mansfield]

A torn cutting from a newspaper with these letters would appear to be the printed version of the item referred to above although there is no original. It is very worn now, and is undated and untitled:

... The men are quite proud of Plug-Street. [Here HW has written in the margin 'L.R.B. & Prussian Guards Nov. 27 – Dec 14'] So much for the lighter side of the story. There is, alas! a grimmer tale belonging to it. Here has been, on a small scale, some of the most desperate fighting of the war. For months there was a bitter and bloody struggle for this position, which is of very considerable military value, and as late as last December the Germans inflicted heavy losses on the gallant garrison. They have little chance now of calling Plug-Street their own, but once more it has been touch and go.

Even today the sniping goes on continually, and occasionally the wood is shelled.

The Watch

Plug-Street represents, in epitome, the soldier's life in the sort of siege warfare that has reigned on the British lines for weeks and months past. Perhaps it is a little better than the weary vigil of the low-lying trenches. There is at least more air and freedom. Death, if it comes, may seem less terrible under the shadows of the trees than in the foul mire of an artificial burrow. But it is terribly wearing. To peep over the parapets on the outskirts of the wood is simply to invite death. To be in the wood at all is to know that at any moment the predestined bullet may find its mark. There is more cheerfulness, certainly there is more real good fellowship in Piccadilly, Plug-Street, than in Piccadilly, London.

Date-stamped APO, B, 47 : 19 JA 15 : Censor 1994
To: W.L.Williamson, The National Bank Ltd., 13 Old Broad St. EC —
readdressed to 11, Eastern Road.

11 January 1915, Belgium
Dear Father, I am writing this in the cottage of a peasant — our rest
billets. It is a small cottage, and occupied by a family whose house
was burned and wrecked by the fighting here. The burned house
in question lies about ten yards behind the German lines, & is the
resort of their snipers, & they have two machine guns in there at
night. However, this is by the way.

As I write, I can hear the sounds of rifle fire in front of me.
There is a large field in front of the house — brown ploughed
earth, pitted here and there with shell holes. In a corner of the
field near the road are three mounds with simple white wooden
crosses on them — three English soldiers graves — their last resting
place. About half a mile in front, over the field, is a cluster of farm
houses — all roofless, many burned, and all telling one tale,
shelling. About three quarters of a mile in front of the farms —
untenanted — is a large field and in the middle of the field a long
line of earth thrown up, and about 100 yards in front of it, a
parallel line. In the space between these lines of earth, one can see
dead cows, huge shell craters, and, just in front of each line of
mounds, a badly made (as an unknowing & unsuspicious observer
would think) and untidy barbed-wire fence.

Behind these mounds are deep ditches, all more or less half full
of water and mud, and curiously made caves. One line of ditches
is occupied by men in khaki, the other by men in grey. The same
observer, if it were possible to stand in the space between the
trenches, would not see a soul. The only sign of human life in all
the vast wilderness and ruin would be the smoke from a wood
fire here, and a sudden shot (sniping) there. That is all — in the
actual trench. Very simple really, but awful to think of. The dead
cows, the ruined crops, the shell wrecked houses, all tell their tale
of misery and desolation.

Let us go three miles or so behind the trenches & see the Field
Artillery. We walk up to where we understand the battery to be,
but see nothing. The guns are cunningly hidden and concealed
from hostile airmen. Suddenly, pang-pang — followed by metallic
screeches — we are shelling the enemy with light shells — shrapnel
from field guns. In the house here, we hear the 'pang' just behind

us, hear the screech of a shell, and look well over the ruined farms in the distance, and soon see a small white dot in the air appear – for all the world like a piece of cotton wool – the shrapnel has burst. The shelling of the enemy's trenches continues, but suddenly stops. Khaki clad figures round the hidden guns dive like magic into places of concealment. Why?

In the air overhead is a speck – hardly moving. It looks for all the world like a kestrel hovering, but its wings are slightly curved. A minute passes, then 'pup' 'pup', little balls of white smoke appear all round it, scores of them. The Taube – for such it is – swings round and makes back towards the german lines – afraid. We hope he has not spotted our guns. If he has, we shall soon have shell upon shell over the house. The Germans will endeavour to silence the battery. After a bit the gunners come out, and 'carry on' with the shelling. We earnestly hope that it is effective, for the German snipers are rather deadly.

If we go back eight or ten miles behind the trenches we will see the heavy artillery. The shells fired by these heavy howitzers are of the percussion variety and are mostly of high explosive, such as lyddite. Our observing aeroplanes, at the risk of their life, fly over the enemies country (that part of Belgium that they hold temporarily being deemed hostile) and, spotting something good to shell, a moving column of infantry, field guns, or heavy artillery batteries, or a farm full of troops, the direction, range etc., is dropped in a message bag, the artillerymen open fire, after locating the position on the map, and the aeroplane signals 'hit', 'miss', 'right', or the position of the shell.

Yesterday we had five large shells at the church here again. Only one burst, but that shattered half the roof and many windows of houses near were blown in. The inhabitants panic for a minute, & then all is calm again. They are used to war.

It is interesting to watch a duel of aeroplanes in the air. It generally ends in the Taube running away. I am sure that we have better air-services now than the Germans, and better artillery. We are eagerly waiting for the Russians, as we know that the whole issue depends on their offensive.

I must now close. Kind regards to Mr. Lockyer.

Yours, HHWilliamson

[Envelope countersigned 'P Jameson' ? – difficult to read]

Date-stamped APO, B, 47 : 19 JA 15 : Censor 1994 (?)

To: Mrs Williamson   17 Jan '15

Dear Mother, I write hurriedly to let you know that I am now on my way to base, where I shall be in hospital. I am suffering from a rather ['severe' crossed out] bad form of 'enteritis' accompanied by rotten pains in stomach & head & am very weak. I have been rotten for 3 weeks. There is no cause for any worry at all. I am very thin and pale but am not downcast. I am writing in the Red Cross train, which accounts for the uneven writing. The arrangements for 'malades' on it are ripping & the authorities are kindness itself. Will drop a card later. Yours affectionately, Harry.

   [Countersigned 'Jameson'?]

This postcard has blue and red lines around the outside edges, with three flags in colour in the centre top (see plate 9b):

Postcard: date-stamped APO, X, 8 [?] 19 JA 15 : Censor 1922

To: Mrs Williamson, etc

No. 1 General Hospital, Brit. Exped. Force. France, Jan 18th 1915

Dear Mother, I am in hospital now: writing in bed. The hospital is an hotel on the sea front. Am very weak and in pain occasionally. Enteritis. Hope you are all well at home. The sea is roaring on the beach about 50 yds away. Please send a little Three Nuns tobacco & 100 Three Castle cigarettes to me at the above address *as soon as poss.* If you delay I may not get them. With love from Harry.

Suffering from the effects of dysentery and trench foot Henry Williamson was returned to England on 26 January 1915.[42] On arrival in England he was taken on a stretcher to the train, supposedly for Birmingham but as the hospital there was full he ended up at the Ancoats Military Hospital at Manchester.[43] While either at the hospital in France or at Ancoats he was presented with KING ALBERT'S BOOK. The printed book label pasted into the inside of the cover states: 'With Mr J. Musker's Best Wishes for a Speedy Recovery and a Victorious New Year. 2nd Western General Hospital, January 1915.'[44] Under this Henry has written: 'H.W. Williamson, Rifle Brigade, 11th Brigade, 4th Division, B.E.F.1914.'

4

Promotion

After a check-up at Ancoats Military Hospital Henry Williamson was moved to its associated convalescent home at nearby Alderley Edge, where he stayed for about a month. At the subsequent Medical Board he was given three weeks' leave and returned home early in March 1915.

His older sister, Kathie, speaking in her old age over sixty years later (after Henry's death) described his return home, which had made a deep impression on her. 'He was a terrible sight; when he appeared at the bottom of Eastern Road we could hardly recognize him. He was very pale and thin. He looked like a scarecrow; his uniform coat was torn and covered in mud. He had dysentery and red puffy swollen feet from being constantly wet and frozen.'[1]

The importance of trench foot can be seen by the fact that Field Marshal Sir John French devoted nearly three pages to the subject in his book 1914,[2] relating that it first appeared around the third week of November 1914, when it was thought to be frostbite, until it was realized that just cold, not frozen, water (usually below 40°F) caused these symptoms which were exacerbated by:

a) Prolonged standing in one position, as is often the case with men deep in mud,
b) Tight puttees and tight boots.
c) Exhaustion and want of food.
d) A natural tendency to feeble circulation, e.g. men who suffered from chilblains.
e) Lying out, after being wounded, in wet and cold weather.

The symptoms are described as ranging from being merely very painful and tender, to the whole foot becoming like a big chilblain, very hot, red and swollen, followed by the toes going black and the foot blue, to the final stage of gangrene. Field Marshal French states that 'the men affected are quite unfit for duty for two or three months at least, especially for duty in trenches in cold weather.' He goes on to state that 'The only real preventative' is to avoid the causes, and then details the instructions that were formulated and issued to all officers in charge, including: 'Boots and puttees should not fit tightly and must be taken off once *at least* every 24 hours and the feet well rubbed and cleaned, and dry socks put on' and etc. He fully realized that this ideal was unattainable. 'In the Ypres region in the winter of 1914–15 many men stood for days and nights up to the middle in water. . . . Indeed a good many were drowned. . . . Treatment does not prevent the man being unable to walk for many weeks without pain. The number of men invalided for "trench feet" during the winter of 1914–15 was over 20,000.' But as a result of experience gained and the adoption of the recommendations this rate was radically reduced to about two per day for the rest of the war. Trench foot was not taken lightly.

The photograph of Henry Williamson taken at this point, a very young-looking man with a white face, shows his overcoat with a ragged edge from hacking off 2 feet of cloth with his bayonet, so there was less cloth to drag in the mud and thus less weight to carry (see plate 1). On an envelope that once contained this photograph, he wrote that his uniform was washed and pressed at Ancoats Hospital, but the coat itself would still have retained much of the clinging sticky yellow clay mud.

On his return from the Front he wrote out some notes for the school magazine *Colfensia*, which appeared under the section headed 'War News'. A second extract from a letter to Leland Duncan (Chairman of the Old Boys' Association) was also included, with several other reminiscences, in an item entitled 'Old Colfeians at the Front'. It is interesting to note the different styles adopted for the two pieces.

All Buffs will be deeply interested to read the following letter from an old Buff, H. Williamson, of the London Rifle Brigade, now invalided home after many weeks of warfare with his regiment in the trenches of Flanders. While in hospital at the base, he met another old Buff, R. W. Barnes, of the London Scottish, a former Captain of the House. The heartfelt good wishes of the House go out to these two old Buffs, with the earnest hope that they will soon be restored to health again. The House is proud to number such among its Old Boys.

'17th March, 1915.

. . . I was invalided home about two months ago, but am now cured, although, of course, I am not very strong; my nerves are a bit "joggy", too.

Trench work is rather monotonous. We relieve men holding them, and are relieved ourselves in turn, regularly.

The first time we went in the trenches we were mixed up with regulars, being, of course, rather nerve-shaken. But the feeling of nervousness soon left us, and we set to work to pump the trenches. I must tell you that the actual trenches were two feet in mud and water, and the harder we pumped, the deeper grew the water (or so it seemed to us). In the trenches we do one hour "on" sentry, and one "off". This is throughout the hours of darkness. During our hour "off" we pump, dig, fix up wire in front (we were about 90 yards from the Germans), fetch rations and numerous other jobs. You can imagine, then, that after three or four days of this the strain is rather acute. The fact of no sleep, and legs, and, in fact, all the body, wet through, does not help to improve the situation.

Now and then we get a shell or two over, and, when very lucky, an attack. We are literally overjoyed when they attack us, for it means a great shooting practice. They attack shoulder to shoulder, and march on our trenches. When (and if) they get within twenty yards they open fanwise, and some sections lie down to allow a clear path for the Maxim fire.

But, generally, they get to the barbed wire entanglements, and there they stop. It is a fine sound to hear thousands of rifles and machine-guns all cracking at once, and now and then a 'rafale' of several batteries of French 75mm guns.'[3]

Old Colfeians at the Front

H. Williamson, London Rifle Brigade (a well-remembered Buff), writes as follows of some of his experiences:

'We have had rather a stiff time at the front. The chief trouble is the mud. We sleep on mud, we freeze on mud, we get mud on our rifles, on our clothes, in our hair, in our food. We were holding the trenches in front of a wood in Flanders. Pumping had to be done day and night, and also bailing, but it availed little. The parapets of the trenches slipped down, the sides fell in, the trench got dangerously shallow. It was impossible to dig, and we were compelled to crouch down in the daytime and wait for the night. When night came we worked in the trenches, put up barbed wire in front (the Germans were about 120 yards off), went and fetched water and rations, and exercised ourselves a bit. All this, remember, under intermittent rifle and maxim-gun fire, and a continuous shower of white rockets that lit up the country for two or three miles around.

Then, when work was done, sentries were posted. Each man did one hour on and one hour off all the night. When wet and freezing up to one's thighs in mud and water the game is apt to get a little trying at times; but, when the relief comes, oh, blessed hour! We troop back indescribably muddy but cheerful. Woolen [sic] caps on most of our heads, some with equipment over goat-skin coat, some with cooking pots on behind, some with fire pails, others with helmets and souvenirs, we reach our billets (peasants cottages) about 1½ miles away, take our soup and then lie down on the straw on the floor.

The stove is burning brightly, we are warm and well filled. A good post of letters and parcels awaits us, "grub" is not scarce. We are men who live in the moment only; we cannot tell when a bullet will find us or a shell hasten our end, but for the moment the room is warm, the roof over our heads keeps out the rain, we are happy and contented. Three days later, another week of wet and mud. Thus our little life goes on. The past appears to have belonged to another world. We hope and pray that it will come again, and know inwardly that, if we are spared, the day is not so very far away when, having done our duty to our country, we shall look back on the days of fighting as but a memory, and not a very pleasant one.'[4]

There is very little primary source material for the following months, certainly no diary or letters, so what Henry Williamson was doing cannot be related in detail or necessarily corroborated. However, it is possible to piece together a broad outline, and to have an overall view of his movements.

In *A Fox Under My Cloak* Henry Williamson shows that Phillip's homecoming in the same circumstances as his own was somewhat strained, and this no doubt reflected the situation in real life. Henry had been through searing experiences during his time in the trenches and ordinary home-life would have taken much adjusting to. Six months previously he had been a 'dreaming youth'. Now he had seen death and destruction on a huge scale. He had been living in appalling conditions. But life within his home and in the surrounding area had hardly changed. Attitudes and opinions about the war were far removed from his experience of life in the trenches. One of the great strengths of the war volumes of the Chronicle is Henry Williamson's ability to show the total scene of the war, so that the reader not only understands what life in the trenches was like but also what was happening back in England in all aspects, from political ideas and arguments, to life in Lewisham and to the Maddison (thus Williamson) family in particular.

Henry's father, William Leopold, was very busy with the duties surrounding his work as a special constable which he took very seriously, and which are well related in the Chronicle. The work connected with the Special Constabulary was quite arduous especially in London. By default it fell to those men who were too old for active service but who wanted to serve their country. Most of them worked at their businesses and professions during the day, carrying the extra burden of work due to shortage of staff with so many men at the Front, and so sacrificing their leisure hours of rest and sleep to fulfill these duties.

Each member was sworn in (normally at local police stations) and was required to undertake four hours duty in every twenty-four hour period. (Later on this was reduced first to three hours and eventually to two.) A truncheon, whistle, notebook and armlet were issued, together with a warrant card bearing the recipient's number, and a badge. Boots and uniforms were not provided until a much later stage. Each company had an inspector, 3 sub-inspectors, 10 sergeants and 90 constables. Official duties included guarding vulnerable points, such as railway arches, canal banks near tunnels, bridges, electricity works and reservoirs. Once air-raids began their work was invaluable in keeping vigil and in assisting with fires and injuries when necessary. Steel 'shrapnel' helmets were eventually issued for air-raid work.[5]

William Leopold Williamson was a Sergeant by seniority as he had been involved since 'Bloody Sunday' in Trafalgar Square in November 1887.[6] His company was attached to Lewisham Police Station. Two small notebooks still exist containing details of the duties he undertook and a meticulous account of canteen takings. In one he notes that his beats were: '1, Hilly Fields; 2, High Street; 3, Hither

Green Station and St. Mildred's; 4, Police Station'. Another interesting item is a list he made of Zeppelin raids. William Leopold served throughout the war and was awarded a long service medal in due course. His uniform and various accoutrements still survive.[7]

Just before his return from his first stint in the trenches, Henry had written to his father that rather curt letter of 10 January about this 'official constable work'. Henry was, of course, writing out of his own experience of the battle bombardment. William Leopold naturally did not take very kindly to such criticism and was rather hurt, according to the *Chronicle*. This, coupled with his disapproval of Henry's tendency to go out with his friends to the local public house, exacerbated their uneasy relationship upon his return.

Henry Williamson now applied for a commission. There is no indication in his archive about this decision but there was a general move by Territorial soldiers to do so at this point.[8] Extrapolating information from *A Fox Under My Cloak* it is possible to work out how Williamson proceeded. Mitchinson confirms that the LRB Colonel, Earl Cairns, was concerned that the LRB might become merely an Officers' Training Corps, and so decided not to recommend men for commissions.[9]

First, Henry visited the 2nd Battalion in training at Crowborough but was given little encouragement, other than the suggestion that he had to apply to the Colonel of the 3rd Battalion in London to sign his papers. Obtaining the necessary 'blue form' from the War Office in Whitehall he applied for the Bedfordshire Regiment. A manuscript note (scribbled on an envelope) in Williamson's archive states that he wanted to join the Bedfordshires to be with his cousin Charlie Boon of Aspley Guise, but 'we never met in France or Belgium and Charlie was killed in action at Beaumont Hamel in November 1916'. He then went round to the Drill Hall in Bunhill Row to get the signature of 'an old officer with gentle face and four rings on his sleeves, with a crown and two stars'. (*A Fox Under My Cloak*, p. 104). This was the Commanding Officer of the 3rd Battalion of the LRB, Colonel H.C. Cholmondeley, CB (Companion of the Order of Bath). The 3rd Battalion was raised on 30 November 1914 and spent five months in London before going under canvas at Tadworth (at which point the command was taken over by Major N.C. King).[10] Colonel Cholmondeley had been Regimental Commanding Officer of the London Rifle Brigade from 1890 to 1901 and had commanded a section of the CIV (City Imperial Volunteers) in the Boer War, receiving the CB.[11]

So Henry Williamson thus obtained his commission, confirmed by the Army List of May 1915 (page 1056g): 'Williamson, W.H., Temp. 2nd. Lieut. 10th Service Btn. The Bedfordshire Regt. 10 April 1915.' The 10th (Service) Battalion was raised in December 1914 and served as a draft-finding unit in the Home Defence Force.

When Henry's commission was confirmed he was not at home. His parents sent two urgent telegrams on 13 April 1915 from Ladywell Post Office, addressed to 'Williamson, c/o Gregg [his Aunt Maude], Hawkhurst, Kent. The first one from his mother timed at 6.56 p.m. read: 'Commission report tomorrow morning urgent Mother', while the second one from his father (who obviously considered his wife's wording not firm enough), was timed at 7.38 p.m. and stated, 'You must come tonight 8.14 report 9.30 sharp tomorrow morning Father.'

Henry now opened an account with Messrs Holt & Co., Army Agents, Navy Agents and Bankers, and on 21 April 1915 he paid in 'By Outfit', £50 and a sum of £31 8s 2d from W.L. Williamson. His army pay entries show a regular monthly sum of £11 12s 6d. As he had been out of the country at the beginning of the year he would not have been able to obtain a diary for 1915, so he tended to jot a few notes into spaces in his 1914 volume. Thus he added onto pages for August 1914 the details of his kit purchases,[12] including 27s 6d for a canvas washbasin, 6s 6d extra for the holdall straps, and £3 5s for a 'British warm'. He wrote a cheque drawn to CSSA on 16 April for £14 1s 7d, which is the total of the clothes part of his kit as shown in the diary entry, while a day or two later two cheques made out to Gamages and another to CSSA accounted for the other items. A further entry of a list of clothing etc would seem to be a check list for packing.[13] It is interesting to note that 'Hair oil' was a required item for an officer!

It was at this time that Henry decided to buy a motorcycle to facilitate his travelling arrangements for off-duty visits. This motorcycle was Henry's first Norton, number LP 1656, and on it he painted the name of his beloved Doris [Nicholson], the girl who with her parents lived at the top of Eastern Road (No. 18, the 'turret' house), with whom Henry was in love. An entry in his Holt's bankbook on 1 May 1915 for a sum of £38 made out to A.H. Rayner would seem to be the relevant payment entry.

The initial Officers' Instruction Course was at Sevenoaks in Kent. Williamson implies in his novels that he did not find the transition to officer very easy. He frequently mentioned this in his later years and it always bothered him. He lacked the background and social graces to carry it off with nonchalance and his efforts to do so meant he committed several 'social gaffes' which were noted by his fellow officers, and which made him feel very uncomfortable and gauche. These served to confirm his feeling of nervous inferiority, which seems to have been a trait that was part of his personality and which he never really overcame, even when a famous author. The course lasted three weeks and consisted of lectures (to which we learn in *A Fox* Phillip paid little attention – and nor would Henry have done).

One of the items in Henry Williamson's archive is a booklet, 'The Principles of War with reference to the Campaigns of 1914–15', a reprint of an article in *The Journal* of the Royal United Service Institution dated February 1915 and delivered as a lecture at the Senior Officers' School Aldershot. Inscribed 'Henry Williamson, Bedfordshire Regt. April 1915' this must have been part of his Officers' Instruction Course. It is incredibly old-fashioned and pedantic in style and one can see why Henry found the course utterly irrelevant (as he shows in his novel) after his real experience of the Front Line.

Another booklet, in pocket-sized octavo and seventy-eight pages long, may have been of better use. It certainly makes fascinating reading as a historical document. It is entitled *Notes From The Front Part III And Further Notes On Field Defences*, collated by the General Staff, February 1915. The Contents page shows it covers many subjects from 'Training in all duties at night; Observation of artillery fire by other arms; Protection of troops from hostile artillery fire; Machine Guns; Sanitation; Frost-bite; Enemy's ruses; Espionage' to 'Cyclist orderlies and despatch riders', to list just a few sections. Standing orders for a division. A short preface states: 'A copy of these Notes should be issued to every officer. It is not intended that this pamphlet shall in any way take the place of the existing Training Manuals, and it should be read in conjunction with the official textbooks.'

There was also 'outdoor work' during which they learned to drill their own squads, and the skills necessary to advance by sign and whistle. Henry shows through Phillip in the novels that he found all this training useless in the light of his experience of battle in the trenches and he did not hesitate to say so.

At the conclusion of the course the commandant read out a list of where each officer was to report. Many were detailed for France. In *A Fox* Henry shows Phillip's (and thus his own) apprehension that he too would be sent back to the Front for he had been following the reports in the newspapers of the Second Battle of Ypres, which were very depressing. Earlier there had been the news of the 'Great Victory at Neuve Chapelle' which had taken place during 10–13 March while Henry was on a brief visit to his cousins, the Boons, at Aspley Guise. The battle of Neuve Chapelle was initiated by General Haig who saw that to capture the village and land to the east of it from German hands was an important strategic objective. Although this objective was quickly achieved, the Germans mounted a fierce counter-attack on 12 March which was repulsed but caused large losses on both sides. Total British casualties were about 12,500 men with an estimated similar German loss. Despite the losses and the problems, this British advance was considered valuable: it raised the prestige of the BEF, both as 'friend and foe', and particularly raised the morale of the troops after a long spell of defensive warfare.[14]

But the news arriving back in England about the Second Battle of Ypres was of a very depressing nature. On 22 April the Germans had attacked using 'asphyxiating gases'. This was against the International regulations regarding warfare. The *Official History* records that 22 April 'was a glorious spring day. . . . Suddenly at 5 p.m. a new and furious bombardment of Ypres by heavy howitzers began [on the French held line] . . . . Two curious greenish-yellow clouds [were seen by observers] . . . a peculiar smell was noticed, accompanied by smarting of the eyes and tingling of the nose and throat. It was some time, however, before it was realized that the yellow clouds were due to the gas about which warning had been received.'[15] The result was chaos as the colonial French line of Algerian troops broke and retired in total disorder, leaving a four mile gap to the north of Ypres for the German Army to advance through. But for some reason they did not press this advantage (they were possibly frightened of their own gas fumes) and halted their advance at 7.30 p.m. This allowed for some Allied reorganization which rescued the immediate crisis. This fearful battle continued for over a month, until 25 May. By that time, apart from the exhausted state of the troops on both sides, there was more or less no ammunition left on either side. British losses were very heavy: 2,150 officers and 57,125 other ranks. German losses were about 35,000 men.[16]

Henry, however, much to his relief, was told to report to

Newmarket, where he was to be attached to the 2/1st Cambridgeshire Regiment. Again, he did not endear himself to his fellow officers. (In *A Fox* he describes them as being drawn from the established provincial middle-class who had been to public school and university.) His behaviour irritated both the elderly Colonel C.T. Heycock, known as 'Strawballs' by his men, and the Adjutant, Captain G.D. Pryor. Other officers were the field officers, Major A. Howell (Indian Army), Major George Bromley Bowes (a newspaper report carries a photograph showing him elderly, balding, fair and with large ears, of the 'well-known firm of Messrs Bowes and Bowes, booksellers and publishers' of Cambridge), and Lieutenant Thomas Hope Formby, of Formby Hall, Formby, Lancashire (the fictional Baldersby).[17] The *Cambridgeshire Daily News* gave full details of Formby's marriage, the first report on 28 July 1915 announcing:

> Forthcoming Wedding: A Cambridgeshire Regiment Guard of Honour. At St. George's, Hanover Square, Lt. Thomas Hope Formby, 2/1st Cambridgeshire Regiment, son of Mr. John Formby, of Formby Hall, Formby, Liverpool, will on Saturday next be married by the Bishop of Chelmsford to Miss Kathleen Ailsa, second daughter of Mr. and Mrs. Andrew Ross of Ardingley, Sussex. There will be a guard of honour from the 2/1st Cambridgeshire Regiment and many officers . . . intend being present.

A later report of the wedding itself shows that the bride was obviously very well connected, several titles being mentioned, and was given away by her uncle, Mr Atlee.

Henry Williamson's son Richard states that the stories of the highjinks that we read of in *A Fox* actually occurred. These show Henry's uncomfortable regime and were repeated to Richard when he was a boy, including the incident of his fellow-officers' court martial. Once, when they were driving through Newmarket together, Henry pointed out Godolphin House and the window of the room that his clothes and furniture were thrown out of during the occasion of the 'subalterns' court-martial' and its ensuing punishment.[18] This behaviour reflected the norm of public school and university ragging, but it was totally foreign and bewildering to a young man who had not had the advantage of either. Henry's own attempts to emulate his fellow officers' pranks only exacerbated his position and were total disasters.

It was not all bad however. A happier side can be seen in the following report from the *Newmarket Journal* on 19 June 1915:

> A concert organised by Lt. T.H. Formby of the 2/1st Cambridgeshire Regiment was given in the Memorial Hall, Newmarket, on Monday evening. . . . Among those present were Col. Heycock and officers . . . and a certain number of civilian guests . . . songs by Capt. M.M. Eastwell . . . were particularly well received. Some capital 'Impersonations of George Robey' by Lt. T.H. Formby evoked an enthusiastic encore. . . . Excellent recitations were given by Lt. Brenan, Pte E. Gatwood . . . Lt. F.C. Jonas' fine interpretation of 'Off to Philadelphia' was lustily encored, and in response he gave 'The Bandolero'. Major Bowes' breezy rendering of 'A Hunting song' was equally well received . . .

There are several other reports of concerts: Captain Jonas appeared most often, the paper noting that he 'has a beautiful voice, and uses it most effectively'.[19]

As for the training that the regiment was supposed to be undergoing, the reader is told in *A Fox* that it was: '. . . much the same every day – 6.30 a.m. under the R.S.M. [Regimental Sergeant Major], parade, after breakfast, at 9 a.m., march away to the great stretches of grassland sloping to woods and the sky, practice advances in extended order, signs by hand and whistle, rush and lie down to give covering fire – in fact the old useless Bleak Hill routine over again' – a matter of expressed scorn by Phillip. 'They never do it out there like this'.[20]

The total impression given is of a battalion run on an old-fashioned system by elderly men who knew nothing of the current war situation and the strategies needed at the Front at that time. The battalion was not going to tolerate the incursion of a brash newcomer who did not know the form. Henry learnt a lot at Newmarket, though not necessarily about war strategy. He certainly learnt certain aspects of how an officer behaved, which only served to reinforce his innate feelings of inferiority.

A newspaper cutting from the *Newmarket Journal* dated 11 September 1915, which Henry pasted into a notebook corroborates a scene from his novel and gives an example of his behaviour:

'YOUNG BLOODS IN THE ARMY' WARNED

Lieut. Wm. Williamson, 2/1st Cambridgeshire Regiment, stationed at Newmarket, was summoned for driving a motor-cycle at a speed dangerous to the public, on the highway in Newmarket on August 26th. He did not appear, and service of the summons was proved.

The clerk read a letter which Lieut. Williamson had written, begging to be excused from attendance in person at the Court, as he had been ill for several days, and was proceeding on sick leave. He expressed regret that it should have been necessary to issue a summons against him. He admitted exceeding the speed limit, and placed himself unreservedly in the hands of the Bench. . . .

Witness: Yes – his speed was quite 25 miles an hour.

Inspector Emsden: It has been decided that in Newmarket anything above ten miles an hour is driving to the public danger. . . .

The Chairman: Defendant will be fined £1. I hope this will be a warning to some of the other young 'bloods' in the Army who are rushing about on motor bicycles.

As the second count, related in the novel, of having an insufficient silencer on his machine is not mentioned in the offical court proceedings one can assume that that hilarious story was an embellishment of Henry's imagination. A cheque made out to 'Clerk of the Justice' for £1 went through his account on 18 September.

Another episode related in the novel is also corroborated in the *Newmarket Journal*, which reported the death of 2/Lt. Joseph Waterton of 2/5th Bedfordshire Regiment who was riding an 'Indian', described as a very noisy motorcycle, and was in collision with a car on the Cambridge/Newmarket road (between Newmarket Cemetery and the golf links) dying at the scene of the crash, the motorcycle being wedged in the bonnet. The paper notes that witnesses to the crash were Miss Constance Ivy (Queenie) Golding and her sister Eileen, who were walking along the road at the time and who comforted the dying man. Here is the basis for Williamson's story of 'Lt. Waterpark's' demise in *A Fox Under My Cloak*, but the newspaper reports (over two or three days) are dated at the end of February 1915, three months before Williamson was posted there, so he was not part of the scenario.

In August the battalion removed to a village just outside Southend for an entrenching and musketry course. A report from the local newspaper reveals a most interesting item. The *Southend Standard* of 12

August 1915 states: 'The Rayleigh Parish Room was crowded last Thursday with the men of the Cambridge Regiment, on the occasion of an excellent concert in which many officers and men took part, augmented by some local talent. There were many encores and a highly appreciative audience throughout. Among the artistes from the Cambridge Regiment were the following: Capt. Jonas, Capt. Eastwell, Lts. Parkes, Williamson and Baxter, Farrow, Koltage, and B. Cooper.'

Despite the totally convincing description of the Battle of Loos found in the novel there is no evidence that Henry Williamson himself was similarly engaged. It is a superb example of Williamson's ability to blend the true facts of the battle front with his fictional story of Phillip's experiences in *A Chronicle of Ancient Sunlight*. By giving Phillip the role of gas officer Henry arranges for him to be at the Front but without attachment to any particular battalion or regiment. He could be in the trenches but he is also able to move about, for example, back to headquarters, where he could overhear official strategy etc. Later, when his part in the battle is over, he is free enough to be able to observe the situation overall from 'the Tower' – the well-known strategic structure overlooking the battlefield.

The decision to use gas had been taken by the British as a retaliatory measure after the Germans' use of it at Ypres earlier in the year.[21] The mechanics of this had been entrusted to 'Special Companies' of the Royal Engineers, under the command of Major Foulkes. The method evolved was to discharge cylinders of liquid chlorine from points twenty-five yards apart. The cylinders at each point were to be handled by two men, one a specially enlisted chemist, the other an infantryman. On opening a valve the gas would rush out and form a greenish yellow cloud which it was hoped would be carried by the wind for two hundred yards, sinking beneath the lighter air and thus incapacitating the enemy troops in their trenches opposite. A demonstration was given to senior officers at Helfaut (where the Royal Engineers were training and where Williamson places Phillip in his novel) on 22 August.

After various changes of plan, the attack was scheduled for 25 September, the gas 'to be lavishly employed on the whole front of attack'. Some 5,500 cylinders were despatched from England and 8,000 men were employed in getting them from the railheads to the trenches. A cylinder emptied in two minutes, so twenty cylinders at each station were needed for the planned forty minute discharge. There were only enough cylinders for fifteen per station so they were to be interspersed with phosphorus smoke candles. 'The care and turning on of the cylinders during the attack was entrusted to the specially raised companies of the Royal engineers and a party of six officers and 180 men – all trained in estimating the direction and velocity of the wind – were detailed from them to each of the six assaulting divisions.'[22]

Henry Williamson wove these details about the gas operations and the battle itself into his story of Phillip's service as a gas officer at Loos with such convincing narrative that it is almost impossible not to believe that he took part in the battle. It is most interesting to follow the passages that he has marked in the Official History and to see them translated through Phillip's progress in A Fox. For instance, a marginal note '23 Sept. Fire & Flood' encapsulates the fire that broke out in Cité St Pierre due to a high-explosive shell and the violent thunderstorm that occurred on X night (the penultimate night before the battle). Even the gas orders given to Phillip are exactly as in the Official History, except that in that volume they are slightly wordier.[23]

One of the main worries was the force and direction of the wind, which was a crucial factor for the use and good dispersal of the gas. The gas officers were specially trained in wind velocity and direction, and their reports were sent to Captain E. Gold, the meteorologist from the RFC (who appears under his real name in Williamson's novel). Wind worry is also a central theme of Williamson's story at this point and he includes General Haig's personal thoughts, which are marked in the Official History and which also appear in Haig's own diary.

Official History

After 5 AM the wind began to increase, but only slightly. At 5.15 AM General Haig gave the order to 'carry on', and then went up to the top of his wooden look-out tower. As the minutes passed so still did the air seem that General Haig began to fear the gas might simply hang about the British trenches.[24]

Haig's Diary

I went out at 5 a.m. Almost a calm. Alan Fletcher lit a cigarette and the smoke drifted in puffs towards the N.E. . . . At one time, owing to the calm, I feared the gas might simply hang about our trenches. However, at 5.15 a.m. I said 'carry on'. I went to the top of our wooden look-out tower. The wind came gently from S.W. and by 5.40 had increased slightly. The leaves of the poplar trees gently rustled. This seemed satisfactory. But what a risk I must run of gas blowing back upon our own dense masses of troops![25]

Both the *Official Diary* and Robert Blake's commentary in the Haig volume criticize Sir John French, whose absence from the official headquarters on the night before battle commenced and his subsequent holding back of the reserve divisions from the front, did not help the situation. On 29 September Haig sent a memorandum to Lord Kitchener explaining the situation: 'My attack, as has been reported, was a complete success. . . . and the reserves should have been at hand *then* . . . the enemy has been allowed time in which to bring up troops and to strengthen his second line. . . . We *were* in a position to make this the turning point in the war . . . naturally I feel annoyed at the lost opportunity.'[26]

In *A Fox* Williamson lays out the key points of this battle through the aegis of Captain 'Spectre' West of the 'Gaultshire Regiment' who has grasped the essentials and tells Phillip what the problems are. All the incidents are verified in the *Official History*. For instance, in *A Fox* the Sergeant Major tells Captain West that both Colonel Mowbray and his Adjutant have been hit and shortly afterwards West himself is wounded, while the *Official History* records that: 'By the time the battalions had arrived at Gun Trench the Commanding Officer of 2/Bedfordshires, Lt. Col. C.C. Onslow, and his adjutant and all four company commanders were wounded (plus 250 other ranks).'[27] So Phillip finds himself in command of the battalion which has been ordered to carry on to the battered cherry tree known to the troops as Lone Tree. The trepidation he feels at this is overcome when the Germans under 'Hauptmann Ritter' surrender. This is based on a real incident which the *Official History* records: 'The leading of the 2/Welch after it had broken through and arrived in rear of the enemy trenches near Lone Tree, which resulted in the surrender of Ritter's force . . . was an exhibition of initiative only too rare on the 25th September.'[28] In the novel Captain Douglas reappears at this point and is suspicious of Phillip, but almost immediately afterwards is wounded — 'a whizz-bang arrived with a scream and crack and shower of chalk and Douglas afterwards was lying on his face, kilt in ribbons, and his backside a mass of blood.' Captain Douglas, it will be remembered, in real life was Douglas Bell who was originally with Henry in the London Rifle Brigade. In March 1915 Bell had taken a commission as Lieutenant in the Cameron Highlanders. He was in Rouen base camp prior to Loos and entrained to Mazingarbe on 29 September. As he records in his own book, *A Soldier's Diary of the Great War*, he was wounded in action on 13 October with 'my kilt in ribbons and my backside in a bloody mess'.[29]

At the close of *A Fox Under My Cloak* there is a message for Phillip to report to the orderly room, where he is told that his exchange to the 'Diehards' had come through. So Henry returns Phillip to England and thus the novel follows again the thread of events in real life.

Henry, in fact, transferred to the 'Diehards' a little earlier. The Army List (page 1385j) notes the transfer of 'Temp. 2nd. Lieut. Henry Williamson to 25th (Reserve) Btn. Middlesex Regt., dated 9 October 1915.' This battalion had been newly formed at Crystal Palace by the Independent member of Parliament John Ward (described in the novel as 'a big heavy man with a large red face . . . had been a navvy on the yellow clay of London'). Ward, having been an agitator for better conditions and pay for navvies, became a trade unionist and from thence gained a seat in Parliament (where he was known as 'Buck Navvy') and on raising the battalion was made a lieutenant colonel.[30]

Williamson joined the regiment at Hornchurch. The only details there are of this period are from his fictional portrait in *The Golden Virgin* which leave one feeling the experience was pretty grim.[31] However, at the end of the year a new battalion was formed and the soldiers, Henry among them, found themselves now stationed at Northampton. At first the men were billeted in the town and carried out normal routine infantry training. Just before Christmas they moved out to a camp to partake in a Lewis Gun Course, where 'The mechanism was explained by a staff sergeant, whose sentences never varied.' [32]

On his return from the allotted four days' Christmas leave Williamson found that he had been posted to the Machine-Gun Training Centre at Grantham. The Army List on page 1563 notes that he was transferred to 208 Company, The Machine Gun Corps, 62nd Division, 187 Brigade. Apart from being in hospital in June and convalescent until the end of October, for the rest of 1916 he was training as a transport officer, learning about the maintenance and firing of machine guns, attending riding school, and learning how to look after horses and donkeys.

There are some small training manuals in his archive which are from this time. One is a slim eight-page booklet entitled *Preliminary Notes on the Tactical Lessons of the Recent Operations* — S.S. 119 — issued by the General Staff in 1916, where Williamson has strongly marked with blue pencil the cover note: 'NOT TO BE TAKEN INTO FRONT LINE TRENCHES OR CARRIED IN ANY OPERATION DURING WHICH IT MIGHT FALL INTO THE ENEMY'S HANDS'. Paragraphs include notes on Clearing Parties; Use of Bombers, 'There is a tendency in bombing operations for more grenades than necessary to be thrown, thus tiring out the throwers prematurely and wasting grenades'; Patrol Work; Use of R.E.; Lewis Guns, Machine Guns and Stokes Mortars, 'Lewis Guns with effect . . . in advance posts . . . machine guns allow an effective barrage to be formed behind trenches'; Use of Flares and Ground Sheets, 'has proved of great value. Their use requires practice, and this must be of the utmost importance.' Although the wording is a little academic, even these short extracts show the detail that officer training involved.

Henry Williamson had further convalescent leave in the summer of 1916. His medical records show that he was admitted to Millbank Military Hospital on 31 May 1916. The report of a Medical Board on 26 June states that 'he is now better but lost weight and is anaemic. He requires a complete change.' The address given is Georgeham. He was given two months' leave. It is at this time that we find him behaving rather wildly with his friend Terence Tetley.[33] There is a photograph of Terence standing next to Henry's motorcycle outside 11, Eastern Road, captioned by Henry as 'in the early summer of 1916'. Additional notes also added to this page state: 'Terence and Me. Top Hat on Sunday & broken boots. Flowers & Condy's Fluid. Horses on Hill. Girls in flat.' This is accompanied by a further, later, expansion.

This note refers to a drunken episode in 1916 when Terence & self went on Hill very early one morning (Sunday) about 3.30 am, wherein we (idiotically) broke into the lavatory & scattered Condy's fluid about on the flower beds — a 'protest' against smug & self-righteous civilians. We also, the next day, put on top hats, old coats & trousers, & with umbrellas mocked the Sunday top-hat parade. In the afternoon, in uniform, we rode horses on the Hill, against regulations. Then we put up flares under hot-air balloons with fuses, to burn high over London — as dummy 'Zeppelin lights'.

Henry also had a great deal of fun with his motorcycle as can be deduced from several cuttings pasted into an army notebook. One is an advertisement for Norton machines from *Motor Cycling*, 17 October 1916, which quotes a sentence of praise from a letter he had written to them, and others are letters printed in newspapers and journals concerning the problem he was experiencing with 'Konking on hills'.[34]

Thus Henry Williamson did not return to France at the beginning of June 1916 to take part in the opening phase of the Battle of the Somme, as Phillip does in *The Golden Virgin*.[35] The battle plan is laid out through the aegis of 'Spectre' West who tells Phillip the battle orders, which are based on an advance up Mash Valley to the Pozières ridge, north-east of the Albert–Pozières–Bapaume road. This was in fact the objective of the 23rd Brigade of the 8th Division, III Corps, of which the 2/Middlesex was part. The relevant passage in the *Official History* has been underlined by Williamson. 'The 8th Division, on the left [of the road], was to capture the German front defences north of the Bapaume road, including the whole western slope of Orvillers spur and the village. It was to push forward to a line facing the German 2nd position between Pozières (inclusive) and Monquet Farm.'[36]

On the following page of the *History*, also underlined (used in later writings), are the details of the operations for laying 'two very large mines' by 179/Tunnelling Company Royal Engineers under the German salient: 'Lochnagar' (under the Schwaben Redoubt) contained 60,000 lb of ammonal while 'Y Sap' contained 40,600 lb. The tunnelling, 1,030 feet long and the longest ever driven in chalk during the war, was carried out in silence, 'the men were barefooted'. The spoil was dislodged with one hand (using bayonet or auger), caught in the other, packed into sandbags and passed out of the tunnel along a line of men seated on the floor. On the final section 'An advance of 18 inches in 24 hours was considered satisfactory.'[37] There were ten of these mines altogether along the length of the British front.

The phrase 'Les Autres Boches!' used by the French sportsman referring to the British troops in 'The Yellowhammer' chapter of *The Golden Virgin*, is authenticated in the *Official History*, in a footnote about 'Rehearsals'. These manoeuvres replicated in every detail the movements for the forthcoming battle and so used up a lot of farmland and damaged and destroyed crops. This infuriated the French *cultivateurs* and the phrase seems to have been in common usage.[38]

Also authenticated is, of course, the appalling fact that this supposedly secret operation was known to the Germans. They had gathered that an attack was forthcoming from their normal intelligence sources, including a speech by Lloyd George on 2 June which referred to 'postponing Whitsun until the beginning of July', which puzzled but alerted them. But they also knew the exact moment of attack from overhearing, by close attention at their listening post at La Boiselle, a telephone message from the Commander of the Fourth Army, General Sir Henry Rawlinson ('Rawly'), wishing 'Good Luck' etc. to the 34th Division.[39] Details of Crown Prince Rupprecht's diary entries regarding this German Intelligence are also in the *Official History*,[40] as are the details of the equipment and clothing of the British troops.[41]

So the morning of that fateful 1 July 1916 dawned – a superbly fine summer's day. Under Brigadier General H.D. Tuson 23 Brigade prepared to attack up Mash Valley and then to advance across the Albert–Pozières road up rising ground to its objective of Pozières village.

Heavy artillery bombardment had been carried out at various times and for eighty minutes' duration during the preceding eight days to confuse the Germans. On 1 July bombardment was carried out for sixty-five minutes only – to give a fifteen minute 'surprise' factor for the attack. The sound of the bombardment was so great that it was heard in England.[42] At 7.30 a.m. in France the artillery barrage stopped. The heavily laden troops of the 11 Divisions of General Rawlinson's Fourth Army scrambled out of their trenches and advanced at the steady walking pace of their instructions to be met by an intensive heavy barrage which created chaos and carnage. The Germans used their pre-knowledge to full effect. 2/Middlesex lost 22 officers and 601 other ranks.[43] The total number of casualties on that first day was 57,540 of which 20,000 were dead.[44]

The Battle of the Somme continued for 140 days; 140 days of relentless fighting; 140 days of advances and retirements, ground gained, ground lost, ground regained; 140 days of death and horror. But with gritted relentlessness the Allies did make some little advance – the Germans were driven back six miles. The battle was finally halted (mainly due to bad weather) on 18 November. Total British casualties were 420,000; French casualties 203,000; German 437,500 – just over one million men.

Williamson did not labour his writings on the Somme Battle. Having set the scene and recorded the appalling event in *The Golden*

Virgin Phillip is one of those wounded on the first day of the battle and returned to hospital in England via the Casualty Clearing Station (CCS) at Heilly and then No. 9 General Hospital at Rouen.[45] Phillip eventually travels to Devon, accompanied by his cousin Willie Maddison, also injured at the Somme, to convalesce at Sir George Newne's home, Hollerday House, in Lynton.[46] Henry Williamson did indeed go on leave to Devon at that time but to the cottage in Georgeham. In August he went down on his motorcycle together with his friend Terence Tetley for company. A photograph in his archive shows them entirely relaxed, swimming naked at Putsborough Sands.

On 29 August he attended another Medical Board at Caxton Hall where he was found to be 'still suffering from the effects of dysentery. He is anaemic & about 1½ stone below weight.' He was considered unfit for General Service for three months, unfit for Home Service for three months and unfit even for light duties for six weeks. He was therefore given a further six weeks' leave.

Throughout 1916 in *The Golden Virgin* there are increasing references to the young girl with 'white even teeth and large china-blue eyes' called Lily Cornford, who is later killed in a Zeppelin raid. The real-life scenario to match this fictional episode is complicated but interesting. Zeppelin and aeroplane raids were rife throughout the war and created havoc throughout the country but particularly in the city of London.

The raid described by Henry Williamson in *The Golden Virgin* is correct in every detail and the facts are all marked in a book entitled *The German Air Raids on Great Britain 1914–18* by Captain Joseph Morris.[47] This raid took place on the night of 23/24 September 1916 and was known as 'The Fall of the Thirties'. There had been an earlier very heavy raid on the night of 2/3 September, 'the greatest airship fleet ever assembled' when sixteen vessels took part. That night was the first time that an airship was shot down by machine-gun fire from an aeroplane. Lt. W. Leefe-Robinson, No. 39 Squadron, went up from Sutton's Farm in his BE2c aeroplane and shot down the wooden Zeppelin *Schutte Lanz* SL 11, which fell at Cuffley village and burned for two hours after hitting the ground. This was a great boost to British morale and a huge blow to the Germans, who thought the airships invincible. Morris's description of this attack, written in formal but graphic tones, is very realistic. Leefe-Robinson was awarded a VC for this heroic feat.

On 15 April 1916 39 Squadron had been formed specifically for home defence. with headquarters at Hounslow, for the immediate protection of London, with two flights, one disposed at Sutton's Farm and the other at Hainault Farm. The idea of Home Defence squadrons expanded rapidly and several more were formed in quick succession. Also in late 1916 gun defences were being organized for London and Morris details seven ground formations in and around the capital – including one at Hilly Fields although this was later abandoned.[48]

On the night of 23/24 September eleven naval airships set out from their bases in Belgium. Two turned back, so Williamson's 'nine' is correct. Morris states 'the three newest and best ships were to attack London'. These were L31 commanded by Kapitänleutnant Mathy, L32 by Kapitänleutnant Peterson, and L33 by Kapitänleutnant Bocker. Mathy was the most well-known and deadly veteran of such raids. The Germans had learnt the lesson of the fall of SL 11 three weeks earlier and approached by a circuitous route to avoid the known defences.[49]

Mathy was active from about 11 p.m. coming in over Rye and continuing to London, and 'by dropping flares he blanketted such searchlights as pierced the darkness to light him up'. He crossed London almost unmolested and got safely away, going out by Great Yarmouth.

Peterson in L32 came in with Mathy, and dropping bombs here and there he approached London at about 1 a.m., bombing searchlight and gun emplacements north of the Thames and then turned to make for home. But he was spotted by 2/Lt. F. Sowrey, 39 Squadron, patrolling the usual run from Joyce Green to Sutton's Farm, who attacked him successfully, bringing the airship down in flames at Snail's Hall Farm at Great Burstead, near Billericay – exactly as described by Henry Williamson in *The Golden Virgin*.

The third airship, under Bocker's command, separated from the other two off the Goodwin Sands and came in to Wanstead at about midnight. He had dropped some bombs but preserved his main load, turning over West Ham where 'gun after gun and light after light got on to his ship'. He dropped his bombs on Bromley-by-Bow and Bow, inflicting 11 deaths and 25 injured people and considerable damage to factories, businesses and houses. He was seen, chased, attacked and hit by 2/Lt. A. de B. Brandon, 39 Squadron, but L33 escaped and continued out to sea. However, in serious trouble the ship returned and then landed intact at Little Wigborough where the crew was taken prisoner.

A week later on 1 October 1916, L31 and Mathy were shot down by 2/Lt. W. Tempest[50] again in a BE2c from 39 Squadron, flying from North Weald Bassett at 10 p.m. for the Hainault Farm/Joyce Green patrol. Tempest spotted a Zeppelin and attacked. The L31 fell in flames and Tempest had to dive alarmingly to avoid being hit by the burning ship which shot past him 'roaring like a furnace'. The L31 fell at Potters Bar just before midnight and with her perished the redoubtable Mathy and all her crew. The death of this hero was a great blow to German esteem.

So the facts in *The Golden Virgin* as given above are correct and L32 was indeed brought down at Snail's Hall Farm. But this was not the raid that bombed Hither Green killing the real-life counterpart of 'Lily Cornford'. That raid took place on the night of 19/20 October 1917, and was known as 'The Night of the Silent Raid'. A mass attack of eleven German naval airships, the largest since the attack on 2 September 1916, set out from Belgium bases on 19 October 1917.[51] Their destination was thought to have been the industrial centre of England, the Midlands. In calm weather they crossed the East Coast between Great Yarmouth and Hull but on having to rise to a height of about four miles to avoid ground defences found themselves caught in a 60 mph gale and were forced beyond their control south-east through England – and eventually France. Morris gives a most graphic description of the appalling conditions these airships and their crew frequently faced from frostbite from the cold, alpine sickness from the height, and enormous buffeting of machines from the elements, so that often neither crew nor machines were functioning in any controlled manner.[52] On this night the main body of airships drifted over London, Morris states, 'quite unconsciously'. The guns and searchlights were forbidden to open up so as not to disclose their whereabouts to the raiders. (*Chronicle* readers will know that Desmond Neville [in real life Terence Tetley] wonders why the gun on Hilly Fields has not fired.) Thus the raid came to be known as the 'Silent Raid'.

In the 'Silent Raid' the airship that concerns this account was L45 commanded by Kapitänleutnant Waldemar Kolle, which came in over the Yorkshire coast at about half-past eight, having left Belgium earlier in the day with enough fuel for a twenty-two hour flight. Rising, like the others, to avoid various attacks, the airship was forced south-east over Leicester and Northampton where she dropped her main load of bombs shortly before 11 p.m. but with little resultant damage. Joan Read has stated that her cargo contained in total two 300 kg bombs, two 100 kg bombs, sixteen 50 kg bombs and ten incendiaries.[53] L45 then followed the London and North-Western railway line to London, dropping bombs on Hendon and Cricklewood, and then Piccadilly, causing a large hole in the road outside Swan and Edgar's Stores, which killed seven people and injured eighteen others. Morris has a photograph of this hole, captioning it as caused by a 2 cwt bomb.[54]

The airship continuing south-east then dropped a 300 kg bomb on Camberwell, and a second one on Hither Green where it fell on Glenview Road, killing five women and nine children and also injuring two men, three women and two more children, and demolishing and damaging several houses. One of the dead was of course 'Lily Cornford', in real life of the Milgate family. In her article Joan Read stated that Lily's father Samuel Lilly Milgate died in hospital five days later, her mother was seriously injured and only one brother, Arthur George Milgate, aged fifteen, escaped lightly. 'The fourteen victims of the bomb were buried in two deep graves dug side by side in "Heroes Corner" in Ladywell Cemetery. Three were members of the Milgate family, two sisters and a brother.'[55]

The airship continued on its way to the Channel and was attacked by Lt. T.B. Pritchard, 39 Squadron, but he was unsuccessful as the airship rose too high for him, and passed out to sea about midnight. L45 was fired at by the French at Auxerre at 6.15 p.m. but again was not hit. Kolle was lost but eventually recognized Lyons and then tried to turn to fly to Switzerland as he was short of fuel. Once more he was fired at unsuccessfully, Kolle thought he had reached Switzerland when over the Haute Alpes and being out of petrol he brought the plane down near Sisteron but realized too late that he was still in France. After a hit and miss landing, when some of the crew jumped out causing the ship to rise again and to be dashed against a hillside, the crew all emerged safely, set fire to the airship, and surrendered. All were interned at Sisteron.[56]

In his story, Henry Williamson wanted to record the tragic death of the young girl 'Lily' Milgate and the details of the Zeppelin raid which killed her and other local people – an important event which he felt must be marked within his overall social history of the area. But he placed Phillip in France at the time of 'Lily's' real death in October 1917. He therefore skilfully encompassed the later raid within the first. There is no evidence to suggest that Henry knew 'Lily' – certainly if he had known her that well one would expect some mention of her in his personal papers. The raid which killed her has no mention in his diary and he was in Felixstowe at that time (see Chapter 6).

At a Medical Board at Caxton Hall on 23 October 1916 Henry Williamson was passed fit for Home Service and so his training recommenced. On 1 November he was promoted to the rank of full lieutenant with the Machine Gun Corps. The promotion appeared in the Army List (p.1565) in the following February, but it was notified in the London Gazette of 21 December.

Two further booklets in Henry's archive give some idea of the training for becoming a transport officer. As their contents are very pertinent to Henry Williamson's work during the following months, it is worth giving some details from them.[57] In the first booklet, Notes on Pack Transport[58] we find, sandwiched between several pink pages of lists of Military Books published by the Authority, ten pages of text plus a selection of illustrative photographs. 'Of all forms of transport, pack transport requires the most unremitting care and closest supervision in order to maintain it in that high state of efficiency without which continuous operations are impossible.'

Details are given on how to fit Pack Saddles and all the attendant accoutrements. The weights that can be carried are stated as 'Mule – 160 lbs, Horse – 200 lbs, Donkey – 100 lbs'. Loading instructions are detailed and the knots to be used for each different process are illustrated. There is a detailed 'Table of Weights' from which one can see for example that a box of 1,000 rounds of .303 charges weighed 80 lb 8 oz, while a pair of saddle bags of ammunition was 19 lb, long crowbars 30 lb, 2½-foot picket posts 5 lb, an 80 ft picketing rope 17 lb, box of biscuits 74 lb, box of preserved meat 78 lb 8 oz, etc. Thus the ratio of these weights, when multiplied up to service even a platoon, to the amount laid down that each animal could carry, makes quite a logistical problem.

The second booklet is a small red volume entitled on the cover The Mounted Officer's Book of Horses and Mules for Transport, and on the title page as The Care of the Horse and Mule and how the harness should fit.[59] The Introduction is worth quoting as it gives an exact feeling of the atmosphere:

The object of this book is to assist those whose duties are with the Machine Gun Transport. It should also be found useful to all Officers who are to be mounted.

As it is considered a point of honour for the Machine Gunner to keep his Gun firing under all circumstances, so it should be a point of honour for the Driver to keep his animal always in a fit condition and ready for any emergency.

This can only be done by the utmost attention to the animals: watering, feeding, grooming, and correct harnessing.

Very often the animal is put down as lazy or bad-tempered when the fault really lies with the man in whose care it is.

The efficiency of the Machine Gun Companies' Transport depends absolutely on the condition of each horse and mule, and too much care and attention cannot be given to their treatment.

The illustrations in this book show exactly the correct position of each part of harness, and any deviation from such position will only result in injury to the animal, create work for the man, and greatly impede the progress of the guns.

Harsh treatment should never be meted out to mules or horse, and this applies particularly to mules, who strongly resent any beating and refuse to be worked as a consequence. But by kindness, coupled with a firm hand, much good work will willingly be done by these invaluable assistants of the Machine Gun Corps.

A list of the sections of the book shows the care that was taken of the animals:

> Horse, Points of (with fold-out illustration showing forty-nine points – e.g. withers, fetlock, cannon bone, etc.);
> The Bridle and how it should fit (it is in seven parts and 'It should be understood that the greatest care should be exercised in fitting the horse's bridle and bit');
> The Saddle and Blanket and how they should fit (seven parts of the saddle and the Correct Holding of the Reins);
> The Correct Position of Rider in the Saddle;
> Officer's Charger Fully Equipped, Marching Order (a fold-out illustration showing detailed nearside, plus hind view and off side);
> Officer's Saddle, Marching Order (instructions on how the blanket should be folded, saddle placed, girths, surcingle, shoe cases, rolled cloak, grooming kit, bit, headstalls, head rope and built up rope, all placed exactly to distribute weight and cause least discomfort to the horse);

Girth Galls, How to keep from;

The Draught Harness for the Mule or Horse (a further fold-out illustration to assist text);

Grooming ('No horse is well groomed unless groomed quickly and with vigour' – some emphasis on disinfectant processes to prevent disease);

Position of various injuries of importance (further fold-out illustration showing in particular the many gall points, plus selection of detailed diagrams in the text);

The Yorkshire Boot for Horses that Brush (rubbing of legs together in motion);

How to Kill a Horse Humanely (handing it a handful of corn whilst you shoot it with a pistol at an exact point on the forehead);

Watering (three times a day at least and before each feed, and etc.);

Feeding ('Horses have small stomachs and should eat in small quantities and often – Morning 2 lb hay & 3 lb oats, Mid-day, 3 lb hay and 3 lb oats, Evening 5 lb hay and 4 lb oats' . . . 'In the Service, a bran mash is given every Saturday evening in place of corn. It opens the horse's bowels.');

The Duties of A Transport Officer [as this is particular to Williamson's duty it is transcribed in full at the end of this list];

Selection of Picketing Grounds and Open Standings (known as lines);

March Routine (Have 'stable', water and feed at least 1½ hours before moving, during which farrier should inspect all animals' feet. Arrange to have a good corn ration in nose-bag . . . an adequate supply of water is as important as food . . . when watering slacken girths and out bits. . .);

General Notes (general behaviour and again emphasizing cleanliness).

THE DUTIES OF A TRANSPORT OFFICER

1. He is responsible for the detailing of all regimental transport. He should arrange a system of detailing transport duties daily, unless transport will be unevenly worked. Otherwise wagons are called out at all odd times, unnecessarily interfering with watering, feeding, grooming and the care of harness. In the case of M.G. Companies, mules worked in single pairs should

occasionally be changed from near side to off, and *vice versa*, otherwise one will always have to bear the driver.

2. The T.O. [Transport Officer] is responsible for the condition of all horses, harness, vehicles, and for all matters which affect their utility, and in order to keep his animals in a good condition he should arrange for the observance of a regular stable routine whenever practicable.

3. He is responsible that the quantity of forage admissible per horse is drawn and expended without waste.

4. That all harness is kept serviceable, and fitted properly to each animal. That the shoeing is kept up to date and that the vehicles are kept properly greased and ready for service.

5. In order that the sick and injured rate of his animals is kept low, he should impress upon his men the necessity of individual care of their charges.

6. When the V.O. [Veterinary Officer] is inspecting his animals, he should arrange his duties so as to be there or detail an N.C.O. to accompany the V.O. during the inspection, and should elicit any information he requires concerning the welfare of the animals under his charge.

7. He should render it impossible for any captured or commandeered horse to be placed amongst his own until such time that they are passed fit by the V.O.[60]

Henry Williamson was now equipped with the knowledge necessary for a transport officer. His training was very shortly to be put to the test in the front line.

5

Transport Officer at the Front

In *Love and the Loveless* Phillip Maddison, as Transport Officer with the 286 Machine Gun Company (MGC), embarks with them to France in mid-December 1916,[1] and Christmas is spent at the Front, although out of line at their base at Colincamps. In the afternoon of Christmas Day Phillip mounts his horse Black Prince and rides off to revisit the scenes of his experiences of the summer and the opening day of the Battle of the Somme. This allows the author to pay tribute to the dead of that battle, and to put into his fictional scenario the anguish that he always underwent in real life at Christmas,[2] and certainly would have felt when he saw this scene a few weeks later.

The actual embarkation of 208 Machine Gun Company, with Henry Williamson as Transport Officer, did not occur until the end of February 1917. This period is very well covered by primary source material: his archive contains his 1917 diary and letters home to his mother, together with a Field Correspondence Book (*Army Correspondence Book*, 152) and a Field Message Book. (These latter contain the carbon copies kept by Henry; top copies would have been sent off to the addressee.) The combination of this material gives a detailed picture with an immediate impression of the atmosphere of not only Henry Williamson's life at that time, but a more general overall view. All the items were written in indelible pencil and the letters tend to be on sheets torn from the Field Message Books – making deciphering difficult but just possible. As before, all grammar and spelling are exactly as in Henry's original holograph material. At this time, as officer in charge of his section, he countersigned all letters, so he was able to be slightly more open than perhaps he would have been if he had known a fellow officer was to peruse them. The code he invented was almost childishly obvious, and would surely never have passed another official censor.

The first entry in his 1917 diary (stamped as passed by Field Office 4491) on 1 January concerns his monthly pay: '£11 12s 6d', and then on 6 January, 'Go to 208 as T.O.'. There he seems to have run into trouble of some sort immediately. On 10 January he recorded cryptically 'All drivers isolated' and two days later '27 new Drivers. Appear fairly good men.' Then ominously on 15 January: 'Heard that am to be fired' and the following day, 'Saw Major McKonnel about my job.'

This was presumably for a reprimand only (not the temporary removal from the regiment that occurs in the 'Life with the Donks' chapter of Love and the Loveless) for the next day, 17 January, Henry went on a week's training to practise getting the animals on and off trains, and moving them and the limbers (a limber consists of two large wheels with long pole arrangements for the harness to attach to, on which carts or guns were mounted for transportation) around the countryside. This was successful for he recorded, 'Entraining. Good results.' The first day they moved to Newark, 'Hard work all day – very frosty', then across to Eakring, 'Good billet. Animals picketted between limbers. Very cold.' On Saturday he took the limbers to nearby Chipstone for further entraining practice – 'Transport late. Rode to range with Gibb, ½ blotto'. They returned to Newark on Monday 22 January and back to Grantham the following day where he heard that orders had come through for the Company to proceed to France on 1 February, found a nice letter from Mrs Nicholson, and 'paid Rose [2nd in Command, 208 MGC] for messing £1 8s 8d'. He went home on weekend leave, taking his gramophone, selling his coat to Gibb for £1 and noting that taxis cost him 13s 6d and his ticket 16/-. On Saturday he met his friend, 'Stany',[3] in town and they 'Went to Romance. Lovely time'. On Sunday he saw Mrs Nicholson who was very nice to him, but returning to Grantham on Sunday night he was 'fed up with life'.

The sailing was postponed and every evening Henry went into Grantham to see either a show or a film, or went drinking with New Zealand sergeants. The cold continued as did the routine work. On 9 February he noted in his diary 'Turned into a remount company' and the next day, 'Transferred a lot of animals to other Coys.' On 11 February he saw 'Capt. King [CO, 208 MGC] re Watch', on 13 February went to the 'Theatre with Montford & Milland, good show, 'Diplomacy'. On 14 February he was 'Strafed like hell by C.O. and Col. Bidder' and the next day recorded; 'Drivers rather sulky. Before C.O. To go abroad on Monday.' But this sailing was again postponed and Henry was 'very fed-up'. On 20 February he got new mules and horses but the very next day recorded 'Poor Cuthbert was run over and killed. Inspection tomorrow by Gen. Gordon.'

Henry Williamson's *Army Correspondence Book*, 152 (*Field Service*) was opened on 6 February 1917. The first page gives a list of 'Drivers 208 M.G. Coy Transport on 14.2.17' (see plate 22a), followed by one or two pages of organizational lists for these drivers. Then follows a copy in Williamson's own handwriting of the 'Orders for Entraining'.

Transport Section 208 Coy.
Orders for Entraining
208 MGC will leave for Service Overseas on 26.2.17
Time of Parade 5.30 pm
Time for refreshments 7.45 pm
Time for arrival at Military Dock 8.15 pm
Train departs 9.30 pm
A hot meal for all grooms and drivers will be served at 4.45 pm. The Transport Section will parade with the Cmp for this meal. The Cmp will be marched to the Dining Hall by the Officer Commanding.
Any casualty in animals is to be reported immediately to the O.C. Transport, direct. No alcoholic drinks are to be taken or received by any of the transport personnel. All animals will be fed with a 1½ feed at 4.15 pm. Animals will be watered at 3.45 pm.

Entraining
a) On arriving at the siding drivers will move their wagons opposite the trucks at which it is to be loaded, and dismount. All drivers will then slacken girths, taking care that they are not left so loose as to enable the saddle to slip off the animals tail, or under his belly during transport. b) Unfasten head ropes and chains. c) Take off bitheadstalls, bits and reins. These will be hung round the neck. d) Remove nosebags. e) Secure traces. f) Slip stirrup irons up the leathers and secure by passing stirrup leather through the irons. g) Horses will be led up platform in single file, with headropes loose being placed alternately right and left of the doorway. Drivers and grooms will take nosebags into compartments with them in readiness to feed if opportunity occurs. All animals must be tied as in the practice entraining, through the ring, round the top bar, round the lower bar then secure. Before leaving the stables on Wednesday all feed bags will be full.

Embarking
If the animals are to be slung onto the transport boat, L/Cpl Stirling and the shoeing smith will be detailed to steady the animals on the deck.
HWW. Lieut i/c TS. 208 MGC 19.2.17.

On Saturday 24 February the 208 Machine Gun Corps 'Left Grantham at 9.30 for Southampton', arriving there at 6 o'clock the following morning with 'No casualties' [i.e. among the horses]. They went on board at 7 p.m. that evening, anchoring in the Harbour overnight and leaving the following day. They arrived after a 'good voyage, at Le Havre without incident at 2 in the morning' on 27 February, and going to the same Rest Camp as in 1914, where Williamson got two new mules and a horse, heard that the English had taken Kut[4] and borrowed 20 francs from Horseley.

Letter: posted from Southampton
To: Mrs Williamson
208 M.G.Coy. BEF. France, 25.2.1917.
Dear Mother,
It is 10 oclock Sunday morning, & we have got to Southampton Docks where I am penning this at the moment. We are expecting to sail tonight, but as yet our transport hasn't turned up (the ship, I mean). We shall be in France on Monday morning and I expect we shall go right up the line.

I hope you got the blankets: will you have them washed: they are my own private property. Will you get my British warm from Jerry,[5] and have it dry cleaned. Tell him I want you to send it out here but dont do so until, and if, I write you.

By the way, when you see a letter of mine with an X at the top, you will know it has a message in it: probably the place we are at: and if it is Ypres I will put a dot under the letters thus 'Y.es, p.resently we r.e.turn ever s.o wet.' Reads Ypres, see?

There is a feeling here that the crisis is almost on us – my own opinion, based upon Lloyd George's speech, and his price for wheat – 80/- this year, & 55/- the next!!, is this -: 'We are at the zenith of our power' – if we can smash Germany up now, well & good, if we can't, we may as well have peace, because we shall never do it if we can't do it this year. I think you will find this is so.

Well goodbye & my love to everyone. I only send my kind regards to my own people: others you can give no message to until I actually write, but I [don't] mind you giving them my address. I am waiting for them to move, comprenez? Well, best of love, Harry.

PS. The mules are very good up to now. We left G' at 9.30, arrived here at 6.

Letter: [marked by HW 'On Active Service' & Countersigned by himself.] *Field Censor* 828
208 M.G.Coy. B.E.F. France. Tuesday 27 Feb. '17
Dear Mother,
Just a line to let you know we had a safe crossing without incident. So far we have repeated our performance of last time, Nov. 1914. [i.e. to Le Havre and Rest Camp]. I have seen the Tanks: they are wonderful things.

The news is very good today, isn't it: we have just read in the papers of the Kut victory, & the Somme affair, which is very cheering. By the time you get this, I shall be round about the place Charlie is now [his cousin Charlie Boon had been killed in action at Beaumont Hamel the previous November – see map p. 215]. If you speak to Gerry, you can ask him where he was, and then you will know where I am. How is everybody?

You ought to hear the artillery here: it is one continuous quaking and heaving of the earth, with blood red flashes always before one – always, always, always. My experiences with the LRB were nothing compared with this now. Must shut up now, as am very busy. Yours with love, Harry.

PS. The Bosche prisoners are a miserable lot. I saw some today.

The Company entrained from Le Havre on 28 February, moving to the front line area and 'arrived at Astreux at 2 in morning (Friday) very tired and fed-up. Went to Forceville.' On 2 March Williamson recorded 'Gave Rose for messing 20 fcs. Are attd [attached] to 62 Div. Guns all day. Rotten billet. Mud. Germans retreating.'

As Henry Williamson recorded at the front of his *Army Correspondence Book*, 208 Machine Gun Company was attached to 62 Division, 187 Infantry Brigade, on 27 February 1917; 62 Division was the 2nd West Riding.[6] Henry also added here; '187 Bgde – Bg. Gen. Taylor. 62 Division – Maj. Gen. Braithwaite. V Corps – Lt. Gen.

Fanshawe. V Army – Gen. Gough. BEF – F.M. Sir D. Haig.' The Commanding Officer of 208 MGC, as already established, was Captain Cecil King and the second-in-command Lt. Clarence Rose.

The role of the Machine Gun Corps, now attached permanently to its allotted division and normally consisting of sixteen guns, was to remain with the brigade and to provide covering fire for its operations, moving in and out of the front line with the infantry. The role of the Transport Officer was to oversee the welfare of the horses and to organize the logistics of movements of guns and armaments and general support, e.g. billets and provisions for both horses and men. The trench maps with their linen backs handed out to officers to which Williamson refers to in *Love and the Loveless* are still in his archive (see plate 20c).

The year 1917 had opened without any particular offensive but with a continual struggle against shelling, sniping and mud. The role of the British Army had been laid down at the Allied conference the previous November, based on General Joffre's scheme. The instructions handed out by Field Marshal Sir Douglas Haig were that the defences should be strengthened to allow more strategic movements of troops and the enemy were to be harassed by 'raids, discharges of gas, and concentrated bombardments' on the fronts of the British Fourth (General Sir Henry Rawlinson) and Fifth (General Sir Hubert Gough) Armies, while preparations were made for a large-scale offensive early in 1917. However, General Nivelle produced a new plan in early December, which delegated a wider front for the British and Haig adjusted his strategy accordingly. The directive for the Fifth Army (which included 62 Division and 208 MGC, and thus HW), holding the area between Lesboeufs and Gommecourt, with Anzac troops on the right flank, was to attack in the direction of Achiet le Grand, with a series of carefully planned advances.[7]

In early February President Wilson of the United States of America had broken off diplomatic relations with Germany (and eventually entered the war on 6 April, with troops ariving in France in late June). Some 50,000 troops of the Portuguese Expeditionary Force now arrived in France, but this extra surge of fighting personnel was unfortunately annulled by the Kaiser's order for German troops to withdraw to the fortified Hindenburg Line. This was a tactical move which much advantaged his armies by giving a greatly reduced line to defend, thus freeing large numbers of troops for other duties; they followed a plan of total destruction as they withdrew which made life extremely difficult for the English armies in pursuit. On the Eastern Front, the situation in Russia was very unstable: by the end of February large protests against the war were being held. Taking advantage of the unrest, the Bolsheviks were stirring up trouble and citing revolutionary tracts leading to riots, including in Petrograd. The trouble escalated so rapidly that the Tsar was forced to abdicate on 15 March – February in the Russian calendar – thus the 'February Revolution', followed in the autumn by the final 'October Revolution'. The summer was marked for those in charge of the Allied Armies by acute anxiety as to which would affect the war first – the demise of the Russian Force, or the hoped for advent of the Americans.

It was established on the night of 25 February that there had been a considerable German withdrawal astride the Ancre Valley when 62 Division relieved the 63rd, who had had a month of heavy fighting with substantial casualty losses. Captain C.H. Hoare, Brigade Major 187 Brigade, on going up the line found it surprisingly quiet and making a considerable recce found the Germans had withdrawn.[8] The continued withdrawal, attacks and subsequent battle can be followed in Williamson's own words as his progress is charted by his diary entries, field notebook messages and letters home. No comment or analysis has been added so as not to interrupt the intensity of Henry Williamson's own detailed commentary, which constitutes a remarkable record of life at the Front in the early part of 1917.

Letter: postmark Field Post Office: 3 MR 1917. Passed Field Censor 1562
Dear Mother,
Just a brief note before we ['watch' crossed out] working. If you dont hear from me for sometime you mustn't worry: of course you comprit that when one is working, especially pushing a handcart [code for a 'push'] one has no time perhaps for weeks. You remember what we saw at the Kings Hall that afternoon? Well, I shall be imitating it in about four hours time: still I have plenty of rum for which G. b. praised. How is Mrs. N.? [Nicholson] Still well, I hope. I have received no letters since I have been here.

Will you please send me a matchbox cover, Bryant & Mays, send it on. The guns are driving me mad: the shells are bursting 200 yards away. I can hardly write properly. I am of course with the guns now. Well, no more now, I have to give my little lads their rum. Goodbye old thing. Tell Jerry I am where he was.

Love to all. H.

Diary: Sunday 4 March: Weather clearing. Went to Beaumont Hamel. [This is where his cousin Charlie Boon was killed in action, Nov. 1916. This must have been a very emotional moment – too much so to mention]. Saw Y Ravine. Terrible place. Deep dugouts. Artillery moving forward. Strafe tonight. Coy. goes in line Tuesday.

Letter: postmark Field Post Office: 5 MR 17. Passed Field Censor 4131
[Written on Machine Gun Corps headed notepaper, and the envelope stamped with MGC crest.]
Dear Mother,   Monday 4.3.16 [NB: mistake in year]
Just a line to let you know I am all right, although you will understand that I am one of the very few lucky ones. We are in rest now, and need it after our experiences. The mud is awful: 2 feet deep: nothing can move, the guns never stop, day or night, & all the windows for miles back are shattered by concussion.

Please write to me as often as you like: letters are always welcome, you needn't send any food etc etc: there are hundreds of canteens out here, where one can buy anything, and the food we get is the very best. I am keeping a diary, which will interest when I come back. Dont believe any rot about the Bosche crumbling: you have only to be out here a bit to realize it is one mighty army facing another mighty army, & to defeat him on land would take millions of guns and lives. Well I am tired so will close now.

The Bosche is only going back because of the mud, nothing can move in it, and we have the disadvantage of fighting over the ground we have utterly ruined: & we will have to build thousands of Nissen Huts, & it will take months to get the guns up. So thats the reason, not because he is 'cracking'. I expect you will read of something in a few weeks time. Well write soon. Love to all Harry. I wrote to Cuthbert [Nicholson] yesterday. How are they all? How is Jerry. Get my warm cleaned & send the April London, Pearsons & Royal every month.

Diary: Monday 5 March: Section officers went to trenches at Miraumont today. Heard we are going to Hamel.

Letter: *postmark Field Post Office:* 10 MR 17. *On Active Service. Passed Field Censor* 4131.
To: Mrs Williamson
[Marked with X to denote the prearranged dotted letter code message which = Miraumont – using a 'w' in place of a fugitive 'u'.]
Dear Mother,
Just a line to let you know I am well and are fit in spite of an awful 3 days & nights. We are in messy rest billets now, & need it too. [The slightly odd wording allows him to fit in his code as above!]

I went this morning to see the ruins of a village which withstood our attack for months, but finally fell to the Naval People. The deep dug-outs are simply marvellous – the steps leading to them were mostly undamaged & very narrow & the dugouts themselves floored, wallpapered, electric lights and beds etc etc. The village itself stood on an eminence and was protected by two roads in the form of a Y, the village being between the two horns, and we had to attack across the horns, and along the stem, so you can see what a strong position it was, as the Bosche could enfilade both the roads from his rear.

Only a few of the dugouts were smashed: our barrage fire accounted for most of them, and they could not get out of their dugouts in time. By the way the date is Monday 5 March, the army out here is beautifully equipped: we have canteens just behind the lines, railways run up immediately the ground is captured, food, clothings, coal, etc, is of the best, all troops get paid. Nissen Huts with stoves & 2 blankets per man keep one warm. There is nothing left of Beaumont Hamel now. All the bricks have gone to make the roads, and the village is one huge desolation and destruction. The work of the Salvage Corps is excellent, nothing is left on the old ground: all helmets, rifles etc are cleared up. I had a narrow escape yesterday. I was going up to the trenches & over came a few Bosche shells and one tore a limber up, & tore a chunk out of my helmet over my left ear: without the helmet I should be in blighty now with a broken shoulder.

Well I cant say any more: did you get my letter from Southampton about the cross on the letter? If so, read, mark and learn & you will learn a few things. I have had nothing from anyone yet. No letters I mean. Love to all Harry.

PS I would prefer to be here anyday, to England. I am, I hope, out to see it through this time.

Diary: Tuesday 6 March: We are relieving the 34th MGC tomorrow. Went to Engelbelmer about billets.

Diary: Wednesday 7 March: Rode over to B.H. [Beaumont Hamel] Beaucourt and nearly to Miraumont today. Awful desolation. Aeroplane down. No letters yet.

Diary: Thursday 8 March: Took over from 34 MGC transport in valley at Hamel. Up at night to Coy. HQ. Road (Railway) badly crumped. Gunners lost 1 horse & G.S. waggon. Freezing at night. Slept in bell tent. Took 24,000 rounds to Miraumont.

Diary: Friday 9 March: Bosche shelled Railway Road a bit. 30,000 rounds to Miraumont tonight. A few whizz-bangs in Suicide Valley (217d) Rose left for HQ.'

Letter: postmark Field Post Office: 12 MR 17. Passed Field Office 4491 [From this point the above details will be omitted unless a change occurs.]

9.3.17 Evening

Dear darling old mother,

Am in the pink, very fit & strong, & daily growing heavier. You may remember in my last, or last but one, letter, I mentioned the name of a ruined town? Well, we are quite near there, altho' the Bosche is a few miles away & likely to go further as you will soon read I expect. We shot 32 last night, a working party.

I have got a lovely Bosche watch & will hang on to it when I get my 'Blighty' (ask Gerald what a 'Blighty' is) & give it to you. I have also *seen* a pair of corsets in a deep dug out here, but I am sure you don't want. Well am tired now, for heavens sake write to me. love – in a hurry. Willie.

Diary: Saturday 10 March: Early morning intense bombardment. Bosche prisoners. Building a dugout. Went to dinner with Canadians. All got tight.'
Diary: memo section: 'Have heard there is to be an attack soon on Achiet le petit & le grand.'

Diary: Sunday 11 March: Note from G.O.C. Brigade to attend at 4 oclock.[9] Saw damning report from Capt. King 'incompetent, useless etc' Road shelled a bit. Five aeroplanes (British) down. 2 Bosche. Preparations for attack on Achiet le petit. 240 prisoners. 15 machine guns.

Letter: 12 March 17

Dear Mother,

Am quite well and fit, but am rather unhappy as I fear I will lose my job – there has been trouble, but anyhow I dont think I shall lose much, it is all work and no pay. So dont be astonished if I go to the artillery or the ASC [Army Service Corps] – I have had more during the last week than I got in 4 months in the Flemish sector. By God, its awful – we are shelled day & night – the roads are barraged and 12inch Hows [Howitzer guns] knock hell into us all day & night, but our guns knock the Bosche to hell & back, & when you get this we shall have done the same – comprenez?

Well I am just going along a — awful road with a little river along it (the only one here) & expect to get a blighty one – 7 of our offrs are back already with Blighty ones. Well, Cheero dear old thing, I don't want any grub or anything except a good pair pyjamas but put your address on each letter to me – I aint had a letter from anyone since I've been out, I expect I will get a good bunch in a day or so – its now Monday time 2.30 in the afternoon.

Diary: Monday 12 March: Artillery ominously quiet early morning. Davy wounded by bomb. Am taking Ammunition through Miraumont tonight. Have a presentiment. 3 letters from home. Took 16 pack mules thro' Miraumont. Got lost. Lost 2 mules. Arrived back at 3 o'clock dead beat. Sent cheque to WLW £20. Bagdad [sic] falls.

Diary: Tuesday 13 March: Dull day, nothing doing. Heard Bosche evac. Irles and 290 prisoners & 15 m. guns. 5 letters. Took stuff up to Beau Regard. Awful [word unreadable – 'ternce', could be short for turbulence?] Shelled & 2000 gas shells. Arrived home 12.30 am. Raining like hell.

Letter: 13.3.17

Dear Mother,

Please send me April magazines. Have seen the March ones. The mud is awful – 3 mules drowned in shell craters last night, it is terrible. Men lie down in the mud & ask to be allowed to die they are so exhausted & beat, it takes one 7 hours to go 4000 yards cross country. The Ger has an 8.2 armour piercing shell here she is a hog — (father will translate) & has already killed ½ my drivers & mules & destroyed nearly all my waggons damn him. Love. William. Dont forget 1. Sweets (caramels etc) 2. Magazines (including Motor Cycle & Motorcycling) 3. 1 pair pyjamas. 4. Sox.

[On the reverse of this letter is a poem:]

Well, old fellow is she dreaming of your coming home one day.
She will never [crossed out – 'stoop to kiss you'] even miss you
should you fall upon the way
[crossed out – 'Whats the use of']
Are you weaving dreams of glory tinged with fames effulgent glow
Or do memories rise and haunt you of your youth of long ago
Does she know you're
[crossed out – 'chilled & weary, tired & forgotten']
chilled & weary stumbling on towards the wire.
What has dimmed your eyes old fellow, in your pictures in the fire.
'Battlefield Poem' by HW Williamson. Lieut. 208 MGC.
With apologies to the editor of the
Royal

Letter: 14 March
[In the same envelope as the previous letter and marked with X indicating code = IRLES.]
Dear Mother,
I am pipped a bit in left arm otherwise OK, am not going to hospital, all right in a week. Sures we've had an awful time. We have pushed the Ger back some. Please send the best indelible pencil with shield, and toffee. Will you take my tunic to the CSSA & have an open collar made. I want to wear it on leave in about 3 or 4 months time. The Ger put over 2000 gas shells last night. Well goodbye, dont forget the mags for April & Motorcycling. All your letters are the same try & vary them old thing.

[And on a further separate page:]

Verses Written on the Ancre — Plain of Picardy
'Suicide Valley'

Mid the thunder of the cannon, as the dusk of evening falls,
And the star shells hang and glitter thro' the broken shell-
scarred walls.
In the corner by the brazier, on an empty biscuit case
Sits a lonely English soldier with the firelight on his face.
And his eyes, a-dream and wistful, watch the flames and never
tire.
He is seeking — always seeking — for the faces in the fire.
Ah, my Paddie, there's a face there more to you than all the rest
Mid the many dear & precious, there is one you love the best.
Ah, tis crowned with such brown tresses, and its beautiful and
true
And of all the world of faces, it the loveliest to you.
And your heart grows cold and weary as a tongue of flame
leaps higher
For the sweet grey eyes dont smile, among the faces in the fire.

[On the back of this is a small rough sketch of his mother.]

Army Correspondence Book, 152 (Field Service)
To: D.H.D.O.S., 62 Division, Engelbelmer.
Will you please let bearer have watch for me, as I am unable to
come up in person. H Williamson, Lt. 208 MGC, Hamel, 14.3.17

Diary: Wednesday 14 March: Raining like hell. Dug out leaking. Slept
till 11 oclock. Artillery waking up. All night intermittent
bombardment by our heavies. Gave Cpl. Bolton 20 fcs. Good
nights rest.

Army Correspondence Book, 152 (Field Service) 15.3.17
To: T. Sgt. [Transport Sergeant Mitchell] Two empty limbers will
leave here by 12 oclock today for Coy. HQ. Each limber will have
six mules and 3 drivers. Double feeds will be carried, and each
driver will take the unexpired portion of the days ration. Time of
return probably late in evening. The picket will have tea ready for
these drivers when they return. The C.Q.M.S. will have rations for
20 men in a bag labelled Lt. Horseley, B Section, which will
proceed with the limbers. H. Williamson. Lt. 208 Coy.

Diary: Thursday 15 March: Bombardment of our heavies all day off & on. Very busy finding billets at Engelbelmer. Saw 34 and 213 MGC. Bombardment intense at night. Achiet le petit the objective. Up all night.

Field Message Book: To: O.C. 208 MGC. 15 March, 2.5pm. Engelbelmer. H.Q.
Town Major has authorised me to take over the billets of 213 MGC, at Belton Park Camp, midway between Martinsaut and Engelbelmer, in a direct line. Aaut. for transport, 177 rank, 10 officers. It appears that only two sections of 34 MG's are going in line, so there is no accommodation for men, H.Q. or C.Q.M.S's stores. To get to B.P.Camp, go thro' Engelbelmer, then down Martinsaut Rd. Camp is on left. HWWilliamson. Lt MGC.
   Addenda. 2.35pm. Belton Park Camp.
   Have just seen the O.C. 213 MGC. He can only let us have accom. for two sections, no accom. for transport or Q.M. Stores. It would appear that approx. 50% 213 MGC are stopping behind at Belton and 50% of 34 MGC at Engelbelmer. The Town Major tells me there is no accom. for us at Engelbelmer. If I might be permitted to suggest something, the T.S. stops at Hamel (where we are more or less 'resting') and that we shift some of the stores to Belton Park. However at the most we can only find 2 huts at BP. I have written to T.M. asking him to find accom. for the remainder at Eng. Shall I shift any stores? HWW.

To: Town Major Engelbelmer. 15. 3pm. Belton.
I find that O.C. 213 MGC can only let us have 2 huts (80 men at a great pinch). He is keeping half his men there, his stores, his HQ and transport (57 animals). Would it be poss. please to find accom. for 100 man and 10 officers, and stores. An officer will be calling on you some time today. HHWilliamson. Lt. 208 MGC.

Field Message Book: To: O.C. 213 MGC. 15. 5.30pm. Hamel. Engelbelmer.
Can you please find accommodation for the 9 officers kits and the Q.M. stores that I am sending up. The mens blankets can be dumped in the two huts the men will sleep in. At the time of writing I have heard nothing further on arrangements in Engelbelmer for the Coy. HWWilliamson. Lt for O.C. 208 MGC.

Field Message Book: To: O.C. 208 MGC. Hamel.
There is a very rough and ready accom for the officers with 213 Cmp billets at Belton Park Camp between Engelbelmer and Martinsaut. It will be rather a crush, but there is a roof and unless Montford can get other arrangements from the Town Major I fear it will have to suffice. HWW.

Diary: Friday 16 March: Shifting into Engelbelmer. Hell of a time all day. Very cold.

Field Message Book: To: Sgt. Mitchell. 16.2.10. Hamel.
Please detail a man to send 6 large feeds to Belton Park Camp – midway between Engelbelmer Martinsaut. The road thro Martinsaut is not to be taken. The transport section will move to Engelbelmer as soon as possible. Also 3 limbers to report at 10 oclock (leave here at 8.30). HWW

Field Message Book: To: O.C. 208 MGC. 16. 5.30. Hamel. B.P.
Can I please have rations for 35 Transport Personnel. I think it advisable for the limbers herewith to remain at Belton Park and the drivers to return with the animals, as I want to shift more limbers. ['If you think it advisable to keep some drivers' – crossed out.]

Diary: Saturday 17 March: Shifted finally into Engelbelmer. Rotten bad accommodation. Cold huts. Trouble with Sgt. Bosche evac. Bapaume.

Diary: memo section: 14486 Davey. 66238 Cpl. Wrighton. Mounted orderly.

Field Message Book: To: Sgt. Mitchell. 17. 12.45pm. Engelbelmer.
Please render to Mr. Rose at once a return of deficiencies in vehicles and harness in the section. This matter is very urgent. HWWilliamson. Lt. 208 MGC.

Field Message Book: To: Sgt. Mitchell. 17. 1.0pm. Engelbelmer.
During the stay at Eng the following will be done. 1) All mules will be thoroughly groomed and cleaned daily. 2) Standings will be cleaned, and if poss. gravel or chalk laid down. 3) Harness to

be thoroughly dubbined and metal work cleaned. 4) Lines to be free of manure. The O.C. will inspect this section at any time. HWWilliamson.

Field Message Book: To: O.C. 208 MGCoy. 17. 1.0. Engelbelmer.
The stat. of the animals is as follows. Officers Horses 7 / Mules (L.D.) 44. Two mules have died & the third has strayed. His description is mule, gelding, 15½ hands, long coat, dark brown with fawn muzzle, lead set of harness without saddle. No. of drivers 24, 1 Sgt. no. of grooms, 5. Spare men, 1 & [?] 3. Ration strength (exc. officers) is 34 men. HWWilliamson.

Field Message Book: To: O.C. Coy.
Description of horse. Gelding, bay, long shaggy hair, 15 hands, condition poor, light draught horse, belongs to artillery. Complete with saddle (no stirrup irons) h.c. & bit, H.C. marked 2 DUR RFA

Field Message Book: To: O.C. 208 MGCoy. 17. 1.15pm. Engelbelmer.
Will you please indent for the following as soon as possible as the matter is extremely urgent. Shoes, mule. Size 14 − 200. Shoes, mule, size 14 − 200 [i.e. shoes for two mules]. Shoes, horse, size 3 − 50 and ditto size 4 − 50. Clipper, horn 1 pair. Rasp farriers, 16 inches. HWWilliamson.

Diary: Sunday 18 March: 'Bosche evac. Achiet & Bucqouy. Evidently falling back on Arras Cambrai Line. Went all day on bomb carrying fatigue. Cavalry in action west of Bapaume. Bengal Lcs. Dgr. Gds. Bosche poisoning wells.'

Diary: Monday 19 March: Still in rest at Belton Engelbelmer. Gave Rose for messing 20 fcs. Raining in evening. Company goes to Miraumont to build Railway.

Letter: 19 March 1917
[Marked with code X = ACHIET − hence 'Cherie' containing four of the letters.]
Dear mother Cherie,
We have not heard from anyone for about a week − heavens knows where the post goes to nowadays. I have had only about 5 letters from you to date − I wish you would date your letters.

Well, I suppose all you in England at the time are rejoicing over the 'fall' of Bapaume — but its rather a funny business after all. I believe personally that the Bosche has done a very clever and good thing for himself — he is falling back evidently (& thus can be no information imparted, as of course we all here get our news from the papers 2 days old) Anyhow, he is falling back on the Arras-Cambrai line, & this will mean a retreat of 21 miles — which is known as the 'Hindenburg' line — designed by Hindenburg & he is popularly supposed to have staked his reputation on its impregnability.

Anyhow anyone knows the wire is ['400 feet' crossed out] 40 yards deep in front of his trenches. In addition we have to go over land which is impassable because there will be no railways (& we must build them) no billets (all the villages he has burned) and water poisoned with Arsenic — so far as we can see there is another 2½ years of trench warfare before we break through — or so the Bosche thinks — but only WAIT a bit and see. Well of course you have read in the papers by this time of the cavalry in action — at least no action for the Bosche has retired according to his own plans — and timetable.

It is merely a case of a cavalry screen being put out in front to feel our way. Of course we knew the Ger was about to hop it, as his heavies for the past two or three days were withdrawn & didnt crump us a bit.

Well I am looking forward to a parcel from you soon, although please dont send anything except what I ask you for, as we get plenty of some things and practically nowt of other things. Now biscuits here are an awful price. What I should like would be toffee, nice chocolates (and if you send bar chocolate send Cadbury's Mexican, a pair of pyjamas, and a cake or so — biscuits & cake are very scarce. Of course all the money you spend on these things must be paid for by me, and Father has plenty of my money, I believe.

Well dont expect a letter from me for a few days or even weeks as we shall be awfully busy tomorrow onwards, and certainly no place or time to write, but I will endeavour to send a p.c. about twice a week.

Well goodbye & love to all. Harry.

Diary: Tuesday 20 March: Raining again. Peronne falls. Bosche retires (walks away) on 80 mile front. Sargeant hurt.

Diary: Wednesday 21 March: Very windy day. Did nothing. Bosche still retiring.

Letter: 21.3.17.
[Marked with X indicating code = BAPAUME.]
My dear Mother,
A very quick letter to let you know that I feel in the best of health and the beastly chip in my arm is now almost well – a very lucky escape for me.

Well things look brighter dont they – on our front at any rate things seem better, and if only the weather keep fine things will be bearable. Did father get my draft for £20 & was it honoured? Will you get those blankets of mine cleaned you will find they are bon things and very warm.

I have just had a letter from Biddy [his younger sister Doris] asking for the loan of my case – she can [have] it (the loan) but I suppose it was the case of 'Please father, Eustace says, can he have the banana on the mantle shelf, 'cos he 'as 'ad' – one of the things I heard t'other night in the Divisional concert party: quite a decent affair – most of them quite first class pros. who have joined up.

We don't get much bread here, & meat (fresh) is very scarce, but we just manage, but biscuits are 6/- a lb!! The messing costs us quite 140 fcs a month. What ever do you mean that Ida was wroth with my letter – did she get one to herself or a swear letter to anyone else. And please dont put 4th letter or anything like that – put the date, as letters arrive at any time, praps tomorrow I shall get one dated 26 Feb & next day one 19 March – we never know. No parcels yet – have you sent any I wonder.

The newspapers amuse us here immensely – we read of the Ger being driven back by our chaps – in reality he is walking away of his own free will, as slowly and as fast as he likes to – I dont think we got more than 12 prisoners on the '85 mile front PUSH' – we call this the German push-bike retreat. Still he is making it rotten for us – this burning and ruining & poisoning is not for spite – thats all rot – its only to hinder us (e.g. no water, therefore greatly increased transport difficulties) as much as possible. I received Father's letter thank him, but when you next write you might let me know about the cheque, & also if he receives any money from S.F.O. [Sun Fire Office] on 24th. Well, bye bye, hope you aint starving yet. Love Harry.

PS. You can write what you like, your letters to me are never censored. Tell me where you think I am in your next.

Diary: Thursday 22 March: Moved in evening in snowstorm to Miraumont. Arr'd 12 midnight. In tent with O.C. Coy.

Letter: 22 March 1917
Dear Mother, I think I have received all your letters to date. Last night I received a parcel with some sox, match box, and butter scotch, for which many many thanks.

I have practically nothing to tell you except that I am not in the danger zone – the reason being that the old fellow has hooked it too quickly, still I expect we shall be 'for it' in a weeks time or so. I am not very well – the bully beef doesn't agree with me, & of course its all that now & has been for the last three weeks, when we had an absolute hell of a time – we were rushed straight up from — where we landed.

Up to the present, I have only had letters from you, Jerry, Stany, Terence, one or two girls, auntie Maude, my tailor, Kathie, Biddy, Father, but the flow has started fairly evenly now. With regard to that joke part, if you repeat the words 'Better 'ome' quickly, & vary a bit, you will get more rhythm & it rhymes better than 'Blighty'.

How is Gerald getting on? I haven't time to write to everyone. With regard to a previous letter of mine. I had rather a row with the chap who is boss here, the result being what happened to me at Grantham with that supervising fellow – only as yet I have heard nothing only I should not be surprised if I were sent away from this Coy. anytime.

Anyhow if I do I will notify you at once, if I meanwhile dont get worse, in which case I expect I shall go into hospital, but I want to avoid that if possible, although it wouldn't be extraordinary, as we have very few originals nowadays: new blood is continually arriving.

At times I get awfully fed up with this game, when I'm cold & wet, and moving to unknown billets with no accommodation, owing to our friend having struck a few matches to paraffin blocks & hey presto, no village: then its absolutely awful – the weather improves, but it freezes a little & the wind is very cold & the rain comes on about 3 times a week & puts everything in about 15 inches of mud.

Well cheero, don't forget to write a bit, & don't always write the same letter, your letters are always the same!!! Love to all, Harry.

Diary: Friday 23 March: Fine day. Mud rapidly drying. Went to Achiet le Petit. Place not half bad, but no sign of Bosche occup. Tear shells. S.F. (to WLW) £10 [This is his Sun Fire Insurance pay.]

Field Message Book: To. O.C.Q.M.S, 23 March. Miraumont.
Please prepare indent for 1000 sandbags from RE dump & ask Sgt Mitchell to give you ½ limber for same this afternoon. HWWilliamson. Lt. 208 MGC

Diary: Saturday 24 March: Fixed up good huts in Miraumont. Rather unwell. Artillery duels up the line.

Diary: Sunday 25 March: Fine day all day. Shifting tomorrow past Achiet le Grand.

Diary: Monday 26 March: Raining like hell all day. Stopped at Miraumont brickfield all day. Shifted to valley near Gomiecourt. Tents.

Field Message Book: To: The Adgt. 208 MGC. 26.3.17
Will you please inform me if the order to Transport Shelters also applies to me. I am at present in a dug-out. HWWilliamson. 208 MGC

Diary: Tuesday 27 March: Gave CHR [Lt. Rose] for messing 20 fcs. Looked around. Everything burnt & destroyed. Parcel from M. Bond. [Mrs. Muriel Bond, a neighbour in Eastern Road.]

Diary: Wednesday 28 March: Bosche balloons up all along the line. Wounded in thumb on right hand. Rode up too near Bosche lines. Parcel with pyjamas & mags from home.

Diary: Thursday 29 March: Gave steward for whiskey (2 bottles) 10.40fcs. Raining all night. Still doing nothing near Gomiecourt.

Letter: 29 March

Dear Mum,

Excuse this bad writing, but I've been hit again, ever so slightly in the right thumb, so I've been wounded twice in this little campaign. It was a crump that burst near me and killed my horse & dented my hat, but didn't hit me except in the thumb, & has only caused a little cut 1 inch long on the inside of the bone. My arm is quite OK now & neither is bad enough for hospital.

We are not far from the Bosche position, in a little hollow, his damn ballons [balloons] can see us. I have a bon little shelter with a Bosche stove in it, we made it. I prefer a hut to a tent if it is warm & watertight, it is raining now. Well about this stove, it is a rare blessing & am going to cart it about with me. It is like this. [Sketch here.] It is 20 ins high, & top is 9 ins in diameter & about 4 or 5 lbs in weight & has a pipe about 6 ft long – my hut is built into a bank and is 6 feet by 8 feet by 5 ft high & the stove is lovely & warm – I have my camp bed in it and change into pyjamas every night. It is about the same as Grantham except less work – rise at 9 have breakfast in a good hut erected by carpenters (we have every kind of trade in this company) good food, bacon, sausages etc etc & good tables & tablecloths & we have a French chef named Carny who is offrs mess cook – we are 10 offrs & 170 men in the Coy you see, which is so much better than a battalion.

Messing costs us about 120fcs a month – of course this doesn't happen always, but only when we are not 'in'. We are as far behind at present as you are from Whitefoot Lane & when we go in I stop behind with the mules & go up over shell plastered roads with the waggons. I have been on the gun bit owing to shellshock & nervous exhaustion (10 days fighting is no joke for anyone on the —) I am permanently with transport – my predecessor is now sleeping his long sleep, which he commenced about 10 days agone, poor fellow he ran straight into the barrage & theres no cover in an open road.

I have saved a lot lately, ask pa if he got my check for £20, & was it honoured? & did he get £10 from Hooton, [Sun Fire Insurance Office pay] if so he has £45 for me & I have £25 so that's £70 & when I came out I had nothing – not bad for 5 weeks is it old thing?

I dont know what Jerry means by not wanting pyjamas – what

about when in rest? We have had no divisional rest yet, that is to say the Div. going out of the line as a whole division. Anyhow I change every night & have a decent bed & blanket & food & servant so its quite OK. I've been through a bit though – 4 times over the top isn't bad is it. [Sentence crossed out in blue pencil.] (Have done this myself – its not quite public news). My blood seems to be quite all right all these scratches heal up easily – the thumb has already ceased paining me, the weather improves its much warmer altho the rain comes down now & then its getting much better.

I can tell you its nice to be here – altho the Ger has cut down trees, blown up each house, poisoned wells, etc etc etc (& broken stoves & put a bomb under each sheet of corrugated iron !!!) Most of his little stoves were done in, but mine wasn't, but a nice little egg bomb was up the chimney ready for the first fire !! I've kept it as a souvenir. He had a piano or two down his dugouts, each one connected to a mine !!!10

Well the country here is grand, we're out of the mud & shell blasted ground, & in lovely, untouched open fields!! The Ger can't have had much stuff here – the fields are green and untouched like the "warm kitchen" but for miles behind our original lines all fields are churned up by men & mules feet, etc etc. I think most of his men have gone away to Italy or somewhere, in which case God help him in May or June !!

Well, am just going to have tea, so will close. Thanks for books & pyjamas & toffee. Can you manage to send me a large cake for the mess (every offr puts his cakes in the mess) & a box or two of biscuits or shortbreads – some of ABC shortbread about 2 doz would be best – send in a tin box of course! Please send Motor Cycling & Motor Cycle & an occasional Daily Mail – we get none here – we're miles from civilisation. Well, goodbye, give my best to Father & the girls & to Mrs. N. [Nicholson] she is a decent child & to Jerry the old humbug – I had a topping parcel from Muriel Bond a Catford flapper yesterday – by the way I am trying to send a few souvenirs home. Will you send some Bachelor Buttons and take my tunic to the CSSA & have an open collar put in instead of that stand up one and tell them to let it out down the back (its too tight) and to lengthen the sleeves 1½ inches. Dont forget as I may be home soon for a staff job (anyhow my leave is on in about 3 months). Love to all, Harry.

Diary: Friday 30 March: Very changeable day. Three guns mounted for A.A. Sent cheque to Cooper's wife 10/-

Letter: to his sister Doris [Biddy] 30.3.17
Dear Biddy,
Your very scrappy letter got me yesterday – dated 24 March. Who is Geoff? and whose car is it? And what make and brake h.p? You seem to be doing the heavy in my absence, nearly as much as I used to do. I hear from several people in Lewisham and Catford & everyone seems to miss me. Apparently everyone knew me. Please answer this letter at length & let me know who Geoff is, who the ell is Captain England or someone? I am very curious & rather riled. I fear I can see Mother & Father alone in the Nest with 'muh' after this war. Its hardly worthwhile coming home nowadays – all offrs on sick leave have to wear that awful band and sick leave has been abolished – its all convalescent homes & then back to duty again. Well, I too am going to stop now. Love to all. Harry. PS How is my fiancee? [This is of course a joking reference to Doris Nicholson.]

Diary: Saturday 31 March: Went out with King [Capt. King, CO] to St. Leger. Saw Hindenburg Line and men working on it. Raining.

Diary: Sunday 1 April: Pay £12.15-. Bosche aeroplane shot down. 1 plane and a balloon near Bapaume.

Field Message Book: To: Sgt Mitchell. Gomiecourt 1.4.17
Much unnecessary trouble is caused by men scrawling their addresses of their various letters right over the envelope. A space should be left for the signature of the officer censoring letters in the lefthand bottom corner. Several drivers letters have to be very carefully censored; Dvr Wishart especially keen must not mention that, for example, they are in tents near a village that has just been evacuated by the enemy, as this might give a hint to the sector the Divsn is fighting in, and must not mention that 'we expect to go into the line is a day or so'. These points must be made clear to all personell of the T.S. HWW Lt. i/c T.S.

Field Message Book: To: T. Sargeant. 1.4.17
RUM: Rum is only to be issued to the T.S. [Transport Section]

individually (ie when not put into tea) under the direct supervision of an officer of the Coy. COLIC, and other cases of sudden illness are to be reported to the senior NCO in that section to the Tr.Offr. HWW

Field Message Book: To: The Adjt. 208 MGC 1.4. 17 Gomiecourt.
Would it be possible, please, for chits and orders to the T.S. for the requirement of limbers to be sent to me, as T.O. Otherwise it is impossible for me to know what mules are out, unless I ask my Sgt for information regarding my section. HWW. Lt. T.O. 208

Field Message Book: To: T. Sgt. 1.4.17
Driver Bevan has been out without feeds for his mules since 12 oclock today. Kindly take necessary action in this matter. I regard this as a very serious breach of discipline. HWW. Lt. T.O. 208 MGC

Letter: 2 April.
[Marked with X indicating code: in this letter the word Croisilles is underlined.]
Dear Mother
Dont forget a cake & send Daily Mail every other day and Motor Cycle & Motor Cycling and the mags. Have you got the souvenirs yet? Sorry I can't get any photos of *Croisilles* for you there isn't a shop left. Am quite well. Don't forget to answer my queries. Sending more souvenirs soon. Love Harry.

Diary: Monday 2 April: Early morning attack on Croisilles & Ecoust, both captured. 40 prisoners. Recd from Ordnance Torch 9/-. Heavy snowstorm all night & 1/2 gale. Brigade going over the top shortly

Letter: 2 April [Marked with X indicating code = CROISILLES.]
Dear Mother,
Just a short epistle to let you know I received your letter dated 28 March. Yes, you are quite right about my destination but you may get a letter with this one that will show you the change.
    I watched an attack at 5 oclock this morning. The warfare has changed a lot – of course we are only scrapping their rearguards & their artillery is only a few guns here & there. Well we got past all the defensive ridges, like the downs, now, & on this hill I stood on

I could see for scores of miles: it was like standing on the Salt Box Hill & seeing the green country for miles away – it is quite possible to ride right up to the Bosche outposts here without knowing where they are.

Well I watched our men going forward at dawn – I was only an interested spectator you see, as I had news of an attack & went up to watch it. The guns gave the village below us hell for a time & then the men went forward, & there was little fire, & an hour afterwards I saw two prisoners wounded & looking very white coming in, & then ten others. So I tied my horse up & stealthily crept up to the village & couldn't see a dam thing. So I went on for a mile or so and to my great surprise & fear I saw a lot of Bosche with machine guns about 150 yds away !!!

And I gave myself up for lost but went on a bit further and found myself in a big trench system with noone about – suddenly it struck me I was in the [crossed out but just readable as –] 'Hindenburg Line'! And I was !!! I can tell you I felt rather windy & started to go back – on the way back I got two Bosche bombs ready to throw as I was unarmed but didn't see a dam thing. I got back to the village after 8 hours away and found my horse frantic with hunger.

I reported my observations to the [crossed out] and one might hear further you never know. And the best part is that if I had known that the Bosche was there I wouldn't have gone for £10000 but I believed all the time that he was miles away !!

Well about that thing you wanted to sell, I should advertise it & you will probably read the advert in the paper about Apr. 10 or evening of 9th. [One hopes his mother understood this message, which was obviously to let her know that an attack was due on 9/10 April!] Tell Ida I am sorry about the letter: it was quite a mistake on my part, and my Sargeant must have got her letter – no wonder he thinks me a 'mad, scatter-brained fellow' – I could tell you a lot about this awful Hindenburg Line but of course I can't, altho' the Bosche is an awful fool, and much behind the times, if he but knew it !!!! Let me know if you get the letter with the Ger identity disc in [this item is in his archive, see plate 25a] and also the parcel of souvenirs – they are very good things to keep.

By the way that letter came from a dead Ger who was killed outside a redoubt near Miraumont – between Grandcourt and

Miraumont, a deep dugout called the 'Pimple' – I found about 20 Gers outside all killed by our chaps and those buttons & that letter came off one. The hat belonged to a prisoner who strayed into my arms near Achiet le Petit a long while ago – he was about 7½ yrs old and I carefully pinched all his private property and hat, & threatened to shoot him if he told anyone. [nb: this is a joke, i.e. the hat was very small.]

In my next parcel of souvenirs I am sending a figure of Jesus I found in Achiet le Grand near a church, and a few cartridges etc etc. Well cheero old thing, don't forget the motor books – we are fighting like gents now – we live in tents and have stores in them & sleep on camp beds & have a mess hut with proper meals, table cloths, syphons of soda & whisky etc in a valley near the Bosche and go out & fight him when we see him – he could blow us to hell if he wanted to but his planes daren't go up, we shoot them down if they do. Don't forget cake – I may be home shortly to form a new company at Grantham – otherwise I am here for life – I rather like the excitement & the mud is all gone. Love to all. H.

Diary: Tuesday 3 April: Very cold in morning. Cheque to Rose 10/-. A few Bosche planes over. Big attack shortly. Had 2 parcels & letters from Mrs. N. & jacket. Raining. 2 balloons near us brought down by Bosche plane.

Field Message Book: To: T. Sgt. Gomiecourt 3.4.17
Notice of the intention of the T. Sgt. or any NCO in this section to bring a man before the C.O. for any reason (crime, complaint etc.) must always be given to the officer i/c T.S. preferably by word of mouth before the man is taken up. HWW. Lt. i/c T.S. 208 MGC

Field Message Book: To: T. Sgt. 3.4. 17
1) Please render to me before 6 pm tonight a confidential report on the junior NCOs in the section. It is to be understood that this is a confidential matter between the officers concerned and yourself.
2) In the event of hostile shelling, all grooms and drivers will at once stand to their animals, and scatter with their animals to the available cover if necessary. This order to be read out on parade, and it is to be understood that neglect of this order will be treated in the same way as a man running in the face of the enemy, or abandoning a gun.

Hostile shelling is taken to mean intensive or concentrated shelling, not a whizz-bang ½ a mile away. HWW. Lt 208

Field Message Book:
Dear Rose,
Do you think the T.S. could have some rum when it's next issued? I write now before I forget. HWW

Diary: Wednesday 4 April: Raining and very foggy. Prelim bombardment Arras way. Rode up the line in evening.

Diary: Thursday 5 April: Lovely sunny day. Rode a buck jumping mule. Rough house. [Two or three words crossed out & unreadable.] Lovely moonlight night. Guns normal. Saw 14 tanks at Mory for Hindenburg Line.

Field Message Book: To: Transport Sergt. 5.4.17
The following points must be made clear to the section.

1) Animals going to & returning from watering, exercise etc, must be kept clear of the camp lines as failure to do this only increases the mud.

2) Limbers returning must draw up into line with the others, and in the correct place.

3) There is a slackness among the drivers in saluting of officers. If this is not immediately improved extra parades will be held to smarten the men up. This slackness is noted both in mounted and dismounted drivers.

HWilliamson Lt. 208 MGC. N.B. The prize for harness etc will be given conditions permitting tomorrow. Harness showing obvious neglect, disciplinary action will be taken.

Letter: to Mother. 5 April 1917
[Marked with X indicating code = CROISILLES]
Dear Mum,
I received on 3rd a parcel from you with biscuits and bulls eyes, and same time books and jersey with letter. The books are very welcome. I shall enjoy reading what I read before the war, but no matter. Mummy dear, my little shack trembles and quakes, the air is full of flashes and thunders, the preliminary bombardment. The iron is rattling like fury over my heads, tis

snowing outside, by the stove is very warm, I have an excellent man and he keep me beautifully.

From what we see the Germans are in a terrible plight at home – they are starving – this is no paper story, but the army knows that the German soldier is broken in morale and courage & the Bosche civilian in all his or her letters whines eternally 'When can we have peace?' There is no food here & so & so & so & so died last week from exhaustion – no food, no wool, dry rot has set in, the events of the last three weeks have astonished everyone out here – Germany has begun to crack!!

Womp, womp, boom, boom, boom, put 50 men in a room with a hammer each & hit as fast as he can, & you get something like it – the birth of the final battle. How long the bombard will last we cannot tell.

Anyhow old thing send the Motor Cycling & let me know if you get the two parcels of souvenirs, & what each contained. When you get this we will have started on 7th week of service. Well dont expect a letter for sometime, but write yourself, and send a cake and Almond toffee (Callard & Bowsers – send a good parcel – take the money from mine but keep an a/c – dont send unnecessary stuff but send 1 tin Bournville cocoa & 2 small tins Nestles sweetened.

Is Kathie married yet. Mrs. N. [Nicholson] sent a topping coat and a decent letter about 2 pages of it being news of someone she calls Doris, I seem to remember the name when I was a tiny boy. [HW is being ironic – this is of course Doris Nicholson, the fictional 'Helena Rolls'.] She asks me to write whenever possible (of course you won't tell her I write to you like this will you?) The guns are quietening a bit – I expect the postman has arrived or something. Just keep an eye on Mr. Arras will you? love Bill. [Henry was often called 'Bill' from his second name William.] Send about 2 dozen stout envelopes. Clean those souvenirs up & put them in drawing room. That bomb is empty so are the cartridges, the cases with red caps are tracer bullets for firing balloons. A Bosche came over our heads yesterday & fired 2 balloons of ours but the RFC offrs in the balloons jumped out in parachutes – the balloons looked just like Zeppelins burning – the Ger plane dived from 2 miles up to ½ mile in about 15 seconds !!!

Diary: Good Friday 6 April: Very fine in morning but raining all evening. America declares war. Bosche counter attacks smashed on our left. Saw Jennings and 201 Coy.

Diary: Saturday 7 April: Rode up line in afternoon with L./Cpls Duval & Nolan past Croissilles. Saw Hindenburg Line & dead Bosches. Got some fine helmets. moving to Mory tomorrow.

Diary: memo section: Zero day approaches. Lens to Arras. Hindenburg Line. French at Reims.

Diary: Easter Sunday 8 April: Shifted to Mory, just in front of batteries, 9.2. hows Bosche planes – camp crumped. Lovely warm day. Saw several old chaps in L.R.B. (2nd Battn)

Field Message Book: To: Transport. Sergt. 8.4.17
All messages to me, requesting leads, limbers etc must be in writing when the distance separating us is considerable, e.g. today, when about a mile. Otherwise confusion is caused. HWW. Lt. 208 MGC

Field Message Book: To: Sgt. Mitchell
16 packmules will be ready to be loaded up at 8 am tomorrow. Please select the fittest and strongest mules for this work. L/Cpl Duval will accompany this party, who will wear steel helmets and respirators. No feeds are necessary. During the absence of the T.O. please pay attention to the following points.
1) Lines to be laid in brick. 2) Rugs laid out and dried on hedges. 3) Shoeing, grooming, harnessing to be laid out for immediate harnessing up. 4) If possible small trenches to be dug, near lines, where men can take shelter in the case of shelling. – narrow trenches, about 2 ft in width, and 5 feet deep.
HWilliamson. Lt. i/c T.S. MGC

Diary: Monday 9 April: Raining like hell all day. Arras bombardment intensive (fury?). Cooper & Case (5fcs) 10 fcs. Heard attack on H.L. [Hindenburg Line] off, thank God. Terrific fire Arras way. Attack by 1st & third armies.

[This is the day that Edward Thomas was killed by a stray shell after the Battle of Arras.]

Field Message Book: To: Transport Sergt. 9.4.17 Mory.
Two limbers will report at 9 today, at the "Old German Dump" near Gomiecourt. This dump is quite near the camp we have just quitted – where the ten trees are. Four limbers will report at crater in Mory for roadmending, at 8.30 am. No limber covers will be taken. HWilliamson. Lt. T.S. 208 MGC

Diary: Tuesday 10 April: Arras attack successful. Australian attack failed. Bosche preparing big blow attempting to retake MORY. Coy. in the line. Big rumours of cavalry action. Bombardment midday at Arras. Beginning to feel the strain a bit – head aches like hell. Sent Carr & Son £1-4-0d.

Field Message Book: To: Sgt Mitchell. 208 MGC 10.4.17
Please detail 4 limbers each with 4 mules to report to O.C. dump on GOMIECOURT Road at 8.45 am tomorrow 10th inst. This R.E. dump is the dump near our last encampment. The remainder of the drivers will carry on with programme as given to you on the 9th inst. HWW. Lt.i/c T.S. 208 MGC

Field Message Book: To: Transport Sergt. 10.4.17
In the event of a move into territory evacuated hurriedly by the enemy, all transport material must be cut down to an absolute minimum. Only 7 rugs will be taken. Drivers will carry a full water bottle; it must be impressed on all drivers that this is to be an emergency, and is not to be touched until permission from me, or any other Coy. officer. – A half limber at once for iron rations. Report to C.G.M.S. HWilliamson. Lt. T.S. 208 MGC

Field Message Book: To: Transport Sergt. MORY 10.4 17
In the event of the enemy evacuating his SIEGFRIED STELLUNG (i.e. HINDENBERG Line) – a very hurried pursuit of him will be carried out. All feed bags – including spares, must be filled to the utmost capacity, and haynets. There will be no room for spares etc in the limbers, which will be filled with guns and S.A.A. [Small Arms Ammunition.] Drivers must roll their blankets in sheet & carry on animals. Please have all toolkits, shoes etc ready for loading. The Coy. is under orders to move at a moments notice. HWilliamson. Lt.

Field Message Book: To: O.C. 208 Coy. 10.4.17 MORY
REF: My conversation with you today, regarding animal strength in this section. We have 7 riders and 45 L.D. animals, of the latter we have WHEEL PAIRS – 14 and LEAD PAIRS – 7. It is therefore possible to move off with 7 limbers (or 6 limbers & water cart) with 4 animals, and 7 vehicles with 2 animals. — Regarding the animals today; 4 teams are on petrol can fatigue, 1 on watercart, 1 on gun (BI) and 1 at Gomiecourt. HWilliamson. Lt. 208 MGC

Field Message Book: To: Sgt Mitchell. T. Sgt. MORY 10.4.17
1) Please have two wheel pairs and one lead pair harnessed up, and ready to move ['within ½ hr.' crossed out] before midnight.
2) You must detail two drivers (wheel & lead) to stand by ready for moving off at any moment, henceforward – if you can guarantee them being ready and hooked in (feeds to be carried) within five minutes, they need not be harnessed up – in any case, the harnessing up must be under five minutes, (5 drivers in all). Please acknowledge. Lt. T.O. 208 MGC

Diary: Wednesday 11 April: Last night attack on H. Line. 14 tanks. Cavalry up and R.H.A. Working all last night. T.S. went back to Gomiecourt. Came up early morning. Bosche sent over 6 8inch h.v. armour piercing shells. L.R.B. sargeant wounded by strafs. Awful snowstorm. Attack by Austr. & 17th Lcs.[Lancers] fails. 10 tanks lost.[11]

Field Message Book: To: T. Sgt. MORY
Your communication noted. Please make all arrangements to move animals back about ½ a mile. A good position will be near the main road we crossed coming here, – about 300 yds in there is a bank at right angles to the road. HWW

Field Message Book: To: Transport Sergt. MORY 1.15pm 11.4. 17
Please send 2½ limbers (empty) to this encampment immediately. Please detail Driver Flynn as one of the drivers, as he knows his way up to the line. They must be here by 2.30 sharp. This is most urgent. HWW

Field Message Book: To: Transport Sergt. MORY 11.4.17
Please detail 3 wheelers and 3 leaders to stand by ready to harness

up and hook at short notice, and to stand by till further orders. Report to me when this has been done in writing with names of men warned. They will be required for the gun limbers. HWilliamson Lt. 208 MGC

N.B. Please prepare a charge against L/Cpl Joy, in charge of grooms, neglect of duty, in omitting to feed the horses before 8.30 am. He will be brought up at Coy. O.R. this morning. HWW

Field Message Book: To: O.C. Coy. 208 MGC MORY 11.4.17
No limbers have reported at the Engineers dump on the Gomiecourt Road, in consequence of your orders this morning. Will they be required please. HWilliamson. Lt. i/c/ T.S.

Field Message Book: To: Transport Sergt. MORY 11.4.17
Limbers Nos A1, B2, C1, D1, will in future be used for gun material only. Even when unpacked (i.e. guns in the line), they will not be used for rations or fatigues of any sort, but will always be available in the event of guns being withdrawn and reloaded. HWilliamson. Lt. T.O. 208 MGC. Approved CBR King. Capt. Commanding 208 MGC.
Note: Please let Pte Hayes cut a cross on tailboards of above limbers – 6in by 6in – and explain to drivers that these are the gun limbers. HWW.

Diary: Thursday 12 April: Great excitement. Bosche broken in north, & expected to evac. H. Line. Artillery all day. Up all night. Gas attack, in early morning (3AM) Friday by English. Great attacks up north. Awful snowstorm. Rose 10 fcs [for Mess expenses]

Field Message Book: To: Transport Sergt. MORY 12.4.17
1. There will be a rifle inspection of this section tonight at 6.30 pm
2. Mules will be rugged up at nights until further orders, except those unclipped during last three months.
3. Lines will be bricked during the day by all available men.
4. Men must be washed and shaved by 7 pm every night.
5. Please include in the ration indent for 4 animals as H.D. – i.e. over 16 hands. We have two horses extra, and only indent for 51 animals.
HWilliamson Lt. 208 MGC

Field Message Book: To: Transport Sergt. MORY 12.4.17 7.0 p.m.
The Coy. may have to move at any moment. ['15 packmules will be saddled up and 8 mules saddled up with G. saddles — to carry ammunition etc.' crossed out and 'see later' added.] Each of these animals will carry on itself a days rations, including hay and waterbuckets. In the event of the Coy. going forward, the limbers will not be used, but all carrying will be done by pack. Drivers will carry rifles and ammunition (for purposes self-defence) Please arrange for all drivers to draw their rations for tomorrow now.

Later. 12 pack mules will be saddled up at 11 *oclock tonight* — these will be mainly for use in B section. All the TS will be paraded and told they must stand by in their shelters, ready to clear off anywhere during the night. For tonight all transport will be by pack. *All drivers must have their gas masks on now, and from henceforward.* In order to enable you to understand what may be the situation and what is required to meet it, the following information is given for your benefit. The 7th DIVISION has got into position that threatens the Hindenberg Line, a withdrawal from which by the Germans is expected. In order to encourage this, BULLECOURT is going to be extensively gassed at 3 am tomorrow 13th inst. If the enemy retires, this Coy. will follow up with packmules. Resistance by scattered parties of Germans may be expected, also gas. You will remain here with the remaining limbers and animals and be prepared to follow on the advance guard. Further orders will be issued as soon as known. HWilliamson Lt. 208 MGC.

Field Message Book:
Dear Rose,
If there is a spare revolver in the stores can I borrow it as I have not one, and shall need something if I go into strange territory. Yrs. HWW.

Field Message Book: To: Transport Sergt. Mory. 12.4.17
These orders will supercede those issued previously, but only as regards numbers. 1) From 11 pm. onwards the following animals will be ready to move at 5 mins notice. (For 2nd Lt Horseley Section) 5 pack mules, 7 saddle mules. L/Cpl Nolan in charge. When this party moves off, the Transport Officer and Pte Case will accompany it for the purpose of reconnoitring roads etc. You will

be responsible to Lt. Rose as soon as I leave. 2) Mr. McKelvey's section (hour of departure will be told you later by Lt. Rose) will take 5 packmules, 7 saddle mules. 3) 2nd Lt. McConnel's section (probably 2 or 3 hours after 2nd party) L.Cpl Bolton, 2 fighting limbers.

Each limber will have 4 mules, and each mule will carry a pack saddle. All the above will move with 1 days rations and fodder.

Diary: Friday 13 April: Saw Jenning. Bosche still in H.L. Fine Day. No post. Guns Arras way quiet. Capt. Pollack came to dinner.

Field Message Book: To: Transport Sergt. Mory. 13.4.17
The orders relating to packmules standing by are cancelled. Two teams (1 team = 4 mules) must be warned now to be ready to move off at ½ hours notice henceforward. The mules need not necessarily be harnessed up, but drivers must always be in a place where you can find them; they must sleep with boots & puttees on, and have their harness ready. They will be required to take guns up the line in the event of a hostile attack. Please note Coy. orders tonight re packmules. HWW. Lt. T.O.

Henry Williamson's archive contains some official documents from this era which consist of several pages concerning the orders and arrangements for the attack on the Hindenburg Line, issued to him over the period from mid-March to the beginning of May, and particularly concerning the orders for 13 April 1917.[12] These give a most interesting insight into the details of this operation.

Field Message Book: Mory. 14.4.17
All animals will graze on the green grass beyond 20 Coy's lines this afternoon from 2.30–4 pm. An ample picket should be detailed to guard these. Animals on returning to lines must be checked. HWilliamson Lt. 208 MGC

Diary: Saturday 14 April: Lovely day. Attack on Bullecourt shortly. Lots of Bosche planes over. Animals grazing all day. Shelled by 9inch guns.

Diary: memo section: Official wire says – 15,902 prisoners, 192 guns since 9th. All Vimy Ridge captured by 1st. Army.

Diary: Sunday 15 April: Early morning Bosche breaks through on our right Coy. standing to. Raining again. Will this bloody weather never improve? Heavy shelling. Bosche takes the guns on our right, but recaptured. No post. Bosche shelled Mory at night but slept through it all. 13inch How.

Field Message Book: To: T.S. Mory. 15.4.17
Limbers moving up to the line are not to use the old Railway track running by the camp, but are to make use of the track behind the Mory lines. This must be clearly understood by all ranks. HWilliamson. Lt. 208 MGC.

Field Message Book: To: Transp. Sargt. Mory. 15.4.17
The four limbers to be ready for fatigue at 5.45 pm tonight. No covers for limbers need be taken. HWilliamson. Lt. 208 MGC. The above of course, includes an NCO in charge. HWW.

Field Message Book: To: Sgt. Mitchell. Mory. 15.4.17
4 limbers will report to Old Ger Dump, Gomiecourt road, at 9am tomorrow 16th inst, unless the Coy 'stands to' at that time. HWilliamson. T.O. Lt. 208 MGC

Field Message Book: To: T.S. Mory. 15.4.17.
Four teams and drivers to be warned now to fall in at ½ hours notice. Take all precautions to ensure that this is done, if required well within the half hour. HWilliamson. Lt.

Diary: Monday 16 April: Fine day early. Raining like hell all night. Letters from Stany, Father, E.R.H. Vll Corps attack fails. Great rumours of French attack down south.

Field Message Book: To: Transport Sergt. Mory. 16.4.17
The number of men and animals to stand by is 2 teams and 4 drivers. Can you possibly make arrangements with T.S. 201 MGCoy so that our animals can graze there this afternoon. Please have all mules clipped with an X this morning during grooming, the X to be on the near side of the neck. A limber may be required to get coal from St. Leger this morning. HWilliamson. Lt. 208 MGC.

On back of next page the following note is written directly in pencil: i.e. not a carbon copy as are all the messages:

> VII Corps advanced at 5.30 failed.
> IV Army front of 5000 [or 8000 – figure could be either] yds between Paget & Gricoust consolidating. 4 off. 400 ord.
> XVII Corps advanced & joins 13 Corps at B29 b 56.
> French 40 division gone thro 3 lines of defence. Ger. routed

Diary: *Tuesday* 17 *April*: F.C. 125 fcs, P.M.C. 50 fcs, Bosche shelled Mory rather heavily. Wrote a lot of letters. No post. French leading Corps ordered to cross the Aisne.

Letter: To Mother, not dated but postmarked 18 April
['To Sgt' – crossed out] Dear ['Father' – crossed out] & Mother.
Thanks for your letters I haven't yet received. I wrote yesterday & again today for something to do. I enclose something of interest to you. Love H. I heard from Jerry a time or two ago. Well au revoir H.
PS Nobody except you & Maristany [*see* Ch. 5, Note 3] writes to me. The enclosed paper is circulated to all troops here so is quite in order for you to show it to people.
[This paper is the printed 'Extracts from German soldier's Letters' – see Note 12.]

Field Message Book: To: Trans. Sergt. Mory. 17.4.17
1) The A.V.C.O. [Animal Veterinary] will inspect effect of [? 'mallein' – word difficult to decipher] tomorrow at 7 am. 2) Please send ½ limber to Achiet le Grand, A.V.C. Mobile Section, to obtain the lime and sulphur today. 3) The two teams are still in readiness B. 4) Letters are being brought to me at anytime, and by different bundles. The time for letters to be handed into my quarters is 6 pm every night. No others & letters will not be taken in at other times except in special circumstances. Men must leave the bottom left hand corner free from writing. HWilliamson.

Letter: To W.L. Williamson, addressed to 13, Old Broad St [i.e. his Bank working address]
Dear Father,   17 April.
A brief note in answer to your long one. First of all I got Mothers parcel with books and cake all right a few days ago. It contained

bullseyes as well. We have heard tonight of a great French success how true I don't know.

Yes, I suppose the war will end soon, I hope so at any rate. The weather is awful a terrible snowstorm a day or so ago. The Bosche is at present putting 1 ton shells over from a 13inch naval gun he has at Douai. You can't hear them coming. It is 10.30 at night & raining like the devil.

I am glad the English have succeeded somewhere at any rate. My experience of the Hindenberg Line is that it is bloody awful. One of our tanks that did come back shined like hell from bullets but the bloke inside was mad. I am sorry I haven't written before but when I see you next I will explain and then you wont wonder. I am sending a cheque for about £10 in the post & you can put it all (i.e. £50) in the D. A/c.

Did you get my 4 parcels – I sent 2 tin boxes of bombs etc, and 3 lovely helmets I got, and a sack of clothing & a saw bayonet. I shant write for a week or so as we are doing another stunt shortly. Well love to all. HWW

Diary:Wednesday 18 April: Cheque to WLW £10 —. Mory shelled like hell, one captain & several O.R. killed. Parcel from home & letters.

Letter: To W.L.Williamson, at the Bank address
Dear Father,   18.4.17
Can now write again feeling much better but raining like the devil. I have an interesting diary can show you when I return.

As for the war well the affair at Arras was a brilliant stroke and a decided victory, but I dont think the effects of it are so great as portrayed by the paper. The battle itself appears to be over. A huge no. of guns were concentrated – and men and after starving the garrison opposite us we captured it or killed it and all the guns – the Bosche guns were so battered that the gunners would not come into the pits to fire – thus the 'neutralization fire' of our counter batteries was very effective.

Man for man I suppose we won – the huge number of prisoners itself speaks for the success of the operation – as by this we know the objectives were taken. Of course we cant help not succeeding everywhere.

The capture of the Vimy Ridge was a brilliant piece of work for the Canadians: this was a ridge overlooking our positions for miles, and many have been the efforts to take it – so deep & well made were the concrete shelters for the guns that in the French attack on it in 1915 they fired over 100 11inch shells into them without even silencing a single battery – but our gunfire blew the whole thing up.

This eternal bad weather is very sickening – it is fine and cloudless one day & then suddenly a snowstorm will blot everything out & the mud will come on again – but not the mud we experienced in Feb. thank God. I had a letter from Hooton a few days ago – he tells me that Brett is now a 2nd lieutenant and still at the W.O.[War Office], so he has managed to do tremendously well for himself.

With regard to my position in this crowd the boss of it is a silent man sort of business. When I had been out here 10 days I was sent for by the General, who said 'I have received this report from your Commanding Officer – I looked & saw a dreadful report – careless, slovenly, no control over men, etc etc. Of course I was absolutely staggered & told him it was a bunch of lies – when I took over this section it was a bunch of waifs & strays and through my unceasing efforts at Grantham I had turned out one of the smartest transports in this Division. The other animals die of cold & neglect – the drivers are slack, but in my section I had 37 drivers & grooms to look after, and 47 mules and 10 horses. Each driver has a set of harness & 2 mules to look after, besides himself, his rifle and equipment etc. They often work all night & day perched up on a donkey absolutely frozen – and never complain – and are always willing – thats my section.

Of course I was greatly distressed at the report, especially as I knew I did not deserve it, but thats 7 weeks ago, so I suppose the report is squashed – anyhow if I had been turned down I should have raised hell.

Anyhow I shouldn't worry now if I were sent back to Grantham – I've had enough of this war – especially in its concentrated form as we've had it since we came out. We've followed the Bosche up step by step & are now 15 miles from his old line of Feb. Some of our poor tanks – oh lord, you people think they are invulnerable – oh dear wait till I see you.

By the way, you might see if my advertisement of my motorcycle appears in the issue of 22 April will you? I expect you people in the country though, will get Sundays papers on Monday

23rd or possible 24th, but keep your eyes skinned, as I must sell it. I should think the most likely papers to advertise in would be the Evening News of 23rd. I hope you get this epistle in time. I don't want to take less than £35 for it, it is worth more. [This is a coded message for a forthcoming battle date.]

I think that letter you wrote me was very excellent: I look forward to long letters like that. I have had several letters from Stany: he is going to join the French army and be allocated to the Brazilian Contingent, as his country is now at war with Germany. I suppose shortly you will be shooting again at the range.

Altho my job is transport officer I go up in an attack just to help a bit & to kill a few Bosche — officially of course to reconnoitre routes for transport but I often go over when it looks quiet, altho last time owing to shortage of officers I went over and got back two days late nearly dead but unhurt.

I do hope you get those parcels all right especially the helmets — write as soon as you get them. Well, must close now with much love H.

Letter: To Mother. 18.4.17
Dear Mother,
Thanks for parcels have received four up to date. It is always raining here. The guns have been silent for the last 2 or 3 days — I suppose we are waiting for the better weather. The last fortnight has been very strenuous, I have got lumbago rather rottenly perhaps it will go when the bad weather goes.

Did you get my parcels — I sent two tin boxes of stuff — empty bombs cartridges etc and pouches — all quite harmless. And I got three lovely helmets — the spikes screw on — and the flat one is a Bavarian, let me know if you got those three and yesterday I sent off a sandbag of clothing I dont want out here and inside a lovely saw bayonet — very rare [see plate 25b]. So you should get 2 tin boxes of stuff — a wooden box of 3 helmets, & the sandbag. Dont forget the Motor Cycling & Motor Cycle. If you read the paper of about the 13th instan. you will see what happens to us — and study father's letter with the cross. I hid for 2 days and managed to get back but pretty dead beat without food. The cake was quite nice we ate it up for tea — the last tea before — well, you remember the last verse of the 'Wooden Shoon' — well repeat it & you will get me.

Watch the paper about 20th of this month and again read pa's cross and you will see your advertisements appear – but 4/6 a line is very much dont you think. [All these references to 'advertisements' can only be coded messages.] Thanks for having tunic done – but cant you have the back widened – it wont matter if he takes that pleat down the back right away.

My leave is due in 5 weeks time – by the time you get this we shall have been out here over 2 months – let me know when you get this – it will be posted on the 18th at the FPO. Please send a little box of envelopes – I've got plenty of paper so dont send any. [This and all letters were written on sheets torn from the Correspondence Book or similar.]

Give my love to all I know – I am sorry I havent written this last fortnight but when I see you next you will grow pale with excitement and my devilish luck – I expect we shall be out for a rest when you get this.

Let me know about the parcels you get – keep everything I send home, including that letter, & show the neighbours that helmet – let them swank over it – the best one I got myself at the 'Cross'. I took it off a man who kicked a wounded Tommy – the Bosche, by the way, still lies there !!! Love to everyone Harry xxxxxxxxxxxxxxxx [& continuing in a coiled squiggle to edge of paper.]

Diary: Thursday 19 April: Rotten day all day. Little shelling on both sides. Attack again postponed. no post.

Field Message Book: To: Transport Sergt. Mory. 19.4.17
The following points regarding letters must again be made clear to all concerned. 1) The address must be in the body of the letter, written along the line. 2) No clue whatsoever is to be given as to the sector, or the locality – To mention, for instance, that 'we are following Fritzy' up is a clue to the fact that the Coy is in the Vth Army, which is the only army operating in the abandoned sector held by the British. 3) It is forbidden to mention that 'Shells arrived at a certain time, and missed us', when it is recollected that a record of *every shell fired* by the enemy is put into a record book, with exact range, direction, & time fired, this order will be understood more clearly. 4) It is *absolutely forbidden* to mention the fact of the proximity of the

batteries. It is probably known that the Coy. is in Mory. Carelessness in this direction could lead to untold consequences. 5) If any of the above are neglected, the letter, or letters, in question will not be posted. HWilliamson. Lt. 208 MGC

Field Message Book: To: T.Sgt. Mory. 19.4.17
One half timber is required to go to 2 Lt McConnels position tonight – to leave here at 7 pm. One team to be taken. Please detail a driver who knows the way, the limber went there the other night. HWilliamson. Lt. 208 MGC

Field Message Book: To: O.C. 208 MGC. Mory. 19.4.17
I recommend the following man for promotion as follows: – 21997 Dvr Flynn to be unpaid L/Cpl – vacancy caused by Pte Duval returned to duty. This man is time serving – was at 1st battle of Ypres 1914, 1915, Somme offensive 1916 (MGC) HWilliamson. Lt. 208 MGC.

Letter: 19 April 1917
My Dear Mother,
You silly ass, you twiddler and numbskull. Last night I got a parcel from you (undated – as usual) and a letter dated 11 April. You mention about the bomb, & crossed it out. We arnt living in the Dark Ages you know and even then, I have told you off and on for the last 3 years that your letters to the BEF are never looked at, never, never, never.

I can put just what you like – never forget that your son is a B.O. – that is British Officer, and as such, he is a mighty power in the present time – and also is treated by all from Fm Haig downwards with courtesy and consideration. Now do you get me?

I sent 2 tin boxes to you – a small one containing coats, buttons, shoulder straps etc. The second with the cap and bomb you got. Now pull yourself together. Do you think for a second I should be such a fool as to send a live bomb? Of course not. Unscrew that cap, & you will find it empty & merely an iron case. That bomb fuse may or may not be alive, but in any case it doesnt matter, it goes off on pulling that wire loop and then only with a sizzling noise, its only the fuse like the fuse of a chinese cracker. That fuse by the way screws into the egg bomb – you pull the wire loop, and 5 seconds after the bomb explodes, that is the action. But in this case I unscrewed the nob and emptied all the ammonal out, so its a dead fuse and an empty iron case. The cartridges too are empty, only the percussion cap is in and that harmless.

For your information I would tell you that the – hush! hush! (forage cap!!!) is mined with 1000 lbs of perdit – so be careful how you put it on your head!!!!

Please when you write, put the date of posting on your letter – thus – 'I got your letter of 11th on the 17th' – then I will know how long it takes – you have been so frightfully vague and delightfully helpless that I shall spank you when I come home.

When you get the helmets let me know at once – when I send some more souvenirs let me know all the contents then I will know what has been taken out – if anything. By the way, guard the helmets – they are exceedingly rare. Your next parcel please send 2 or 3 packets of Callard & Bowsers toffee – one likes to chew all day.

1 mile across the field guns are going trump, plump, pump, pump, plumb as fast as you can say it – I expect it means a Bosche attack or something, and an infantry S.O.S. rocket has gone up, meaning 'barrage fire'.

I have just inspected my sections rifles, field dressings, discs, gas helmet and respirator. It is just 7 oclock evening of Wednesday, or it may be Thursday, anyhow it is the 19th. In ½ hour I shall sit down to soup, stew or roast, vegetables (no spuds for past week) sweets, savoury, coffee, whiskies & soda. Then I shall go into my tent – put coal on the fire, light my candles, read, or add up my money again, gaze at a photograph, & get into a topping bed of four blankets made on a camp bed. Perhaps 10 seconds from now we shall have some shells over – they killed a lot in the next field yesterday & then perhaps a — will creep by, ready for the — line, and then the 60 pounders only a few hundred yards away will strafe, then the 9.2 hows will cough, & womp, out go my candles – when the heavies only a few yards away fire, out goes my candle – poing, & then a noise like a tramway – over goes a 300 lb shell to the Bosche. Please send the M.C. (both) when they come out – send them in a wrapper each week – if you really dont want to do it, just tell me & I will give an order to a bookseller – it is silly always waiting for things that never turn up. I should have thought it not a very hard thing to do – it gives me great pleasure to read them regularly and I may not have much chance to read many more, three of us are left at present – two of my pals are still lying in the wire of the — line. It is a month at least since I wrote for those two 1d weeklies, & I send you stuff you know.

Well how is Kathie? Thank her for that delicious toffee — I havent heard from Jerry for a long while. What exactly do you mean by the statement that the Clarks live at the top of the Hill — have the other people moved then? Not that I care much, my earthly troubles are over, or as good as over, I cant see how anybody can escape all whats portending. I suppose we shall try our luck again shortly, & the Bosche dont exactly love a machine gunner you know.

The only thing to look forward to in this awful monotonous wildness is the post — sleep I get in plenty at present, and food, but inside I am never peaceful — even if I go back to England there is no peace for me, & one gets tired of eternal theatres, picture palaces and beer. I have no friends now — except Stany — and certainly it would appear he misses me — we had such a bon time together in London — we used to go where all the good music was, and sip beer at the Cafe Moniqua, and indeed have a bizarre and bohemian time — but thats all over and done with now — never more will we listen to the Valse Triste and imagine ourselves unhappy but happy in each others company — never more shall we play billiards in the Black Bull before a warm fire till 8.45 & then to a bon show at the Hippodrome — finish, finish. Shall I ever hear my gramophone again I wonder?

Do you remember that evening I came in to get those records & gramophome? When I went out, I mean. And old Terry and I enjoying ourselves innocently on my dear old bus, the pride I took in that exhaust pipe — those jaunts down to Hawkhurst — all over. Gone are the wild birds, the dawn, and the dew — and away yonder the heavies pound away to cut the wire, the gunners clean up their Vickers guns, & examine field dressings, for soon —— and a few more mothers will be broken-hearted. I dont know whether I should send you this letter — if I thought it would put the wind up you, I wouldn't — but I think you know that at times I despair at the greyness of everything, and then when I write in these moods you will understand me a bit more — by tomorrow I shall be glad to be alive again — by tomorrow, who knows?

Dont forget, dear Mummie, if I get wounded, have my photo in the Kentish Mercury, dont forget. And if it is willed, & I dont think it is somehow, that I join dear old Charlie, well, dont worry — I

1. Henry Williamson on leave after his first stint in the trenches, November 1914–January 1915, when he was hospitalized with dysentery and trench foot. He had hacked off about 2 feet of his trench coat with his bayonet to relieve the weight of wet mud.

2. The cover (all that still exists) from the journal of the London Rifle Brigade issued to Henry when he enlisted in January 1914.

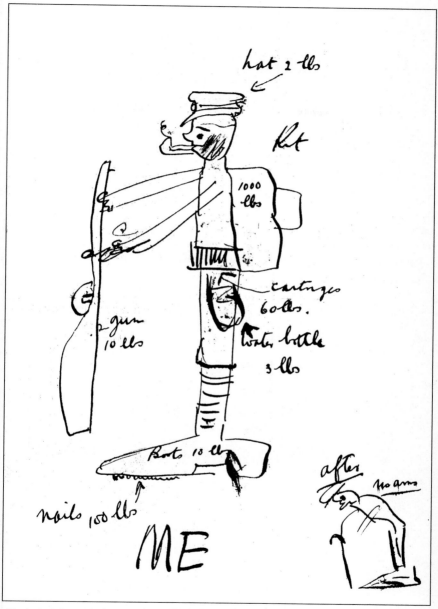

3. A sketch made by Henry Williamson on the back of a letter sent from training camp in September 1914, after a long march.

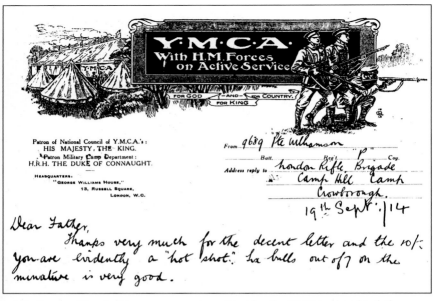

From 9689 Pte Williamson
Batt. "P" Regt. Coy.
Address reply to London Rifle Brigade
Camp Hill Camp
Crowborough.
19th Sept: /14

Dear Father,
Thanks very much for the decent letter and the 10/-
you are evidently a "hot shot". 1x bulls out of 7 on the
miniature is very good.

4. Letters written by Henry on paper provided by the YMCA: a) to his father on
19 September 1914; b) to his mother on 8 October 1914.

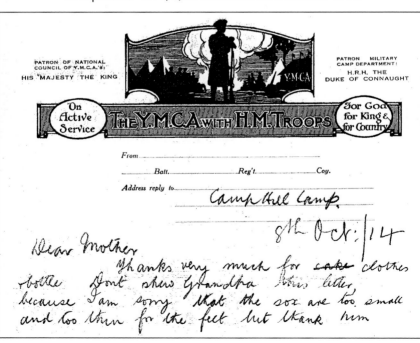

From
Batt. Reg't. Coy.
Address reply to Camp Hill Camp.

8th Oct: /14

Dear Mother
Thanks very much for ~~cake~~ clothes
& bottle Don't show Grandpa this letter
because I am sorry that the sox are too small
and too thin for the feet but thank him

94.A. CAMP OF 2ND BRIGADE 1ST LONDON DIVISION. CAMP HILL CROWBOROUGH.

5. The camp of the 2nd Brigade 1st London Division, Camp Hill, Crowborough. Henry sent this postcard to his older sister Kathie, 1 October 1914: 'This is a little bit of our camp.'

YMCA
With H.M. Forces
on Active Service

FOR GOD   AND   FOR COUNTRY.
FOR KING

8 oclock Weds morning.

Order just arrived "Battalion will embark on Saturday" (destin. unknown) may therefore be in London anytime before that Saturday. Dont come to Crowbro will wire if we are coming to 'Town. Or if we entrain anywhere. May be go to S. africa. love Henry

6a. Henry's postcard sent from Crowborough shortly before embarking for France, and war, for the first time.

6b. Roland Barnes, a school-friend from Colfe's, who enlisted in the London Scottish. The postcard is signed on the back 'Yrs aye Roland'. Henry has noted that it was taken 'after Messines, day after Hallowe'en 1914'.

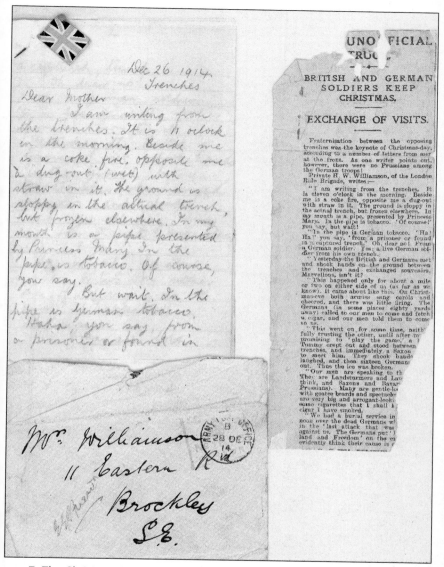

Dec 26 1914
Trenches

Dear Mother

I am writing from the trenches. It is 11 o'clock in the morning. Beside me is a coke fire, opposite me a dug-out (wet) with straw in it. The ground is sloppy in the actual trench, but frozen elsewhere. In my mouth is a pipe presented by Princess Mary. In the pipe is tobacco. Of course, you say.

But wait. In the pipe is German tobacco. Haha, you say, from a prisoner or found in

Mr Williamson
11 Eastern Rd
Brockley
S.E.

ARMY POST OFFICE
28 DE
14

7. The Christmas Truce, 1914. A letter from Henry to his mother from the trenches, 26 December 1914, and its subsequent printing in the *Daily Express*.

With
Best Wishes
· for a ·
Happy Christmas
· and a ·
Victorious New Year.

From
The Princess Mary
and Friends at
· Home ·
· · · ·

8. The Christmas card sent with her photograph by the Princess Mary to all soldiers at the Front. Still in the original small envelope, this was a precious relic that Henry kept all his life.

9a. The tin containing tobacco (still inside the lead foil packet) and cigarettes sent by the Princess Mary to all soldiers at the Front, with Henry's own matchbox.

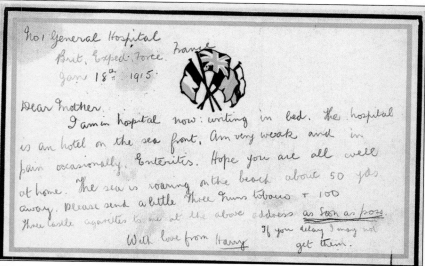

No 1 General Hospital
Brit. Exped. Force. France
Jan 18th 1915.

Dear Mother.

I am in hospital now: writing in bed. The hospital is an hotel on the sea front. Am very weak and in pain occasionally. Enteritis. Hope you are all well at home. The sea is roaring on the beach about 50 yds. away. Please send a little Three Nuns tobacco + 100 Three Castle cigarettes to me at the above address as soon as poss. If you delay I may not get them.

With love from Harry

9b. A postcard sent by Henry to his mother from hospital in France, January 1915.

10. This photograph was taken in March 1915 after Henry's return from a month at a convalescent home in the Midlands.

Army Form E. 511.

If this certificate is lost or mislaid no duplicate of it can be obtained.

DISCHARGE CERTIFICATE OF A SOLDIER OF THE TERRITORIAL FORCE.

T.F. RECORD OFFICE
No. 5/682/15
Date 16/4/15
LONDON

This is to certify that (No.) 9689 (Rank) Private
(Name) H. W. Williamson
(Unit) 5th City of London Regt (L.R.B.) who was enlisted
to serve in the Territorial Force of the County of London
on the 22nd day of January 1914,

Here state cause of discharge as detailed in the Regulations for the Territorial Force.

is discharged in consequence of * Having been Gazetted to a Commission in the 10th Battn Bedforshire Regiment
and that his claims have been properly settled.

His total service in the Territorial Force is 1 years 78 days, including
Nil years 318 days embodied service.
Service abroad, viz., in France Nil years 84 days.
Medals, Clasps, and Decorations Nil.

(Signature of Officer Commanding Unit) J G Adamson
(Place and Date) London April 9th 1915.

(7 13 9)   W 5752—1330 100,000 1/11 H W V   Forms E. 511.   COL.

NO TERRITORIAL FORCE RECORD OFFICE,
LONDON.

11a. Certificate of Discharge from the Territorial Force, 9 April 1915.

George R.I.

George by the Grace of God of the United Kingdom of Great Britain and Ireland and of the British Dominions beyond the Seas, King, Defender of the Faith, Emperor of India, &c. To Our Trusty and well beloved Henry William Williamson Greeting. We reposing especial Trust and Confidence in your Loyalty Courage and good Conduct do by these Presents Constitute and Appoint you to be an Officer in Our Land Forces from the Tenth day of April 1915. You are therefore carefully and diligently to discharge your Duty as such in the Rank of 2nd Lieutenant or in such higher Rank as We may from time to time hereafter be pleased to promote or appoint you to of which a notification will be made in the London Gazette and you are at all times to exercise and well discipline in Arms both the inferior Officers and Men serving under you and use your best endeavours to keep them in good Order and Discipline. And We do hereby Command them to Obey you as their superior Officer and you to observe and follow such Orders and Directions as from time to time you shall receive from Us or any your superior Officer according to the Rules and Discipline of War in pursuance of the Trust hereby reposed in you. Given at Our Court at Saint James's the Tenth day of April 1915 in the Fifth Year of Our Reign.

By His Majesty's Command.

Henry William Williamson
2nd Lieutenant
Land Forces.

11b. Document of Commission as a 2nd lieutenant, 10 April 1915.

12a. Details of kit purchased on promotion in April 1915.

12b. A packing checklist at about the same time.

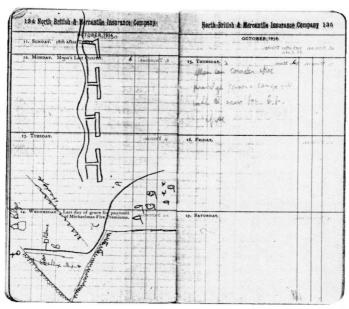

11. SUNDAY. 18th after Trinity.

12. MONDAY. Moon's Last Quarter.

13. TUESDAY.

14. WEDNESDAY. Last day of grace for payment of Michaelmas Fire Premiums.

15. THURSDAY.

16. FRIDAY.

17. SATURDAY.

13. Notes made in Henry's 1914 diary during the Initial Officers' Instruction course 1915.

19. SUNDAY. 1st after Easter. Low Sunday.

Lent

20. MONDAY.

Concealment aircraft
movements slow
communications hampered
flanks.
method attack

23. THURSDAY. St. George.

Apl

21. TUESDAY.

little artillery
counter attack preserve
no higher control
Attack on a wood.

24. FRIDAY.

22. WEDNESDAY.

fight for edge
interior.
celebrating

engineers

25. SATURDAY. St. Mark. New Moon.

14. Newly commissioned; this photograph is inscribed on the back in his mother's handwriting 'Harry April 1915'.

15a. A group of fellow officers 1915–16, inscribed on the reverse by Henry when writing the *Chronicle* novels: 'Phillip M [i.e. HW himself], not used, [sitting left to right] Flagg the Grimsby Fishmonger, Captain Bason, not used'.

With Love to Willie from his old Pal – Stany.

15b. Henry's Brazilian friend Eugene Maristany.

16a. Henry with his friend Terence Tetley (1918).

16b. Terence Tetley with Henry's sisters, Biddy, on the left, and Kathie, on the right.

17. 'Very much the Officer' – Henry on joining the Machine Gun Company, November 1916.

18a. Henry's father, William Leopold Williamson, in the uniform of a Sergeant of the Special Constabulary.

18b. The uniform still exists, together with his medals, armbands, truncheon and whistle.

18c. Pages from his notebook, detailing Zeppelin raids.

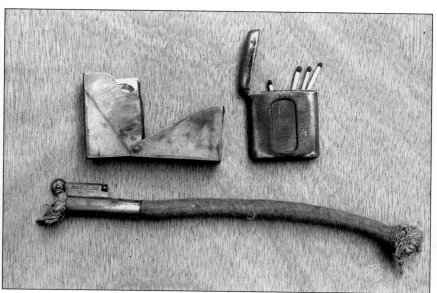

19. Items that have survived: a) Henry's uniform jacket; b) his identity disc; c) his water bottle; and d) his fusée and matchboxes.

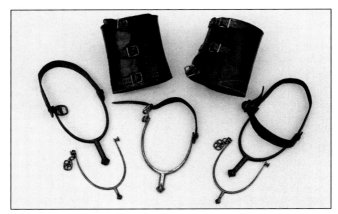

20. Further surviving items: a) Henry's riding and dress spurs, and leather gaiters;
b) personal items, his bone toothbrush, khaki block and brush case; c) a selection
from a considerable number of trench maps.

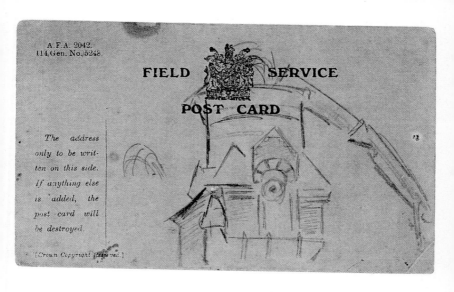

21. Sketch of the 'Golden Virgin' at Albert made by Henry on an Official Field Service postcard.

14·2·17.   Drivers 204 M.G. Coy Transport.

Sgt   Mitchell
L/Cpls   Nolan   Cpl 16.4.17.   Grooms
L/Cpl   Stirling   ret 24.4.17   L/Cpl Joy
           Bolton   sick 29.4.17   Pte   Slate
Dvr   Beer   sick 29.4.17 cc   Cooper
           Douglas   Franklin
           Twells   Pte   Finch
           Ogden   Vetters
           Thomas   CS course   Balmer Pte Case
           Fox   Cold Shoer
           McKay   Hughes   Pte Hayes Frith
           Cooper
           Allison   Stitcher
           Finch   Pte Hayes.
           Tracey
           Dawley   H.Q. Transport
           Askew   Pte Palmer
           Walker
           Lymon   Dvr Smith ...
           Norris   28.3.7.
Mob.   Wright   returned to duty 10.4.17
           Bentley   altd
           Wishart   Parkinson
           Bevan
L/Cpl   Flynn 10.4.17.

Spare drivers (as gunners) L/Cpl Duval, Dr. Martin.

22a. Henry's List of Mule Drivers in 208 MGCoy Transport Section in February 1917, taken from his Field Notebook.

22b. MGCoy officers: i) McClane and McConnel; ii) 2 Lt. C. Horseley; iii) 2 Lt. C.F. Wright.

Bécourt
Dec '15

208 M.G. Coy. May '17 at ERVILLERS.

23. A page from an album in Henry's archive. The four outer photographs are of 208 MGCoy, May 1917 at Ervillers; the centre one is of graves at Bécourt in December 1915.

24a. 2 Lts McConnel and McClane at Gomiecourt in April 1917.

24b. HW and Lt. Tremlett, DSO, Beaumont Hamel, March 1917.

24c. HW with a crashed British plane at Gomiecourt.

25. German souvenirs sent home by Henry from the Front: a) cloth *feldgrau* cap, shoulder tag, leather helmet, and identity tag; b) German bayonets, including the 'saw bayonet' mentioned in a letter home to his mother; c) close-up of the German helmet from the battlefields.

26a. Nominal Roll Transport Section 208 MGCoy, April 1917, from Henry's Field Notebook.

26b. List of Henry's belongings made at 44 CCS, Colincamps, June 1917, after he had been gassed.

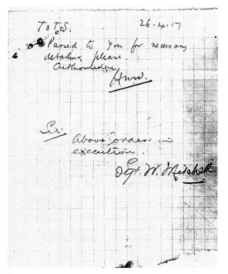

26c and d. These messages are still in the envelope used to send them at the time.

27a. A page of photographs showing Henry's convalescence at Trefusis in Cornwall, summer 1917, including a side view of HMS *Implacable* which features in the *Chronicle*.

27b. Henry with nurses and fellow officers at Trefusis.

28a. Captioned by Henry Williamson himself: 'Group of Convalescent Officers at Trefusis, Aug. 1917 + denotes since killed in action. 2 Lt. Griffin MC, Capt. Johnson M.C. Cheshires, Lt. H.W. Williamson 1st Bedf. R., Maj. Banns R.G.A., 2 Lt. Catlin A.S.C., + Major Traill M.C. East Yorks. ——, Lt. H. Martyn D.L.I., Lt. Goodall A.S.C., + Lt. Percy Worral R.F.C.'

28b. Henry leaving Trefusis 'in the governess cart' for the Devonport Military Hospital at Plymouth.

28c. At Plymouth with his friend Gibbo, September 1917: 'Gibbo sometimes stuck on a Charlie Chaplin moustache while wearing an eyeglass with his usual languid manner.' (*A Test to Destruction*)

29. Two photographs of Henry in the uniform of the Bedfordshire Regiment, taken on the same day: one formal, the other touched up to look more like a portrait.

30a and b. A postcard sent by Henry to his father from Felixstowe.

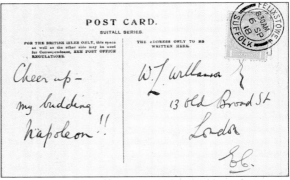

POST CARD.

SUITALL SERIES.

FOR THE BRITISH ISLES ONLY, this space as well as the other side may be used for Correspondence, SEE POST OFFICE REGULATIONS.

THE ADDRESS ONLY TO BE WRITTEN HERE.

Cheer up –
my budding
Napoleon !!

W. J. Williamson
13 Old Broad St
London
EC.

30c. Henry and his partner Milling, winners of the men's doubles at a Regimental Tennis Tournament, Felixstowe, August 1918.

30d. Taken in Folkestone in early 1919, on the steps of the house occupied by Mabs Baker (the fictional 'Eve Fairfax').

31a. Henry with his father and two sisters in the garden of 11 Eastern Road towards the end of the First World War.

31b. A close-up of the miniature medals on his uniform jacket.

31c. Uniform badges and the only medal to be recovered after a theft in the 1960s.

32a. Henry standing among battlefield graves on his honeymoon in 1925.

32b. The same visit: in the Ancre Valley.

32c. Captioned by Henry: 'These German crosses, black as a wasteland of charred thistles at the Labyrinth, Arras. 36,000 graves in chalk. Crosses extend beyond horizon.'

shall have only gone a little way away, and shall not worry about bikes, or friends, or, other friends, then.

Well goodbye dear mother, at least au revoir a bit longer, my only worry is the monotony: — food, weather, stove, money, bed, all right, and only a fluke will kill your loving son, Harry. XXXXXXX Give my love to my old woman up the road. [Mrs Nicholson]

Diary: Friday 20 April: Sent pass book off and parcel boots and bombs. No post again. New section arrangements. Nothing doing today.

Army Correspondence Book, 152 (Field service): 20.4.17
The Transport Section from today will be divided into four subsections, a, b, c, and d respectively. Each subsection will be under an NCO. Drivers of limbers A1, A2, A3 will be in subsection a, B1 B2 B3 in subsection b etc. The NCO in charge of a subsection will be responsible to the Transport Segeant for the prompt turning out of limbers, pack mules etc under his command. Whenever possible, subsections will group together in bivouacs — the subsection NCO will see that his section of the camp is clean, and that all the standing orders of the Coy. and TS refering to Gas Alarms and shelling etc are carried out. Spare men, attached men, shoeing smiths etc will be under the T SGt. Grooms will be as heretofore. The 18 members of a subsection on inspection parade will stand two paces behind the centre man of his subsection. Fatigues etc will be done by subsection in rotation. HWilliamson. Lt. MGC 208.
Copies to: O.C. Coy, T.O., T.S.

Army Correspondence Book, 152 (Field service): To: TS 20.4.17
Please render to me as soon as possible a nominal roll of each subsection, and of attached men, smiths etc. Each s.s. NCO will report to you any difference of harness, mules, personal kit etc as soon as it occurs. Until Lt/Cpl Stirling returns, his s.s. will be under Cpl Nolan, but render his section separately, & let the drivers understand they are Stirlings section. Your duties, generally speaking will be the same as before, this system should relieve you a bit. HWW.

Army Correspondence Book, 152 (Field *service*): 20.4.17
NOMINAL ROLL TRANSPORT SECTION
Subsections
A: Martin, Davy; Norns, Fox; Vetters; – Cpl Nolan
B: Douglas, Mobbs; Hughes; Allison; – [L/Cpl Bolton crossed out]
C: Nixon, Bevan; Lyman, Young; Cooper; – L/Cpl Stirling
D: Walker, [Benn/Hosp]; Twells, Willis; Flynn, Askew; – [L/Cpl
Flynn crossed out]

H.Q.-: Tracey ; W.Ct -: Bentley, Parkinson; Runner -: Wishart;
Farriers -: Frith, Thomas; Stitcher -: Hayes; Batman -: Case
Grooms -: Slate, Franklin, Cooper, Finch; – L/Cpl Joy
HWilliamson Lt. T.O. 208 MGCoy.

Field Message Book: To: Transport Sergt. MORY. 21.4.17
A) There will be a parade for all men in the section who require
new boots at the Coy. stores this afternoon at 2pm. B) Great care
must be taken to keep the inside of the breast collar and wither
trim scrupulously clean. Neglect of this kind will lead, as at
present, to breast galls. There will be an inspection of the breast
collar and wither tens tonight at 6.30pm – absolute cleanliness
inside being the main point. HWilliamson. 208 MGC.

Field Message Book: To: Sgt Mitchell. Mory. 21.4.17
Many galls, wither, breast, and in some cases, back, are occuring
in the section, particularly in the case of wheel animals.
Whereever possible the wheel animals so galled will take the place
of lead animals, and vice versa. This will be arranged by you as
soon as the section is in. HWW. Lt. 208

Diary: Saturday 21 April: Fine day. Many Bosches planes over. Camp
shelled at 3 am Sunday morning. Mule wounded. Harness
destroyed. Lost tunic, breeches, [word unreadable -'bruntteary'?],
field glasses, and revolver.

Diary: memo section:

| Bet Mclane | 5fcs | 5fcs | hostilitie dont cease July 31 |
| McKelvey | 5 – | 5 – | Bosche ex-France May 31 |

Letter: 21.4. 17

Dear Mother,

Today, Saturday 21st, I sent off a parcel containing my boots and an orange in each – again the latter is quite empty. Please let me know when you get same. I am writing you a lot because I am doing nothing at present – the calm before the storm you know – all storms nowadays – you understnd me?

By the way the little Bird wrote me and said he is not going to be married on Sunday as I wrote in my last but it is postponed until the 27th or the 28th [i.e. attack dates] – as he postponed this four or five times, I expect he is getting rather fed up with his firm and meanwhile his future ma-in-law gets *stronger and stronger*. Still he is a *bully* lad, and his *courting* [NB – code for Bullecourt] has been very vigorous dont you think. Let me know your opinion when you write next.

Well there is absolutely nothing to say so I will shut up – today we begin our third month over here!! Dont forget what I told you about your letters. Love H.

PS. If by any chance you find a greyish powder in any of those eggs, merely empty it in the garden NOT in the fire. There is always a millionth chance of a full one going in by mistake, but they are quite harmless unless it is lit by a match – unscrew the screw and shake – if nothing comes out is is empty – if grey brickdust falls out its all right to pour it out in the garden. Dont get the wind up – out here we kick them aside, ride over them, the horses kick them, but if you put them in a fire (i.e. not be concussion) they go wallop. But I am sure they are the ones I specially emptied.

Letter: 21.4.17

Dear Father,

I am quite well thankyou. I hope you like the enclosed cutting, one of the most awful lies I have ever read anywhere in any paper. Remind me when I come home & I will tell you what really happened. Yours with love, Horace.

Diary: *Sunday 22 April*: Bosche planes over camp in morning, 400 ft up, 140 mph. Shifted to Ervillers in evening.

Field Message Book: 2 Lt. A.P. McCleave. Mory. 22.4.17
Please send those men not actually bathing back to camp immediately. The Coy. has to move tonight. HWilliamson. Lt. for O.C. 208 MGC.

Diary: Monday 23 April: No sleep last night. Intense bomb. early morning. Four times in and out of Fontaine – fighting with clubbed rifles. Lovely day.

Army Correspondence Book, 152: To: O.C. Mobile Station AVC [Auxiliary Veterinary Corps]. 62nd Div. Ervillers. 23.4.17
We have a mule hit by shellfire in near foreleg; it is unable to walk. It is in our own mule lines at MORY: we have shifted and are now at Ervillers. Can you please arrange for an ambulance to be sent immediately. Another mule hit in the back for admittance please. HWilliamson. Lt. 208MGC. 187 Inf. Brigade.

Army Correspondence Book, 152: To: O.C. 208 MGC. ERVILLERS.
The ADVS [Assistant Director Veterinary Surgeon] inspected the animals this morning, and was very dissatisfied with the condition of the mules. He remarked that some were apparently neglected, and wasting away. I explained this was the case with some animals, the reason being hard work, irregular watering and feeding (due to fatigues), the poor quality of the fodder and corn, and the under-establishment – this being 1GS [General Service] waggon, and six mules. He has authorised me to protest in the event of too frequent fatigues. I also explained that rest at night was broken at intervals by the proximity of battery at MORY. HWilliamson. Lt. 208 MGC.

Diary: Tuesday 24 April: A.D.V.S. ['arounded'? – difficult to read] – straffed like hell over the mules. Still perfect weather. Rose 50 fcs. Saw first lot of swallows.

Army Correspondence Book, 152: To: T. Sargeant. ERVILLERS. 24.4.17
Please render to me for signature an indent for the number of haynets and nose bags & water buckets that are deficient. In Indents which may be in, you may disregard as the indent will be marked 'repetition'. Feeds will be madeup into feed bags and waterbuckets from hence forward, and given in them.

Will you put the poorly conditioned mules by themselves, as they will need special attention in the matter of feeding & watering. Linseed, when available, will be made into a pulp and given to the sickly ones — soaking for 24 hours will suffice. *The line orderly will be responsible for the collection of bags and buckets after the feeding. HWW.*

Letter: 24.4.17
Dear Mother,

I received your parcel containing biscuits & toffee yesterday for which many thanks.

The weather is beautiful now — we are living under canvas on one of the lovely slopes of ground — once a huge rolling wheatfield, for which this part is famous — the downs untouched by shellfire — all the terrible desolation of the Ancre battlefield is miles behind us — and the newer desolation of the havoc caused by our guns is in front of us — a couple of miles or so — at last we are having a well-needed rest.

The sky above is a lovely rich blue — flecked here and there with small fleecy patches of white — smoke caused by the archies when a plane attempted to come over a few moments ago at about 15000 feet up. Right along the sky for miles are our sausage balloons — watching, directing, photographing, ever ready to be pulled down, or worse still, jump out in parachutes in the event of a big Roland diving down from 15000 feet to 1700 feet in about 30 seconds & firing the bag.

The Roads are splendid now, and we have a lesser evil, Dust. Soon it will be almost unbearable, and the flies will begin to worry us, and the lice as well perhaps. The mules feel the better weather already. The thin emaciated dreary-eyed mud-caked mules of March are now rolling in the warm stubble, and braying with thankfulness to their God — the Sun.

In the vast blue above the newly arrived swallows wheel and call and from yonder grim and black wood of Loqueast [see map at end showing Front line on 18 March 1917 where Loqueast Wood is marked on lefthand side nearly halfway up] the cuckoo sings. Spring is here with its promise of life and hope — and Death.

The guns in the distance are firing lazily and slowly — soon they will bang and crash, and send their screaming missiles of destruction into the wire forests ahead — behind which the grey clad troops crouch in dugouts — weary, and with the fear of the future in their souls.

Now overhead a dull droning is heard, and miles up appear six planes crashing through space — a British fighting squadron of a new type — triplanes with a speed of 140 miles an hour. Perhaps we shall soon hear a dull and far away pop, pop, pop — another squadron has been sighted, but instead of the circles they wear the black cross. And perhaps a plane with two humans in it will hurtle down through space to crash and shiver into the brown stubble — but still the cuckoo will call with its haunting cry, and suddenly with a cry of anguish we will think of Holwood Park or Fox Grove Woods and our stolen escapades in there during schooldays — and remember how we would hare off at the sight of a farmer — or climb for the rooks eggs just about this time, only years ago.

I 'spose the blue-tits still sing as they search the newly opening buds for insects? and the pigeons still fly with a clatter of wings through the beech trees in the Park. The old oak is still there, perhaps with the same owl in it, but a younger and strange human watching it. The lakes in Holwood still glisten in the sun, the same carp splash among the water lily leaves — Nature is unchanged in England.

Here the earth will soon vibrate with the thunder of the guns — tons of earth will be blown skyhigh in huge black fountains — the shrapnel will burst in white soft clouds above the wire — Hell itself will be let loose, and soon the beauty of the spring will disappear, and shattered trees and torn earth alone be left — and among it, pathetic little bundles of wasting flesh will strew the ground. Here one will be lying quietly, peacefully, as though it fell to the ground in a natural manner, there a figure will lie, clay and earth in its hands, torn up in the mad final frenzy. And the sky will still be blue, and at night the stars will shine out — and the hooting of the owls and the crying of the lapwings will be interrupted by the tearing rending guns, and the harsh staccato rattle of the machine guns.

Enough.

Well Mother, I am tired of writing so goodbye. Write to me again soon & send the Kentish Mercury occasionally. Love H.

Diary:Wednesday 25 April: Peace rumours. Much colder. Still resting.

Field Message Book: To: Sergt. W. Mitchell. 26.4.17 Ervillers.
In future reveille for the T.S. will be at 6.30 am. An NCO will report to me as soon as the animals are fitted up ready for filing away for water. (This only applies to early morning). Animals that have to be hooked in will be fed and watered *an hour before* time of hooking in. If water at the troughs is not available before 7 am, water buckets will be filled overnight. It must be impressed on everyone that severe results may occur if animals are not watered *before* feeding. Severest disciplinary action will be taken in the event of non-compliance with the above orders. To be read out on parade. HWilliamson. Lt. 208 MGC.

Field Message Book: To: T.O.C. 208 MGC 26.4.17
Description of horse strayed onto the T. Lines on 25.4.17. Bay mare, light draught, 14.2. Blaze, stocking near hind, 2 L.O. off hind. HWW

Diary: Thursday 26 April: Doing nothing. Mess cart to Albert. Continuous artillery fire all night (British). Letter from Stany.

Army Correspondence Book, 152: [Written directly in pencil – not duplicate.]

> Bluebells pray, blue as the sea
> Ring out your secret softly to me
> Tell me if, far away, over the sea
> Someone is living their life for me.
> Bluebells faded grey as the sky
> Whispered the message through the sky
> Tell her I think of her, kiss her goodbye
> Spring come again, Love cannot die

Army Correspondence Book, 152: To: O.C. 208 MGC 26.4.17
Sir, On the morning of the 23rd I ordered the Transport Sgt to water the horses in a pond on the Arras–Bapaume road just outside the village of Ervillers and near the camp. He did not bit the animals up to water here as we should not have passed through a village. Meanwhile I rode into the village to look for better watering accommodation, for although a notice board pointing to the watering hole indicated that the horses could be watered there, the water was not good. In the villages I

ascertained that proper accommodation was available in the form of watering troughs. I rode back in time to stop the horses being watered in the aforementioned pond, and beckoned the men to follow me. I beckoned from about 50yds, and consequently did not see that the animals were without bits. The leading man, Pte Finch followed my horse and when I turned up to the troughs he was stopped by the MMP. [Mounted Military Police] HWilliamson. Lt. 208 MGC.

Army Correspondence Book, 152: To: TS. ERVILLERS. 26.4.17
1) Men must be ready to file out to water at 7 am, 11.30am, and 4pm each day. All feed bags must be prepared during or before the watering.
2) Now the weather has improved, more attention must be paid to metal work. The CO expects to find a great improvement in this direction immediately.
3) Mules or animals ordered for parade in the early morning must be watered and fed *an hour before* the hour of parade.
4) The ADVS is very particular about grooming. Constant supervision by the NCOs is necessary to ensure good grooming. HWilliamson. Lt. 208 MGC.

Letter: 26.4.17
Dearest,
Just got your letter saying you got helmets – good. Dont know the regts – one is artillery. – Am in hurry to catch post. What is Tetley in now? Thanks for toffee & Cycling. Aren't those helmets good souvenirs? the spikes screw on top. The flat fellow is Bavarian. Write soon send Kentish Mercury. Love Harry. PS Guns going like hell.

Diary: Friday 27 April: Weather threatening. Attack again postponed.

Army Correspondence Book, 152: To: OC 208 MGC ERVILLERS. 27.4.17
Sir, Nineteen (19) men are deficient of iron rations in the TS. The losses are made up as follows.
Neglect: Drvs Mobbs, Nyman, Beer, Hughes
Stolen: (Engelbelmer) Drvs Bentley, Vetters, Walken, Norris, Cooper.
Unserviceable: Drvs Wells, Fox, Young, Finch, Silate, Cpl Nolan, L/Cpl Joy.

Not issued: Drvs Askew, Bevan, SS Frith.

With reference to those not issued, the train at Hauvre station moved off before issue was complete – the remainder being bundled into the train. The CQMS [Company Quarter Master Sergeant] was informed of this at the time.

Ptes Willis and Parkinson consumed theirs in the trenches by order of an officer.

HWilliamson. Lt. TO 208 MGC

[At this point there is a page with two German stamps pasted on and the comment 'Found on dead German near Croisilles. April 1917'.]

Army Correspondence Book, 152: To: T.S. 27.4.17

Ref, the attached lists. On the list signed by yourself there is a def. of iron rations, 19. On the unsigned lists, only seven are marked as deficient. Please explain *immediately*, and state which of the lists I am to take as correct. The words 'complete kit' are very vague – does it mean personal kit? If so, separate articles should be named. I can't possibly make a return from these lists, with such discrepancies. HWW

Army Correspondence Book, 152: To: OC 208 MGC ERVILLERS. 27.4.17

Return of men innoculated twice, more than 12 months ago.

11143 Franklin, 73115 Mobbs, 34854 Lyman, 36273 Martin.

Innoculated once, more than six months ago. Nil.

HWilliamson, Lt. TO 208 MGC.

Army Correspondence Book, 152: To: O.C. 208 MGC.

The following articles are required by the TSection, (lost by accident, negligence, or unserviceable.)

Pantaloons, 4. Iron Rations, 12. Cap comforter, 5. Puttees, 6 prs. Cap cover, 5. Spurs, 7 prs. Knife, 4. Clasp knives, 9. Field Dressings, 2. Spoon, 3. Socks, 29 prs. SD cap, 2. Coat British warm, 1. Cardigan, 1. Shaving Brush, 1. Rifle covers, 7. Mess tin, 9. Mess tin covers, 3.

HHWilliamson.

[and added underneath] Drivers 63745 Davy, H.O. 36273 Martin, W.F.

Army Correspondence Book, 152: To: OC 208 MGC ERVILLERS
Sir, Can I have two drivers from the Coy lent to my section please,
as I have only 22 drivers but 47 mules. This matter is urgent as no
one driver can look after more than two mules. I am informed
that Sgt Mitchell has gone down to the base. HWWilliamson. TO.
Lt. 208 MGC

Diary: Saturday 28 April: Inspection of transport by Corps & B. de
Staffs. Good. Heard concert in open air.
Diary: memo section: Watering in shellholes. Watering without bits.
[This must refer to the complaint about procedure by MMP on
23.4.17.]

Diary: Sunday 29 April: McKelvey goes to [difficult to decipher –
'CARNIERE'?] Good weather still holding. Bosche planes over.
Feeling very lazy. Heard from mother.

Diary: Monday 30 April: Mules being overworked. Divisional relief
soon after the attack. Beer and Bolton to hospital. Parcel from
home. Awful accident to T.M.B's. [Suggest this is Trench Mortar
Bombs.]

Army Correspondence Book, 152: To: O.C. 208 MGC 30.4.17
L/Cpl Bolton and Drv Beer have been admitted to hospital. Drvs
Duval and Wright having been returned to duty with the Coy, and
Drv Smith admitted to hospital, wounded, and Drv Thomas on a
course of coldshoeing, the section is short of trained drivers. We
have two attached men who are not trained. The cooks cart has
two drivers now. Would it be possible please for the section to
have more drivers attached to it, as at present we have only 22
actual drivers, excluding Cpl Nolan. HWilliamson. TO 208MGC

Diary: Tuesday 1 May: Still fine day. Few Bosche planes over. X day
today [i.e. three days before attack]. Batteries & bulbs for lamp
arrived. Few mules lousy.

Field Message Book: To: Sgt. Mitchell. Ervillers. 1.5.17
The C.O. will inspect the harness on or about the 3rd inst. Men
must clean this, the brass and metal work first, in their own time.
There will be an inspection of harness by me on the 2nd inst, at

6pm. Drvs Allison, Bevan, Lyman will be available for all fatigues until the evening of the 4th inst. In addition you will inspect their harness about 8pm (to give them time to clean it) every evening. This is in the nature of a punishment. HWWilliamson, Lt. 208 MGC

Letter: 1 May PRIVATE PLEASE
Dear Mum,
Thanks for letter of 24 which I got on the 29th. No I dont want to write to Efford, he really doesnt interest me I wish you would choke him off & not write to him. History repeats itself in all the cases doesnt it — here is Mrs. E. coming to see you with his photo — do you remember what I asked you to do etc etc, its all the same old game I suppose, and now Ive got the bird from the N's [Nicholsons] — I wrote a month ago a long letter — I'm not going to write any more there, even if they write me — washout!

Do you think I care a damn about any cousins or not, of course not, I've never had anything except very faint interest in these people and what small interest I did have is now gone. However your letters mentioning these little things are very interesting although I personally am not writing them again in this war unless I am compelled to in courtesy.

I hope you are not all starving at home, I am glad you got the sword bayonet OK — it wont explode by the way. [This bayonet still exists in Williamson's archive — see plate 25b.] You might let me know pa's birthday will you I dont want to forget it. Do you ever see the Tetleys, what do they say, I dont write to them but would like to hear a bit of news now & again.

['Would you send out my Brownie' — crossed out] Could you buy a folding pocket thing for me, you can get a good miniature vest one for about 35/ — & send it out as soon as poss with ½ dozen spools, one of those tiny things but dont get a cheap one — pa will give you the money, & a few records of me will be good, eh? Dont forget. Well must look at the donkeys now — love Harry.
PS. I may be home soon — I am done up, one of two left now.

Diary: *Wednesday 2 May*: Rode up line. Flynn to MORY copse. Coy. went up the line. Bosche intermittent shelling.

Field Message Book: To: T.Sgt. 2.5.17
Please detail two fighting limbers of B section to parade this afternoon, hooked in by 2pm. L/Cpl Flynn will be in charge of party. Blankets, waterproof sheets will be taken, water buckets to be filled. 1 water bucket for each animal, and fodder for two days. (also unconsumed portion of days fodder). HWWilliamson. Lt. T.O.

Field Message Book: To: O.C. 208 MGC. 2 May.
Map ref. of L/Cpll Flynn is B16 a 9.1.

Letter: 2 May 1917
Dear Mother,
Thanks for parcel of sweets etc, also the batteries & bulbs arrived yesterday from the stores. By the way you will be surprised to hear that Bert is going to be married tomorrow (3rd) and from what he writes me it is going to be a very swell affair – it will be the biggest war wedding this year – fancy the Rt. Hon. Bert marrying an actress, in spite of his noble pa!! St. Martins-in-the-Fields, the ceremony will take place. [He had evolved an elaborate coded message to disguise the real content, but it is fairly obvious that it means an attack for 3 May!]

Well thanks for parcels. The guns at present are bombarding all along the line, we are certainly waking him up. I would like to tell you an awful lot, but I can't. Well, must close now – give my love to all at home. Well, cheerio. love H.

Letter: 3 May – Dawn
Dear Biddy,
Thanks for letter. Am just going over the top, so will write a hasty note. Give my love to mother. The Ger is putting an awful barrage up – the day is just breaking, we are over in 20 minutes. Am just having a cup of tea before rejoining the men who are lined up waiting for the artillery to open – it does in 7 minutes. Well cheero. Give my love to all. God bless you all. Harry.

Diary: Thursday 3 May: Z Day. Zero hour 3.45.[13] Intensive barrage right up North & down to Bullecourt. Rumours of failure – prisoners in cages – walking wounded. 187 Bde smashed up, ¾ Coy missing at evening. No shelling in rear areas. 7th Div. again attacks in evening. Montford killed.

Field Message Book: To: O.C. 208 MGC. Ervillers. 3.5.17. 5.30am.
No casualties in T.S. 2 signs herewith. HWWilliamson, Lt. 208 MGC.

Field Message Book: [Here there are two messages superimposed on the same sheet – so very difficult to read and shows confusion of situation.]
To: Capt. King. MORTHOMME / To: Cpl. Nolan . 3.5.17
Herewith 1) 50 rations, 2) coat, 3) [?] if needed. Left camp 7.30pm. ½ limber at once. report to Capt. King near [?] (aeroplane) at Morthomme (Coy. HQ) Send Bevan. He knows the way. Instruct the [corporal?] to send 1 cook field machine order & 2 days rations and 4 dixies in the limber.

Field Message Book: To: C.Q.M.S. 4.5.17
Please send 40 rations (8 sacks of 5 each) and 1 jar rum in half limber to Coy. HQ. at Homme Mort. The ½ limber will leave here at 4am. Please arrange with mess Cpl to send 4 tins sausages, some tea and sugar and rations for 8 officers for a day with the limber. Report to me when arrangements are made. Arrange with Sgt Mitchell for limber and driver (send L/Cpl Joy with the limber).

Field Message Book: [this message crossed out] To: 2 Lt. A.P. McClane. Ervillers. 4.5.17. 12.11am
Message noted. Am sending rations (+ one jar rum) for 90 men and 8 officers. Limber leaving lines at 4 am, destination C.H.Q. Mort Homme. HWWilliamson LT. T.O. 208 MGC
[substituted by this one] To: 2 Lt. A.P. McClane. Ervillers. 4.5.17. 12.30am
Your message (undated) received. Am sending rations for 90 men and 8 officers (including extras for later). No time mentioned, so am sending now. HWWilliamson. Lt. T.O. 208 MGC.

Field Message Book: To: O.C. 208 MGC. ERVILLERS. 4.5.17. 1.45pm
2nd Lt Wright proceeding with 15 gunners after dinner. You say 'Rations tonight will be as last night'. 18 bags of 5 (ie 90 rations) went up last night (plus for 8 offrs). Will send same amount up at 4pm tonight, unless I hear by messenger to the contrary. Please state if RUM is required.
HWWilliamson. Lt i/c Rear Party.

Field Message Book: To: Lt. Rose. M.H. ERVILLERS. 4 May. 1.45pm.
Herewith 4 shelters, + posts. The water cart follows. Can you
please return this. We have tanks here, but nothing to fill them
with, as you have all the petrol tins. If you can concur, I will send
you the w.c. up every morning, and you can fill up from it. If the
cart is damaged, we are certainly done for as regards water. (Note
– I *can* fill (if needed) up with water buckets, but this is altogether
too filthy a practice to carry out.) HWWilliamson. Lt i/c R.P.

Field Message Book: To: O.C. 208 MGC. ERVILLERS. 4.5.17. 3.20pm
Herewith: 1) Cpls Harris + Hutchings. 2) 1 cook, 5 Dixies, Camp
Officers mess stuff. 3) Fresh meat for 100 men, bacon for 100
men, and rations for 100 men. (In the event of the Coy stopping
there tomorrow, 5th, will send cold meat and potatoes for 100
men. If they come to Ervillers, cold meat and potatoes will be
ready tomorrow, 5th. 4) Maggone + Welland with stuff for
officers. Post with Signalling Corporal. No papers today. If you
want water cart will send up to fill cans with. Am not sending
men's post until casualties are known. Will 4 chargers be stopping
there? (am sending rations for 8 mules and 4 horses herewith).
HWWilliamson, Lt. i/c Rear Party.

Diary: Friday 4 May: Gen Gough pleased with 62nd Div., why, God
alone knows. 7th Div. badly cut up – apparently H.L. too damn
strong for us at present. Another attempt at night fails. Coy. badly
mauled. Have been very lucky.

Letter: 4 May 4 oclock
[Written on a long thin strip of brown paper.]
Dear Mother,
Am well, am at present commanding a battalion or whats left of
it. My address is same. Am sending this back by scout telephonist,
dont expect you'll get it, as the barrage is absolutely awful. No
time for more. By the time you get this shall be enjoying myself I
hope. The air is full of flying splinters & smoke from shells & the
dust is awful. Love H.

Field Message Book: [Scribbled in pencil and thus not a message as
such – presumably a roll call of men present or men injured.]

Gunners:	Mr. Wrights party	
	Sgt Jones (at H.L.)	
	6 men	
A Section :	2 ['stragglers' crossed out] men from line	
	8 A section	1 TS
B	2 men	2 [word unreadable]
C	L/Cpl Tyler	20 drivers
	2 gunners from line	4 grooms
D	Lt Wright	1 Batman
	Sgt Jones from line	
	4 carriers from line (attd mg)	
	4 gunners 1 carrier [crossed out] attd man	
HQ	1CQMS 1 Postman	
	2 Storemen	
	1 [unreadable]	
	2 cooks	
	1 Mess Cpl	
	1 mess cook	
	5 batmen	
	3 watermen	
	3 orderly Room staff.	

Field Message Book: To: Lt Rose. Ervillers. 4 May. 8.30pm
Herewith two chargers for officers coming back. Am sending up at the trot 3 limbers, as I expect you will need the third. Rations with limbers following horses. HWWilliamson.

Field Message Book: To: Cook Corporal. 4 May. 8.45pm.
Please have two dixies of water on boil for C + D sections, expected to arrive about 10.30–11pm at camp. HWWilliamson. Lt. 208 MGC

Diary: Saturday 5 May: Early morning HAC [Honourable Artillery Company] & Warwicks attack again. Fail again. Evening Devons & Welch try again. Barrage at 10 oclock. Sgt Mitchell a casualty. Bosche attack smashed. Raining in evening.

Diary: memo section: A.C. Montford, 79 Crofton Road, S.E.5
Lt. Laubernburgh, 22 MGC
[Addresses of dead men; HW obviously intended to write to their families.]

Letter: 5 May

[Marked with X denoting code = FAILED.]

Dear Mother & Father,

I thank you for your lovely letter, received two days ago. Well we are out now at last thank God – the horror of the last two days is still on me. I feel awfully lonely, as most of my pals are with Charlie, one of who, a 2nd Lt who lives at Crofton Park, will get the VC (posthumous) [i.e. 2/Lt. A.C. Montford]. I cant tell you what happened but you can guess when I say nothing about our affair. Well, well, better luck next time.

The paper states that the ['submarine peul' ? – difficult to read] is great. Well the war cant last for ever, can it? My bag was 2 prisoners (lousy and with skin disease – all yellow from dugout life). I think thats about all we took. Well I expect to be peaceful till about the time I first went to Devon last year – meanwhile my leave is due soon. Love H.

Diary: Sunday 6 May: Awful rot in papers about our attack. Wrote a lot of letters. Whole Coy. out 2 miles to mobile A.V.C. Fine day. Had fine time with T.O./22 MGC (tight). Still in Ervillers.

Army Correspondence Book, 152: To: O.C. 208 Cmp. 6.5.17

Number of P.H. helmets in T. section numbered under 50 is 22. I have 2 unserviceable also. HWWilliamson. T.O.

Army Correspondence Book, 152

208 M.G.Coy.

Transport Section   6.5.17

ROLL

Cpl. Nolan   L/Cpl in charge

A.	1 – Martin, Davy	2 – Norris, Fox	3 – Velters	–
B.	Douglas, Mobbs	Askew, Hughes	Allison	–
C.	Cooper, Bevan	Lyman, Young	(Cooper)	L/Cpl Stirling
D.	Walker, Wishart	Twells, Willis	(Fly)	
			(Askew)	
			Flynn	(L/Cpl Flynn)

H.Q.	Tracey	Grooms:	Ivy
W.C.	Bentley		Slate
M.C.	Parkinson		Franklin
Farrier:	Frith		Cooper
	Thomas (Course)		Finch

Stitcher: Hayes
Batman: Case

HWWilliamson TO
Lt. 208 MGCoy

Army Correspondence Book, 152: To: H.Q. 187th Bdge. ERVILLERS.
6.5.17
I am short of three drivers. Can these please be replaced as soon as possible, as there is no-one to look after their animals.

HWWilliamson. Lt. for O.C. 208 MGC.

Army Correspondence Book, 152:
Transport Programme. ERVILLERS. 6 May
6am Reveille. 6.15 Grooming. Stables. 7 Watering. 7.30 Feeding. 8.45 Parade – cleaning lines, grooming etc. 10.45 Break. 11 Watering. 11.30 Grooming. 12.30 feeding. 2pm Harness cleaning. 4pm Watering. 4.30 Feeding. 7.30 Hay.

From henceforward each driver is responsible for the cleanliness of his harness. Harness showing neglect, the driver will be to blame. The line orderly is responsible for the cleanliness of the lines during the day. 2nd Lt Stirling will inspect the animals twice a day in order to dress bites, kicks etc. The times of the above programme will be strictly adhered to. HWWilliamson. T.O. 208 MGC.

Diary: Monday 7 May: Mess Pres. 80 fcs. Bde out of line. French take 5800 prisoners. Raining at night. Tremlett DSO. McConnell MC. Me nothing. Case & Copper 5 – 10 fcs. Cash 125 fcs. 2 Gordons take Bullecourt.

[There follows a message from the Transport Sergeant to Williamson as Transport Officer.]

[From Transport Sergeant's Message Book.] 58. May 7 / 17
To: Transport Officer. 208 Machine Gun Coy.
Sir, Ref. my 54 under date May 1st. The C.Q.M.S. informs me that he is not yet in receipt of same. I append a copy also additional list of requisites.

From: Sgt. W. Mitchell

Copy of [Transport Sergeant's Message appended to above] No. 54 May 1st.
Nosebags g.s. 15. Haynets 30. Water buckets 20. Dragropes 10. Straps drag ropes 20. Clippers horse 1 pr. Ropes picketting 66ft. 1. Additional: Ropes picketting 66ft. 1. Drag ropes 12. Straps drag ropes 24. Oil wood preserving paint (service).

Diary: Tuesday 8 May: 'Grooms (for soap etc) 5 fcs. Raining all last night and till midday. Sgt. comes back. Intense fire at 9.35 pm. another attack (counter attack on Bullecourt).

Letter: 8 May 1917
Dear Father, Today it is raining like hell so I do nothing but sit in my tent, read, smoke, & write letters. We had some good news yesterday – Bullecourt has at last fallen, after four attempts. We know the reasons now why the Boche left his Ancre positions – they would have been child's play to take compared with his Hindenburg line.

I think you at home will just about be able to see what happens if you read our official reports – and the German reports. I have found the latter strictly accurate in all details. We of course dont mention our failures only our gains. Now at the Arras battle a month ago we had a brilliant victory – the Bosche said nothing or very little – we said a lot. On the 3rd – quite as big an operation – we say little & the Bosche says a lot. Both are true. Get me? The French appears to have done well lately.

People who read accounts of Beach Thomas, Phillip Gibbs etc, will get a hopelessly erroneous idea of affairs out here, according to them nothing withstands our artillery – they say we merely have to bombard a position, & it falls. Nothing is more misleading. If we dont get our objectives but all get killed instead – they say the "fighting here is most intense".

Well how are all you people getting on at home? Out here the monotony is the worst thing – am getting awfully fed up with the same old meals, the same old routine. Well goodbye. love to all. Harry.

Army Correspondence Book, 152: To: O.C. MGC. 9.5.17 ERVILLERS
Sir, I have to report that the forage delivered to this unit is insufficient. We have been drawing 7 80lb bags of oats and 3 bales of

hay. We have 54 mules and light draught horses and each animal is entitled to 12 lbs of oats and 12 lbs of hay per diem. (G.R.O. 1399 – Forage.) With the present issue of oats (560 lbs) only 10½ lbs approx is available to per animal. Regarding hay, G.R.O. 669 only 10 lbs per horse is drawn at railhead – this should make our total weight of hay 540 lbs. One bale of hay weighs about 120 lbs. Only 360 lbs approx. is being drawn by this section. Condition of the animals cannot improve rapidly under the present scale of forage.

HWWilliamson. Lt. T.O. 208 MGC

Diary: Wednesday 9 May: New Officer arrived. Hellish windup at midnight. Gas attack. Still at Ervillers. Bde at Ervillers.

Letter: 9 May

Dear Mother, Your letter with one from father got me today (8th) – but this will be posted in at the P.O. at 11 oclock on the 9th. I am sorry to hear about Uncle Harry & his bike – I hope everything was insured.

I am afraid Father doesn't quite understand me about the sale of my motorbike but you must look between the lines for the solution. For some reason the auction went awfully badly indeed, if I had known about the bad market I wouldn't have sold at all, anyhow I am utterly disappointed and have lost an awful amount of money (for me) and all for nothing. However I suppose the war is responsible for a lot of people losing their money. However I was too hasty, I should have studied the conditions better first. [That is all, of course, a further 'coded' message, presumably 'I' stands for those that planned the attack.]

You ask for war news – well I am afraid I cant give you much. Apparently the Bosche is awfully strong, and appears to know exactly when anything is going to happen – his intelligence corps is wonderful – even better than ours. I saw one or two mouldy prisoners, but nothing like the Arras stunt, when 17000 men were taken in four days by the 1st & 3rd armies.

Father says 'everybody is interested in my doing, & there are many enquiries, notably from a young lady at top house'. Who is the young lady pray? I know of no young lady, unless it is the one you mentioned next door to the Tetleys, if so, she is about 45 I think, & I dont really know her. You might let me know when you write next will you.

I will endeavour to send you a Bosche pack soon but dont give the N's [Nicholsons] one of those bombs. I had intended to send one but am not going to write any more − [sentence thoroughly crossed out] (that was silly). As for the New Zealand stunt its all off. I shant go with a man who is silly enough to get married − I will "hare" off with Maristany to Brazil − they will make me a G.S.O.1 in their army (GSO1 being General Staff Officer 1st Grade − usually a Col. on the DW staff −)

My address is 208 M.G. Coy − attached 187th Inf. Brigade, 62nd Division, but I think just 208 MGC will find me. I have hellish rows with my O.C. but we get along all right − he is rather a snotty fellow. Dont forget that vest pocket kodak will you.

By the way what I wanted doing with my tunic was − sleeves lengthened 2 inches − open collar, and let out down the back − it was too tight round the chest and too tight round the belly and ribs. Please ask the Stores to do it − I must have a decent tunic for leave − & will you get my boots field polished like a mirror, and also a 6d tablet of Properts (white) Paste for white buckskin strappings. I don't expect I shall be home before July 1 but I might be 'one never knows do you?'.

Once again I will tell you − your letters to me are never censored, mine are liable to be censored at Base, but not in most cases (unless you see "opened by Censor" on) they are not seen except by yourself. Well must close. Love HWW.

Army Correspondence Book, 152:
From: Lt. HW Williamson TO 208 MGCoy. ERVILLERS 9 May 1917. Confidential.

To: O.C. 208 MGC.
Sir, I have to report that this morning L/Cpl (act Cpl) J. Nolan came to me with a request that he might see the O.C. Coy. The reason he gave me was that he wished to revert to the rank of driver. I asked him why. He replied that Sgt Mitchell appeared to be very disatissfied with his work, and that as he (Nolan) was of junior rank he could not say anything. Cpl Nolan said that Sgt Mitchell had made the remark to him that things had been a 'complete box-up during his (the Sgt's) absence'. I spoke to Sgt Mitchell who said 'from what he could see, things had been going very badly. I reminded him that I was in command of the section, not him, and that the allegation reflected very badly on me. I then called Cpl

Nolan and he appeared very dissatisfied and still wished to revert. I told both the NCO's that I should refer the matter to the C.O.

During the sickness of Sgt M. Cpl Nolan has been of the greatest assistance to me. I gave him a programme of work, which he carried out in all details. He appears to have splendid control over the men, and I believe they follow his orders with the greatest willingness. If, through this trifling matter, Cpl Nolan is permitted to revert, the section will suffer, as all the men will know the reason, and it will have a very bad effect on the discipline of the men. I should be extremely sorry, personally, and as T.O., to loose Cpl Nolan. He is an old regular soldier, with three good conduct stripes. He has a marksmans certificate with the 3rd Gordons.

[The message ends here halfway down the page.]

Field Message Book: To: Transport Sergt 208 MGC. Ervillers. 9.5.17
Four limbers are required for the 187th T.M.B. next door at 10. One team each limbered wagon only – in future for fatigues only, two animals will be sent with each limber. If the limbers are loaded above the top of the limber they will be overloaded. Each driver will be responsible to me that on these fatigues the limbers are not overloaded. Cpl Nolan will be ready to proceed with me from the camp at 9.45 – my horse, my groom, and a horse for Cpl Nolan. The inspection is cancelled for us. Follow routine orders. HWWilliamson. Lt. TO.

Diary: Thursday 10 May: Parcel from home (WLW £10 per L.C.& W) and M. Bond. Raining in evening. Intelligence states Bosche in very bad way over raw material.

Army Correspondence Book, 152:
Orders for Transport, for 11 May. ERVILLERS. 10.5.17
[NB: written out as vertical list] Reveille 6am. Groom till 7. Water 7 oclock. 7.30 Feed. 9 – 11 Grooming, cleaning lines etc. 11 watering. 11.30 – 12.30 grooming. 12.30 feeding. 2 – 4 grazing under grooms. 4.30 Drivers on harness cleaning, feeding. Kit inspection at 7pm. HWWilliamson

Army Correspondence Book, 152: To: ERVILLERS. 11.5.17.
The following order will be read out to the rank and file of the T.S. In future parades for harness cleaning will only be ordered for

special parade inspections etc. After 14 May, each driver will be held directly responsible for the cleanliness of the harness, and the freedom from rust of the metal work. 'Cleanliness of harness' means freedom from accumulated dirt, and softness of leather due to careful and frequent oiling and dubbing. Only inclement weather will in future be regarded as an excuse for this not being carried out. Oil for cleaning work and dubbing for harness can be obtained on application to the T. Sgt. This order will be enforced strictly after 14th May. HWWilliamson. Lt. T.O. 208 MGC

Army Correspondence Book, 152: To: Sgt Mitchell. ERVILLERS. 11 May. Reveille from henceforth will be at 5.45 am. L/Cpl Joy should have in the Grooms Section the following as marked with a *. (articles in brackets are probably used up). (10 tins saddlesoap) 3 Turkey sponges.* (5 tins brown polish) (14 lbs silver sand) 5 Polishing cloths. (1 beeswax) 9 headropes white*. 5 double brushes*. 3 mane combs*. HWW.

Diary: Friday 11 May: Still fine. Bet Horsely 50 fcs about pear. Letters from Jerry, Stany, & Tetley.

Letter: 11 May
Dear Mater,
Thanks for vests recd yesterday. We are very busy, as we have many new drafts, and shortly shall kill a few more Bosches I expect. There is no leave. Love to all. HWW.

Dear Biddy,
Just a hasty line to you. Will you send a small parcel including sweets etc *and a pipe* (about 1/6) and about 100 woodbines etc to this man – 68348 Driver G. Bevan, 208 MGCoy, BEF France – with a note stating you have heard he is a lonely soldier, & would he care to accept etc etc etc. Dont mention your connection with me but sign your proper name and address. You might write him a letter, & mention that a parcel is coming. Make it a decent one up to 10/- or so & Father will give you the money from my a/c. No time now, love Harry.

Diary: Saturday 12 May: Colonial bombardment at 3.45. 91 Brigade over the top at Bullecourt. Letters from Stany, Elles, Penelope.

Field Message Book: To: Sgt. Mitchell. 12.5.17
N.C.O.'s in future, except when specially warned, or under special circumstance will not do piquet duty [i.e. on picket lines with the animals]. HWW.

Diary: Sunday 13 May: Raining. Still resting.

Diary: Monday 14 May: Taking rations to Bullecourt tonight. Shelled a bit and about 200 phosgene gas shells sent over. Found magpie's nest in bush near front line. Returned at 12 oclock. New offr.

Field Message Book: Ervillers. 14.5.17
Pte Parkinson is permitted to drive mess cart of 208 MGC (Ref. D.R.O. 5,6, – 14.5.17) HWWilliamson. Lt. T.O. 208 MGC.

Field Message Book: To: Transport Sergt. Ervillers. 14 May.
All horse transport vehicles on fatigue will carry in feed bags one feed and also hay to the capacity of the bag. The M.M.P. have strict instructions to report any driver without feeds and hay. Ref. D.R.O. 516 of 14th May. You will inspect all limbers and vehicles leaving the lines to see that this order is observed. HWWilliamson. Lt. T.O. 208 MGC.

Letter: 14 May
Dear Mother,
Thankyou for the little letter. Of course you always pile the agony on, dont you. Why am I a hero? I tell you frankly I would rather be here than at home – because out here I cant spend money, and also I have quite as good a time. I shant be going in any more attacks – as it is proved, thank God, that a T.O. is essential to send up supplies etc during one. All the T.O.'s out here chuckle to one another and say "haven't we absolutely got a soft job etc etc" On transport one sees & hears all the strafing but just comfortably out of the unhealthy zone. Of course one may die any second by hostile shelling, but even then, one has a sporting chance of seeing the war through.

With a tent to live in, a good bed, good food, and fine weather, the only thing that bores one is the monotony, but even then what is England nowadays? No friends, beer an awful price, no petrol, taxes – bah – give me France at least till October 1917 when the bad filthy weather starts. Well mother, I am glad Jerry went to Carr – the latter is awfully decent – I owed him money for a year & he never complained. [In about four or five letters held in his archive written to Jerry (Gerald) Simpson, HW urges him to get his uniform made at Carr's.] I have sent several people there too, and will get stuff there after the war.

By the way an officer was cashiered once for giving away his locality in a letter – so now you know why I rarely mention the war. Russia looks black, doesn't it. It would be awful with 2000000 more Bosche out here, with guns, wouldn't it? Do you know the present infantry strength on the Western Front (of the Bosche) I mean? I dont know but I should guess about just over a million. People talk rot about 6 million Germans in France, but youll find I'm right.

Well Mother, will you please give an order to a newsagent to send me, on Tuesday – the Motor Cycling and on every Thursday – the Motor Cycle. Now please, IS THIS CLEAR. You can pay him for a few months in advance, but dont forget I want each paper sent separately, it will only cost him or rather me 3d per week – *and please get it done*. I think this is about the fifth time I've requested you to send it – surely it isnt asking too much is it? And I should like the Kentish Mercury, regularly please. I asked about the MC etc whilst in England – I have missed 3 months issue by your not doing it.

Now please dont forget. You needn't worry about them – simply pay the money & leave them my address, & the things done. For heavens sake let this be the last request for these papers. Well I cant write any more now. Love to all. Harry.

Diary: Tuesday 15 May: Weather threatening. News of Bosche retiring to DROCOURT–QUEANT line. Very quiet all night.

Field Message Book: To: Sgt Mitchell. 15.5.17
The enemy is reported to be withdrawing to his DROCOURT-QUEANT line. If this is so, there is a possibility of the Coy. moving out at very short notice.
HWWilliamson. Lt. T.O. 208 MGC

[A further message from Sgt. Mitchell underlines the supply problems.]

Army Correspondence Book, 152: To: Transport Officer. 60. 208MGC
Sir, Will you please sanction undermentioned requisites for indent.

Sgt. W. Mitchell.

Whips drivers, 6. Head Chains, 6. Brushes dandy, 10. Brushes body, 10. Comb curry, 12. Rifle cover, 7. Baggage straps, 24. Rubbers, horse, 10. NB. The CQMSgt, in reply to my enquiry, states that he has not yet received from the Company orderly groom the list for indent submitted May 1st, No. 54, and also a copy of same under date of May 7th. No. 58. Sgt. W. Mitchell.

Letter: 15 May 1917 [written, unusually, in ink]
My dear Mother,
Thanks for the two bundles of papers etc arrived today. By the way, you never answered my query about how many boxes of souvenirs you got – I sent two tin boxes off, then a box of helmets, then a sandbag. You have acknowledged the three latter, but what about the first box? It would be best to begin always – 'I received yrs of -th yesterday – or today.' I keep a record of letters sent & then would know what you get and when.

Well Mother dear I am getting on quite well thankyou. We hear tonight of another German retreat – how true I cant tell but you will know by now I expect.

We are having tomorrow some sports in the Transport Section – mule jumping and bare back racing – but I expect this retreat will stop it. Well I'm going to bed now, so goodnight. Don't forget Kodak will you? Well goodnight. love Harry.

Diary: Wednesday 16 *May:* Weather changing for worse. Went to ASC [Army Service Corps] Mule races in afternoon. No Bosche retirement.

[The following programme for the mule races, printed in capital letters almost certainly by Sgt. Mitchell, on a loose sheet was placed in the *Army Correspondence Book.*]

PROGRAMME
1. MULE RACE (SADDLED)
2. MULE RACE (BARE BACK)
3. HORSE RACE (GROOMS)

4. JUMPING COMPETITION (CHARGERS)
5. INTER SUB SECTION WRESTLING ON MULES
6. V.C. RACE (DRIVERS & GROOMS)
7. JUMPING COMPETITION (MULES)
8. HARNESS STRIPPING COMPETITION
9. CIVILIAN RACE (MULES)
10. DRIVING COMPETITION (PAIRS)
11. DRIVING COMPETITION (TEAMS)
12. MULE RACE (PAIRS)

Field Message Book: 16.5.17
L/Cpl Harris (208 MGC 62nd Div) is permitted to ride on the mess cart. HWWilliamson. Lt. T.O. 208 MGC

Diary: Thursday 17 May: Took rations up to Embankment near Bullecourt at night. Hellish bloody time. Cash. 125 fcs.

Field Message Book: From: Lt. Williamson. To: O.C. 208 MGC. 17 May 17. Reference your chit. The limbers usually proceed to corner of cemetery on the road only 70 yds from the embankment. Except when I ride with the 1st. limber, the drivers come under the orders of Lt. McConnell, as soon as they report to him. Reference to the first part of your chit, it was my intention to go tonight at 7.30. HWWilliamson. Lt. 208 MGC.

Army Correspondence Book, 152:
To: Transport Officer. 208 Machine Gun company. May 17 / 17
Sir, in view of probable bad weather, have I to send the animals out to graze, or carry on with harness cleaning? Sgt. W. Mitchell.

Army Correspondence Book 152: To: O.C. 208MGC. ERVILLERS. 17 May.
The following articles are needed to replace articles inserviceable. [List as per Sgt. Mitchell's above, again highlighting supply problems.]

HWWilliamson. Lt. 208 MGC

Diary: Friday 18 May: Awfully tired and fed up all day. Many planes over. Rose 80 fcs [for Mess expenses]. Had letters from Mrs. N., Roy [Nicholson, her son], Stany, Fairy, Dorothy M. Felt much better.

Letter: 18 May

Dear Mother, Am awfully tired – have just got up after one of my frequent all night and early morning touches – and last night we ran into a barrage of tear and phosgene shells, and had to hare off to the right over shell pitted ground to get out of the way. Well my eyes are very painful and for the moment Im fed up. This letter wont be posted till 19th midday.

Well old crockery rat, in brief – I got the vests, the papers, the toffee with KM [*Kentish Mercury*] & Daily Mail, in fact all youve sent. Re the Kodak, dont of course put what the parcel contains – the act of taking photos is forbidden – that's all, but of course hundreds have them.

I saw a man today or rather last night come in from the front, he had been wounded on 3rd and been there ever since – without food & water – his right arm was shattered and stinking green!! Yet he was cheerful. I saw some of the famous P [Prussian] Guard prisoners today – got a watch!! Well cheero love from Harry. Haven't heard from N's yet. I have a complete short rifle for father, will bring home on leave. PS please send some envelopes.

[and in the same envelope]

Letter: 19 May

Dear Mother, Just a line to tell you I am quite well. I am dead beat, as I was up all night in a relief, shelled to hell with tear shells & crumps. Dont send envelopes – got heaps of them. Well this is my fourth month and not a sign of leave yet – oh my hat I am bored stiff – I love the life (except the strafes of course) but am pining all the time. Thank God I'm a transport officer & dont go up again to the awful slaughter they call our front line – with the Bosche grinning 1000 yds away in a position much stronger than Beaumont Hamel, with his concrete dugouts & machine guns, & his tearing 5.9 inchers.

They say our dead out there are being stripped by him, he wants the clothes for making paper!!! Still when we do finally get in those trenches – we will call it even!! love Bill.

PS. I wish Father wouldn't tell people I'm a hero – I'm not – & they will think I'm conceited or something.

Diary: *Saturday 19 May*: King [Capt. C.R. King, CO] goes up line. Feeling very tired. Bosche planes over camp. 600 ft up. Great artillery strafes at night.

Letter: [Not dated but it would have been 20 May 1917 – posted 22 May.]
Dear Mother, Am going down the line a bit for 5 weeks to do a Signalling Course – why I dont know – I am very fed up with losing my Transport job but don't worry – they wont get me in the infantry. I will return to the Coy – as T.O. I hope, but I don't know. You can address my letters to the 208 MG Coy as before, as I will arrange for them to be sent on. Well till 24 June I shall be well out of the fighting: I shall be at the vth Army Corps H.Q. Well will write when I have further news. I have just returned from special duty in London. [No further information about this is available – see below.] Well Cheero Yrs with love H.

Diary: *Sunday 20 May*: Divsn fire in morning. Rumours of big attack by 3rd Army. Proceeded to 6 wks course of R.E. signalling at BIHUCOURT. Hamilton acting T.O. Damn nice crowd here – evidently in for a tophole time.

Diary: *Monday 21 May*: Rather dull – artillery going ceaselessly. Rode up line to see CBR [Lt. C.B. Rose]. Snubbed again by the bounder. Hellish Bosche shelling. Determined to stop all this nonsense. Parcel from Carr.

Diary: *Tuesday 22 May*: Raining heavily. Went to A le G [Achiet le Grand] to cinema in evening. Fine show. Horse [Horseley, his fellow officer, not an animal] didn't turn up.

Letter: 22 May
Dear Mother, Just a short note to let you know I am O.K., and a staff job at last!!! And on Army Staff Corps too !!! I got it by luck – went to the W.O. [War Office – there is no detail or confirmation of this rather extraordinary event] the other day special duty, & came back to a course, & clicked at once.
My address is HWW – M.G.C. attd Vth Army. Corps HQ – Signal School – B.E.F. I'm here at least till July 1, when I shall probably get leave. The Bosche is miles away now and I am where I got

those crucifix I sent you, you will probably remember it. Well cheero, dont forget all news of people, Kentish Mercury *every* week & M. Cycle & M. Cycling. love H.

Diary:*Wednesday* 23 May: Cash fcs 100. Richardson (PMC) 25 fcs. Case 10 fcs. Fine day. Poor old Tremlett killed last night. Awarded the D.S.O. same morning. Letters from Stany, DW, FR, Jerry, Mother, Efford.

Diary:*Thursday* 24 May: Fine day. Wrote to Roy & cheque to Faulkners for spurs 11/-. Went with fellows to Picture Palace, Achiet le Grand. Good show, fans, lights, pukka seats etc.

Letter: 24 May.
Dear M. Quite well, miles from line. Herewith flowers from Achiet le Grand cemetery. Herewith your cutting. Much worse than that – thats nothing. Am 'mentioned'. Writing tomorrow. Parade at 6.30 am tomorrow, flag drill. Tired. 11.30pm now. Get me? Will write to Boon. This Coy has got: 1 VC (officer – posthumous) 1 DSO (officer – posthumous – killed tonight !!!) 1 MC, 3 DCMs (men) 2 MMs, 2 Offcs mentioned, 5 men ditto, out of 9 officers & 120 men! Record for a MGC Coy out here, all for work on 3rd May. Au revoir till 25th. Love Harry.

Diary: *Friday* 25 May: Good day. Wrote long letter to Mrs. N. Bosche shelling with 8in naval gun. Am going to be sent back from course tomorrow.

Letter: 25 May.
Dear Mater, Have been chucked out of the course as I know damn all about signalling – my address therefore as before. Dont be surprised if you see me home shortly as I might get leave any minute. Well love to everyone. Yrs with love. Harry. PS Did you get those violets?

Diary: *Saturday* 26 May: Sent back from Signalling Course. Good. Very rotten report however. Strafed by G.O.C.

Diary: *memo section*: Field allowance till 26 inst. Damaging report. Business of limber (no apology) – May 21 – Rpt. on Cpl Nolan. ?Horse

Diary: Sunday 27 May: fine day. Doing nothing in Ervillers. Shelled by 6 inch H.E. shrapnel & 13.5 naval gun.

Diary: Monday 28 May: Brigade commences shifting to Bihucourt. Applied for transfer to another Coy. Tremletts DSO official. Saw 206 Coy.

Diary: Tuesday 29 May: Capt. King went on leave. Coy. going out tonight. Am going to Ecoust with limbers on all night stunt. Rainy day.

Letter: 29 May
Dear Mother,
Am quite well. I was sent back from the Signal School as no bon. Tomorrow we are going out to rest. I am transferring by the way, to another Coy – at least I have applied for it – I could never agree with my C.O. and now he's back again I am going. However continue to address to MG Coy as before.

Why couldn't father get that thing? [the Kodak camera] Surely he didn't tell them what it was for, did he? Hundreds are being sent out, but in an ordinary way in an ordinary [probably 'parcel']. Well there is no news – I am fitter than I have ever been before, & hope you all are.

Well my love to everyone. Harry. The Motor Cycling is arriving thanks.

Letter: 29 May 6.30 pm
My Dear Mother,
Thanks for your letter and also the Royal. They came very quickly having been sent on the 24th – you must have had my letter quickly from the School. Yes I was in the place where I got those pansies from – only now we are out altogether at a village on its immediate right – that is about ½ mile from it only in a field.

Our O.C. goes on leave today: he is 2nd officer to go – I have applied for a transfer as T.O. to another Coy. as I cant get on. I might go to the 7th Division but I am not sure. I might get leave soon now. I shall only know the morning I go, and I catch the 3.30 train from Railhead, which is where I got the pansies.

Well it is 6.30 and at 9 I should leave here to go up the line with 3 limbers to get the guns out, & probably will return about 5 in the morning, very tired, at least not tired, as I am used to working for hours at a stretch without food – and its quite an ordinary thing to work all night on transport.

Well when I get leave the first intimation you will get will be a telegram from Folkestone – dont rush about with wind up thinking of an unshorn dirty soldier, as I should be in winter time, but remember I bath every morning and get my hair cut when necessary, have polished boots, & four meals a day, and in fact live exactly the same as at Grantham, with the exception that the food is much better cooked & better quality. Occasionally one gets fed up – but on transport there is just enough danger (e.g. tonight – a few crumps over, & gas shells, & an unlucky hit will finish us, mules & all, but really the risk is not one millionth that the infantry, poor devils, run!) Well give my love to everyone. Dont forget the K. Mercury. The others arrive regularly. Before I've done tonight I shall have ridden a matter of about 40 miles. Will post this on 30th if I am OK. Love Harry.

Diary: Wednesday 30 May: Raining a bit. Arrived Bihucourt 4 am. Went to concert in evening. Lost revolver.

Diary: Thursday 31 May: Kicked on head by Tommy [Tommy was a mule]; 2 drivers badly thrown. Very fine weather.

Field Message Book: To: Sgt Mitchell. 31.5.17
Please render to me tonight return of requirements. 1) Tunics, hats, breeches, puttees (unserviceable). 2) Underclothing, socks. 3) Small kit. 4) Harness, drag-ropes, straps, hay nets, spoke brushes etc + general transport requirements. Allowance must be made for a further ten days wear, as the articles will probably only arrive here after ten days. HWW

Field Message Book: From: T.O. 208 MGC. To: O.C. 208 MGC. 31.5.17
I recommend the following man to be L/Cpl. 67104 Dvr Fox. G. this man is one of my best drivers, he is smart, intelligent, and altogether an example of the best type of soldier. HWWilliamson. Lt. T.O. 208 MGC.
[Then in pencil – i.e. not a 'sent' message but a note to himself]
'heads – 3½ prs – kept till 9.30 with only 6 animals. Wagon lines ordered to be cleaned at 4pm, not done at 10pm. Asked why? Told

off 6 men road, 4 watch animals, 12 on lines – remainder cleaning
harness (9pm). At 10pm no-one cleaning harness. Asked why?'

Army Correspondence Book 152:
[Message from Sgt. Mitchell, his serial number] 68
To: T.O. 208 MGC. May 31/17
Sir, the following is a list of deficiencies in the section.
Spoke brushes 10, limber covers 5, spanners wheelers 2, whips
drivers 6, whips long reins 1, dandy brushes 6, water buckets 10,
hay nets 20, harness buckets 15, ropes picketing 66 ft 2, posts
picketing 5 ft 6. Personal kit: tunics 3, breeches 10, cap 1 (7½),
puttees 7, boots 2, capbadge 2, trousers 1, numerals 1 pr, Field
dressing 1, jack spurs 1, razor 4, p.h. helmet 4, table knife 3,
housewife 5, mess tins 5, tear shell goggles 8, washing soap 10
lbs, mess tin cover 3, clasp knife 2, comb 2, towel 4, fork 1, ration
bags 1, tooth brush 1, cap comforter 1, spoon 1. Spring Punch
saddlers – one. Needles saddlers – 1 packet.
[Not signed but in Sgt. Mitchell's handwriting.]

Army Correspondence Book, 152: To: O.C. 208 MGC. May 31.
The following is a list of requirements in the Transport Section.
[List as above.]   H. Williamson Lt. T.O. 208 MGC

Army Correspondence Book, 152:
From: T.O. 208 MGC To: O.C. 208 MGC 31 May
Two full limbered G.S. wagons have been detailed by Bgde T.O. to
report to Bgde HQ. I have had no notice of this, the order being
given to my T. Sgt. Is this an order? HWWilliamson Lt. T.O. 208
MGC

Diary: Friday 1 June: Heart to heart talk with Rose. Feeling very ill.

Letter: 1 June
Dear Biddy,
Thanks for your note. No, dont send any more parcels to Bevan.
He didn't write the letter – I was away when the letter was
written but I should imagine the Sergt composed the answer in
order to impress one I suppose what a genteel fellow he was . . .
Bevan wont write or read or do anything – he is quite a mule.
    Well write soon. I am leaving this Coy soon – we are having a

good time at present. I may get leave in a month or so, or if I go to this other Coy., in 3 or 4 month – I dont really care. Love H.

PS. was kicked on the head today & laid out, am therefore with a rotten headache [see diary entry 31 May].

Letter: 1 June
Dear Mater,
Please dont send any parcels to me as I dont expect to be with this Coy after a day or so as I have been very ill the last week or so, and expect shall have to go into hospital. Well mother I hope to God I am not going to have dysentery again, for I am not at all keen to leave France – but I shall be very glad to leave the Coy as I have had a rotten time since the new C.O. came. Well cheero dear – theres nothing to worry about. love Harry.

Diary: Saturday 2 June: Went in evening to concert at Achiet le Grand. shelled by 15 inch naval guns in morning. Very hot.

Diary: Sunday 3 June: Still hot. Bosche shelled Sapogny with 15in crumps. Wrote several letters. Bombed at night by planes. Feeling rotten.

Army Correspondence Book, 152: To: O.C. 208 MGC 3 June 1917.
Reference attached. We have no wheelwright. It is not clear whether the CHQ of this RE Coy is at point H8a58 [a map reference but figures are difficult to read] or whether their dump is there. HWWilliamson. Lt. 208 MGC

[HW was obviously asked to send a wheelwright to the RE Coy. He had no wheelwright and so sent a carpenter instead as the following message shows.]

Army Correspondence Book, 152: To: Sgt Mitchell. BIHUCOURT
Please detail 1 full limber to report to O.C. 461 Cmp at Sapignes tomorrow at 9.30. A carpenter from the Coy will accompany it. The driver to take attached authority, and bring same back. HWWilliamson. Lt. 208 MGC

Letter: 3 June

Dear Father,

How are you all getting on? I am not very fit – feel rather run down and weak – have had a touch of enteritis the last two or three days, and I might get a few days leave in England, as really I am fed up to the back teeth with the war.

A *tremendous* crash has just sounded outside & I rushed out of my tent and saw about 200 yds away a tremendous column of smoke and bricks – he has started shelling with 15 inch naval shells – hellish things that you cant hear coming as they travel faster than sound. I expect another will come in a moment – he is putting them over at eight minute intervals.

Well father after 4 months of continuous warfare on the Ancre and against the — line I am really fagged out. My work hasnt been extra dangerous – but we have been incessantly shelled – and working as I have all day and all night – the nervous strain is too much. you would be surprised how awful it is to go 6 miles up & 6 miles down the line every night – right up to the gun positions – shelled like hell all the way – stinking horses, broken limbers, gaping shell pitted roads – urgh, I am tired of it all – and really shant be sorry if I am sent into the hospital here – in which case I might go down to the base.

Well my love to you, Harry. PS. I have some souvenirs for you in my kit.

Diary: Monday 4 June: Lovely day. Rose at 12. Saw chit from G.H.Q. asking for report on my conduct.

Letter: 4 June

Dear Mother,

Thanks very much for your letter dated 29 May. All I can tell you about myself is that I am very unwell – having been in a considerable period up the line while the Bosche was sending over Phosgene gas – I got quite a lot of it – and my insides generally done in & done up – those long sweats up the line night after night, usually through hellish shelling and dead horses, and gas etc. have just about fed me up.

I expect I shall have to go to hospital if I cant pick up. Four months of this is enough for anyone, and any rate, I shall get out of this unit, with which I am absolutely fed. Well old girl, you will be pleased to hear I am feeding on eggs and lime juice — and half of that I usually spew up. Well have you sent the camera — if not dont send it. Dont send any parcels but books etc will get to me. Well cheero, I havent the energy to write more. I shall go, if I dont improve, to a convalescent camp where I got those pansies, & if lucky — thence to the base. love Harry.

Letter: 4 June
[Addressed to his father at the Bank, 13 Old Broad St.]
Dear Father,
Just a line to let you know I am quite all right, but rather sick with phosgene gas and dust and filth and stenches etc etc. If I am lucky enough to come home on a month or so's sick leave, I will bring you about 3 lbs of good baccy, my accumulated rations. love Harry.

Diary: Tuesday 5 June: Rather hot. Went to Achiet le Grand today to pictures with McClane.

Diary: Wednesday 6 June: Letters from Tetley, Stany, I. Large, Wright. Wrote back to Wright.

Diary: Thursday 7 June: Inspection by Col. Badham. Not bad turn out. Hellish bombardments from Flanders front. Messine etc captured by 2 Army.

Diary: Friday 8 June: Went sick this morning. Medicine & duty. Raining in evening. Letter from Stany. Cheques — Cooper £1.15 Case 10s. Gassed at B. [Bullecourt] Field cashier (100frs).

Diary: Saturday 9 June: Admitted to Field Ambulance Hospital. Very sorry to leave the section, but damn glad to leave Coy. Raining a bit in evening. Spewing all night & day.

Diary: Sunday 10 June: Dull day. Went to 44 CCS [Casualty Clearing Station] at Colincamps. On milk diet. Great thunderstorms in night.

Letter: 10 June
Dear Mother Sweet,
Am in hospital at the Pansy Place, and am getting better. I hope to be sent somewhere to the seaside for a fortnight to recuperate:

these last four months have been fair devils to me from every point , however, if I am to go down the line from here I am struck off the strength of the Coy. and shall be posted to another one, as Transport Officer, if I can possibly manage it. However I might get right away to Blighty if they start clearing the hospitals out for a push. Do you see theyre pushing up North where I used to be with the LRB? Love H.

Letter: 10 June
Envelope printed 'ON ACTIVE SERVICE' Passed by Field Censor 681.
    44 Casualty Clearing Station (C.C.S.)
My dear Mother,
As you can see by the above I have got out of the Field Ambulance and am now at Colincamps. I expect to go down to the base shortly, so perhaps it would be as well if you didn't write me at this address.

It is a nice place – in a big marquee of course but the patient is very feeble as I have that cursed milk (nestles tinned) only to live on.

The other officers, about 20, here seem remarkably well & fit – they lark about all day and eat like wolves – there are two other gas cases here besides me – one, poor devil, will die soon I expect. Well I am all right but a little feeble. Well goodnight ma, dont send any more parcels or papers as I shant get them. Well goodnight. Love H.

Diary: Monday 11 June: Much fitter. Am going to base by next train. Hurrah!

Diary: Tuesday 12 June: Several cases sent to Warloi today, Clearing Hospital. Shall I stop? Pains again.

Diary: Wednesday 13 June: Fine day. No sign yet of train. Most inspiring news in form of telegram from GHQ.

Letter: 14 June
Dear Mater,
    How are you? I am much better but sick, sick, sick, all the time even milk turns me up. This gas is awful thank god I only got a whiff of it.

Hurray I am going down to the base in a day or two – as soon as a train comes. I wrote to Auntie Maude and Cuthbert N. this morning. He has written me a lot. Will you get some arm protectors put in my best tunic in case I come home.

I've been out 18 weeks now. The war will be over this year: there are all the signs of an imminent collapse on the Bosche's part – look – he lost one of the strongest positions in this war at Messines Ridge and nothing can withstand our massed artillery. The Bosche is demoralised. Well cheero, no address at present. Love to all. Harry.

Diary: Friday 15 June: Arrd Rouen No. 8 Gen. at 7.30 am. For England by first boat ! Good spot.

Letter: 15 June.
Passed Field Censor 320. Rouen. [Marked by HW] 'Urgent and Private'
Dear Mother,
Please get those protectors for armpits in my new tunic at once – big ones under the lining – you probably know by this time that I am for England on the first boat which leaves any time – probably tomorrow morning Saturday – I will wire you as soon as I get to a hospital. Mother, I thank God I am out of that inferno. I was for a rest at Doulons as I was run down & the last night up at Bullecourt the Bosche put a hell of a lot of salvoes of crumps over – blew our ration wagon up and killed a driver and blew my tin hat off and destroyed my gas respirator. Then he suddenly changed to gas shell – we ran right into the barrage on the track you see, and I got a fair dose of phosgene – which has a deadly action on the heart and system – next morning I was down & out and the ambulance came for me. I expect I shall go into some hospital in London, then to a convalescent home, then 3 weeks leave, & then back again to the BEF – I dont want to see Grantham again ever. Well dont forget to keep silent about my homecoming I want it as a surprise. This hospital is a bon place – I live on champagne and fried plaice & chicken now !! Love Willie.

Diary: Saturday 16 June: Feverish. Boat in. Expect to go early tomorrow morning. Temp. 102 !!

Diary: Sunday 17 June: Am leaving today for hospital ship 'West Australian' 'Helpless' case. Temp. 101 !! Left Rouen at 4 pm. Left tunic behind. Awful hot in boat.

Diary: Monday 18 June: Arrived S'hampton 8 oclock am. Left for London 1pm and Sussex Lodge Hospital at 5 oclock. Bon spot — civvy doctor. Cash £3-3-1. Wired mother & Stany.

6

With the Bedfordshires

In response to Henry Williamson's telegram Eugene Maristany went to see his friend in hospital the very next day, where he promptly borrowed some money. Henry's diary records for Tuesday 19 June: 'Good hospital this. Lent Stany £1. Collars, shirts from Carrs. Fine day.' The following day he was up and went out with Stany, seeing 'M.S. – Nice girl but flighty' (there is no indication whom M.S. is) and was visited by his father and sister Kathleen, but not by his mother. However, the next day Henry left the hospital and returned home where he 'Saw all' including the Nicholsons ('except Mrs. & W.') and recorded 'Very nice reception. Roy [Nicholson] is a topping kid. Board tomorrow.'

At the Medical Board on 22 June he was considered unfit for General Service for three months, unfit for Home Service for two months, and unfit for Light Duties for one month. He returned home, noting that he lent 'Stany' a further £1 8s 6d but the next day had quarrelled with him and was already bored with the life at home: 'Brockley – fed up'.

A week later, on 29 June, he travelled down to Cornwall to an Auxiliary Hospital for Officers, Trefusis, at Falmouth, one of many houses turned into convalescent homes for sick and wounded soldiers.[1] The next two days were spent yachting and 'fooling around generally'. The contrast could hardly have been more extreme. On 7 June he was at the Front in the middle of a most fearful battle but within three weeks he was sailing in the gentle waters of Falmouth estuary. This was a harbour haven in every sense of the phrase. Photographs of Henry Williamson during this period of convalescence at Trefusis show him very relaxed, playing tennis, boating, and friendly with the nurses. In his novel series he transfers this period to the following year, 1918, where the details, allowing for his story line and some artistic licence, would appear to be as they were in real life.[2]

On 3 July Henry Williamson's diary contains a terse but all important entry: 'Began story'. There are no details to flesh this out, no reasons given for this most dramatic step, and no indication of progress. He was in a highly nervous state at this point, which is pinpointed in that diary entry for 1 June: 'Heart to heart with Rose. Feeling very ill.' The strain of the constant bombardment coupled with the difficulties he faced within the regimental company structure combined with his own psychological make-up meant his nerves were stretched practically to breaking point. In a note added into his 1917 *Army Correspondence Book*, 152 written in red ink, signed and dated '29 November 1957 while writing Novel No. 7' (*Love and the Loveless*) Henry wrote:

Note made by HW looking at this book, possibly for the first time since the entries were made in France in the Spring of 1917.

On 3 May 1917 an attack was made on the *Siegfried Stellung*, (Hindenburg Line) before which the Company had moved with the rest of the Fifth Army, with its sign of a Running Fox, following the German retreat from the Somme positions in February, March and April. The attack on 3 May was a failure, several officers in the Coy were killed (Montford and Tremlett DSO among them) and many infantry in the division. While the C.O. (Capt. C.R. Redmony King) was at his battle HQ, I was in charge of the Company details left with the Transport. Reading these orders of mine, I am surprised that I was so able or competent. But in March 1917 I had an 'adverse report for inefficiency' by Capt. King, and again in June 1917, when my name was not included amongst those officers fit for promotion. My section was well-run, the animals cared for despite the morass we were in (Feb–April) but the Sergeant was a conceited, rather pert man, who undermined my authority: but it is perhaps fair to say that I was perhaps too much a stickler for 'correctness', in the poor wintry conditions. He got away, 'sick' to the base. Captain King did not like me, nor I him. He was a very quiet man, with a mild manner, which concealed what he thought – until he suddenly acted, and we had all 'had it'. He also got rid of 2nd Lt Wright, a farmer and stout fellow, whose manner was a bit gauche, but Wright was a good officer. This was after a newspaper scandal, in which Wright's farmer brothers, in Wisbech, Cambridgeshire, tarred and feathered one of their wive's lovers, at night, and left him to die, for all they cared, in a field. I met 2/Lt. Wright again in Norfolk in 1937, and I must say, he was a grim, rather abrupt little man.[3] HWW. (writing novel no. 7) 29th Nov. 1957.

The adverse reports referred to in this note and in Henry Williamson's personal papers, as related in the previous chapter obviously did worry him greatly at the time. At the end of his 1917 diary there is written on the inside cover, very faintly and now only just readable, a note which Williamson presumably copied from this second adverse report. 'I do not consider this officer qual. to hold higher rank. Work of unsatisf. nature wh. with the Coy. shows lack of tact in handling men and I can't regard him as a reliable ofcr.' This report is noted in his diary as arriving on 8 July while he was at Trefusis.

My personal feeling, having read every item available in Henry's archive, is that, apart from his physical symptoms, he was suffering from some form of nervous breakdown at this point and that this is one of the reasons why his convalescence went on for so long. His diary records that his next Medical Board, was due at Caxton Hall on 22 July but on Saturday 21 he was instead 'Boarded at Falmouth M.H. [Military Hospital] Conv. leave 3 mos. Unfit G. S. [General Service] 3 mos.' A note attached to this report from William Banks, Doctor in Charge, Trefusis Auxiliary Hospital, dated 21 July 1917, states: 'Lt. Williamson has during the last ten days begun decidedly to improve. But in my opinion he will need much longer than the time he has already had under treatment before one can report him recovered.'

It may be that he turned to writing at this point as an outlet for his highly charged nervous state, as an 'occupational therapy' during those long summer days in Cornwall cut off from his friends and family. There were already several 'war' books on the market, including Henri Barbusse's Le Feu,[4] and he may well have thought that he could emulate these.

On 31 July he noted 'Battle of [Third] Ypres started in rain.' Field Marshal Haig had planned a major offensive for the second half of 1917. Officially the Third Battle of Ypres (Passchendaele) lasted from 21 July to 6 November 1917. Beginning with a massive bombardment which lasted ten days, the Vth Army under General Gough, attacked on 31 July. The Allied objective was to capture the whole of the Passchendaele–Broodseinde Ridge. Fearful fighting raged in what was virtually a bog of deep mud until the final action on 6 November when the Canadian troops attacked and gained Passchendaele. The Anzac (Australian and New Zealand) troops were involved in the first attacks while the Canadians finally took the ruins on 10 November.

At the point when Henry Williamson himself returned to England suffering from the effects of a gas attack, Phillip in the novel *Love and the Loveless* merely journeys to England for ten days' leave. He then returns to 286 Machine Gun Company (MGC) at the Front to find that the Division has been transferred to the Fifth Army (under the command of General Sir Hubert Gough) where he takes part in the attack on St Julien evenually culminating in the advance on Passchendaele in September and October. Williamson, therefore, is able to create the structure which allows him to describe this period, including the English mutiny at Etaples in early September 1917.[5]

Williamson's own diary entries for August 1917 are almost non-existent, merely noting that it rained at the beginning of the month and that he attended another Medical Board at Devonport Military Hospital on 29 August, but with no note as to the outcome. He had left Trefusis that day (in the governess cart, the photograph (see plate 28b) in his archive giving proof of the description in the *Chronicle*) for Devonport Military Hospital at Plymouth. September is almost equally bereft of entries with only a few brief notes which mostly refer to cashing money for his requirements. But it was at this time that he met the man known as 'Gibbo' (see plate 28c). He attended a Board at Devonport on 24 September where it was noted: 'He has greatly improved and is now fit for light duty.' The Board recommended three weeks' leave for he was still 50 per cent unfit.

On Monday 15 October, after three weeks' leave, Henry noted in his diary: 'Joined 3rd. Beds.' (and in the front of his 1918 diary wrote that he was in 'A' company). This is corroborated in the official records: 'Lieut. H.W. Williamson joined 3rd. Bn. Bedford Regiment on 15.10.17 Signed for Major General, Commanding Harwich Garrison, Felixstowe, 18 October 1917.' The Third (Special Reserve) Battalion of the Bedfordshire Regiment was stationed at Landguard Fort just outside Felixstowe in Suffolk. This Battalion was mobilized in 1914 and served in defence of the East Coast of England throughout the war.[6] Williamson gives no details of his life at this point and diary entries are mainly limited to money transactions and notes on letters received and sent. There are no references whatsoever to 'Lily' Milgate or the Zeppelin raid that killed her. On Monday 19 November he recorded: 'Board due' (the report of this stated, 'the bowel symptoms have disappeared but he is weak and debilitated' – he was still considered unfit for General Service). On Wednesday 28th Henry wrote: 'Snowing', on Thursday 29th, 'Bourlon Wood attack failed', and the next day, Friday 30th, 'Bosche counter attack. Transport lost.' These references are to the Battle of Cambrai.

This battle,[7] the first great tank battle, commenced on 20 November 1917 when 381 tanks went forward in massed formation in what was virtually a surprise attack. Initially this gained a great victory, but which, yet again, the Third Army was unable to take advantage of, having to fall back to a defensive position, enabling a crippling counter-offensive by the German Army on 30 November. On 4 December Field Marshal Haig ordered withdrawal: all territorial gain was lost and British casualties totalled 43,000.

Perusal of Henry Williamson's markings in his copy of the Cambrai volume of the *Official History*[8] shows how he built up the background for *Love and the Loveless*. Noticeable is the 'Third Army Plan for the Battle of Cambrai' where it states: 'The object of the operation is to break the enemy's defensive system by a *coup de main* . . . to seize Cambrai, Bourlon Wood, [etc] . . . The essence of the operation is surprise. Prior to attack firing must not be over the normal daily average of past three months: camouflage of movements, preparation of battery boards and calibration of guns of utmost importance.'[9] A smaller detail can be found on page 15 of the *History* where Williamson has marked information about the huge fascines made by a Chinese labour company with a marginal note: 'Capt. Cox': '. . . enormous bundles of brushwood; each containing 75 faggots, 10 feet long, [bound by] chains'. A footnote on this page adds: '400 tons of brushwood were used and the whole of England had to be searched to provide the 12000 feet of chain. Each fascine weighed 1¾ tons . . .'[10]

The arrangements for movements of troops and equipment into position are also underlined by Henry, particularly the section headed 'The Advance Towards Bourlon'[11] which details the arrangements of 186 Brigade (of 62 Division, 2 West Riding, commanded by Major General W.P. Braithwaite). The commanding officer of 186 Brigade was Brigadier General Roland Boyes Bradford – known as 'The Boy General' – who took over the brigade on 10 November 1917 and at twenty-five years of age was the youngest Brigadier General in the British Army.[12] Williamson's narrative in the novel follows the real battle plan, procedure and outcome exactly.

The orders for 62 Division were contained in '62nd Division Order No. 78: 16 November 1917', signed by Lieutenant Colonel C.R. Newman, General Staff and can be found in Appendix 11 of the 'Cambrai' volume of the *Official History*.[13] These state that on zero day (20 November) IV Corps was to attack the German Trenches between the Canal du Nord and the Trescaut/Ribecourt road; 62 Division on the left nearer the Canal du Nord and 51 Division on their right. The essence of the attack was to be secrecy and speed. Within 62 Division, 185 and 187 Brigade were to attack through the 'Blue line' to the 'Brown line' (these were objective lines of demarcation plotted on the map) with the 186 at first in reserve but to push through after capture of the 'Brown line' and drive the enemy back to the village of Graincourt and the final objective of the 'Red line'.

On Y/Z night 186 Brigade was to move into Havrincourt Wood and proceed as per orders to Graincourt. Sixty tanks of 6 Battalion Tank Corps were allotted to 62 Division, of which thirty supported 185 Brigade and thirty, 187 Brigade. Machine guns were to mount a barrage at Zero Hour and when this task was over they were to revert to the control of their Division. So it was that 213 MGC thus reverted to 186 Brigade with rendezvous at zero plus two hours east of Havrincourt, to support their advance. The main aim of IV Corps, to push forward advanced guards of all arms to capture Bourlon Wood on Z day, was considered of great importance.[14]

The progress of the battle as found in *Love and the Loveless* follows the exact progress of the real battle as found in the *Official History* in the section 'The Advance Towards Bourlon'.[15] On 20 November 186 Brigade 'with the approval of Major General Braithwaite and at the express wish of its commander who appreciated the value of time, moved off from its assembly position in Havrincourt Wood at 9 a.m.'[16] Brigadier General Bradford continued forward taking Graincourt and beyond. The next day far in advance of any other forward movement and although ordered not to advance further, he 'saw no reason why it should deflect him from the attack of his immediate objectives'.[17] This is followed immediately in both the *Official History* and Williamson's novel by the episode of the 2/4th Duke of Wellington's cavalry capturing a totally unprepared column of 200 German infantry who marched up the road from behind them. The platoon of the Duke of Wellington's let them pass and then attacked from the rear.

'The Boy General' with 186 Brigade was allotted twenty tanks, the 11th Hussars (from 1st Cavalry Brigade) and two squadrons of King Edward's Horse. Its objective included Anneux and surrounds and if successful on to Bourlon. Machine-gun barrages were to be laid on

Anneux but the Official History notes that 62 Division had much trouble in getting its field artillery forward; 'only one road was available and that, in places was axle-deep in mud'. In the novel Williamson records this information as an entry in Phillip's diary[18] and subsequently uses this fictional diary to give a précis of the progress of the battle as it is laid out in the Official History.

He writes about the visit of Field Marshal Haig thus: 'the Commander-in-Chief, accompanied by Major General R.H.K. Bulter, Deputy CGS and Major General R.L. Mullens . . . had ridden up to the ridge near Flesquières to view the battle-front.'[19] Then 'Relief of 62 Division by the 40th (119, 120, 121, Brigades) who went on to Bourlon Wood whilst the 62nd were put onto forward road work.' On 25 November the relief was reversed and 62 Division were in position before midnight 'although hostile shelling inflicted some casualties upon the 186th Brigade'.[20] The security of Bourlon wood and the ridge was still the imperative objective as it overlooked Cambrai.

In Britain on 23 November the church bells rang to celebrate what was being seen at home as a great victory. The rejoicing was premature.

On the night of 28/29 November, 62 Division was relieved by 47 Division commanded by Major General Sir G.F. Gorringe : 'a harassing and somewhat costly operation conducted in a bombardment of gas shell'.[21] In Love and the Loveless Williamson structures his narrative by delaying the relief of 62 Division for twenty-four hours and then has Phillip direct his men, instead of south-west to Demicourt, via a mistaken route going south-east to Le Quennet farm and then west to Gouzancourt, thus running into the German attack on Gonnelieu and Gouzancourt on the night of 29/30 November. Williamson has marked several sentences in the section on Gouzancourt in the Official History[22] including the stand made by Brigadier General Vincent ('Vincent's Force') in Gauche Wood[23] and the attack on the Germans in Gouzancourt Wood by the 1st Guards Brigade who, after a successful attack, were able to utilize the contents of a supply train which fed them for forty-eight hours.[24]

At this point in his fictional story-line Williamson returns '286' to Ribecourt where they learn that their commanding officer 'The Boy General' has been killed. Brigadier General Bradford was indeed killed at the Battle of Cambrai on the night of 30 November 1917 by a shell not far from his headquarters.[25] He is buried in the British Cemetery at Hermes. The departure of 62 Division into the rest area had been cancelled because of the downturn in the battle, and they were being held in reserve while 186 Brigade was ordered to move to Lock 7 of the Canal du Nord to support 2 Division.[26]

One further detail from the novel commands interest here. The *Official History* confirms that General Byng, Commander Third Army, did feel that machine gunners were an undisciplined section 'trained as specialists, not as soldiers', and ordered that special attention to discipline and *esprit de corps* should be built into future training. Although Byng blamed the men, it is shown that it was his own lack of understanding of the situation and conditions that was the main problem.[27]

Thus Williamson utilizes the real events and manipulates them to fit into the structure which he wanted within the sequence of events in the narrative of his novel: bringing in as much detail of the final and important but devastating Battle of Cambrai as was possible. Once he has achieved this, Williamson has Phillip contract a fever and sent home to England to join the Bedfordshires at Felixstowe in the final chapter of *Love and the Loveless*, thus linking the fictional story with his own life : 'Posted to C company, to share a billet in No. 9 Manor Terrace with a subaltern named Allen.'[28]

Williamson's entries in his diary for December 1917 are very sparse. A short note encompassing expenditure scribbled on 8 December states: 'Uniform £42.10, Linen £3.4, Watch etc, £13.10, Camp equip. £11.7.' While on the following page is written in slightly wild handwriting:

> Rsbd Rsbd in my lady's hair
> Tell me Did she think of me when she placed you there
> Does she know I gathered you
> Kiss yr petals
> Wet with dew
> Ah' I wonder if she knew
> Tell me would she care.
> Rsbd Rsbd now you have the power
> Just to tell my love to her
> Every passing hour
> Night and day my secret grows
> Light the real heart of a rose
> Ah I wonder if she knows
> Tell her little flower.

There is very little primary source material to show what Henry Williamson did while at Landguard. But as he puts Phillip there in the *Chronicle* novels in prosaic conditions, there is no reason not to presume that what Phillip was doing Henry did in reality. Thus we can assume Phillip's letter to his mother telling her that he was working in the Orderly Room as assistant adjutant described the situation in real life. It is quite plausible that an officer of his rank and seniority would have been engaged in such a way. The only difference being that this would have begun in the middle of October 1917:

Manor Terrace was a brick and slated row of workmen's cottages built on the edge of the shingle bank near the mouth of the river Orwell. Landguard Camp extended south almost to the estuary, where from the slips and hangars of the Royal Naval Air Service arose the great flying boats which patrolled that area of the North Sea under Harwich Command. To the hutments of the 3rd (Special Reserve) Battalion the Gaultshire Regiment at Landguard came all those men and officers, after convalescence from wounds and sickness, from the various fronts in France and Flanders, Italy, Salonika, and Mesopotamia. Phillip had acquaintance with most of them, since, being assistant adjutant, it was his job to receive each new arrival.

A Test to Destruction, Chapter 1, 'The Staff of Life'

Henry Williamson seems to have settled down at Landguard Fort. He was safe and, as the sentence following the above quotation states, 'a regulated life had given regulated thoughts'. In his archive is a small red bound book with the Bedfordshire Regimental Crest on the cover containing the *Rules of the Officers' Mess 3rd. Bn. Bedfordshire Regt.* signed by Captain R.B. Knight (presumably Mess President at that time) and 'approved' by Lieutenant Colonel Lord Ampthill, Commanding 3rd Bedfordshire Regiment Landguard 21 August, 1916. Its contents emphasize the punctiliousness and civility of an army officer's life, laid out in a series of precise sentences covering the whole code of behaviour, giving a unique flavour of that era.

Breakfast is served from 7.45 to 9 am (9.30 am on Sundays); Luncheon, 1 pm to 2 pm; Tea 4 pm to 5 pm; Dinner 8pm. All officers present in the Mess will stand up when a visitor enters, when the Commanding Officer enters, and when a Field Officer enters (but need not stand up more than once to the same officer). . . . It is always customary to say 'Good Morning' to

Senior Officers in the morning and 'Good Evening' when entering the Mess for dinner. . . . Punctuality at Dinner is a matter of courtesy to the other officers and is invariably expected. . . . No officer will leave dinner until the wine has been round [I would presume this to mean the port wine]. . . . Under no circumstances is bad language to be used in the Mess. . . . Officers who are dining out will write their names on the warning out slate by 5 pm daily. Officers failing to do so will be fined 1/6d . . . .[on guest nights the deadline was 2 pm and the fine 2/6d]. . . . The Mess will be closed at 11 pm. Officers remaining in the Mess after that hour will be fined 6d for each hour after 11 pm. . . . All officers are forbidden to stand drinks. . . . No member of the Mess staff is to be reprimanded by anybody except the Mess President. . . . Any complaint must be entered in the Book set aside for this purpose. This will be found on one of the tables in the ante-room. . . . Early morning tea can be brought to officers' quarters by officers' servants. . . . Mess bills must be paid by the 7th of every month. . . . All breakages will be charged individually, but wilful breakages at six times the value of the article. . . . Cigarette and Cigar ends are not to be thrown on the floors of the Mess but placed in receptacles provided for that purpose. The same applies to matches. . . . Cards – The Points played for are not to exceed: Bridge, 1/- a hundred. . . . Members should not shout for waiters but ring the bells provided.

Most importantly for his psyche Williamson liked his Commanding Officer, Lord Ampthill (Lord Satchville in the novel) and according to *A Test to Destruction*, the eighth volume of Henry Williamson's *A Chronicle of Ancient Sunlight*, his fears about his adverse report lessened when he realised that others far more senior to himself had also been *stellenbosched*, including the lieutenant colonel who had commanded the 2nd Battalion and Lieutenant General Sir Launcelot Kiggell, Haig's own Chief of General Staff.[29]

So the year turned, 1917 ended and 1918, which was to be the last year of the war, began. *A Test to Destruction*[30] steps outside his immediate narrative and opens with a powerful overview of the situation.

In the winter of 1917–18 the Great War for Civilization . . . still engaged. . . .

This battlefield, upon which there had been continuous fighting for three and a half years, could be seen at night from aircraft as a great livid wound stretching from the North Sea, or German Ocean, to the Alps: a wound never ceasing to weep from wan dusk to gangrenous dawn, from sunrise to sunset of Europe in division....

... all combatants ... were coming to the end of their endurance upon both the Home Front, and the Western Front — that deadly area where millions of husbands and sons had fallen, in the coastal sandhills besides the Channel: in the brown, the treeless, the grave-set plain of Flanders; among the slag-heaps and derelict pithead-gear of Artois; upon the chalk uplands of Picardy and Champagne; in the forests of Argonne and Alsace extending in the neutral country of Switzerland — where below mountain peaks, under the snow, wild flowers lay resting as still within their corms and bulbs as the human dead upon the battlefield.

As the great battles of the Spring of 1918 broke upon France and Flanders, so the flowers of the upland valleys arose with blooms as fugacious as human hopes for the outcome of the war, which, it was said everywhere, would decide the fate of the world.

A Test to Destruction, Chapter 1, 'The Staff of Life'

Henry's diary for the opening months of 1918 contains only the briefest of entries which mainly concern his money transactions and barest details of appointments, but he did note that he was off sick with 'flu from 7 January for about a week. He also frequently recorded receiving letters from Terence Tetley and sending him money (this amounted to several sums over the duration of the war).[31] An important entry appeared on 18 January when he noted: 'Between Verdun and Laon about March 1' showing he had access to information about the forthcoming German Spring Offensive. He probably learnt this through his secretarial duties as Assistant Adjutant, as indeed Phillip does in the novel.[32] On 23 January, Henry's monthly Medical Board passed him for home service only and on 28 January he noted 'Air Raid. Began Musk. Course'.

There are two Army booklets in his archive which he has signed and dated 'Bedfordshire Regt. 1918'. One is entitled Extracts from General Routine Orders issued to the British Armies in France by Field Marshal Sir Douglas Haig, GCB, GCVO, KCIE. 'Part I: Adjutant-General's Branch' issued by General Headquarters, 1 January 1917' which contains 124 pages concerning the minutiae of army life, with rules covering such subjects as what to do when dealing with the effects of sick, wounded or dead soldiers, Censorship orders, Courts-Martial, duties of the Regimental Paymaster and Field Cashiers (who dealt with 'Money in the Field for Private Purposes'), Censorship and Trench Magazines and so on. It quite bizarrely opens with what troops were to do if in the presence of a low-flying aircraft: 'An aircraft requires an open and clear landing place and alights in the direct line in which it is travelling.' And continues with equal obviousness to state that troops in the vicinity will halt (but not in the direct line of flight), will not scatter in the direct line of flight and if necessary will lie down to avoid being struck by the propeller!

The other is a small four-page pamphlet entitled *Précis of Lessons learnt from the Experiences of a Division in the Cambrai Operations 30 November to 6 December 1917*, which consists of extracts from the report of 2 Division as an 'excellent example of how a successful defensive battle should be conducted.' 2 Division was positioned between Bourlon Wood and Moeuvres from 26 November 1917. 'The subsequent story is one so brimful of heroism that it deserves to take its place in English History and to be a proud day in the lives of all those splendid British soldiers who, by their single-hearted devotion to duty, saved what would have been undoubtedly a catastrophe had they given way.'

This booklet may well have been handed out at the musketry course Henry attended, as emphasis is laid on 'the effective use of the rifle, the Lewis and Machine guns, and Stokes' Mortars'. . . . Great care had been taken during training periods to encourage musketry and train infantrymen and Lewis gunners in the art of using rapid fire. . . . The men had marked confidence in their rifles and hundreds of men actually killed Germans, and in future, it will not be difficult to encourage musketry. . . . Great stress had been laid during the training on the constant practice of rapid fire. This was well repaid. . . .'

Despite the fact that he was attending the musketry course, a few days later on Friday 1 February, Henry Williamson went on leave. On the Saturday night he 'went to a dance at St Cyp's Hall and saw DN [Doris Nicholson] home. Slight advance but said nothing.' (The church of St Cyprian was located near his home in Eastern Road, between Adelaide Road and Ivy Road. The church was destroyed in the Second World War.) Henry saw DN again the following morning on the Hill, on the Monday met her at lunchtime and on Tuesday 5 February recorded: 'Drunken episode with DN and Hippo. Oath not to return to Brockley. Evening with EFM [Eugene Maristany], no sleep.' His leave ended the next day and he returned to Felixstowe. The following day he 'Paid Mess bill – £11.19.5' (thus obeying the Bedfordshire Regiment's rule that mess bills had to be paid on the 7th of each month). The next

Monday he 'sent off 2 tales to DN (anon)' showing that he had spent a productive weekend practising his writing skills. The musketry course ended on 13 February when Williamson also recorded that he 'sent EFM £7'. There was another few days' leave during 22–7 February; again he saw EFM, lending him yet more money, and also 'saw DN midday, incident of damson tart'. (How teasing not to know more of this incident!)

On 27 February he attended yet another Medical Board where it was stated that, 'There have been no symptoms of dysentery since his last Board' but he was still 'debilitated and under 20 per cent fit', and was given a further two months' Home Service but two days later, on Friday 1 March, he recorded: 'Bosche drive will begin within 14 days, between Verdun & Laon. Switched name from H.S. list to Overseas.' This provides evidence that the incident in the opening chapter of *A Test to Destruction*, where Phillip burns his most recent medical sheet classing him as B2 and instead types his name on the 'A' list, has some basis.[33] This was an extraordinary, not to say heroic, action for someone who was mortally afraid of the battle front line.

However, in real life Henry Williamson did not embark for the Front as early as does Phillip in the novel. In the fictionalized version he wanted to record the whole of that momentous battle for posterity. In fact Henry noted in his diary on 21 March: 'Bosche drive begun between Scarpe and Oise'; and on 22 March: 'English front broken at St Quentin. Retire to Peronne, Ham, Bapaume line.' He was granted leave during 22–6 March and noted seeing Terence Tetley and Eugene Maristany, who paid back £3. The entry for 26 March is too faint to read properly but it seems to be about the Canadian involvement. Then on 27 March: 'Return Felixstowe 5 a.m. Left for Victoria 9.30 a.m. Crossed to Boulogne 11.30 p.m. to IBD at Etaples. Up the line tomorrow, to 8th Battn.'[34] Unfortunately, the following pages in his diary are missing and there are no letters or papers of any sort for this period.[35] However, his novel *A Test to Destruction* covers the action in great detail so it is possible to piece together from that what was happening.

This action was part of the massive German Spring Offensive of 1918. The Russian removal from involvement in the war in the late autumn of 1917 and, after a long peace conference, the subsequent signing of a peace treaty between the Central Powers and the Ukraine on 9 February 1918 and finally with Russia itself on 3 March, released that (large) part of the German Army engaged on the Eastern Front and allowed them to realign on the Western Front during the winter months. The Allies were now facing a huge force. The Americans were not yet involved in great enough numbers for it to be of significance and it was obvious that the Germans, under the command of Major General Erich Ludendorff, needed and intended to strike before that came about. It is known that Ludendorff's main objective was to destroy the British Army, at this point greatly depleted by the battles of the previous autumn but still the biggest bane of the German Army.

Haig needed massive reinforcements to counteract the growing numbers of German troops being amassed for attack. These had not been forthcoming. The government while paying lip service to the need did nothing to resolve it. This is clear from many contemporaneous sources including the *Official History* itself. The history of the Bedfordshire Regiment also states that Haig was not given reinforcements and that the heavy losses of the Third battle of Ypres could not be made good. The only course left was the reorganization of troops, hence the consolidation of battalions that took place during the early months of the year in all regiments.

The time and place of the German attack was well forecasted. (This can be seen from Henry Williamson's own knowledge at his base in the home service on the east coast.) The Germans began a series of preliminary bombardments on about 9 March. The British Front was lined up thus: General Byng commanding the Third Army in the northern sector and General Gough the Fifth Army (which had been transferred from the Ypres area during the winter) on the southern two-thirds. The main offensive began just before 5 a.m. on 21 March with a massive bombardment along the whole front from the River Oise on the southern end to the River Scarpe (running through Arras) on the north. This bombardment of heavy guns, mortars and gas shells lasted for five hours.

Between 21 and 24 March the German advance moved inexorably forward with heavy British losses as they fought and retreated before the onslaught. By the time Henry Williamson crossed the Channel on 27 March to join the 2nd Battalion of the Bedfordshire Regiment the first fierce phase of the offensive was over. In the earlier reorganization the 2nd Battalion had been transferred from 89 Brigade to 90 Brigade but still remained in 30 Division. Lieutenant Colonel H.S. Poyntz was in temporary command of 90 Brigade, his previous job as C.O. of 2 Battalion being taken by Major R.O. Wynne, DSO.[36]

On 21 March, 30 Division, and thus 2 Battalion Bedfordshire Regiment, was in the battle zone in the St Quentin sector near Savy, generally known as Picardy.[37] Dawn was accompanied by thick fog. The German attack worked its way steadily forward through the battle zone and on 23 March this attack was greatly intensified. C Company's trenches were captured but A and B Companies held on doggedly until they were surrounded. Only a small remnant escaped. That afternoon the brigades on the flanks were driven back and 90 Brigade was ordered to retire to Ham, and later went into reserve across the Somme. The 2nd Battalion then took up position east of Verlaines to cover the withdrawal of 89 Brigade from Ham. On 24 March further withdrawal was ordered to behind the Canal du Nord and the battalion was given the task of defending the bridge at Buvenchy. By then 30 Division was reduced to two weak brigades, and the 2nd Battalion itself to 7 officers and 134 other ranks. The enemy was checked but a further heavy attack forced 2 Battalion into retirement to Solents. On 26 March it was in position at Bouchoir and again attacked heavily. On 27 March a last stand was made on the Arvillers–Folie road where the following day they were relieved by French troops. Between 21 and 28 March the Regiment lost 15 officers and 554 other ranks.[38]

Williamson would seem to have transposed at least the idea, and possibly some of the details, of the action of the 4th Battalion of the Bedfordshire Regiment which was with 63 Division in a sector to the east of Cambrai into his novel *A Test to Destruction*. In the *Regimental History*[39] he has marked sentences concerning their Commanding officer Lieutenant Colonel J.S. Collings-Wells, DSO, who formed a small party of men to cover the withdrawal of the battalion from an exposed position it had gallantly defended. On 27 March, 4 Battalion was ordered to Bouzincourt to counter-attack the German capture of Albert. Collings-Wells, knowing his men were exhausted, led the attack himself, even after being wounded, until he fell dead. He was awarded a posthumous VC for this.

The volume of the *Official History* for the opening phase of the battle is not in Williamson's archive (although he could have consulted it elsewhere). The second volume for 1918, which is there, opens on 27 March, the day Henry himself went out to France.[40] At this point 2nd Battalion the Bedfordshire Regiment, as part of 30 Division, was moved out to rest 'and thence it went up to Ypres to take over a sector on the Passchendaele Ridge'[41] as indeed does the fictional 2nd Battalion of the Gaultshires who on 1 April [from their camp at Bresle] 'marched over the hill to Baizieux and down again to Warloi, through country untouched by war . . . up the long rising road to Varenne coming in late afternoon to the railway sidings at Ascheux [about 10 km north-west of Albert].' This route can be traced on a large scale map of the area. The subsequent train journey to the north with its circuitous route and continual interruptions took the best part of two days.[42]

On arrival in the Ypres arena 30 Division joined the 2nd Army. The *Official History* notes that 'This Army received some of the most battered divisions, . . . [includes the 30th].' 'The 2nd Division of the Second Army contained only the very exhausted 30th and 36th Divisions.'[43] They had been sent to reinforce the British line against the German offensive in Flanders called the Lys Offensive (after the River Lys) which was the area of the ST GEORGE attacks.[44]

The passages referring to this battle are marked in the *Official History*,[45] but very lightly, merely noting the outline of the exact time of movements of troops and action taken. There are a great many more markings concerning the official battle strategies on the part of Haig and Foch especially in the 'Reflections' chapter at the end of the volume.[46] Thus when one compares the sparsity of the marked references for the Battle of Messines with the amount of detail in the battle scene in *A Test to Destruction* one assumes that he had no need to look these details up because he knew them, despite the lack of official corroboration and the fact that 30 Division itself was positioned further north at Poelcapelle. Williamson does state in the novel that a group of men were 'lent pro tem to the Scottish Division, to help hold the high ground from the Menin road to Wytschaete. As you know, the ridge extends to Messines . . .'. But the German Army was still in the ascendant and Hill 63 was taken on 11 April.[47]

Another marked passage concerns the '21st Composite Brigade' formed due to the weakness of 30 Division. The 21st Brigade went into the line astride the Ypres–Commines Canal of the Bluff on 9 April, and the '1st. Composite Battalion' under the command of Lieutenant Colonel R.O. Wynne held the line from the Bluff to the Caterpillar. Phillip commands a composite battalion at this point in the novel.

Henry Williamson's own diary entries begin again on Thursday 18 April: 'Left Hall-Walkers Hospital in Regent's Park.[48] Board at Caxton Hall, in week's time.' He then had a few days' leave, noting on Sunday 21 April that he 'saw Tetley from Havre. Went to see Lilac

Domino & S.D. Allen went overseas'. He returned to his unit at Felixstowe the following Wednesday and on Friday 26 April attended his routine Medical Board (i.e. instead of the one at Caxton Hall) for which the official report states that 'he has been doing ordinary duty since his last Board' and also that 'he has now no symptoms of dysentery'. However, he was still recorded as 'under 20 per cent disabled'. His diary for Tuesday 30 April recorded: 'Heard Westy killed. Tremendous fighting in France. Wish I were there.'[49]

Henry's diary entries for the early part of May are terse and mainly concern a quarrel between himself and Terence Tetley: 2 May: 'Rec'd letter from THT re finality of friendship'; 7 May: 'Wrote letter to THT of explanation'; 9 May: 'Letter from THT enclosing my letter − seal broken & obviously steamed'; 12 May: 'Saw THT' but no details are given. On 14 May he played tennis with Doris Nicholson and they listened to the gramophone afterwards. The next day he returned 'Felixstowe 3 p.m. Fed up. Posted to 'C' company. Know no-one.' The following Monday, 20 May, he recorded: 'Asked for medical board. Want to be in France. No life in England.' At a Medical Board on 27 May it was recorded 'that he appears to have recovered from his dysentery. His general health seems good − he shows no sign of any disease.' He was at last passed as 'A − Fit for General Service'.

On 6 June he was once again on leave and on most days recorded that he played tennis with Doris Nicholson. On 12 June he visited the Royal Academy with Mrs Nicholson; on 13 June he noted that he had a 'nasty' letter from Terence Tetley, and he returned to Felixstowe on Sunday 16 June. On 18 June he states in his diary that he attended a Medical Board and was given '3 months' Garrison duty. I asked to be sent out, but they said I was still shaky.' The report of this Board does not appear in Henry's official records.

Henry was writing at this point for he recorded on 21 June that he sent a story called 'Money Moon' to Doris Nicholson. On 27 June he wrote: 'Am i/c [in charge] company. Little to do. Boche seems active still but crisis is over'. The following day the entry reads: 'Swam in early morning with Billjohn my little terrier. Feel better.' July contains several entries of early morning swimming sessions and tennis (presumably with army duties in between). From various notes one can deduce that he and Terence Tetley were continuously at odds with one another. However, during a weekend leave he met up with Terence recording: 'Blackheath, incident of horses' (which can be found in the novel) – and at this point quarrelled with Doris Nicholson: 'Finish'.

On 18 July he recorded: 'Foch's counter offensive begins which will end the war'. The *Official History* notes that on the 24 July 1918 'at the final turn of the tide in favour of the Entente, Marechal Foch . . .'[50] From then on by a continuous series of offensives and battles the Germans were forced to retreat until finally in November Mons was once more in Allied hands and by 11 November the Front Line ran roughly north from Sivry on its southern end to Granimont in the north. The enemy was defeated. These battles were no less bloody and awful than those in previous years but they played no part in Henry Williamson's life, either real or fictional, so are not recorded here.

The entry in Williamson's diary for 1 August 1918 reads: 'Linden Day [underlined]. Tennis with Ld. Ampthill & two others.'[51] The next day he noted: 'Swam 7 a.m. with Ld. A. & others. He a bearded Viking.'

On 14 August Henry recorded: 'Began my book again, after 5 months interval.' There follows several references to his writing, with some chapter analyses preceded by the entry: 'Writing at night. Door locked.' Interspersed are domestic and financial details including the fact that he won the men's doubles (with Milling) in the Regimental tennis tournament (see plate 30c) but 'Lost everything else'.

Once again there seems to have been a high degree of turmoil in Henry's life which is reflected in the diary entry referring to 'finishing' with Doris Nicholson. There is a most interesting entry on Wednesday 4 September: 'Failed Air Force. Not fit. Hell.' At the end of the month, on 27 September, he was seen by the doctor. 'M.O. sounded my lungs and said I have a dull patch. Hurray. Will solve everything.' The following day, 28 September, however, the situation changed graphically: 'Am going to India! My transfer to Indian Army came through! B1 category no bar!!' On 2 October he heard the embarkation details and the next day noted, 'Lord Ampthill spoke to me awfully nicely about leave. He said I could go tomorrow. Working party parade 7.15 am.'

While on leave he recorded that he typed out his manuscript (he did this in his grandfather's house next door), and that he had read the finale of his story to the Nicholsons. He also noted in a memo to himself that he would need 'New Kit & Riding Boots' and there is a list of people to see and say farewell including Maristany and Terence Tetley. He visited Terence at Selby on 19 October, where

Tetley was 'i/c AA gun'. Henry caught 'flu there, and immediately noted in his diary 'Is it rapid consumption?' He had to spend a few days in bed, returning home on 24 October.

A telegram recalled him to Felixstowe on 28 October where he learnt that he would sail on 4 November. He returned home the same day and went to a dance with Doris Nicholson that evening. The next day he recorded that he sorted out his finances, paying the money held by his father into his account at Holt's Army Agents Bank, and buying a £100 war bond for £77 10/ − (this is also entered in his bank book) and on 31 October, 'Gave a farewell dance at St Peter's Hall. Bubbly etc. Went very well. Danced with D.N. Paid Carr £10.' (Carr was his tailor.)

This celebratory farewell was, however, a little premature for on 3 November he learned 'Orders cancelled', and recorded the next day, Monday 4 November: 'Won't sail − awaiting fresh orders.' During the next two days he spent considerable time with the Nicholson family. On 6 November he 'saw McCready re France / says I am going to India. "Farewell" to DN at lunchtime' and the next day the momentous 'War Ending'.

Martin Gilbert in *The First World War* relates the scenario that pertained during the last days of the war. Although on the battlefields soldiers were still fighting during the first few days of November 1918, the German armed forces were in chaos as mutiny spread throughout the navy, army and factory workers. A general strike was called by the Socialists within the Reichstag. The Kaiser was in despair at this revolt and the collapse of the Imperial German power. He fled to the neutral Holland as the terms of the Armistice were accepted by the German Government.[52]

Henry Williamson was recalled to Felixstowe on 8 November and on 11 November his diary contains the announcement all had been waiting for: 'Armistice signed at 5.30 this morning. Bands playing, guns, sirens, etc etc. PEACE! Wrote Mrs. N.'

The *Official History* states:

The Armistice was signed at 5.5 a.m. on 11 November, and at 6.50 a.m. the following message was sent to Armies from Advanced G.H.Q.

'Hostilities will cease at 11.00 hours today, November 11th. Troops will stand fast on the line at that hour. . . . Defensive precautions will be maintained. There will be no intercourse of any description with the enemy until receipt of instructions from G.H.Q. Further instructions follow.'

. . . hostilities, both on the ground and in the air, were continued until the last moment.[53]

Gilbert's book goes on to quote John Buchan who was witness to the final moment:

Officers had their watches in their hands, and the troops waited with the same grave composure with which they had fought. At two minutes to eleven, opposite the South African Brigade, at the eastern-most point reached by the British armies, a German machine-gunner, after firing off a belt without pause, was seen to stand up beside his weapon, bow, and then walk slowly to the rear.

There came a second of expectant silence, and then a curious rippling sound, which observers far behind the front likened to the noise of a light wind. It was the sound of men cheering from the Vosges to the sea.[54]

The next day Williamson prosaically recorded that he bought a further £50 war savings certificate for £38 15s (paid for by cash he had received from Holts Bank the previous day – he had presumably finalized his account prior to the proposed embarkation for India) – and 'wrote my tale' and sent letters to Terence Tetley and his mother. Unfortunately this latter letter is not in his archive; it probably contained his thoughts on the end of the war and would have been of great interest. His diary entries for 19 and 20 November record the last moments of the war:

Tuesday 19 November: 20 German submarines to enter Harwich tomorrow at 12 am. No cheering.

Wednesday 20 November: Saw scores, painted dragons on bows, saw-edge to cables over conning towers etc. Crews all to attention entering Orwell estuary.[55]

Henry Williamson's life seems to have become fairly mundane at this point, reflecting perhaps a reaction after the tension of war. His diary entries are very sporadic and consist of brief notes of whom he received and sent letters. His Christmas leave began on 9 December and although he saw Doris Nicholson, by the casualness of his diary entries their friendship seems to have been waning rapidly. Terence Tetley was also on leave, and their quarrel obviously made up (although only temporarily) for they went around together for a few days.[56]

Henry did not return to Felixstowe on 20 December when his leave was supposed to end – the note 'Ret. Felixstowe' is crossed out – and instead leave seems to have been extended over Christmas for the entry for 27 December reads 'Return to Shorncliffe'. This was for duties first at the No. 1 Dispersal Unit, and later at No. 3 Rest Camp Folkestone, on what would appear to have been fairly undemanding duties organising troops returning from the Front, no doubt similar to those he was involved in at Felixstowe as Assistant Adjutant.

Details of his life at this time can be found in the third chapter 'Metamorphosis' of my biography, *Henry Williamson: Tarka and the Last Romantic*.[57] Suffice it to summarize here that he now began to write seriously and continuously and became involved with a lady noted in his diary as 'Mabs B.' [Baker] who was the wife of a fellow officer, and whom appears as 'Eve' D'Arcy Fairfax in his novels[58] (and see plate 30d). After the demise of that relationship he met Gwendoline (Doline) Rendle, a very sensible firm young lady who was a great help to him during his early attempts at writing, criticizing but encouraging his work.

There is no 1919 diary but Henry did paste several cuttings into an Army notebook which mainly concern his purchase of and exploits with a new Brooklands Road Special Motorcycle.[59] Most important, during this time at Folkestone Williamson found a copy of the book that was to be central to his thinking and writing. He was browsing in a bookshop at some point in the spring or early summer when he came across a copy of Richard Jefferies' *The Story of my Heart* which he read in rapt attention to the end. This book, an outpouring of mystical and spiritual growth, was for him a revelation of total truth (his personal revelation on the road to Damascus) and influenced him greatly. His writing aspirations were strengthened and deepened from that time. Jefferies' ethos was to write 'the Truth' and Henry Williamson took this onto himself as if it had been a cloak that Jefferies had bequeathed to him, and which he wore for ever afterwards. He started a folio sized 'Journal' at this time in which to record all his thoughts and dedicated it to Richard Jefferies.[60]

After a holiday in August spent at the cottage in Georgeham in the company of 'Mabs B.' (over which he concocted a complicated story that she was his dead wife's sister for the benefit of the Vicar's wife – a story which inevitably was to rebound on him in later years) Henry was posted to Brockton Camp at Cannock Chase in Staffordshire. Very shortly after he was sent for by the Commanding Officer as he wrote many years later in an article for The Strand Magazine entitled 'When I was Demobilised':[61]

I was then with the reserve battalion at Cannock Chase, and I had done with the war. I had discovered myself as a writer, and spent my days in my asbestos cubicle writing, and reading Galsworthy, Shakespeare, Shelley, and Richard Jefferies.

I was immensely exhilarated by the world I had discovered my true self to be part of. I wanted to write the truth as I had seen it, and to do this it was necessary to keep myself entirely apart from my fellows. Parades, what were parades? I had done with parades!

So I stayed in my cubicle, eating biscuits and making tea, and occasionally going into mess dinner at night. I knew nobody there, and avoided speaking to them, as to strangers. I had a racing motor-cycle, the first post-war model turned out by a famous Birmingham firm, and sometimes went to Stafford to buy food, and meet acquaintances in the bars of hotels.

After two or three weeks of such irregular conduct, during which time I had ignored all chits summoning me to the orderly room, from both assistant adjutant and adjutant – both junior in service to myself – I was sent for by my colonel. He said curtly that I must hand in my papers.

He had been through the war from the beginning, and so I apologised to him for my conduct. He said he was glad I had apologised; and then I told him, in halting words, that I was possessed by an overwhelming feeling to devote myself to writing. We shook hands, while my eyes could not see properly; and the next day I left on my motor-cycle for London and demobilisation. A few formalities at the Crystal Palace, and I was out again, a free man.

Henry Williamson was demobilized on 19 September 1919. He may have physically left the Army, but spiritually and emotionally he never left it. His experiences of the war were part of his soul and his being, a catalyst that gave rise to his life as an author, and in particular to his writings about that war. A metamorphosis from which he emerged to a new beginning.

7

Beyond Reality:
Henry Williamson's Writings about the
First World War[1]

When Henry Williamson was demobilized in September 1919 he was almost twenty-four years old. In the essay 'When I was Demobilised'[2] he gives us a very clear picture of his thoughts at that time:

It was then that I felt lost; [for] all my years since boyhood – a very long time to me – the Army had been my home, indeed it had been my entire grown-up world. Now I had no world, except the shadowy and diminished sphere of civvy life which had been steadily dissolving since 1914. I could hardly speak to my parents; there were hardly any light-rays between our worlds.

I remember going slowly round the streets of Sydenham, wondering what I could do. At last I went to London, to stay in a hotel and visit some of my war-time haunts. But I might have been a ghost. I drank beer alone, yet with imaginary comrades.

The next day I went to the Army bankers to see about my 'blood money', or gratuity. This was payable at the rate of 180 days' pay for the first year of commissioned service, with 90 days' pay for every subsequent year or part of a year. I found I had nearly £300 to come. Of this, £100 had already been spent on the racing motorcycle. [Williamson also received a disability pension for some years – of which a regular sum of £13 a month paid into his account would appear to be this.]

I wrote at night, and loafed about during the day. I ran into some of my friends and we hailed one another with crys of happiness. . . . It was a strange world. . . . There was an ex-Officers' Association, to which I and a friend went, putting down our names for jobs. Any jobs; at home or abroad. We learned that what we were in the Army was of little use in the new world we were now becoming accustomed to. . . .

Gradually we were absorbed into the post-war. The battlefields were cleared up. Tens of thousands of Poles and Italians filled in the craters with long-handled shovels; tens of thousands of rusty dud shells and fragments of steel were collected into dumps.

We used to say during the war that it would take a hundred years to clear up the Somme battlefields; actually it was done in little more than half a hundred months. As for the human souls that once trudged there, in sweat and terror, in cold and mud and in heat and choking dust, they, too, became in time indistinguishable from the civilian world of which they had once been so derisive. . . .

So it came about that I left London and went to live in a cottage in Devon by myself, to meditate and to write the truth as I saw it, to clarify what we fought and died for – a new vision of the world.

Henry Williamson had, of course, been working on a novel for some time now[3] both during the last months of the war and while earning his living as a journalist in Fleet Street.[4] When his book was accepted by a publisher, he made the decision to leave home and to live in North Devon. His life as a writer had begun in earnest, but it was to be some time before he wrote about the war.

Williamson joined the Bedfordshire and Hertfordshire Regimental Association at an early stage; Issue No. 2 of its magazine, dated July 1920, is in his archive and there is also a list of members for 1923 on which his name appears. Elected Council members included: Colonel Lord Ampthill, GCSI, GCIE; H.C. Cressingham, DSO; R.R.B. Orlebar; Lieutenant Colonel R.O. Wynne, DSO (with an Australian address); and Major E.S.M. Poyntz, no doubt the son of Lieutenant Colonel H.S. Poyntz, DSO, whose name appears on the general members list. These people have all played their part in the preceding chapters. In April 1922 the magazine was given a new format and a new name *The Wasp* (this name derives from the regimental black and orange striped tie). Henry's archive copies of the magazine extend to 1935.

Also in Williamson's archive is *The Ypres Times*[5] running from Volume 1, No. 2 January 1922 to 1932. This was the Journal of the Ypres League whose President was Field Marshal Earl French of Ypres and Vice-Presidents Field Marshal Earl Haig, Field Marshal Viscount Allenby and Field Marshal Lord Plumer of Messines. The editorial of Issue No. 2 echoes Williamson's own thoughts for the rest of his life:

With the din and merriment of Christmas still about us, the thoughts of Old Comrades are likely at this season of the year to be reminiscent. . . . We shall remember those who stood shoulder to shoulder with us, whose bodies are now mingled with the sacred soil of Flanders.

Williamson did not include any of his war experience in his early cycle of novels *The Flax of Dream* beyond that of the hero Willie Maddison's reminiscences in thought and conversation. His purpose here was to show the 'before and after' aspect of life, and particularly to lay out his 'Policy of Reconstruction' – his ideas on how education reflects the thought processes of politics and the establishment, and how this in turn affects the thought processes of the next generation.

At this time in his life Henry leaned towards communism. There is a pair of identical photographs in his archive showing him with an incipient beard, both marked with the same date in 1922. One of these, printed on page 79 of my biography, is signed 'Yours ever, Henry Williamson' while the other is signed 'Comrade Williamson'. This communist tendency is evident in *The Pathway*, the last volume of *The Flax* tetralogy. The hero, Willie Maddison, has decided leanings towards Lenin's philosophy as revealed in a conversation with the vicar, Mr Garside: 'He [Lenin] designed a new way for humanity; or rather slung the old bag of rubbish overboard – all the old mass virtues – those virtues arising out of mass fears, distrust, jealousy, and held together by dividends.' Willie Maddison denies being a member of the Communist party, but the reader is made very aware that that is where his sympathies lie. Further evidence can be found in *Goodbye West Country*, where in the mid-1930s Williamson discussed his more recent thoughts about Hitler and set them out more succinctly: 'So with Hitler . . . Here at last is someone who has perceived the root-causes of war in the unfulfilled human ego, and is striving to create a new, human-filled world. I tried to show the same things . . . through Maddison in *The Flax of Dream*. That was about 1927 [i.e. when writing the final version of *The Pathway*]. It [*The Pathway*] was the point of view of the ex-soldier, made coherent, real. Before this [i.e. his new thoughts about Hitler and the new Germany in the mid-1930s] I'd seen hope only in Lenin's point of view.'[6]

One of the books in Henry Williamson's archive is *Imperialism. The Last Stage of Capitalism* written by Lenin, and published by the

Communist Party of Great Britain in 1917. Lenin's short Preface ends with the words: 'I would hope that this little book will help the reader to understand the fundamental economic question, without the study of which modern war and politics are unintelligible – to be more precise, the question of the economic nature of Imperialism.' In an equally short Introduction, Lenin reiterates: 'We are going to show, briefly and in the simplest way, the connection between and the reciprocal values of the chief economic features of capitalism.' One can see immediately on reading this book how it coincided with Henry's thoughts at that time. When in later years he found that communism had taken the wrong (and evil) path he looked to what he thought would follow the road that paralleled his own thinking – namely the new Germany (for Hitler had risen to power because he had been instrumental in ridding the country of communism) and then in Britain in 1937 to the party headed by Mosley, the British Union. Williamson thought the British Union would put into place the economic policy based on agricultural reform, which was central to his own thinking. Fascism itself was never his interest.

Williamson's leaning towards communism in the years following the war almost certainly came mainly from the influence of Henri Barbusse, the author of the acclaimed war novel Le Feu (Under Fire)[7] which won the prestigious Prix Goncourt in 1917. Barbusse was born in 1873, son of a French journalist and playwright and a Yorkshire mother, and was forty-one years old and already an experienced writer when the war broke out. His first book, a volume of poetry was published in 1895 titled Pleuresses. As a student he came under the influence of the rearguard of the French Romantic movement and its leader the troubadour poet Catulle Mendes, whose daughter he married. By the time L'Enfer (Inferno) was published in 1908 when Barbusse was thirty-five years old, he had matured into a poetic realist with a fierce and sombre power. The controversy over the violent imagery of this book made Barbusse's reputation as a writer.[8]

War intervened. Barbusse's poor health was against his enlistment but he persevered and became a soldier. His experiences, related in Le Feu, changed his attitudes completely, and the closing chapter of this powerful book reflects this: 'equality' is being discussed by the few soldiers left alive. These thoughts equate exactly with Williamson's own as can be seen.

The peoples of the world ought to come to an understanding, through the hides and on the bodies of those who exploit them one way or another. All the masses ought to agree together. All men ought to be equal. . . . When all men have made themselves equal, we shall be forced to unite. And there'll no longer be appalling things done in the face of heaven by thirty million men who don't wish them. . . . Ah, you are right, poor countless workmen of the battles, you who have made with your hands all of the Great War, you whose omnipotence is not yet used for well-doing. . . . There is not only the prodigious opposition of interested parties — financiers, speculators great and small, armour-plated in their banks and houses, who live on war and live in peace during war . . . their faces shut up like safes. . . .

Barbusse was at this time a left-wing socialist rather than a communist. He did not join the communist party until 1919 and even then it was a defiant gesture against the French government rather than a personal conviction.[9]

It is now evident that Barbusse's thoughts coupled together with the revelation of Richard Jefferies' writings, with their mix of mystical and socialistic trends,[10] provided the literary influences that set Henry Williamson on his life's work.

After the war, apart from joining the Regimental Association, Henry Williamson took an active interest in wartime affairs. For instance, there is a service sheet in his archive, for a service he attended on Sunday 16 November 1924 at the Cathedral Church of St Alban for the presentation of the Colours of the 1st Battalion of the Bedfordshire and Hertfordshire Regiment (amalgamated in 1919).

In May of the following year, with five books already published, Henry Williamson married Ida Loetitia Hibbert,[11] daughter of an officer of the Cheriton Otter Hunt, whom he had met while gathering material for his proposed 'Otter Story' later to be published as *Tarka the Otter*. The first part of their honeymoon was spent at an isolated farm near Dunkery Beacon on Exmoor and then the young couple left for France and a tour of the Battlefields. On this visit Williamson kept a *Notebook* recording his thoughts which are of great interest and give his impressions on his first return only seven years after the end of the war. The emotions that arose as he surveyed the scenes of the fighting and even more of the cemeteries of the dead, are powerful evidence of the turmoil within him and of the split in his soul that he could not reconcile.

The first stop was Amiens Cathedral on 23 May 1925 where he noted the various memorials on the pillars: 'Newfoundland contingent . . . Sixth Regt of U.S. Engineers . . . 600,000 men of Armies of G.B. & Ireland . . . Royal Canadian Dragoons . . . Australian Imperial Force . . . New Zealand Div. . . .' His last note here was about the French Memorial: '*A la mémoire des soldats de la paroisse Notre-Dames morts pour la France* — sculpture of dead soldiers, with old man, & matron with child weeping. Stone.'

The bride and groom continued to the Ancre valley where Henry wrote many entries in his Notebook. A selection is quoted here:

Walked from Albert to Beaucourt-Hamel. Explored Y Ravine, and was drenched by rain. . . . Tall black dead trees, branchless, poplars, standing in marsh. At evening a wild chorus of bullfrogs began. . . . Baillescourt Farm rebuilt, much bigger. Long grasses over battlefields. . . . No gunflashes lit the whitewashed wall of our room, the trains from Arras rolled noisily past the window, and a star moved across the curtain. The dug-outs of Y Ravine have subsided, the timbers break with a touch. . . . Rust and mildew and long green grass and frogs. The Ancre flows swift and hostile as before, gathering the green duckweed into a heaving coat as of mail, & drowning its white water-crowsfeet. . . .

What is to be found in this valley now? The answer is nothing. . . . Why have I a war-complex? Terrified by war, I now love to let my mind dwell on the immense destructive power & desolation of war. Is this a form of neurosis? I love to imagine guns flashing, & troops marching, and the vastness of our army's movements & operations. This is, of course, in retrospect, very different from the war that actually *was*.

Hindenburg Line Walked from Achiet to Croisilles . . . & walked up sunken road to Hindenburg Line. Remembered. Trenches filled in but dug-out shafts remain. Deeper than the Somme dugouts. Concrete blockhouses every 50 yards. Trenches over slope of hill. No direct observation upon them — they see all that comes over the grassy skyline. No wonder we failed on May 3, 1917 and afterwards! The sunken lines lying before the position, and parallel to the lines, were a death-trap, as machine guns from the village (Bullecourt) swept one end, & from the fields, the other. . . .

Watched German graves at St. Leger being dug up and brown bones and scraps of rags being shovelled into boxes, roughly in the shape of coffins. Brown bones, black rag scraps. The tall blond Flemish workmen picked them up and chucked them in. . . .

An Englishman supervised with a French sergeant. The Englishman stood there to see that no English dead were exhumed by mistake, for Germans in war often buried friend and foe together. But not in peacetime! . . . The bones of the slain may lie side-by-side at peace in wartime, but in peacetime they are religiously separated, each to its cemetery. . . . But now, they prepare for another war, so that the babes in the cradles will be slain in the wasted corn.

Hindenburg Line, near Bullecourt. Saw a simple cross of poplar at the edge of a cornfield. It was formed of a stick stuck there, & the cross was bound with a withy. The stick was in green leaf. . . . Oh, the concrete machine gun places in the corn! The peasants are working there now, digging out thistles. The corn is knee-high, & the turtle doves are here!

Below Vimy Ridge. 28.5.1925. Arras is a dirty pimply spattered pocked place; thank sun & rain that England is green . . . .

Written at Neuville St. Vlaast. 2 p.m. 30.5.25. Have just seen the German Cemetery at La Maison Blanche, on the Bethune–Arras Road. 36,000 black crosses, with white names & numbers thereon. Packed close together, two by two back & front, the wooden crosses are planted in the chalk. No flowers grow here, except the strays of the old battlefield – charlock, poppy, & bindweed. They look in disgrace and unfriended. Black, black, black, thirtysix thousand of them, stuck in the white chalk. In a field adjoining was a concrete machine gun shelter, burst open, with its iron girders rusty and clawing heaven. The grass was long about it. Larks sang above – always singing larks in France. Black, black as charred thistles, pressed together, unloved, stark, black, the graves of the hated invaders! . . .

Down the straight road again, & one comes to La Targette, where English & French cemeteries lie together. How a spirit of loving kindness hovers around this English cemetery! Flowers are here . . . The simple stones, each carved with a cross & badge & name, are clean, and the lawns around them are weeded and mown. Contrast to those black thistles higher up!

Next is the French cemetery. White crosses, wide spaced, & the place is tended, & flowers are grown here. Gardeners are at work. Each cross bears the tri-colour – blue, white, and red. The spirits of the slain may breathe here – there is elbow room.

Rochincourt, where we stayed two nights to explore Vimy Ridge . . . & the concrete gun pits in the wood over the crest, has a gallic cock on its war memorial, crowing on a broken gun barrel. . . . Oh, do the dead feel cock-crowing triumph over the dead German cannon-fodder? The crowing is for the industrial magnates, the Lens versus Ruhr mine-owners, not the poor unknowing, simple dead! I seem to remember that a cock crew elsewhere & then Peter wept bitterly. . . . The hawthorn blooms, & its scent is heavy in the warm May days, the nightingale sings by Achiet le Grand station, and I, I can find no rest, no answer.

The German Cemetery Again. Black as thistles – the unwanted thistles that the farmer & his wife deracinate through the long days. One sees them in the corn, with armfuls of docks, charlock, & thistles. The green & undulating cornfields, with rusty shells piled by the cart tracks, & barbed wire pressed like bales of rank hay, thrown into craters where mossy water stagnates, reeds grow, & the ghastly croak of the frogs creeps forth. Black as a burned place, bitter and black as frost and fire, a frost of silence among the black crosses – the invaders burned & laid waste, & now their unwanted bones lie in a burnt waste.

Dommage de guerre . . . At Rochincourt, under the Vimy Ridge, La Veuve Marchand . . . her son died at Verdun. Now she looks after the English gardeners of the cemetery, & has done so for four years. . . . She is a clean, red-faced woman, with quick shuffling feet, & cleans her new floors every day on her knees, with pail & swab. Her rooms have little furniture. She awaits *dommage de guerre* for furniture. . . . Poor little veuve, her son's portrait (enlarged from a snap) looks down from the wall. She has a splendid cooking [range] porcelain & enamel faced, with a design of birds & flowers; but no son.

Messines & Wytchaete. 1.6.1925 Watched frogs in water of mine craters. Listened to bloody degenerate lache Belgians in a cafe on Whit Monday. Talked yesterday with the woman of Le Gheer, whose house I explored on Xmas Day 1914. She remembered the dead canary.

Here the honeymoon visit notes abruptly end, to be followed immediately by: '4 Nov. 1926 Attended the re-union dinner of the original L.R.B. survivors − "Chyebassa dinner", named after ship that took us from Southampton to Havre on 4/11/14. This is a copy of Lt. (now Capt.) Fursdon's map he sketched for me on one of the cards − map of Plug-street wood & trenches.' This is followed by the map and notes on his comrades whom he now met for the first time since the war. These are notes which he obviously made with his writing in mind − he had already determined that he would write a second series as a follow-on from his Flax volumes, which would show the life of Willie's cousin Phillip and his involvement in the war. He could little know at that point how many years it would be before he would be able to begin, nor how the enterprise would grow at that time, fifteen volumes of which five are on the war.

D.H.BELL − keen, dark, double-life. This man took G.E.W. [Henry's mother − see main text] round Crowboro' Camp in '14, & regretted he could not take her in the 'officers' mess, as he was not himself an officer! At dinner, 12 years after, he showed curious double strain . . . . Afterwards he went to Cameroons, became Capt., M.C., obviously he was a sahib officer; & yet also the old comrade, but they conflicted. . . .

HOLLIS − slow of speech, red face, just as in 1914! Same old Hollis! No thought, no change. John Bull. Solid, nice, kind, loves beer. Never hilarious; solid, old red-faced Hollis.

BLUNDEN − 'lance-corporal Blunden.' Slight impediment in speech. Small narrow face, dark close-set eyes; deliberate. Root of an oaktree. Arm off now . . . Never got angry with men; talks a sort of dialect; messenger at the Gresham before the war, wears a top hat; is now a messenger; just the same Blunden. . . . He was 25 in 1914; . . . He loved it when times were worst, was very happy in the line. The oak in its leafy glory, the last of English spirit; Blunden, small, narrow, almost insignificant, is of that oak; but a root of it, exposed. In fact a hero.

CHAPPELL BROS − Went to Public School − sons of a City tailor − sort of veneered but good boys. I did not like them; they did not like me. Perhaps it was because I was a filthy snob regarding Martin Sharman & Co. − the 'Leytonstone crowd'. Survival, this mood of mine, from the Sun Fire Office of 1914. A la J.V. Brett. Coulson was of their "tent", & I fought him in the moonlight before Xmas Eve, & was properly 'hided' by him.

DIPLOCK – cpl in 1914; became C.S.M. [Company Sergeant Major], taken prisoner in March 1918. Changed from a mild, pleasant little man, rather soft, to an iron-thewed man. He served longer with LRB than anyone else. . . .

FURSDON – Platoon commander – Devonian. Confessed to me his worry in 1914 was lest he should do the wrong thing, and so lose his men – not his commission; but his men.

HENSHAW – Sergeant. 'Granny' Henshaw. Became R.T.O. [Railway Transport Officer] after May 1915. Rather got 'naggy' under the influence of flooded trenches. . . . Grannie Henniker (as I shall call him) had gone through the war, & never changed his outlook.

HINMAN – the handsome, rather self-confident person. . . . Centre of group – he'd been drinking & boasting of his 'rum-running' prowess. Hinman became Lt. Col. in war, gaining DSO & MC [in 1956 Williamson queried this as he could not find it in the LRB record]. His runner got it him as much as anything. . . . An interesting character study; I must pursue him. . . . Scout in 1914, with bicycle. Big calves and body.

JOHNSON – Company Commander in Oxford. No moustache now; brownish, big man, his eyes are wide open. Now a parson.

POTHECARY, Major D.C.M. – short, sturdy, popular, heavy-jawed, charming, happy. Best spirit and nice to all. Sahib. Sherborne School. Great contempt for Alec Waugh [friend of HW, met 1920].

There are two menu cards for the 1926 dinner in his archive, one has Fursdon's rough sketch of the Front Line on it which Henry copied into his notebook; the other has the signatures of most of the 'P' Company survivors present that evening.[12] Henry attended the *Chyebassa* dinners for several years but later they were amalgamated into a larger regimental unit and he found he could not face them. There is also a menu card for a Bedfordshire and Hertfordshire Regimental dinner in 1928 which contains the signature of Captain C.O. Whitfield. Whitfield was an officer who had seen service in Egypt and who joined the 3rd Battalion Bedfordshire Regiment at Felixstowe while Williamson was there. They became friends and Henry wrote several letters to him over the years. However, Henry also gave up going to these dinners in due course.

The following summer, with the typescript of *Tarka the Otter* safely at the printers, Williamson made another visit to the battlefields. This time in the company of his brother-in-law, William Busby, the husband of his younger sister Doris (Biddy), who had been an officer in the Tank Corps. Henry again entered his thoughts into a small notebook, filling sixteen sparse pages, dated 3–10 June 1927:

Calais – names Romantic on board – . . . Hazebrouck. Hotel St. Georges. . . . The Square, which way did we march in . . . Poperinge – Skindles – officer's club – five houses down, Toc H. adjoining chemists (man like Hindenburg) . . . Toc H. greyish front, 2 stories up . . . [postcard reproduced in HWSJ, no. 34, September 1998]

He may have stayed on to attend the unveiling of the commemorative tablet in the London Rifle Brigade cemetery at Ploegsteert on Sunday 19 June 1927. In fact this may well be why he made this trip as he had noted the 'unveiling in the spring' on the *Chyebassa* dinner card the previous autumn. However, the commemorative book on the unveiling in his archive does not include his name on the list of those attending, but he could easily have attended unofficially – a photograph of the event shows a large crowd of people present.[13]

All the notes from this trip were used in the story of *The Wet Flanders Plain*. Henry, however, wrote them up first as a series of articles to help pay for his pilgrimage. The *Daily Express* accepted four of these and published them under the general title 'And This Was Ypres'; the first 'Vlamertinghe' appearing on 20 July 1927, the second subtitled 'Goldfish Chateaux Mystery', the third 'How Troop Trains arrived at "Pop"' while 'Hotel Skindles', the fourth one, is not in his archive.

On 12 June 1928 Henry Williamson was awarded the Hawthornden Prize for Literature for his book *Tarka the Otter* published in the autumn of the previous year. He was now famous and thus a marketable commodity. He wrote to his wife's mother: 'One has arrived.' This award was a prestigious advertisement for his succeeding books and provided a sales surge for *Tarka* and especially for *The Pathway*, the last volume of *The Flax of Dream*, which was published that autumn. It received much attention, with almost rave reviews in America. This meant that Henry was in huge demand by newspapers and magazines to produce articles, many of which tended to have nature themes. But there was also an intense production of articles with a 'war' theme including the previously unsold pieces written up from the battlefields pilgrimage of June

1927, now taken by the *Daily Telegraph* and elsewhere. Of course, the autumn of 1928 also marked the first really important 'war anniversary' – ten years from the Armistice.

The most important of Henry's articles appeared in a series in the *Daily Express* on 17 September 1928, entitled 'I Believe in the Men Who Died'. The *Daily Express* headed the article thus: 'This most moving and brilliantly written article, by the winner of the Hawthornden Prize for 1928, is in continuance of the now famous *Daily Express* new series in which distinguished men and women are reaffirming their faith in certain things that, for them, matter most in life.'[14]

The article 'I Believe in the Men Who Died' appeared with a few small changes the following year as a prologue entitled 'Apologia pro vita mea' in *The Wet Flanders Plain*. It opened with a cameo scene of ascending the church tower at Georgeham. This church tower is a recurring theme in Williamson's work and had a symbolic significance (akin to William Golding's *The Spire*). It was also used as a symbol in the essay 'Surview and Farewell' from *The Labouring Life* where Williamson reflects and philosophizes on life.[15]

This tower, above and beyond the real world, is a symbol of total goodness, a confessional, a place where only truth can be spoken. Williamson was not religious from an establishment point of view, but he had a deep, innate, idea of the powers of good and evil, of darkness and light – Christ and Lucifer and the duality of the whole of life and history. Hence his 15-novel sequence *A Chronicle of Ancient Sunlight* and its portrayal of good and evil, where he shows the evil root causes of the First World War and builds up to the ultimate example of duality of nature that was to be found in Hitler and the Second World War. Williamson called Hitler Lucifer, the Light Bringer, the angel once equal to Christ but who, when tempted, gave way to evil and fell into everlasting damnation (as opposed to Christ who withstood temptation and thus rose to everlasting life). Williamson's supposed allegiance to fascism started as a genuine admiration for what he thought was being achieved and became an attempt to understand and portray the facts of the history of our age. When he was misunderstood, he remained silent, neither explaining nor defending himself. A mixture of stubborn, arrogant pride and genuine deep hurt and puzzlement would not allow him to put matters right. If people misunderstood, then that was their affair.

However, all that was in the future. At this point, as he rode the crest of the wave made by the Hawthornden, his deepest thoughts were with his comrades of the war. The following quotations from his central essay 'I believe in the Men Who Died' show the depth of his feelings. The italic sections, which appeared in the newspaper, gave greater emphasis to his thought than the version which appeared in The Wet Flanders Plain.

The great sound [of the bells] sweeps other thought away into the air, and the earth fades; the powerful wraith of those four years of the war enters into me, and the torrent becomes the light and clangour of massed guns that thrall the senses.

I take the weight and strength of the barrage, and grow mighty with it, until it becomes but a seam of sound nicked with flashes and puny in space and time controlled by the vaster roar of stars in their age-long travail through elemental darkness. I see all life created by those flaming suns of the night, and out of life arises a radiance, wan and phantasmal and pure, the light of Khristos.

The wraith of the war, glimmering with this inner vision, bears me to the wide and shattered country of the Somme, to every broken wood and trench and sunken lane, among the broad straggling bells of rusty wire smashed and twisted in the chalky loam, while the ruddy clouds of brick-dust hang over the shelled villages by day, and at night the eastern horizon roars and bubbles with light.

And everywhere in these desolate places I see the faces and figures of enslaved men . . .

Until in the flame and rolling smoke I see men arising and walking forward; and I go forward with them, as in a nightmare wherein some seem to pause, with bowed heads, and sink carefully to their knees, and roll slowly over, and lie still. Others roll and roll, and scream . . . while the dust and earth on my tunic changes from grey to red.

. . . the soldiers feel they have been betrayed by the highsounding phrases that heralded the war, for they know that the enemy soldiers are the same men as themselves, suffering and disillusioned in exactly the same way. . . .

The bells cease, and the power goes from me, and I descend again to the world of the living; and if in some foolish confiding moment I try to explain why I want to re-live those old days, to tear the Truth out of the past so that all men shall see plainly. . . .

I must return to my old comrades of the Great War – to the brown, the treeless, the flat and grave-set plain of Flanders – for I am dead with them, and they live in me again. There in the beautiful desolation of rush and willow in the forsaken tracts I will renew the truths which have quickened out of their deaths:

that human virtues are superior to those of national idolatry, which do not arise from the spirit: that the sun is universal, and that men are brothers, made for laughter one with another: that we must free the child from all things which maintain the ideals of a commercial nationalism, the ideals which inspired and generated the barrages in which ten million men, their laughter corrupted, perished.

The summer is beautiful to men of all nations, and every man was once a little boy with an imagination.

I have a little boy now; a wild little innocent who looks at birds in the sky, at poppies and bumblebees and dandelions and thinks no mean thought, and sees no harm anywhere. . . . Must he, too, traverse a waste place of the earth; must the blood and sweat of his generation drip in agony where poppies have grown, and corn?

The revised book version ends: 'until the sun darken and fall down the sky, and rise no more upon the world?'

Here one can see all those elements of 'Above and Beyond', of poetic and Romantic truth, and indeed of religious truth, found at the essence of a great deal of Williamson's work. The tremendous cacophonous clanging of the church bells was a catalyst releasing him from reality to express himself through the medium of a great nightmare vision encapsulating in a few hundred words the essence of those years of battle, his fallen comrades and his thoughts. This was his desperate plea – on how to put the world right and ensure that war should never happen again – a plea on behalf of children. 'I Believe in the Men Who Died' was Williamson's credo for the rest of his life as he emphasized by changing the title to 'Apologia pro vita mea'.

This article made quite a deep impression on the public at the time. In October 1928, the *Adair Monthly* (an American publication) reprinted it: 'We have received numerous requests from our readers to reprint this article by an ex-officer in the British Army which appeared in the *Daily Express* of 17th September, 1928.' The *Express* article was read by a young German student studying languages. He sent a letter of response to the editor which was printed on 1 October 1928:

Sir, . . . Recently I saw a copy of the 'Daily Express' containing an article "I Believe in the Men Who Died" by Henry Williamson. Believe me, that essay, those poetic phrases, made such an impression upon me that I could not refrain from sending my sincere thanks to you and to the author.

I love my country with my whole heart . . . but is it not necessary, now more than ever, for the young people of the European nations, who must rebuild on the ruins of old Europe, to learn to know and to understand one another?

We revere the dead of all nations who bled in the war, for they died for a great idea – for a new Europe. We, the young, who live, have the duty of reconciling the nations who hated each other by means of that respect and reverence for the war's victims.

We want no books, plays or films that uphold overthrown ideals: we want a future in which the struggle is only for peace . . . .

With compliments, W.R., Mainz, Germany.

These sentiments, exactly echoing Henry's own, must have done a great deal to reinforce his faith in his new ideal.

The *Daily Express* also published a series of articles by Henry Williamson entitled 'The Last 100 Days'; these were factual accounts of the progress of the war during its final phase as though they were a commentary of something happening at that time. The first one appeared on 11 August 1928 headed: 'Ten years ago there began at Amiens the series of terrific engagements that were to culminate in the final collapse of the German military machine. The *Daily Express* has asked Mr Williamson, who served as a soldier of the line, to describe from time to time in these columns the principal events of the last hundred days of the war.' These short pieces appeared at intervals (roughly weekly) up to the tenth Armistice anniversary on 11 November.[16]

There was also an article by Henry Williamson in the *Radio Times* for 9 November 1928, headed 'What we should Remember and What Forget'.[17] A short editorial introduction was set into the middle of the page: 'Mr. Williamson writes in this article of the war which he himself knew for four years and the thoughts which today trouble the mind of a poet who was once a soldier.' The article is a plea for understanding not just the rights and wrongs of both sides of the conflict, shown through the allegory of the graves of the dead of either side, but for the future. Henry's words included a letter from an ex-German soldier he had met on the pilgrimage visit in the cemetery at Arras.

We all – you English, French and Germans, and all others – have to join and teach the coming generation the lesson of peace and understanding. . . . Let us join as brethren do, and forget; let us rebuild what was destroyed, and grow strong in confidence to each other and so help to *save* mankind. . . . you having been a soldier of the line, must detest war. What we write should become our dogma and our duty. . . .

[This reinforced Williamson's own thoughts and he continued:]

Future generations will see those [war] years as the supreme paradox of the old ways of European thought, when millions . . . enslaved themselves to a set of ideals which inevitably would destroy them. . . . These are the things, done in the name of honour and patriotism − the immaculate white exterior of the sepulchres of our minds − we should scorn, and cast out of ourselves, and so forget; and when this has been done we shall remember that the sun is universal, shining on all countries and all flags, and that all men are like ourselves. . . .

An article which appeared in *Britannia* on 9 November 1928 called 'The Valley' (of the Ancre) became the last section of *The Wet Flanders Plain*:

I was . . . a man who had lost part of himself, and was only now beginning to find it again. For years the lost part had lurked in the marsh, seeing wraiths of men in grey with coal-skuttle helmets and big boots, wraiths of men in khaki, always laden and toiling, wraiths of depressed mules, . . . wraiths of howitzers flashing away their shells with stupendous corkscrewing hisses upwards, wraiths of pallid flares making the night haggard, while bullets whined and fell with short hard splash in the shadowy and gleaming swamps of the Ancre.

Henry attended the 'Ten Years' Anniversary Remembrance Service on 11 November 1928 on behalf of the *Daily Mirror* and his piece on this appeared the following day.[18]

. . . 11 a.m. A note deep and sonorous, another deep note from Big Ben, and we are launched into silence and olden time. Whitehall is a chasm, filled with grey silence, and the people are the dead: I am dead, but there is no Valhalla, only a strange immensity of twilit silence . . . . The maroons crash, it is finished. . . . We hope that we are really awakening; we who are the Posterity of the Lost Generation. . . .

At the beginning of 1929, Henry Williamson gathered together all his articles from the pilgrimage visit preparatory to publishing them as a single volume. He approached C.W. Beaumont, 'Publisher of Belles Lettres' (as his letter headings announce in a flourish of lavish green ink) in January 1929, sending him his manuscript of 'the small travel diary *They Only Fade Away*. Beaumont wrote back, 'I have been much impressed by its beauty and sincerity', and agreed to publish it, subject to his usual terms being agreeable. Henry did not find the terms agreeable but after a further exchange of letters they reached a settlement and on 23 February Beaumont thanked Williamson for his 'revised MS of *Ten Years After*'. A further letter dated 27 March shows that Henry had changed the title yet again, although printing had commenced and Beaumont was preparing a prospectus (all of which put up the costs which were partly charged to Henry by way of reduced royalties). The title was not mentioned but it was, of course, *The Wet Flanders Plain*. This limited press edition was published on 12 June, followed later in the year by a trade edition by Faber with a Dedication to C.R.W. Nevinson, the war artist whose work appears as the frontispiece of this present work.[19] It was published simultaneously by Dutton in America. The penultimate paragraph contains the sentence that was to be the key thought of Williamson's philosophy for the rest of his life: 'What you seek is lost for ever in ancient sunlight, which rises again as Truth.'

Douglas Bell's *A Soldier's Diary of the Great War* was also published in 1929. Bell had asked Henry for help with the book. Henry read the manuscript which was Bell's war diary, made several suggestions and revisions and sent it off to his friend Richard de la Mare at Faber & Gwyer, who accepted it and published it anonymously. Henry wrote a fourteen-page introduction for the book. It is interesting to compare Bell's descriptions of the early phase of the war in the LRB with Williamson's own experience and subsequent writing. Henry's 'Introduction' tends, it has to be said, to be a little condescending as can be noted in the sentence: 'We call such creations works of genius when they are made; such is *Le Feu*, by Barbusse. Our Diarist merely . . .'

In the autumn of 1928 Jack Squire (Sir John C. Squire), well known literary critic and editor of the *London Mercury* and a member of the committee for the Hawthornden award, introduced Henry to the Tasmanian-born artist William Kermode. Kermode, who had served in the war, had made lino-cuts of war scenes and wanted someone to write short caption-like paragraphs to go with these. These lino-cuts are very well known and are still incredibly powerful, stark and dramatic. Henry's first sight of them obviously struck a deep chord in his soul and he was immediately inspired by the project, deciding to write a full-length book himself, thus rather relegating the lino-cuts to second place.[20] Kermode stuck to his guns and insisted the story-line must reflect the 'cuts' and that both must be on equal terms. The result was a literary masterpiece, entitled *The Patriot's Progress*, which was highly praised by Arnold Bennett:

> It is short, and it is not a novel. It contains very little concerning the supposed-to-be chief military (and civil) diversions . . . . It is the account of the war-career of a plain, ordinary man, John Bullock, who entered the army with a dogged sense of duty, and left it minus a leg. The author has not drawn John Bullock as an individual, John Bullock is Everysoldier, and *Everysoldier* would have been an excellent title for the book.
>
> The account is simple, and awful, absolutely awful. Its power lies in the descriptions, which have not been surpassed in any other war-book within my knowledge. . . . No overt satire, sarcasm, sardonic irony in the book. Yet it amounts to a tremendous, an overwhelming, an unanswerable indictment of the institution of war . . .

It is no coincidence that the title echoes John Bunyan's *A Pilgrim's Progress* and an analogy can be drawn between the two books. *The Patriot's Progress* is a morality tale. John Bullock is the archetypal common soldier fighting patriotically for a cause he does not understand. He is unintelligent, unimaginative, but grimly determined, facing every horror, first of brutal initiation into army life and then that of the trenches, with the futility of battle, until the inevitable result of a shell wound and leg amputation, and a return to the mindless non-understanding of life in England.[21] But having planted the suggestion to his readers that there is a connection between his book and Bunyan's, Williamson does not follow the obvious path of onward progress that Christian took. Indeed for Williamson's central character 'progress' is an ironic allusion. There is no progress. The book is divided into five 'Phases'. They merely mark the inevitable progression of total futility.[22]

Williamson's tight control of his subject matter in this book and his use of structure and language show a great growth in maturity and skill, but a further strength of the book lies in its visual impact, particularly in early editions, where design, illustration and text combine to make a visual whole. Kermode's lino-cuts portray the very essence of the horror of war. This is enhanced by the choice of the dark bold type font. But the real effect comes from the fact that there are no paragraph divisions, and the text runs on, thick and black, in a continuous monotonous flow which highlights the monotonous grind of the war stone.

T.E. Lawrence sent a long letter, giving the book praise and selecting many little phrases and words that he had found particularly pleasing.[23] Henry's answer details his frustration over the whole enterprise and particularly, 'Damn! I wanted 60,000 words recreating the Etaples mutiny; now I've popped it off in 600 words. I used all the stereotyped details of war books [of course he didn't]: reserving the fresh ones for my *real* war book . . . 500,000 words – 1894–1924. *The Hopeful Life.* 3 volumes. I'm flinching from beginning.' It was to be another twenty years before he wrote his '*real* war book' – then he used five out of the fifteen volumes of *A Chronicle of Ancient Sunlight* and about 1,000,000 words.

Modern editions of *The Patriot's Progress* carry an explanatory Preface by Williamson which first appeared in 1968, in which he prints in full both Arnold Bennett's review and the letter from T.E. Lawrence. In that edition there was also a two-page Epigraph, which included a copy of *The Times* obituary for William Kermode. It ended with words which epitomize the effect that the war had on Williamson for the whole of his life:

That battlefield . . . seen at night from aircraft (including Zeppelins) as a great livid wound stretching from the North Sea, or German Ocean, to the Alps, during four and a quarter years: a wound never ceasing to weep from wan dusk to gangrenous dawn, from sunrise to sunset of Europe in division . . . .

Similar words can be found in *A Test To Destruction* also published in 1968, where Williamson sets out an overview of the war at that point, but his use of these words at the end of *The Patriot's Progress* was not just for dramatic purpose. They are surely a pointer to the source of his idea for the book – a source that was an overwhelming influence on him in the years after the war, the writings of Barbusse:

And there amid the baleful glimmers of the storm, below the dark disorder of the clouds that extend and unfurl over the earth like evil spirits, they seem to see a great livid plain unrolled, which to their seeing is made of mud and water, while figures appear and fast fix themselves to the surface of it, all blinded and borned down with filth, like the dreadful castaways of shipwreck. And it seems to them that these are soldiers.

The streaming plain, seamed and seared with long parallel canals and scooped into water-holes, is an immensity, and these castaways who strive to exhume themselves from it are legion. But the thirty million slaves, hurled upon one another in the mud of war by guilt and error, uplift their human faces and reveal at last a bourgeoning Will. The future is in the hands of these slaves, and it is clearly certain that the alliance to be cemented some day by those whose number and whose misery alike are infinite will transform the old world.

This quotation comes from the opening chapter 'The Vision' of Henri Barbusse's *Le Feu*. Barbusse wrote *Le Feu* in six months while in hospital recovering from lung problems caused by an explosion in the trenches. This opening scene in *Le Feu* is somewhat surreal. Set in a sanatorium (the sanatorium in which Barbusse himself was recovering) the group of people in the scene are the patients of a ward. They are 'above and beyond' in a physical and a metaphysical sense. 'They' can be considered singular – their conversation is the fevered thoughts and imaginings of a person ill enough to be near to death, a hallucinated vision as they look down on the appalling scenes that that war will inevitably bring – just as in the vision that Williamson had in the bell tower when he too looked back at those appalling scenes. *Le Feu*, based on Barbusse's trench diaries, is a record of what it meant to be a private soldier of an infantry section day by day, in and out of the line; it is a living record of a profound and terrible human experience. So is *The Patriot's Progress*, and so too in a different way are the war volumes of *A Chronicle of Ancient Sunlight*.

Another pointer to Williamson's thoughts about Barbusse is found in *The Wet Flanders Plain* where he mentions the author to the French family with a shell-retarded son. They knew the work and told him that a German soldier had been there only the previous week, who had also read Barbusse and found the experiences in the book to be equally true for German soldiers.

Interestingly, where *The Wet Flanders Plain* opens with the sound of church bells catapulting Williamson back into the vision of war, so his essay 'Reality in War Literature',[24] written at about the same time, opens in a similar way. But here it is a car suddenly slowing down in the lane outside that provides the catalyst.

Barbusse plays a major role in 'Reality in War Literature'. 'Those of us interested in books begin to talk of the appearance of the great war book that shall stand somewhere near *War and Peace*.[25] Barbusse's *Le Feu*?' Williamson then quotes from *Le Feu* and continues: 'That is the writing of a man who has sight: and who can translate sight into words. . . .' Then as the essay gathers pace, Williamson compares each book he mentions against *Le Feu*, to their detriment.

It has already been seen that Barbusse influenced Williamson's thinking and leaning towards communism in the years after the war, but this influence goes even deeper. Barbusse's ethos is Williamson's ethos. Towards the end of *Le Feu*, there is an argument that is totally central to Williamson's thinking, in the chapter entitled 'The Refuge'. This is an ironic name for the place where the wounded are taken and which Barbusse described as an absolute hell-hole. A wounded aviator mumbles semi-deliriously to himself, making awful sense:

Up there, from the sky, you don't see much you know. . . . Last sunday morning I was flying over the firing-line. Between our first lines and their first lines . . . it's not very far; sometimes forty yards, sometimes sixty. To me it looked about a stride, at the great height I was planing. And behold I could make out two crowds, one among the Boches, and one of ours, ... Then I understood. It was Sunday, and there were two religious services being held under my eyes – the altar, the padre, and all the crowd of chaps. The more I went down, the more I could see that the two things were alike – so exactly alike that it looked silly. One of the services – whichever you like – was a reflection of the other, and I wondered if I was seeing double. . . . Then I could hear. I heard one murmur, one only. I could only gather a single prayer that came up to me *en bloc*, the sound of a single chant that passed by me on its way to heaven. . . . I made out two voices from the earth that made up the one – '*Gott mit uns!*' and 'God is with us!' – and I flew away.

Now think of it! Those two identical crowds yelling things that are identical and yet opposite, these identical enemy cries! What must the good God think about it all?

We know that Williamson always felt great anguish over the fact that the soldiers of both sides of the conflict thought that they were right and that God was on their side. He discovered this on that fateful Christmas Day in 1914, and it marked him for the rest of his life.

The last chapter of *Le Feu* returns to the 'great plain' exposition of the opening vision scene. That pre-vision has now come to pass. The few men left alive have sunk exhausted into the mire of a totally flooded plain. They are surrounded by a desolation relieved only by the bodies of the drowned dead. Dawn arrives.

Sinister and slow it comes, chilling and dismal, and expands upon the livid landscape. . . . My still living companions have at last got up. . . . They move and cry out . . . They are struggling against victorious spectres, like the Cyranos and Don Quixotes that they still are. . . .

But their eyes are opened. They are beginning to make out the boundless simplicity of things. And Truth not only invests them with a dawn of hope, but raises on it a renewal of strength and courage. . . .

And while we get ready to rejoin the others and begin war again, the dark and storm-choked sky slowly opens above our heads. Between two masses of gloomy cloud a tranquil gleam emerges; and that line of light, so black-edged and beset, brings even so its proof that the sun is there.

These same visionary thoughts about the sun are found in Richard Jefferies' more mystical writings. How Williamson found a copy of *The Story of my Heart* in a Folkestone bookshop in 1918 and its subsequent influence on his thought and writing is well known. In Jefferies' work the idea of sunlight – ancient sunlight – is propounded as the essence of life itself.

It was the phrase 'ancient sunlight'[26] that particularly caught Henry Williamson's imagination and it became the core of his own philosophy. His self-appointed life's task, Romantic and Quixotian though it may have been, was to prevent the world falling prey ever again to the predatory evil of war. He had a vision of a perfect world where all would be brothers under an ancient sunlight which had shone since time began and would continue to shine through eternity – a world where greed and war would not exist, and where Truth alone would obtain. There is no way that he could have succeeded in such a task even apart from the fact that his purpose has tended to be misrepresented (although some of that has been his own fault). But despite being misunderstood by many he remained true to his self-appointed purpose, and in the course of endeavouring to achieve this he wrote some of the finest books of the twentieth century, particularly those concerning the First World War, ever the most important element in his life.

This chapter has examined Williamson's earlier writings of the immediate post-war period on the subject but, as has been established, from the very beginning of his writing career he had always planned a parallel series to his early tetralogy *The Flax of Dream*, which would have Willie Maddison's cousin Phillip as the central character and which would encompass those war years so noticeably not included in *The Flax* (when his psychological war wounds were still too raw and painful for examination and exposure).

Williamson set out his own criteria for the book that would stand up against Tolstoy's *War and Peace*, the epitome of war books, in that early essay 'Reality in War Literature' – a book that would encompass: 'the sense of reality in action, verging on the unreal, as though time were being withdrawn from the world and the power responsible were endeavouring to substitute a Fourth Dimension, which was beyond control and dragging life backwards into chaos.'

It is obvious now that he was referring to his own work, not then written but structurally planned in his mind, the work that we know as *A Chronicle of Ancient Sunlight*, as the work that would meet that criteria. He did not begin properly to write this series of novels until 1949 when his return to Devon and subsequent second marriage gave him the impetus of a fresh start, a second wind. Then he worked solidly for twenty years to produce the eventual fifteen volumes, one of which appeared almost every year. This was a prodigious feat: the volumes average about 200,000 words each, and apart from the task of writing much research had to be undertaken, especially for those five First World War volumes. Apart from the *Official History* there are over 200 other books about the First World War in his archive and a very large number of them contain notes which show how carefully he checked every detail. Proof reading of any one volume necessarily overlapped the writing of the next. Add to that the fact that Henry was a compulsive revisionist, for example there are about twenty versions of the penultimate volume *Lucifer Before Sunrise*,[27] and one can begin to appreciate what he achieved.

The intensity of his feelings about the war itself, its effect on his life, and his knowledge of the enormity of the task ahead of him can be seen in an extract from a 'Journal' he kept in December 1946, written in a school exercise book:

Christmas time is always, as it approaches, a sensitive time for me, & I tend to immolate myself, turn towards death and darkness, & have a picture of myself eating nothing, keeping alone & perhaps walking to exhaustion point for several days without food, sleeping out in the rain & cold & so reduce myself to a ghost. . . .

Christmas Day 1914: the awful rain of the November month; the freezing trenches 3 ft. deep in yellow clay & water; . . . I want to write the Phillip M. novels with all the details, every single detail, being the cause of a later effect, in all the characters. This has never been done in literature, & it is my dream & has been since 1919. Such a work, if produced, would be accepted by all human beings. . . . But, O God, it will take every ounce of my strength & will require years of calmness & serenity. . . .

To resume:— Christmas Day 1914, the fear & dread of our Noman's Land wiring party, coming after the nightmare attack over the same ground on 19 December, when we were shot up & screamed in fear as we fell & hid in 4 ft. of greenish shell-hole water, & I raved in my mind for what Mummie would feel if I were killed — me DEAD, oh God save me, O Christ save me, I am lost, O Jesu help us, we all thought & wept — Christmas Day followed after a quiet moonlight Eve when the 'Huns' heard us but did not shoot. Not one shot went off from their trenches in the turnip field only 50 yards away — & we worked with a lightness & joy until 2 am & then filed back to the water dripping blockhouses. . . The next day the miracle was manifest. . . .

This is an emotional outburst which is not found in Henry's published writings on the war and it contains the essence of everything he felt and stood for.

Williamson actually returns to Tolstoy's *War and Peace* in *Lucifer Before Sunrise* where Chapter 14 is entitled 'War and Peace'. Although he is referring to the Second World War at this point, his thought arises from the powerful influence of his experience of the First World War:

> If I do not survive this war who will write a novel of our times, transcending 'War and Peace'? . . . no European writer of the future worth his salt will fail to strive to understand the phenomenon of the conflicting views of this war. . . . He must create 'character, environment and action' out of a common humanity and relate all the effects of peace to all the causes of war.

Gathering all these points together we can now see what Henry Williamson was trying to achieve in his writing about the First World War, the 'Fourth Dimension' he was seeking – a dimension which goes 'Beyond Reality'. Examination of his writings (the two earlier books *The Wet Flanders Plain* and *The Patriot's Progress* and the five war volumes of Henry Williamson's *A Chronicle of Ancient Sunlight*) shows us that Henry Williamson's purpose does indeed go far beyond the mere retelling of his own experience, encompassing the whole spectrum of the Western Front – a total experience of those four years of war. In examining his fictional work against the reality portrayed in this volume one gains the deepest respect for the structure and skill inherent in his writings. The interweaving of his own experiences and those of his contemporaries, coupled with his meticulous research into the overall war scenario, resulted in a tour-de-force. His books stand as a vital memorial to all those who took part in that war.

Henry Williamson's owl colophon, which appeared at the end of every one of his books.

Appendix

The Western Front, 1914–18.

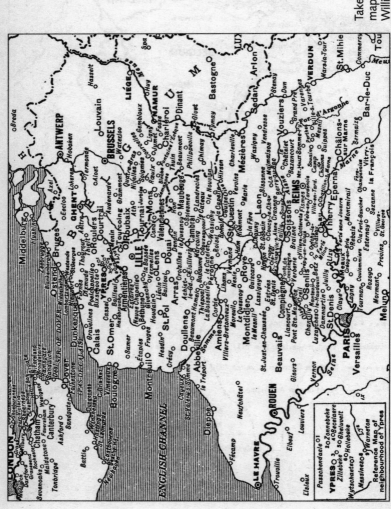

Taken from a small loose map found folded in Williamson's archive.

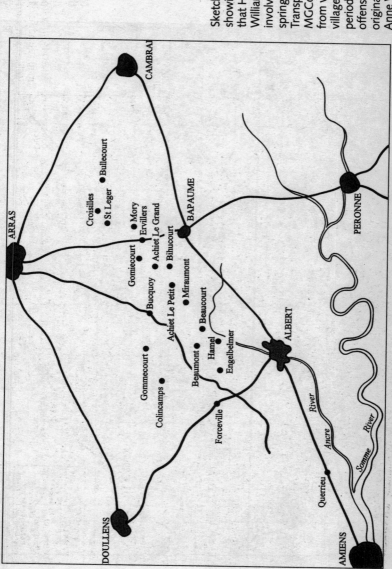

Sketch map showing the area that Henry Williamson was involved in during spring 1917, as Transport Officer, MGCoy. He moved from village to village over the period of the offensive. (From an original drawing by Anne Williamson.)

Map showing the situation at the Front on 18 March 1917 from Henry Williamson's archive

Notes

The following abbreviations are used throughout the Notes:

Henry Williamson: HW; The Henry Williamson Literary Estate Archive: HWLEA; The Henry Williamson Society: HWS; The Henry Williamson Society Journal: HWSJ

PREFACE

1. Henry Williamson, *A Chronicle of Ancient Sunlight* in fifteen volumes (Macdonald, 1951–69). The five 'war' volumes are: vol. 4, *How Dear Is Life* (Macdonald, 1954, 1984; paperback edn Sutton Publishing, 1995); vol. 5, *A Fox Under My Cloak* (Macdonald, 1955, 1984; paperback edn Sutton Publishing, 1996); vol. 6, *The Golden Virgin* (Macdonald, 1957, 1984; paperback edn Sutton Publishing, 1996); vol. 7, *Love and The Loveless* (Macdonald, 1958, 1984; paperback edn Sutton Publishing, 1997); vol. 8, *A Test to Destruction* (Macdonald, 1960, 1984; paperback edn Sutton Publishing, 1997). (These are main editions only; other editions have been published.)

2. Henry Williamson, *The Wet Flanders Plain* (limited edn Beaumont Press, 1929; Faber, 1929; Dutton USA, 1929; new edn with introduction by Richard Williamson and additional material, Gliddon Books, 1987).

3. Henry Williamson, *The Patriot's Progress* (Geoffrey Bles, 1930; with new preface and epigraph by HW, Macdonald, 1968; paperback edn Little Brown, 1991; paperback edn, Sutton Publishing, 2004).

4. Letter: HW to Captain Sir Basil Liddell Hart, 9 July 1939 (Copyright © Henry Williamson Literary Estate). Copy of letter: Basil Liddell Hart to HW, 22 July 1939. Both in the Liddell Hart Centre for Military Archives, King's College, London. For further illumination on HW's actions and state of mind at this time, see Anne Williamson, *Henry Williamson: Tarka and the Last Romantic* (hereafter *Henry Williamson*) (Sutton Publishing, 1995, paperback edn 1997), pp. 227–8, and chapter 6 'The Last Romantic', pp. 187–205, where it is shown that he was a Romantic rather than a Fascist. His involvement with the British Union in the late 1930s was purely because he thought the movement would stabilize the agricultural industry (he came from farming stock and became a farmer himself in 1937) and that they were also working for a peaceful solution to the looming threat of war.

5. Anne Williamson, *Henry Williamson* for further information.

6. *History of the Great War, Based on Official Documents. Military Operations. Belgium and France,* in several volumes published by Macmillan over many years. (Hereafter, *Official History.*) Individual volumes are referred to in situ.

7. Henry Williamson, 'Reflections on the Death of a Field Marshal', *Contemporary Review*, vol. 218, no. 1265 (June 1971), pp. 303–13. This arose out of the film *Oh What a Lovely War!*, which has scenes lampooning Haig and his wife. Williamson does not criticize the film itself, acknowledging its merit, but seeks to redress the balance on Earl and Lady Haig, drawing on his own experience as a soldier of the Western Front. Williamson points out that the German war historians considered Haig to have been 'a master of the field' and that after the war Haig worked tirelessly and unceasingly with the British Legion on behalf of ex-servicemen until he died worn out at the age of fifty-eight.

8. Recent research has revealed that Galsworthy's mother, Blanche Bartleet, and HW's great-grandmother Eliza Bartleet were cousins. See Anne Williamson, *Henry Williamson*, paperback edn p. 9; also Anne Williamson, 'Biographical Matters', HWSJ, no. 32, September 1996, 'Frankley-Hagley: An examination of the relationship between John Galsworthy and Henry Williamson', pp. 50–5.

CHAPTER 1: A DREAMING YOUTH

1. Henry Williamson, 'The Last Summer', *Sunday Times Magazine*, August 1964. Reprinted in Henry Williamson, *From A Country Hilltop*, ed. John Gregory (HWS, 1988).

2. Colfe's Grammar School still exists today. Details about HW's schooldays can be found in Anne Williamson, *Henry Williamson*.

3. Henry Williamson, *Dandelion Days*, vol. 2, *The Flax of Dream* tetralogy (Collins, 1922, rev. edn, 1930). This book gives a very accurate picture, although fictionalized, of the author's schooldays. Here Colfe's School is translated to the West Country and is called Colham.

4. Henry Williamson, *The Lone Swallows* (Collins, 1922). A collection of natural history essays.

5. William Wordsworth, *The Prelude*, Book I, 1850.
> 'Fair seed-time had my soul, and I grew up
> Fostered alike by beauty and by fear.'

6. Further information about the family connection can be found in Anne Williamson, *Henry Williamson*. Williamson invariably spelt the name Boone with a final 'e' although the official record on the war memorial recording Charlie's death spells it without. A family member has confirmed 'Boon' is correct.

7. The question of the Georgeham cottage is examined in Anne Williamson, *Henry Williamson*. The background of the cottage and the family use of it has not been entirely resolved, but they had access to it and HW visited it several times during the course of the war before finally going to live there in 1921.

CHAPTER 2: PRIVATE 9689 AND THE LONDON RIFLE BRIGADE

1. This is the official date on HW's 'Certificate of Discharge' from the London Rifle Brigade on taking up a commission in April 1915.

2. *How Dear is Life*, p. 95.

3. K.W. Mitchinson, *Gentlemen and Officers: The Impact and Experience of War on a Territorial Regiment, 1914–18* (Imperial War Museum, 1995), p. 19.

4. Ibid., p. 21.

5. *Short History of the London Rifle Brigade*, compiled Regimentally (1916). This volume is in HW's literary archive. There is no author's name mentioned in the book but there is a letter inside from Col. Norman C. King (Commanding Officer 3rd Battalion, LRB, during First World War) to Williamson written in 1941. Col. King had just read *The Story of a Norfolk Farm*, 'with surprising interest because I am a Cockney born'. He had deduced that Williamson had been in the LRB from his reference to 'Plug Street' and offered to send HW a copy of 'Col. Bates's Short History' – which the present volume obviously is (although Williamson probably already had this book as there are two copies in his archive). The frontispiece of this volume is a photograph of Lt. Col. N.C. King, TD, Comdg. 3rd Battn, Lt. Col. A.S. Bates, DSO, Comdg. 1st Battn, and Lt. Col. G.R. Tod, Comdg. 2nd Battn.

6. Mitchinson, *Gentlemen and Officers*, p. 13.

7. *Short History, LRB*, p. 2.

8. Ibid., p. 6.

9. Mitchinson, *Gentlemen and Officers*, p. 22, states that this team was '60 men under Captain Husey and Sgt. Dick Wallis'; *Short History, LRB*, states the team was under Capt. Husey and Lt. Large. This is only briefly mentioned in *How Dear is Life*, where Phillip is parading with his company in Hyde Park after mobilization led by 'Captain Forbes, sturdy and red of hair, brows and moustache – the fiery Forbes who had led the famous record-breaking London–Brighton march' (p. 146). Although HW would not have wanted to draw attention to the LRB within the fictional scenario he was creating with the 'London Highlanders' (in real life the London Scottish) he could not resist the reference to Husey's famous exploit.

10. Mitchinson, *Gentlemen and Officers*, p. 25.

11. Ibid.

12. *How Dear is Life*, p. 126.

13. These headlines are taken from a page depicting facsimile newspapers from *News In Our Time: Golden Jubilee Book of the Daily Mail 1896–1946* (Associated Newspapers Ltd, London, 1946). This volume is in HW's literary archive. I am sure that this is where HW himself obtained the headlines he used in his novel, rather than the original newspapers. This book contains one or two manuscript notes in the margin (although not on this page) mostly expressing irritability with the *Daily Mail* commentary, especially where dates are not expressly noted on news items Williamson wanted to refer to. There is also a very agitated note by Henry contradicting the opinion given of the Kaiser, shown in a very bad light in this book. I think that it is from this volume that HW thought up the idea of Richard Maddison taking the *Daily Trident* (i.e. the *Daily Mail*). The description on the opening page of this book of the placard hoardings used as advertisements, particularly the colours, corresponds exactly with the description in the novel and Richard's thoughts about taking it on a regular basis when it came out in

1896. HW was not even one year old at that time, therefore this cannot be a 'memory'.

14. Ibid.

15. 'Captain Forbes' is Capt. Husey (later Lt. Col. R.H. Husey, DSO, Commanding Officer 1st Battn, LRB, August 1916–August 1917, and Dec. 1917–May 1918), despite the fact that in the novel he is in the 'London Highlanders' (the London Scottish). 'Baldwin' was in real life Williamson's fellow soldier in the LRB, Private E.W. Baldwin, who was killed in action in May 1915 at Menin Gate (see Mitchinson, *Gentlemen and Officers*, p. 277). In his novel Williamson has him killed in the London Highlanders' first offensive at the Front. This device would have been to simplify his storyline: he had wanted to record Baldwin's death, but by the time it occurred Phillip was no longer at the Front (nor was HW himself) so he transferred it to an earlier date. Mitchinson, *Gentlemen and Officers*, has a photograph captioned 'Henry Williamson's friend, Baldwin'.

16. The commandeering of horses is referred to again in *How Dear is Life*, p. 147: 'They saw more drivers of carriages, carts, and even a milk float, being interrogated by soldiers wearing spurs and bandoliers.' That horses were commandeered is borne out in Mitchinson, *Gentlemen and Officers*, p. 32, where he describes how there was some confusion in the provision of equipment (priority would have been given to the regular army) which explains the 'activities of the LRB in trying to round up sufficient horses and carts from the streets around Bunhill Row'.

17. 'Old Bird' is F.W. Lucas, the Headmaster of Colfe's Grammar School; 'Duncan' is Leland Duncan, an old boy who was by that time a distinguished historian (he was the author of *A History of Colfe's Grammar School*, a tome presented to the boys as they left school, and other volumes), chairman of the Old Boys' Association, and editor of their magazine. Rupert Bryers was one of Henry's great friends from school, who left in 1912 and who features in Williamson's books. He enlisted in May 1915, was missing and presumed killed in September 1916. (Ref. Leland Duncan, *Colfe's Grammar School and the Great War*, 1920.)

18. There were two Barnes brothers who had been at Colfe's Grammar School during 1907–12, Rowland and Leslie. Both served in the London Scottish. This is Rowland, who joined in June 1914. (Ref. Duncan, *Colfe's Grammar School and the Great War*.)

19. Mitchinson names this man as Sgt. Cook 'Tootsie' Hands, a reservist with over twenty years' regular service. Mitchinson, *Gentlemen and Officers*, p. 36.

20. Mitchinson refers to *Chyebassa* as 'formerly an Orient Line cattle ship'. In fact SS *Chyebassa*, built in Belfast in 1907, speed 12 knots, tonnage 6249, was a cargo vessel belonging to the British India Steam Navigation Company and was one of six sister ships of their C-Class, designed for main liner service with accommodation amidships for cabin passengers. These ships traded between Middlesborough and London to Antwerp, Bombay and Karachi.

The history of this company can be found in W.A. Laxton and F.W. Perry, *The British India Steam Navigation Company Limited* (World Ship Society, 1994). The reference to SS *Chyebassa* states: 'The *Chyebassa* was in home waters at Middlesbrough on the outbreak of war and was taken up as an Expeditionary Force transport on 7 August. . . . Among her tasks she transported 1/5 London Regt. (London Rifle Brigade) from Southampton to Havre in November 1914, forging a link between the Brigade and the ship which was cemented by the presentation of the ship's bell after she was sold out of service. The *Chyebassa* was released from transport duty in March 1916 and then came under the Liner Requisition Scheme between 1917 and 1919.' On 8 December 1917 she was torpedoed by UC25 in the Mediterranean but did not sink and was taken to Malta and repaired. *Chyebassa* gave long and good service to the British India Company and was finally sold in 1938 for £11,500 at Antwerp. She was broken up in Italy the following year. (I am indebted to Brian Dolan for researching this item.)

Strangely, although Mitchinson, *Gentlemen and Officers*, refers to Williamson in his text, and quotes short passages from his novels and the tape made by HW for the Imperial War Museum, he does not include Williamson's name on the list of those who embarked for France on the *Chyebassa*. Furthermore, there are several names of survivors listed on the post-war *Chyebassa* reunion dinner menus that are in Williamson's literary archive that also do not appear on Mitchinson's list. It is surprising that apparently an official list was not made and kept in the Regiment's own records.

What Mitchinson does clarify and endorse is that when HW left for 'overseas service' he was technically under-age (albeit by only one month). As borne out by HW's letters, volunteers were supposed to have passed their nineteenth birthday. 'Others like Harding . . . and Williamson were also under age but managed to convince the authorities that they should not be left behind.' (Mitchinson, *Gentlemen and Officers*, p. 33.) This may be the basis for Williamson's often repeated claim that he was under-age when he volunteered, for which he has been greatly criticized but which on this technical point can be seen to be correct.

Mitchinson has an entry for 'Harding' (as above) on p. 280. As an employee of the Sun Fire Assurance Office, who joined the LRB in Feb. 1914 with a number very close to Williamson's own, he is possibly 'Edgar' from *How Dear is Life*, although HW does not appear to have used him in a war context in the novels.

21. Mitchinson, *Gentlemen and Officers* p. 43.

CHAPTER 3: IN THE TRENCHES – CHRISTMAS 1914

1. *Short History, LRB,* gives a list of thirty names of officers on embarkation: Lt. Col. W.D. Earl Cairns (*Commanding*); Lt. Col. (Hon. Col.) C.G.R. Matthey, VD (*Second-in-command*); Maj. N.C. King, TD. *Captains:* A.S. Bates [later Col., DSO]; M.H. Soames; R.H. Husey; C.H.F. Thompson; H.F. MacGeagh; J.R. Somers-Smith; A.C. Lintott; Hon. Maj. C.D. Burnell. *Lieutenants:* R.E. Otter; J.G. Robinson; G.H. Morrison; E.L. Large; P.A. Slessor; H.B. Price; A.G. Kirby; G.H. Cholmeley. *Second-Lieutenants:* K. Forbes; G.H.G.M. Cartwright; W.L. Willett; H.L. Johnston; C.W. Trevelyan; H.G. Vincent; G.E.S. Fursdon; G.C. Kitchin. *Adjutant:* Capt. A.C. Oppenheim, KRRC. *Quartermaster:* Lt. J.R.S. Petersen. *Medical Officer:* Maj. A.D. Ducat, TD.

Mitchinson, *Gentlemen and Officers*, states that the actual number of 'other ranks' varies according to the source consulted – but there would have been over eight hundred, whatever the final figure might have been.

2. *Official History*, 1914, vol. 1, 3rd edn (Macmillan, 1933). Compiled by Brig. Gen. Sir James E. Edmonds, CB, CMG. See map on p. 15. This particular map is undated and does not give a strictly accurate picture as the German Armies are depicted as along but outside the Belgian border while the BEF is in situ. By the time the BEF was in situ the German Armies had advanced well into Belgium. However, it does show the overall strengths of the various forces.

3. There is a newspaper cutting in Williamson's literary archive of a letter from Maj. Gen. F.R. Bingham, undated and addressed to the Editor of *The Times*, which sheds interesting light on Gen. Sir Smith-Dorrien's stand at Le Cateau: 'Sir, As Volume I of the *Official History* of the War has just appeared giving the details of the retreat from Mons, the following may be of interest:- I was Chief of the British Section of the Military Inter-Allied Commission of Control in Germany from 1919 to 1924 and had occasion to meet General von Kluck, who commanded the German First Army in 1914. On one occasion I asked him if he had any message for General Sir Horace Smith-Dorrien who had fought against him at Le Cateau. His answer was, "Yes, tell the General that if he had not stopped and fought as he did at Le Cateau, I should have turned the flank of the British Army and taken Paris." I am, Sir, yours, F.R. Bingham, Major-General (Retired) etc.'

However, Field Marshal Viscount French of Ypres, KP, OM, etc., in his book *1914* (Constable, 1919) criticized Smith-Dorrien's decision as contrary to the battle plans, and thus causing problems.

4. Although it does not have any place within this immediate story, the enormous losses suffered by countries other than Britain during the First World War must not be forgotten. France and Belgium, of course, and other Allies, particularly British Dominions, suffered greatly. Equally fierce fighting on the Eastern Front also decimated the Russians, but meant that the German force had to split in order to hold both fronts at once – the supreme weakness of the Schlieffen Plan (prepared by Count Alfred von Schlieffen in 1905, it assumed the Russian Front would be weak and easily held, allowing attack of France via Holland and Belgium to be completed in six weeks).

5. John Terraine, *The First World War 1914–18* (Macmillan, 1965), p. 34, relates that Sir John French stated he was preparing to retreat in full; this brought Lord Kitchener furiously to Paris on 1 September to countermand this and order cooperation with France. (No reference given for this statement.)

6. *Official History*, 1914, vol. 1, map.

7. Ibid., p. 456 ff. and Sketch 21.

8. HW's letter to his father dated 19 September 1914 states 'The London Scottish (Barnes is in it) is in Paris'. This seems extraordinarily good intelligence for a lowly private to have acquired so quickly. Even if Barnes had written to him he surely would not have been able to mention such a fact. This shows that Williamson had very good knowledge of the London Scottish, either through

Barnes or some similar contact, which would have given him a sound base when he decided to put Phillip in the 'London Highlanders' in *A Chronicle of Ancient Sunlight* in due course.

9. J.L. Lindsay, *The London Scottish in the Great War* (1925) quoted in Mitchinson, *Gentlemen and Officers*. A full examination of the movements etc. of the 'London Highlanders' as in Williamson's novel and the actual movements of the London Scottish at this time can be found in Peter Cole, 'The London Highlanders', HWSJ, no. 14, September 1986, pp. 6–17.

10. *Official History*, 1914, vol. 1, p. 307. These numbers differ from those given in Lindsay, *The London Scottish*, which states 394 killed.

11. French, 1914.

12. These dates and times would appear to be taken from the *Official History*.

13. French, 1914, p. 262–3.

14. *Short History*, LRB, p. 9.

15. *How Dear is Life*, chapter 18, 'Lines of Communication', pp. 216–17.

16. *Short History*, LRB, p. 9.

17. Capt. J.R. Somers-Smith – see list of officers given in note 1 of this chapter.

18. HW added the place-names into the margins of his copy of the *Short History*, LRB as they had to be left out at the time of publishing but these names are well known today.

19. *Short History*, LRB, p. 9.

20. Ibid., p. 10.

21. Mitchinson, *Gentlemen and Officers*, p. 44.

22. The Official Records state that there was a clearing hospital at St-Omer. This would seem to be the only place that HW could have met Barnes.

23. At this time a Second Lieutenant and Officer of Williamson's platoon, G.E.S. Fursdon was later promoted to Captain. HW met up with him again at the *Chyebassa* reunion dinner in 1926, and some contact was maintained. It was Fursdon's son John who married HW's second wife, Christine, after their divorce in 1968. See entries in Anne Williamson, *Henry Williamson*.

24. *Official History*, 1914, vol. 2, p. 460.

25. *Short History*, LRB, pp. 10–11.

26. Ibid. Romarin was a tiny hamlet to the south-west of Ploegsteert.

27. This is reference to a visit made by Henry and his mother, accompanied by her father, Thomas Leaver, and other family members, to visit his sister Kathie at the convent she attended in Thildonck (north-east of Brussels) in Belgium. See Anne Williamson, *Henry Williamson*, p. 23. This visit appears in *Young Phillip Maddison*, vol. 3 of *A Chronicle of Ancient Sunlight*, chapter 28, 'Jaunt to Belgium'.

28. This statement is a mystery. There is no evidence within HW's literary archive to suggest that his grandfather was ever in the army and researcher Brian Dolan has not found his name in Army Records. He was a quantity surveyor by profession, and appears as such or similar in all census records found. It is possible that Henry has made a mistake here and referred to his grandfather when he meant some other member of the family. However, HW does make him 'Captain' Maddison in the *Chronicle* novels and in real life he

married the daughter of Capt. Josef Luhn (of German nationality but who may have been fighting in a British contingent), which suggests that there could have been an Army connection.

29. *Official History*, 1915, vol. 1, p. 5. The reference to Brig. Gen. Hunter Weston, 11th Inf. Bde, has this marginal note 'Hunter-Bunter' by Williamson. Hunter Weston is the person who had the idea of naming trenches etc. to make them more easily recognized and accessed.

30. *Short History*, LRB, p. 11.

31. *Official History*, 1915, vol. 1, p.5, reference to duckboards and Williamson's marginal note.

32. *Official History*, 1915, vol. 1, p. 12.

33. *A Fox Under My Cloak*.

34. *Official History*, 1915, vol. 1, p. 19 and Appendix 8, p. 380.

35. Mitchinson, *Gentlemen and Officers*, p. 48.

36. *Short History*, LRB, pp. 12–13.

37. Tape made by HW for the Imperial War Museum, copy in the HWLEA. Quoted by Mitchinson, *Gentlemen and Officers*, p. 48. This tape in its entirety is quite muddled and repetitive. Although of interest it should not be considered as a totally accurate record of the truth.

38. *A Fox Under My Cloak*, p. 25.

39. A photograph of troops wearing these goat skin jerkins appears in Philip J. Haythornthwaite, *A Photohistory of World War One*, photograph 83, captioned: 'In the winter of 1914 a most unusual garment was issued to the British Expeditionary Force: Goatskin coats and jerkins to combat the cold weather. Nicknamed 'Teddy Bears' by the British troops, the garments came in all colours and designs which may be observed from this company parade just behind the front line in late November or early December 1914.' This is one of the few photographs in the book where the troops' regiments etc. are not detailed, which is a great pity since one of the men looks extremely like HW. There is also a photograph of LRB men wearing these garments in Mitchinson, *Gentlemen and Officers* but taken after Williamson had left the Regiment.

40. Mitchinson, *Gentlemen and Officers*, pp. 52–3.

41. *Official History*, 1915, vol. 1, p. 23.

42. The date given on the official form detailing his service with the LRB on gaining his commission; see plate 11b.

43. Information about the hospital is held in the archives of Manchester City Library and I am grateful to the archivist, Mrs Sarah Sherratt, for sending a brief outline. Ancoats Hospital started life as the Ardwick and Ancoats Dispensary in 1828. Eventually it moved to larger premises in 1873 and was able then to make provision for beds and became a voluntary hospital run by subscription and benefactors. In 1904 funds allowed for a convalescent home to be built nearby at Alderley Edge. This finally closed in 1967. There is apparently no reference to its use as a military hospital for the duration of the First World War in the records.

44. *KING ALBERT'S BOOK: A Tribute to the Belgian King and People from Representative Men*

and Women throughout the World, published by the *Daily Telegraph* in conjunction with the *Daily Sketch*, the *Glasgow Herald*, and Hodder and Stoughton. No publication date is given but it must have come out as 1914/15 turned. This extraordinary collection of tributes and thoughts on war includes numerous reproductions of paintings (in full colour and tipped in). I quote from the editor Hall Caine's 'Introduction' at length because despite its hyperbole, it does sum up the state of war and the hopelessness of the Belgian situation in a way that official accounts cannot by their nature do: 'The immediate object of this Book is to offer, in the names and by the pens of a large group of the representative men and women of the civilised countries, a tribute of admiration to Belgium, on the heroic and ever-memorable share she has taken in the war which now convulses Europe, and at the same time to invoke the world's sympathy, its help and its prayers for the gallant little nation in the vast sorrow of its present condition. . . . During the past fateful months, Belgium has fought not only her own battle but also the battle of France, the battle of Great Britain and the battle of Freedom. . . . But she has paid a terrible penalty. . . . A complete nation is in ruin. A whole country is in ashes. An entire people are destitute, homeless and on the roads.'

The list of names of the contributors is illustrious, and the volume is worth consulting as a phenomenal product of the time.

CHAPTER 4: PROMOTION

1. In conversation with Richard and Anne Williamson.

2. French, 1914, pp. 288–90.

3. *Colfensia*, 1915, pp. 23–4.

4. Ibid., p. 43.

5. Details taken from *The Times History of the War* (The Times, 1919), vol. XX, chapter CCXCIX, 'Special Constables', pp. 377–96.

6. See *The Dark Lantern*, vol. 1 of *A Chronicle of Ancient Sunlight* (Macdonald, 1951, 1984; paperback edn Sutton Publishing, 1995), p. 110: 'Round Trafalgar Square, with its memories for Richard of Bloody Sunday of November 1887, when as a constable specially enrolled, he had been on duty with others in a vedette just off the Strand in Northumberland Avenue. . . . An evil agitator, John Burns the socialist, and a traitor to his class named Robert Cunninghame-Graham, had been sent to prison for their parts in what might easily have become an insurrection, but for the determination of all good men and true. A red-bearded Irish ruffian named George Bernard Shaw, after making an incendiary speech, had escaped.'

Williamson sets out very nicely here Richard Maddison's hidebound attitude regarding established order; calling the now highly respected GBS a 'ruffian' pinpoints this. Henry must have heard his father's views on this at length. Thus the author brings into his tale an interesting real-life incident that happened before the opening of the *Chronicle* novels. However, although the main details are correct historically he did use a little poetic licence.

Brian Dolan checked The Times indexes for 1887 and found several reports of Socialist meetings and marches but references are to 'disorder' rather than 'riot'. The incident referred to would appear to be that reported in The Times, 5 December 1887, p. 10, col. 6, headed 'The Police and the Socialists': 'The people were invited by a handbill, which was widely distributed over the metropolis during the week, to come to Trafalgar-square yesterday afternoon in their "myriads" to protest against "Police rule in London". Certain Socialists made an appearance there yesterday, backed up by a few well-known Home Rulers in and out of Parliament. At three o'clock [presumably the time for the meeting] it was very quiet and neither police nor people were to be seen. But a quarter of an hour later, when the public houses had closed, crowds began to collect. . . . The police were as rapidly increased and the mob followed certain Socialists across to the Union Club. . . . Rushes were made from time to time by the unruly, and a large number ran down Whitehall booing at the police. The police arrangements for maintaining order were complete in every way. The avenues leading to the square were well protected. . . . The special constables were not in evidence but bodies of them were ready in barracks and other places. . . . Maj. Smith had also over 1,700 special constables detailed for duty. They fell in at half past 2 o'clock in the afternoon on the Thames embankment.'

This report goes on to show that Mr John Burns (who in HW's archive copy of Pear's Encyclopaedia [45th edn, no date] is referred to as 'b. 1858 – a prominent Parliamentary Labour representative. A working man and a friend of working men and came into prominence during the great strike of dockers [Aug/Sept 1889]') and Mr R.B. Cunninghame-Graham (Pears, 'b. 1852 – a well-known author who has written numerous works on Spanish-American life') were actually addressing a demonstration in Glasgow – but Cunninghame-Graham had not attended due to illness. The gathering was smaller than expected and John Burns had said he was 'ashamed of the apathy of the Scotch workmen' and 'he feared that Mr. Cunninghame-Graham and himself would get six months imprisonment . . .'.

George Bernard Shaw (b. 1856) was not mentioned in this report, although there are veiled references to 'Socialists'. Shaw had, of course, written many Socialist pamphlets and was prominent in the Fabian Society formed in 1883 with Socialist aims.

A letter printed in The Times on 21 October 1887, headed 'Socialist Disorder' and complaining about the 'present disgraceful outbreaks near Trafalgar-square' shows these disruptive meetings continued over quite a long period that autumn.

7. We learn how seriously William Leopold took his work and how strict he was via the Chronicle, particularly by the grumblings of Special Constable 'Sailor' Jenkins, who lived in the same street and who is seen from the 'Notebook' entry to be in real life Horace F. Welch of No. 8 Eastern Road.

8. In the Chronicle Phillip is encouraged to do this by Tom Cundall: 'All the county regiments are taking on a dozen and more service battalions, for Kitchener's New Armies. You'd get your pip tomorrow, if you applied. Get a blue

form from the War Office at once, man! Then get your Colonel to sign it. Simple!' (*A Fox Under My Cloak*, p. 104.) Tom Cundall's real-life counterpart was Victor Yeates, the friend from Colfe's, who was later – when dying of TB – to enlist Williamson's help in writing his own book, *Winged Victory*.

9. Mitchinson, *Gentlemen and Officers*, p. 85.

10. Maj. Norman King, TD, had gone out to France with the original 1st Battalion in November 1914 but had been invalided home and was promoted to Lt. Col. It is he who wrote to HW in 1941 and sent him a copy of the *Short History*, LRB. Lt. Col. Earl Cairns also left the 1st Battalion through ill health in March 1915 and the command was taken over by Maj. A.S. Bates, now promoted from the rank of Capt. that he went out with on 4 November 1914, and further promoted to Lt. Col. by 1916, with DSO. Short History, LRB.

11. Ibid.

12. Williamson's description at this point in *A Fox Under My Cloak*, chapter 9, 'In Clover', p. 130, of the Regimental badge as 'a star of many rays embossed in the centre with a wild ox with big horns' is a disguising factor; the badge of the Bedford Regiment contained a deer showing antlers in the centre.

13. In the novel Phillip also buys a regimental brooch for Helena Rolls (Doris Nicholson in real life). See Anne Williamson, 'Helena Rolls Brooch', HWSJ, no. 33, September 1997, pp.48–9.

14. *Official History*, 1915, vol. 1, Battle of Neuve-Chapelle, pp. 74–156.

15. Ibid., pp. 176–7. Mention of this can be found in *A Fox Under My Cloak*, chapter 10, 'Helena', p. 162, including the making of home-made gasmasks. Reference to these can be found in several volumes, including *The Times History of the War*, vol. XXII, p. 385, which shows a picture of a special constable wearing a thick wad of cloth over his nose, mouth and chin and tied behind his head. A note underneath states: 'Hundreds of thousands of these respirators were hurriedly made by the people and sent to the Western Front after the Second Battle of Ypres. They were, however, speedily replaced by more efficient gasmasks.'

16. *Official History*, p. 355.

17. Names of officers of the Cambridgeshire Regiment are found in The Army List, columns 1565–8, and include Lt. Col. C.T. Heycock, Maj. G.B. Bowes, Maj. A.A. Howell, Capt. G.D. Pryor (Adjt.), Capt. W.P. Cutlack, and Lt. T.H. Formby. (Research by Brian Dolan.)

Who was Who, 1929–1940 shows that Charles Thomas Heycock, MA, FRS, was a lecturer firstly at King's College Cambridge and later reader in Metallurgy at Goldsmith's. He had been Colonel Commanding of 3 Cambs. V.B., Suffolk Regiment, Infantry CUOTC, and 2/1st Batt. Cambridgeshire Regt. Born in August 1858, he died in June 1931.

Thomas Hope Formby died in action on 13 October 1916 at Thiepval and was gazetted as Capt. after his death. His death was reported in the *Cambridge Independent Press* (oddly dated 24 August 1917), which gave details of the attack on the Schwaben Redoubt on 14 October 1916: 'The morning before the attack the Commanding Officer took all the officers who were going over in the attack with him over the whole ground, or as much of it as the enemy would allow them to go over. In this reconnaissance two officers were lost – Capt. Formby and Lt. Scott.' (Information sent by Peter Cole.)

Brian Dolan checked Formby's administration of effects (granted to his widow living in Sutton) which show that he was not well off at all, the amount being a paltry £10 9s. 4d.. However, he no doubt would have had expectations from the family property at Formby Hall in Lancashire had he lived. (Research by Brian Dolan.) Entries are also found in the Regimental history, *The Cambridgeshires 1914 to 1919*. Further information confirming the fictional identities of these characters is contained in a letter from HW to John Gregory, written in the 1960s.

Peter Cole has found several references to members of the Cambridgeshire Regiment in local papers which confirm various details given in HW's writings. Some have been incorporated into the present text.

18. *A Fox Under My Cloak*, chapter 14, 'Spree Continued', p. 218.

19. Capt. Frank Charlton Jonas, 1 Cambs., died 31 July 1917 at St Julien. He is Capt. 'Jonah' Whale in the novels.

20. *A Fox Under My Cloak*, chapter 11, 'Life is Fun', p. 167.

21. *Official History*, 1915, vol. 2, pp. 151 ff.

22. Ibid., p. 160.

23. Ibid. See also report of Lt. White in Appendix A, *Short History, LRB*, which bears out these details.

24. Ibid., p. 171.

25. *The Private Papers of Douglas Haig, 1914–1919*, ed. Robert Blake (Eyre & Spottiswoode, 1952), p. 104.

26. Ibid., p. 105. Soon after this Sir John French was dismissed from the command and Gen. Haig was appointed in his place.

27. *A Fox Under My Cloak*, p. 318. Casualty figures are from the *Official History*, p. 233. An investigation into the complexities surrounding the fictional Capt. 'Spectre' West (and other characters) can be found in HWSJ, no. 34, September 1998.

28. *Offical History*, 1915, vol. II, p. 394.

29. See *A Fox Under My Cloak*, pp. 325–6, and also *A Soldier's Diary of the Great War*, anonymously published by Douglas H. Bell with an introduction by HW (Faber & Gwyer, 1929), pp. 140–1. Bell fought at the Somme and was awarded the MC. He then served in the RAF.

30. *A Fox Under My Cloak*, p. 242. Lt. Col. John Ward (1866–1934), CB (1919), CMG (1918), was a most interesting and active man. He had founded the Navvies Union in 1889, and was Independent MP for Stoke-on-Trent 1906–29 and member of the Trades Union Committee. He served in the Sudan, gaining Khedive's Star, medal and clasp, and in the European war in Siberia 1918–19. Awarded the Croix de Guerre, France, Italy and Czecho-slovakia, Cossack Atarman. As Colonel of the 25th Middlesex Regiment he raised five battalions for The Duke of Cambridge's Own (Middlesex Regiment).

An interesting reference can be found in Charles Thomas Perfect, *Hornchurch during the Great War*, (Benham and Co. Ltd, 1920), pp. 154–5, in a section on the use of the camp at Grey Towers by various battalions. (Photocopies of text supplied by Essex Record Office.)

'THE NAVVIES' OR PIONEERS' BATTALION (26th Middlesex Regiment)

> 'Canst work i' the earth so fast? A worthy pioneer!'
> (Shakespeare: *Hamlet*, Sc. I, Act v.)

For some time after the departure of the "Sportsmen" from Grey Towers the camp remained unoccupied, but in the following November the 26th Middlesex Regiment, popularly known as the Navvies Battalion, arrived under the command of Colonel John Ward, M.P. This fine body of men was drafted into Kitchener's Army for special work, and as their name implied, was very largely on the manual rather than on the fighting side of warfare; the Battalion was, however, in nowise lacking in a military sense.

Although their stay with us was short and produced nothing out of the common, it must be said to their credit that their conduct was all that could be desired, and they were in every way quite sensible of their responsibilities as soldiers of the King. Their general bearing was probably somewhat of a reflection of the great example set them by their chief. During the time they were in camp there was no regular Church Parade of the Battalion at the Parish Church, but instead a service was generally held on the Parade Ground, at which Colonel Ward usually gave a short address, which always contained some sound and good advice to his men. This service was held at 9.30 o'clock, and those who wished were therefore free to attend service at one or other of our places of worship, and every Sunday morning a commanding military figure might be seen at the service at our ancient Parish Church. This was Colonel John Ward, and with him was always one or more of his officers.

The 'Navvies' had a fine band, and, headed by their mascot, a splendid goat, helped to enliven our village during their stay. Afterwards this band did excellent service in assisting recruiting in many of our large midland and northern towns.

Some kind Hornchurch friends were in the midst of making preparations to give the 'Navvies' a Merry Christmas, but within a few days of the Christmas festival, the battalion received news to vacate the Camp, and on December 21st they, too, marched out of Grey Towers en route for the railway station and another camping ground.

31. *The Golden Virgin*, chapter 2, 'Grey Towers', pp. 41ff. The complicated scenario surrounding Williamson's fictional portrait of Capt. Kingsman and including Julian Grenfell's poem 'Into Battle' is discussed in Anne Williamson, 'Some Thoughts on "Spectre" West and other elusive characters', HWSJ, no. 34, September 1998.

32. *The Golden Virgin*, chapter 7 'Christmas 1915', p. 109. This episode is reminiscent of the poem 'Naming of Parts', written in 1946.

Today we have naming of parts. Yesterday
We had daily cleaning. And tomorrow morning
We shall have what to do after firing. But today,
Today we have naming of parts. Japonica
Glistens like coral in all of the neighbour gardens
And today we have naming of parts.
'Lessons of the War: 1, Naming of Parts', Henry Reed, (1914–86)

This poem may well have been published as Williamson was writing this volume, thus giving the impetus for his thought.

33. Terence Tetley was a Sapper in the Royal Engineers, No. 1513. He saw service in France from 28 May 1915, and was awarded the 1915 star. He appears on the 1918 Army List as in Royal Field Artillery (Special Reserve) and was commissioned as a Second Lt. in March 1918 in Royal Garrison Artillery 17 March 1918. (Research by Brian Dolan.) The relationship between Williamson and Tetley had a certain ambivalence and deteriorated from this point.

34. See Anne Williamson, *Henry Williamson*, pp. 52–3, where details about the motorbike are expanded.

35. *The Golden Virgin*, Part Two, 'The Somme', pp. 205 ff.

36. *Official History*, 1916, vol. 1, compiled by Capt. Wilfred Miles (Macmillan, 1938), p. 373.

37. Ibid., p. 375. In his fictional account Williamson has also added the details about dissolving the chalk with vinegar which are detailed on p. 325 of the *Official History*, where also can be found 'One auger actually penetrated into a German officer's dug-out unnoticed by the enemy'. (See *The Golden Virgin*, p. 242.)

38. *Official History*, p. 262, note 1.

39. *The Golden Virgin*, pp. 274, 276, and also *Official History*, 1916, vol. 1, p. 376.

40. *Official History*, 1916, vol. 1, p. 316.

41. Ibid., p. 313.

42. We read in *The Golden Virgin*, pp. 287–8, that Richard Maddison heard it on his early morning walk on the Hill, which adds to his feeling of happiness as he goes home for his cold tub and bacon breakfast. Heavy irony on HW's part.

43. *Official History*, 1916, vol. 1, p. 387.

44. Ibid., p. 483.

45. Williamson has marked the reference to the CCS at Heilly in the *Official History*, p. 282, with 'Phillip goes here'. He took details of No. 9 General Hospital at Rouen from Monica Salmond, *Bright Armour* (Faber & Faber, 1935). Monica Salmond was the sister of Julian Grenfell and a nurse at this hospital. For further details see article by Anne Williamson in HWSJ, no. 34, September 1998, p. 91.

46. This was a real place but it had actually been burned down three years previous to the incident in HW's novel. For background information see Peter Lewis, 'The Lynton and Barnstaple Railway and its Founder', HWSJ, no. 32, September 1996, pp. 24–34.

47. Capt. Joseph Morris, BA, AFRAeS, later RAF, *The German Air Raids on Great Britain 1914–1918* (London, Sampson Low, undated). This substantial book gives

authentic and objective details of this aspect of the First World War. In his preface, Joseph Morris states that 'during the war 9,000 German bombs of a total weight of 280 tons were dropped on British soil in the course of fifty-one airship and fifty-two aeroplane attacks. In all, 1,413 persons were killed and 3,408 others were wounded, London suffering more than half of the casualties.' This book relates in full detail every raid and the measures taken to counter them. Six accompanying maps show the menacing routes taken.

48. Ibid., p. 160.

49. Ibid., chapter XII, 'The Fall of the Thirties' (i.e. airships with the number 30-plus involved), pp. 136–48.

50. This pilot becomes the fictional Tom Cundall in the novel, who was Victor Yeates in real life. (See references in Anne Williamson, *Henry Williamson*.) Please note that Victor Yeates was not actually involved in this skirmish.

51. Morris, *German Air Raids*, p. 178 and frontispiece map.

52. Ibid., p. 177.

53. Joan Read, 'The Zeppelin Raid', HWSJ, no. 18, September 1988, p. 38. Strangely William Leopold Williamson does not give any details for this particular raid in his Special Constable's notebook. The area was on his beat, and one would think, as it killed so many local people, that it would have merited more detail than usual. The only explanation is that he was away on holiday at that point. In Williamson's novel, Richard Maddison attends the explosion and is stunned by the bomb.

54. Morris, *German Air Raids*, p. 182.

55. Joan Read, 'The Zeppelin Raid', HWSJ, no. 18, September 1988, p. 38.

56. Morris, *German Air Raids*, pp. 181–3. There is also folded inside this book a cutting from the *Weekly Dispatch*, Sunday 21 February 1926, of a long article by Sir William Nott-Blowers, City of London Police Commissioner 1902–25, entitled 'London's Air Invasion' detailing some of the more spectacular raids.

57. Some of these details can be found in the opening chapter of *Love and the Loveless*.

58. Army 40 / W.O. / 3140, *Notes on Pack Transport*, 1916.

59. Second Lt. R.J. Day, *The Mounted Officer's Book of Horses and Mules for Transport* (Ernest Day & Co., 1916).

60. Ibid., pp. 39–40. The book ends with a section somewhat curious and surprising in an Army textbook – 'The Horse's Prayer'. In his novel Williamson twists this slightly by stating that a copy of this prayer was given to each officer by courtesy of 'Our Dumb Friends' League'

CHAPTER 5: TRANSPORT OFFICER AT THE FRONT

1. A detailed comparison of HW's fictional Machine Gun Company with the MGC of real life was made in an article by Peter Cole, 'The 286th Machine Gun Company', HWSJ, no. 18, September 1988, pp. 30–7. Cole had no primary source material at that time and the meticulous nature of his research can be seen when compared with the account here where HW's own papers reveal not

only his own movements but the real names of many of his compatriots, and thus the 'fixing' of some of his fictional characters.

Henry Williamson added a note into his Field Correspondence Book 152 dated 29 November 1957 as follows: 'In No. 7 Novel [of the Chronicle – Love and the Loveless] I have not used as characters all those of 208 Company with whom I went out from Grantham in Feb. 1917. I have used, instead, Capt. Roy Colgate, with whom I nearly went to France as T.O. but he was suddenly sent out, leaving his embryo company at Belton Park, to take command of another Coy. already in France; where he was killed. He was a splendid fellow (for me) & is Jack HOBART in my novel: at time of writing this, I have just ended the fox-hunt chapter. I knew "Pinnegar" at Grantham, but he did not go out with No. 208 Coy. I have used him in No. 7 novel, because he links up with the later Norfolk novel.'

'Teddy Pinnegar' was Freddy Tranter – see Anne Williamson, Henry Williamson, p. 228. Note that as he did not go out with 208 Coy. then Peter Cole's assumption that Lt. Clarence Rose is the basis for Pinnegar at this point (by default) can be presumed to be correct.

Capt. (temp) R. Colgate, MGC, died of wounds 12 July 1916. He appears on the Army List February 1916 as in the Royal Fusiliers (City of London Regt.), 32 Service Bttn. East Ham.

2. See Anne Williamson, Henry Williamson for references passim, particularly p. 257, of examples of the anguish Williamson felt at Christmas throughout his life; a period when he was spiritually and emotionally with his comrades in the trenches reliving the scenes of the Christmas Truce of 1914.

3. 'Stany' is the character who in the novels is Desmond Neville's Brazilian friend 'Eugene'. Williamson refers to Stany on several occasions in later letters in this chapter, and also in his diary, and on one occasion calls him 'Maristany', thus Stany was his diminutive for Maristany. The clue that definitely connects Stany to 'Eugene' is revealed in the letter in which Williamson refers to Stany in connection with joining the Brazilian army.

4. Kut was a town situated on the River Tigris at a strategic point where a confluent joined it to the Euphrates (both joining and issuing into the Persian Gulf). It was necessary to take control of Kut before control of Baghdad could be achieved. The battle in this area was being conducted by the British Mesopotamian Expeditionary Force, which included large numbers of Indian troops, against the Turks. Kut was the symbolic centre of an area of the disastrous fighting known as 'The Fall of Kut' when about 12,000 troops had surrendered to the Turks on 29 April 1916. Kut was retaken by the British and Indian troops on 24 February 1917. Baghdad was regained on 11 March. (Ref. Martin Gilbert, The First World War (Weidenfeld & Nicholson, 1994).) Gilbert states that over 7,000 Indian soldiers were killed on the Western Front in 1915, 1,700 at Gallipoli, but that in Mesopotamia over 29,000 were killed. This is a sharp reminder of the fate of the soldiers of our allies. Gilbert shows the full contribution of the Indian soldiers: 'In Delhi, a monumental arch records the Indian losses, India's contribution in blood to the Allied War effort.' (Gilbert, p.

245.) Their efforts should never be forgotten. Although the Mesopotamian Battles are not part of Williamson's life or fictional work, it is important to record that he was aware of the total arena.

5. 'Jerry' was Henry Williamson's cousin, Gerald Simpson (b. 1892), younger brother of Hubert (b. 1888), sons of Sidney St. Paul Simpson and Maude (née Leaver). This family had emigrated to Canada but had returned to England to live in Adelaide Road, Brockley, in 1909. Gerald was first a gunner and then a lieutenant in the Royal Field Artillery (RFA) – Regimental number L/9102. He first went to France on 10 February 1917. (Research by Brian Dolan.) Thus his role in the Chronicle as Gerry Cakebread appears to be directly based on real life: 'Gerry had got into the Gunners, the RFA, and was at the Shop – Woolwich'. (A Fox Under My Cloak, p. 145.)

The role of the elder brother Hubert, the fictional 'Bertie' Cakebread, would, however, appear to differ. It is Hubert Cakebread who, in the novel, introduces the young Phillip to the LRB Drill Hall in early 1914 and he is described on p. 145 of A Fox Under My Cloak as 'wearing the Lilywhites chequered band round his cap, with the gold-braided peak of the Guards'. But Dolan has found no army records at all for Hubert Simpson. He has discovered that he was married in Eastbourne in 1909. (Thus there is no basis for the fictional version that he was Phillip's rival for the attention of Helena Rolls – see HWSJ, no. 33, September 1997, p. 48 'Helena Rolls' Brooch'.) A letter to Henry from his Aunt Maude in 1917 seems to suggest that Hubert was farming and it may be that he was not fit enough for service.

Readers interested in Williamson's family tree should consult Anne Williamson, Henry Williamson, or the more detailed article: Anne Williamson, 'Roots', HWSJ, no. 31, September 1995, pp. 6–27.

6. 62 Div. (2nd West Riding) was a 2nd line Territorial Division commanded by Maj. Gen. Walter Pipon Braithwaite from 23 December 1915 to 28 August 1918. See E. Wyall, The History of 62nd (West Riding) Division, 1914–1919. Gen. Braithwaite, GCB, KCB, Bath King of Arms (1865–1945), had a distinguished military career, gaining many medals and military honours, including GOC (General Officer Commanding) of Western Command, India 1920–3, Eastern Command 1926–7, and ADC (Aide-de-Camp) General to the King 1927–31 when he retired. For further details see Who Was Who, vol. 4.

7. Official History, 1917, vol. 1, compiled by Capt. Cyril Falls (Macmillan, 1940), chapter 3, 'The Opening of the Year 1917', Sir Douglas Haig's instructions, pp. 60–4. This volume is not in Williamson's archive.

8. Ibid., pp. 94–5.

9. Williamson would have been brought before the General Staff Officer 62 Division, Lt. Col. The Hon. A.G.A. Hore Ruthven. It is his signature that appears on the Divisional Order, No. 36. This Order and the ensuing 'Orders for the Hindenburg Line, May 1917' are reproduced in HWSJ, no. 34, September 1998, pp. 26–34.

10. Official History, 1917, vol. 1, relates almost exactly the same instances of booby-traps – see 'Retreat to the Hindenburg Line', pp. 148–9.

11. It is interesting to compare the scenario as seen, understood and recorded by HW at the time with the overall view as described in the Official History, 1917, vol. 1, 'The First Attack on Bullecourt, 11 April', pp. 357–70: 'On the front of the V Corps, held by the 7th Division until the morning of the 5th and then by the 62nd Division, the 18 pdr batteries . . . were advanced by sections to the neighbourhood of Croisilles and Ecoust, and began wirecutting on the 7th. . . . No gaps could be found by the Australian patrols. . . . The operation of the Fifth Army was therefore postponed.' It was then proposed that on the morning of 10 April tanks would be brought in from the quarry at Mory Copse under cover of darkness to penetrate the wire, allowing 62 Division to attack their objective of Hendecourt while the Australians advanced on Riencourt. The tanks did not appear and the attacks had to be aborted, and later reinstated for the following morning, when despite massive problems, there was some initial success. Then a misunderstanding of the exact position led to a confusion of orders, and artillery support asked for was not given, leading to ultimate failure and much loss of men.

12. These orders and the 'Extracts from German Soldiers' Letters' (see further paragraph) and other similar documents are printed facsimile in the HWSJ, no. 34, September 1998.

13. For an account of this battle see the Official History, 1917, vol. 1, chapter 18, 'The Battle of Bullecourt, 3–17 May 1917', pp. 455–81, which is summed up by the words: '. . . at Bullecourt a fierce and bloody struggle, in which the British side from first to last six divisions were engaged on a few acres of ground, raged for a full fortnight.' (p. 456). Throughout, the Australian Anzac Corps fought bravely and well on their right flank. The Battle of Bullecourt was a subsidiary action – a 'flanking operation' to the main action, which was the Battle of Arras, 9 April–30 May 1917. The Official History records that on the first day of the attack, 3 May 1917: 'On the front of V corps the 62nd Division (Major-General W.P. Braithwaite) attacked with all three brigades in line.' (That is, 185, 186, and 187 Brigades; p. 463.) 'The 187 Brigade (Br. General R.O.B. Taylor) . . . attack fell into confusion equal to that of 186 Brigade.' (p. 465). 'The 62nd Division could not renew the attack on a large scale. It had engaged all its battalions and suffered nearly 8,000 casualties.' (p. 465).

The battle continued backwards and forwards until on 12 May: '. . . the British held the whole village [Bullecourt] except the Red Patch' (an area marked red on the maps by the British for special attention; p. 475) with some further gain the following day.

'On the 15 May came the last and biggest counter-attack. It extended over the whole front of the captured position, which it was designed to capture in its entirety. There was an intense bombardment during the preceding night, causing heavy casualties and destroying much of the work done to secure the defence of the position in the Hindenburg Line. The British protective barrage was put down, though the field artillery batteries were enveloped in gas, and the counter-batteries followed suit. The flashes of explosions, the fantastic firework display as rockets of all colours were flung up, calling, it might be, for aid, for fire to lengthen, or fire to shorten – no observer could in the confusion recognise signals or even tell whose were the rockets – made a truly awful and infernal battle picture, of which the din was fitting accompaniment.' (p. 476). Much of Bullecourt was retaken by the Germans.

On the night of 15/16 May, 173 and 174 Brigade (58 Division) relieved the exhausted men, with Maj. Gen. H.D. Fanshawe in command, who set about recapturing the village. This included a frontal attack on the Red Patch by 2/5th London (London Rifle Brigade) which was successful. The Germans evacuated Bullecourt, and the battle was officially over. However, further attacks continued to take place on the one hand to support the Australians but mainly to disguise from the Germans the fact that the battle was over, for Field Marshal General Sir Douglas Haig had decided to move his offensive back to Flanders.

'The British losses at this battle were extremely heavy. Those of the 1 Anzac Corps numbered 292 officers and 7,190 other ranks. Those of V Corps were about 300 officers and 6,500 ranks of which 62 Division lost 143 officers and 3,284 other ranks. The total casualties were therefore over 14,000, or a thousand a day.' (p. 479).

CHAPTER 6: WITH THE BEDFORDSHIRES

1. See Lady Ursula Redwood, Trefusis Territory, privately printed 1987, for descriptions of the house; also Henry M. Jeffery, FRS, 'On a Tudor Mansion at Trefusis in Mylor', in Journal of the Royal Institution of Cornwall, vol. 10, pt 37 (1891) pp. 399–402. The description of this house is virtually the same in its details as the house Williamson ascribed as the fictional Maddison family home, i.e. Capt. Maddison's home at Colham in 'the West Country'. See Anne Williamson, Henry Williamson, pp. 57–8 and note 7 on p. 338.

2. A Test to Destruction.

3. Readers of Williamson's Chronicle will recognize the character of 'Lt. Bright' in the saga of Second Lt. Cyril Wright. Peter Cole, 'The 286th Machine Company', states that Wright was a Cambridgeshire man, who commanded 'D' Section of 208 MGC and that the War Diary notes that he went on 'special leave' on 19 May, returning to the Infantry in the autumn.

4. Henri Barbusse, Le Feu, 1916. First English edn translated by W. Fitzwater Wray (Dent, 1917). Awarded the prestigious 'Prix Goncourt' in 1917. It is known that Williamson did once have a copy of this book. It is referred to by Ann Thomas in her article 'A Visit to Henry Williamson', John O'London's Weekly, 25 June 1932, reprinted in HWSJ, no. 10, October 1984, pp. 30–7, exact reference on p. 34. The copy is no longer in his archive, which is a great pity as it may well have contained notes, and almost certainly the date on which he obtained it, which would have helped in understanding the influences behind his own thoughts and writing. One feels that he probably did read this book at a very early stage, as there are so many other early war books in his archive. Further discussion will be found in chapter 7.

5. Love and the Loveless, chapter 18, 'Mouse to Lion', p. 314 and chapter 15,

'Mutiny', pp. 251–67. This account of the English mutiny at the Infantry Base Depots (IBD), Etaples, in early September (9–12) 1917 was published in 1958. Research by John Homan and Paul Reed reveals that this was almost certainly the first description of the mutiny to be published in print. (See letter from John Homan in HWSJ, no. 16, September 1987, p. 37, and letter from Terry Russell in HWSJ, no. 15, March 1987, p. 54.) Reed and Homan believed at that time that the only other book to treat the subject was Allison and Fairley, *The Monocled Mutineer*, published in 1978 (twenty years after Williamson's book) and on which a television series was based shown in four parts during September 1986. However, Henry Williamson himself had mentioned the mutiny in *The Patriot's Progress* (pub. 1930) (p. 127 John Bullock sees this) thus 48 years before Allison and Fairley. See present volume p. 206, for HW own comment. There was never an official pronouncement on the incident, as records for Etaples for that period do not apparently exist. Gilbert, *First World War*, only gives the incident brief mention, p. 360.

In chapter 15, 'Mutiny', of *Love and the Loveless* Phillip meets at Etaples a young major called Traill, second-in-command of Phillip's depot, with three wound stripes and a Military Cross. 'The pale delicacy of his face was emphasised by dark wavy hair. Clean-shaven, gentle-voiced, Traill looked to be about twenty years old.' The two men became friends during Phillip's short stay at Etaples.

This officer was in real life Maj. (Temp) Colin Balfour Traill, MC. He was awarded the MC 'for conspicuous gallantry and devotion to duty' driving an attack on Oppy Wood, 3 May 1917, where he was wounded in the face and head and blown off his feet by another shell, but continued with the attack. He was convalescent at Trefusis at the same time as HW and there are several photographs of him in HW's archive, one of which is captioned 'My Friend' by Williamson with his name and regiment; here HW has written 'West Yorks Regt. killed March 1918', elsewhere 'East Yorks.' Traill was in 10 East Yorks Regt. and was killed in action on 28 June 1918, by the blast from a British shell falling short.

Neither Traill or HW were present at this affair at Etaples, as both were still on convalescent leave in the West Country. Speculation about how Williamson obtained this information has to remain open. In any event he knew about it personally, in default of any official information being available.

6. Maj. Gen. Sir F. Maume, KCMG, CB, D.Lit., *The 16th Foot: A History of the Bedfordshire and Hertford Regiment* (Constable, 1931).

7. The Battle of Cambrai is described in *Love and the Loveless*, chapter 20, 'Victory', pp. 333 ff.

8. Official History, 1917, vol. 3, 'The Battle of Cambrai' compiled by Capt. Wilfred Miles (HMSO, 1948). In the Preface, Brig. Gen. Sir James E. Edmonds (main compiler of the *Official History*) criticizes the Commander of the Third Army, Gen. Julian Byng (who succeeded Gen. Allenby on 7 June 1917) for his mishandling of the Cambrai operation.

9. Ibid., Appendix 1, pp. 306–7.

10. Ibid., p. 15. In later life Williamson often referred to the make-up of these

fascines – the joining together of many small parts to make one large strong whole – and his view of 'fascism' was greatly based on that definition: joining together for strength and the common good, not the vile dictatorship that the word connotes today.

11. Ibid., pp. 84 ff.

12. *Love and the Loveless*, chapter 19, 'Flanders Sanatorium', pp. 323–6. Phillip meets the new brigadier in a dugout and is shocked to find him so young and with so many decorations.

13. Printed in the *Official History*, 1917, vol. 3, 'Cambrai', Appendix 2, pp. 358–64.

14. Ibid., Appendix 1, 'The Third Army Plan', p. 307.

15. Ibid., pp. 84 ff.

16. Ibid., p. 84; *Love and the Loveless*, pp. 334 ff.

17. *Official History*, 1917, vol. 3, p. 86; *Love and the Loveless*, p. 339.

18. *Official History*, 1917, vol. 3, p. 112 and footnote 1; *Love and the Loveless*, p. 343.

19. *Official History*, 1917, vol. 3, p. 112; *Love and the Loveless*, p. 343.

20. *Official History*, 1917, vol. 3, p. 147; *Love and the Loveless*, p. 344.

21. *Official History*, 1917, vol. 3, p. 167; *Love and the Loveless*, p. 346.

22. *Official History*, 1917, vol. 3, 'Gouzancourt', pp. 185–1902.

23. *Official History*, 1917, vol. 3, p. 186; *Love and the Loveless*, p. 352.

24. *Official History*, 1917, vol. 3, p. 190; *Love and the Loveless*, p. 354.

25. *Official History*, 1917, vol. 3, p. 224, footnote 1.

26. *Official History*, 1917, vol. 3, p. 224; *Love and the Loveless*, p. 354.

27. *Official History*, 1917, vol. 3, p. 301; *Love and the Loveless*, p. 355.

28. *Love and the Loveless*, p. 360. The fictional Lt. S.D. Allen as can be seen was actually a soldier in the Bedfordshire Regiment.

29. After the German counter-attack on 30 November 1917 (the Battle of Cambrai) the War Cabinet asked Field Marshal Sir Douglas Haig for a full report. Haig himself set up a Court of Enquiry in France at Hesdin towards the end of January 1918. *Official History*, 1917, vol. 3, 'The Battle of Cambrai', pp. 294–301. There is no mention here of criticism of Lt. Gen. Kiggell, CGS, beyond a euphemistic 'broken down in health' (p. 55), but Brian Dolan's research shows that he was indeed '*stellenbosched*'. (The term *Stellenbosch* is historical military slang and means 'supercede without formal disgrace'.) His entry in *Who was Who* is impressive but *Macmillan's Dictionary of the First World War* shows the problem clearly: 'Kiggell went to extraordinary lengths to reinforce Haig's natural optimism, including the suppression of intelligence to support the latter's arguments. A strong advocate of "Breakthrough Tactics" his influence upset other BEF commanders and there were calls for his removal before he collapsed with "nervous exhaustion" in late 1917, becoming commander of forces on the Channel Islands on his recovery in early 1918.' (p. 269) (i.e. an appointment out of harm's way.)

The Commanding Officer of 2/Bedfordshire was Lt. Col. C.H. de St. P. Bunbury (attached – his actual regiment was Alexandra, Princess of Wales Yorkshire Regiment) and details can be found in the War Diary of 2/Beds,

Nov–Dec 1917. Col. Bunbury went to hospital on 1 November and Maj. Wynne, DSO, assumed command in his place. Col. Bunbury then proceeded on leave on 3 November. He rejoined the battalion in the line on 21 December but proceeded sick to Field Ambulance the very next day. Further details not known.

30. *A Test to Destruction.*

31. One extraordinary letter from Tetley, postmarked from 'Shoeburyness' but undated, asks for money because he says he is 'living in three messes' at once and thus had very high expenses. There is an obvious hint of blackmail in this letter which, when linked to inferences in other archive material, seemingly stems from some homosexual experimentation in their youth.

32. *A Test to Destruction*, p. 381. Phillip has to attend and take notes at a meeting between Lord Satchville and Col. Mowbray, who discuss the forthcoming offensive. One presumes HW attended a similar meeting.

33. *A Test to Destruction*, chapter 1, 'The Staff of Life', p. 22.

34. This is a clerical error on Williamson's part. 8 Battalion Bedfordshire Regiment was disbanded at the end of January as part of the reorganization of the Army to meet the new threat and the troops amalgamated into other battalions. It was 2 and 7 battalions that were at the Western Front at this time (the 1st was in Italy) and it was 2 Battalion that Williamson joined.

35. There is no official corroboration anywhere of Williamson having been on the Front Line at this point. However, the details in his diary prior to this show most definitely that he was planning to leave and did indeed leave for France on 27 March. It is known that the War Office was in great turmoil over the German breakthrough and sent out everyone they could. Perhaps Williamson was sent out on a fairly mundane task, such as escort to a battalion of men going out, and once he arrived was asked to continue with some further task, which took him to the Front Line and this was either not recorded due to some confusion, or is a record that has been entirely lost.

36. Maume, *The 16th Foot*, chapter xi, 'The Great War 1918', pp. 198 ff.

37. Hence 'Roses of Picardy'. HW's mention of this song in the last chapter of *Love and the Loveless* can be seen as a quite deliberate structural pointer.

38. Maume, *The 16th Foot*, pp. 198 ff.

39. Ibid.

40. *A Test to Destruction*, chapter 8, 'Prachtige Kerl', p. 142. Henry's arrival can be traced, hidden towards the end of the chapter: 'At Bresle [Bresle is south-west of Albert, north of the Albert–Amiens road, about ⅓ distance along] a draft of nearly four hundred men arrived with nine officers from the IBD at Etaples. . . .' Immediately after this Williamson inserts a summary of the German Battle plan, noting the MICHAEL attack, which had begun on 21 March and was now virtually over, and the MARS attack on Arras, which began the evening of 28 March (repulsed).

41. Maume, *The 16th Foot*.

42. *A Test to Destruction*, p. 143. The description of the route march from Bresle to Ascheux is so detailed that it must be fairly certain that Williamson took part in

it, thus supporting the theory that he was possibly (if nothing else) acting as escort to a draft.

43. *Official History*, 1918, 'March to April', compiled by Brig. Gen. Sir James Edmonds (Macmillan, 1937), p. 140, footnote, and also on p. 146.

44. *A Test to Destruction*, chapter 9, 'ST GEORGE I' where Williamson sets out the overall plan: 'The situation in Flanders during the first week of April 1918 was that VALKYRIE [north of Arras to Lens] and ST GEORGE I were mounted, and preparations for ST GEORGE II were well forward.' The ST GEORGE area was the scene of several separate battles; Williamson was concerned with the Battle of Messines, which was defended by IX Corps of the Second Army and began on 10 April 1918, and which included Hill 63 and Wytschaete.

45. *Official History*, chapter 11, 'The German (Lys) Offensive in Flanders' to 'The Battle of Messines', pages particularly marked are pp. 212–14.

46. Ibid., chapter 25, 'Some Reflections', pp. 456–90.

47. The 'Special Order of the Day' that Maj. Bill Kidd reads in Williamson's novel while in the 'Staenyzer Kabaret' is word for word the same as that sent out by Field Marshal Haig, dated Thursday 11 April 1918, 'TO ALL RANKS OF THE BRITISH ARMY IN FRANCE AND FLANDERS'. *A Test to Destruction*, chapter 10, 'Bill Kidd's Hour'; *Official History*, 1918, Appendix 10, 'Special Order of the Day' p. 512. This is not marked by Williamson, the inference being that he would have had a copy at the time. Bill Kidd is based on Bill Child (see AW, biog., p. 288)

48. There is no corroboration of Williamson having been in Hall-Walker's Hospital at this point. He did not attend the board at Caxton Hall but instead his routine board at Felixstowe, which was in the Harwich Garrison, where it was reported that, 'He has been doing ordinary duty since his last Board & states that he now has no symptoms of dysentery.' It has not been possible to reconcile the conflicting aspects of this episode. The only explanation I can offer (as previously stated) is that he was detailed to go to France for some reason (despite it being technically against the rules because of his sickness category at that time) and that, being unfit, perhaps he collapsed at some point while out there, or was taken ill on the boat home, and was therefore told to report to the hospital for a check-up on return but was found to have nothing wrong and proceeded as normal. It is possibly significant that the Board was at Harwich Garrison (and not at Landguard itself) where his movements would not be known – and thus the fact that there was a peculiarity would not necessarily be noticed. I have examined his diary entries with great care and they do seem to me to have been contemporaneous. He was preparing to go to France. He went to France. In the light of the newly released medical records (PRO - WO 339) one cannot say that he certainly would have taken part in the battle he describes in his novel. However, one cannot rule it out entirely, despite the fact that there is no corroboration. In HW's novel 'Spectre' West does query the fact that Phillip is at the Front, so in real life an officer may well have noticed the discrepancy, and insisted HW had a check up at the hospital on his return.

49. No details of anyone corresponding to this name and date have been found. This entry adds greatly to the mystery of the identity of the fictional

'Spectre' West. This whole question is addressed in my article 'Some thoughts on 'Spectre' West. . . .' HWSJ, no. 34, September 1998, pp. 86–88.

50. Official History, 1918, vol. 5, 'September to November', 'The Advance to Victory', chapter 36, Reflections', pp. 570 ff.

51. In A Test to Destruction this is the day that the 'Gaultshire' Regiment celebrates with much ceremony at the 'Duke of Gaultshire's home at Husborne Crawley' the Battle of Minden. Minden was indeed captured from the French (who had taken it a year previously) on 1 August 1759 during the Seven Years' War. Information on the Battle of Minden is taken from an old edition of Pear's Encyclopaedia in Williamson's archive. Williamson's elaborate scenario seems to be a most wonderful flight of fancy. HW must have found the alliterative connection between Linden and Minden and the coincidence of the same day an irresistible stimulus. One wonders what the real Beds. Regt. made of it!

52. Gilbert, The First World War, p. 493.

53. Official History, 1918, vol. 5, p. 552.

54. John Buchan, The King's Grace (Hodder and Stoughton, 1935), p. 203, quoted in Gilbert, The First World War, p. 501.

55. These short entries are described more fully in A Test to Destruction, chapter 18, 'Nightshade', which Williamson ends with the poignant words: 'Such weariness; such sadness.'

56. This was temporary. The two men were never truly reconciled to each other and Williamson had uneasy thoughts about Tetley throughout his life as various references in his papers prove, many of which refer to the amount of money he had lent him during this time. There is a decided inference within his personal papers that these money transactions involved an element of blackmail which arose from a homosexual relationship earlier in their friendship. (HW also, of course, lent a great deal of money to Maristany.)

57. Anne Williamson, Henry Williamson, pp. 63 ff.

58. A detailed examination of this period can be found in Anne Williamson, 'Save his own soul he hath no star', HWSJ 39, (Sept. 2003) pp. 30–60.

59. Ibid., pp. 63, 71.

60. Ibid., pp. 71–2.

61. Henry Williamson, 'When I was Demobilised', The Strand Magazine, 1945.

CHAPTER 7: BEYOND REALITY

1. The war volumes of A Chronicle of Ancient Sunlight have been dealt with to a large extent in the earlier chapters and readers can find the background to their writing in the present author's recent biography, Henry Williamson: Tarka and the Last Romantic. This chapter will concentrate on the period of the 1920s when Williamson's thoughts and actions were still freshly influenced by his war experiences, culminating with the writing of A Wet Flanders Plain and The Patriot's Progress.

Space restrictions preclude the inclusion here of many other details of Williamson's involvement with war writings, some of which, for instance his support for Victor Yeates and his book *Winged Victory*, can be found in Anne Williamson, *Henry Williamson*. Other examples can be found in the HWSJ, for which a detailed index is available on the website. Some of HW's later articles on the First World War, arising from a return visit to the battlefields in the mid-1960s and including his long three-part essay 'The Somme — just Fifty Years After', have been published by the HWS in *From a Country Hilltop*, ed. John Gregory (1988) and others in *Days of Wonder*, ed. John Gregory (1987). Williamson also contributed 'The Christmas Truce' in *History of the First World War* (Purnell, for BPC Publishing Ltd in cooperation with the Imperial War Museum; a magazine in 128 parts published in the late 1960s), vol. 2, no. 4, pp. 552–9.

2. Henry Williamson, 'When I was Demobilised', *The Strand Magazine*, 1945.

3. Henry Williamson, *The Beautiful Years*, vol. 1, *The Flax of Dream* tetralogy. Apart from references in my biography, see also Dr J.W. Blench, 'The Apprenticeship of a novelist', pt 1, HWSJ, no. 17, March 1988, pp. 5–19; also, Dr J.W. Blench, 'Henry Williamson's *The Flax of Dream*', HWSJ, no. 20, September 1989, pp. 5–27.

4. Further details can be found in Anne Williamson, *Henry Williamson*. Williamson's 'Fleet St.' articles were published as *The Weekly Dispatch*, ed. John Gregory (HWS, 1983). Williamson's essay 'The Confessions of a Fake Merchant', a biographical chapter of his time as a journalist, was first published in *The Book of Fleet Street*, ed. T. Michael Pope (Cassell, 1930).

5. Not to be confused with *The Wiper's Times*, the trench magazine produced during the war itself under amazingly difficult conditions. HW contributed the Foreword when this was published (together with its successor, *BEF Times*) in facsimile (Peter Davies, 1973).

6. *The Pathway* (Cape, 1928) and *Goodbye West Country* (Putnam, September 1937). In a letter to T.E. Lawrence, dated 1 May 1928, Williamson states: 'I feel rather a sneak, because <u>Pathway</u> I suppose is Bolshy to the core. An attempt to reconcile Jesus and Lenin, which may mean that I feel I have them both in my pocket. O what a conceit.'

7. Barbusse, *Le Feu*. As stated previously Williamson's copy is no longer in his archive. The edition used here was a library copy of Dent's 1969 reprint, 'Everyman's Library' No. 798, from which the information about Henri Barbusse has been taken with reference to the excellent introduction by Brian Rhys.

8. Henri Barbusse, *L'Enfer* (1908). Described as a violent and terrible book, *L'Enfer* is a series of stories seen by an eye looking through a spy-hole into an empty room and imagining the scenes it sees therein.

9. After the war Barbusse founded an Ex-Soldiers Republican Association and in 1919 held an international congress of soldiers from both sides (Allies and German) at Geneva. He also showed his sympathies with the growing Communist party in France, publishing a 'Letter to Intellectuals' but he did not sign the card as a party member. However, the French Government, in an attempt to quash both institutions, prosecuted Barbusse for his activities and imprisoned the communist leaders. Outraged, Barbusse then immediately 'signed' and so became a full communist member. He founded the *Clarté* group, which published an international review that Barbusse edited. By 1928 much of

Barbusse's energy went into fighting fascism. But although he spent much time in Moscow, he was still in many ways outside the communist movement, retaining an individual approach. He founded a weekly paper *Monde*, which he edited until his death in 1935 from a recurrence of his lung trouble leading to pneumonia while in Moscow for the VIIth Congres Internationale.

10. See references in Anne Williamson, *Henry Williamson*. See also Dr J.W. Blench, 'The Influence of Richard Jefferies Upon Henry Williamson', pt 1, HWSJ, no. 25, March 1992, pp. 5–20; pt 2, HWSJ, no. 26, September 1992, pp. 5–31.

Richard Jefferies (1848–87) had detailed knowledge of rural England and wrote a large number of books. He first came into prominence with a long letter in *The Times* on the plight of the agricultural labourer, especially shepherds, in Wiltshire in the early 1870s. The more prosaic side of his nature can be seen as decidedly socialist while there was also the opposite mystic stance of *The Story of My Heart* (1883), which is an outpouring of mystical thoughts and which is the source of Williamson's phrase 'Ancient Sunlight'. In *After London* (1885) there is a vision of future disaster arising from industrial civilization with a 'back to nature' message, rather similar to Barbusse's opening chapter in *Le Feu*. Williamson had access to the whole range of Jefferies' books from (so he tells us) his own grandfather, and certainly from his first wife's father, Charles Hibbert, who had a large collection. I have found no reference in HW's early papers about the metaphysical poet Francis Thompson, the other great literary influence on Williamson. In later life he frequently mentioned that his Aunt Mary Leopoldina had sent him a volume of Thompson's poetry while in the trenches. See references in Anne Williamson, *Henry Williamson*. A thin, tattered volume of Thompson's work is probably this item.

11. Readers interested in the background to Williamson's courtship and marriage should consult Anne Williamson, *Henry Williamson*.

12. This sketch and the *Chyebassa* signatures are reproduced in HWSJ, no. 34, September 1998, pp. 40, 41.

13. *Ploegsteert 1927*, the official publication for the unveiling of the Commemorative Tablet in the London Rifle Brigade Cemetery at Ploegsteert on Sunday 19 June 1927 to the 91 officers and 1,839 other ranks who were killed during the war. Printed by the Athenaem Press, 1927. Henry Williamson made a further visit to the battlefields in 1964 to write a series of articles for the *Evening Standard* entitled 'Return to Hell', including a visit to Plugstreet Wood, an evocative and moving description of the area. It included a photograph of the grave of Rifleman Reuban Barnett, a Jewish lad who was killed in action on 19 December 1914, aged fifteen years. These articles reprinted in *The Wet Flanders Plain*, new edn 1987, Gliddon Books.

14. This article was reprinted in a volume containing the articles from three newspaper series (*Is Prayer Answered*; *I Believe*; *How I Look at Life*): 'Three Subjects Discussed by Famous People in a Series of Articles that made History in Daily Journalism' (*Daily Express*, undated but late 1928). Also of interest to Williamson readers is the fact that the first article in the *Is Prayer Answered* section is by J.D. Beresford, billed as 'one of the most distinguished of present-day novelists'. J.D.

Beresford, as reader for Collin's publishers, recommended Williamson's first work and thus helped to set Williamson on his writing career.

15. Henry Williamson, *The Labouring Life* (Cape, 1932). 'Surview and Farewell', pp. 455 ff.

16. These articles are printed in HWSJ, no. 34, September 1998.

17. Henry Williamson, 'What we should Remember and What Forget', *The Radio Times*, 9 November 1928. Reprinted facsimile in HWSJ, no. 27, March 1993, pp. 40–1.

18. Henry Williamson, 'Ten Years' Remembrance', *Daily Mirror*, 12 November 1928. Reprinted in HWSJ, no. 18, September 1988, pp. 28–9.

19. A short article on the background to C.R.W. Nevinson and 'A Group of Soldiers' is printed in HWSJ, no. 34, September 1998, pp. 94–6.

20. Further details can be found in Anne Williamson, *Henry Williamson*.

21. Reading Williamson's description of L. Cpl. Blunden made after the *Chyebassa* reunion dinner in 1926 (see p. 196), it would not be, I feel, too fanciful to suggest the possibility that Blunden would have been to some extent the original for John Bullock – certainly the physical description (changing amputated arm for leg) and temperament fit John Bullock, although the text is based on Williamson's own experience.

22. For critical analysis of *The Patriot's Progress* see John Onions, *English Fiction and Drama of the Great War, 1918–39* (Macmillan, 1990), chapter 4, 'Aldington and Williamson: The Ironic Mode', pp. 68–83; and Bernard Bergonzi, *Heroes' Twilight* (Constable, 1965; Macmillan, 1980; revised edn Carcanet, 1996).

23. Further details can be found in Anne Williamson, *Henry Williamson*, p. 133.

24. Henry Williamson, 'Reality in War Literature', *The London Mercury*, January 1929, reprinted with additional material in Henry Williamson, *The Linhay on the Downs and Other Adventures in the Old and New World* (Jonathan Cape, 1934). A copy of the typescript in his archive has a note written by HW in 1968 stating that it was written in 1928. That was the version printed in *Linhay* but an extant early manuscript is signed and dated 12 December 1926. Williamson tried to place the essay in several journals, including *The Ypres Times* (whose editor refused it saying it would sit uneasily between their covers), before it was taken by *The London Mercury* – after he had won the Hawthornden Prize for Literature. The ms version is printed facsimile in HWSJ, no. 34, September 1998.

25. The influence of Tolstoy's *War and Peace* on Henry Williamson is discussed more fully in HWSJ, no. 34, September 1998; Editorial, pp. 4–5.

26. For further information of source and influence see Anne Williamson, *Henry Williamson*, pp. 65–6.

27. Henry Williamson, *Lucifer Before Sunrise* (Macdonald, 1967, 1985).

Bibliography

Those who wish to understand the full story of Henry Williamson's life and work may find it useful to consult my recent biography *Henry Williamson: Tarka and the Last Romantic* (Sutton Publishing, 1995, paperback revised edition, August 1997), and also the *Journals* of the Henry Williamson Society, which contain a vast variety of material and writings. The September 1998 issue, no. 34, entitled *Reality in War Literature* (ISBN: 1-873507-13-5) and devoted entirely to the First World War including material which it has not been possible to include here, is virtually a supplement to this present book.

I. ON THE FIRST WORLD WAR

Main works consulted by the author:

Gilbert, Martin, *The First World War*, Weidenfeld & Nicholson, 1994.
History of the Great War, Based on Official Documents. Military Operations. Belgium and France. Main compiler Brig. Gen. Sir James E. Edmonds, CB, CMG. Published by Macmillan in several volumes over about twenty years.
Mitchinson, K.W., *Gentlemen and Officers*, Imperial War Museum, 1995.
The Private Papers of Douglas Haig, 1914–1919, ed. Robert Blake, Eyre & Spottiswoode, 1952.
Terraine, John, *The First World War 1914–18*, Macmillan, 1965.
The Times History of the War in 22 volumes, The Times, 1921.

Other references can be found *in situ* in the Notes.

II. ON HENRY WILLIAMSON'S LIFE AND WRITING

The Aylesford Review, 'Henry Williamson: A Symposium and Tribute', vol. II, no. 2, special issue (winter 1957/8), ed. Father Brocard Sewell.
Bergonzi, Bernard, *Heroes' Twilight*, Constable, 1965; Macmillan; 1980; revised edn Carcanet, 1996.
Farson, Daniel, *Henry: A Portrait*, Michael Joseph, 1982.
Girvan, I. Waveney, *A Bibliography*, 'Introduction' reprinted in HWSJ, no. 31, centenary issue, September 1995, pp. 74–6.
Lamplugh, Lois, *A Shadowed Man*, Wellspring, 1990; revised edn Exmoor Press, 1991.
Murry, J. Middleton, 'The Novels of Henry Williamson' in *Katherine Mansfield and other Literary Studies*, foreword by T.S. Eliot, compiled by Mary Middleton Murry, Constable, 1959.

BIBLIOGRAPHY

Onions, John, English Fiction and Drama of the Great War, 1918–39, chapter 4, 'Aldington and Williamson: The Ironic Mode', pp. 68–83, Macmillan, 1990.

Price, Bernard, Creative Landscapes of the British Isles, Ebury Press, 1983: Henry Williamson entries pp. 109, 132–5.

Seago, Edward, Peace in War, 'Henry Williamson', portrait and essay, pp. 49–52, Collins, 1943. Reprinted in HWSJ, no. 31, centenary issue, September 1995, pp. 83–5.

Sewell, Father Brocard (ed.), Henry Williamson: The Man, The Writings – A Symposium, Tabb House, 1980.

West, Herbert Faulkner, The Dreamer of Devon, Ulysses Press, 1932. Reprinted in HWSJ, no. 31, centenary issue, September 1995, pp. 62–70.

Williamson, Anne, Henry Williamson: Tarka and the Last Romantic, Sutton Publishing, 1995; paperback edn 1997. The official biography.

The Henry Williamson Society Journal, ed. Anne Williamson, contains reviews, correspondence, reminiscences, original and fugitive texts by, criticism of, and articles based on research into, Henry Williamson's life and writings. Its wide and varied content has greatly added to the knowledge and understanding of this foremost writer. The latest issue, no. 34, Reality in War Literature, September 1998, is available to non-members at £7.50. Back copies and a detailed index are also available from the Society's Publications Manager:

John Gregory, 14 Nether Grove, Longstanton, Cambridge, CB4 5EL

III. HENRY WILLIAMSON'S BOOKS ON THE FIRST WORLD WAR

The Wet Flanders Plain, limited edn Beaumont Press, 1929; Faber, 1929; Dutton USA, 1929; edn with introduction by Richard Williamson and additional material, Gliddon Books, 1987; paperback, ditto.

The Patriot's Progress – Being the Vicissitudes of Pte. John Bullock, illus. William Kermode, Geoffrey Bles, 1930; edn with new preface and epigraph by Williamson, Macdonald, 1968; paperback edn Little Brown, 1991; paperback edn Sutton Publishing, 2004.

How Dear is Life, vol. 4, A Chronicle of Ancient Sunlight, Macdonald, 1954, 1984; paparback edn Sutton Publishing, 1995.

A Fox Under My Cloak, vol. 5, A Chronicle of Ancient Sunlight, Macdonald, 1955, 1984; paperback edn Sutton Publishing, 1996.

The Golden Virgin, vol. 6, A Chronicle of Ancient Sunlight, Macdonald, 1957, 1984; paperback edn Sutton Publishing, 1996.

Love and the Loveless, vol. 7, A Chronicle of Ancient Sunlight, Macdonald, 1958, 1984; paperback edn Sutton Publishing, 1997.

A Test to Destruction, vol. 8, A Chronicle of Ancient Sunlight, Macdonald, 1960, 1984; paperback edn Sutton Publishing, 1997.

Days of Wonder, introduction Richard Williamson, ed. John Gregory, Henry Williamson Society, 1987.

References are also found in some of Williamson's other books, e.g. Goodbye West Country (Putnam, 1937).

A full bibliography of Henry Williamson's books can be found in Anne Williamson, *Henry Williamson: Tarka and the Last Romantic* or on application to the Henry Williamson Society.

Readers interested in the Henry Williamson Society should contact :

Sue Cumming, 7 Monmouth Road, Dorchester, Dorset DT1 2DE

The Society maintains a comprehensive website at: www.henrywilliamson.org

Index

Achiet le Grand, 89, 93, 99, 103, 109, 119, 154, 155, 159, 161, 193, 195

Achiet le Petit, 94, 97, 103, 109

Adair Monthly, 201

Adelaide Road (Brockley), 176

air raids, 76–9, 230–1n

air ships, 15; 76–9 *see also* Zeppelins

Aisne, Battle of the, 30

Aisne, River, 34, 35, 119

Albert, 74, 75, 133, 179, 180, 193

Albert, King of Belgium, 11, 33, 35, *see also* KING ALBERT'S BOOK

Alderley Edge (convalescent home), 57

Allen, Lt. S.D., 172, 181, 237n

Allenby, Maj. Gen., 33, 36; as Field Marshal Viscount, 189

Allies (in the First World War), xiii, 75, 89–90, 167, 178

Allison, Dvr. (208 MGC), 137, 142

American troops, 178, *see also* United States of America

Amiens, 202

Amiens Cathedral 1925, 193

Ampthill, Lt. Col. Lord, (Commanding 3 Beds Regt), 173, 182, 189

ancient sunlight, 209, 210

Ancoats Military Hospital, Manchester, 56, 57, 224n

Ancre, the 90, 144, 160, 193, 203; *and see* plate 32b

Anneux, 170

Antwerp, fall of, 28, 30, 33, 35

Anzac troops (Australia and New Zealand), 89, 167, 235n

Armistice, xi, 183

Armies in France, Extracts from General Routine Orders to British, 175

Army, British, *see* British Army (subdivided into armies, brigades, corps, divisions; for regiments *see* individual names)

Army Correspondence Field Book 152, HW's, 84–163 *passim*

Army, French, *see* French Army

Army German, *see* German Army

Army Lists, HW mentioned in; page 105g, 63; page 1385j, 72; page 1563, 72; page 1565, 80

Army Service Corps (ASC), 151

Arras, 35, 99, 110, 111, 112, 113, 117, 120, 144, 145, 178; in 1925, 193, 194, 202; 234n

Artists' Rifle Brigade, 24, 40

Artois, 175

Arvillers, 179

Ascheux, 180, 239n

Aspley Guise (Bedfordshire), 3, 17, 62, 65

Asquith, Mr, 10, 28

Astreux, 88

Avebury, Lord, 1

Australian troops, 89, 113, 114, 167; memorial in Amiens Cathedral, 193

B——, Mabs ('Eve Fairfax'), 185, 186

Badham, Col., 161

Baggy Point (Devon), 4, 6

Baghdad, fall of, 94

Baillescourt Farm, 193

Baldwin, Pte E.W. (LRB), 11, 45, 220n

Banks, Dr William (at Trefusis), 167

Bapaume, 74, 98, 99, 101, 106, 177

Barbusse, Henri, (*Le Feu – Under Fire*), viii, 167, 191, 204, 207–8, 235, 241

Barnes, Roland W. (Colfe's and LRB), 24, 27, 39, 58, 220n, 222n; *and see* plate 6b

Barnett, Reuben (Rifle Brigade), 242

Bates, Col. (LRB), 36, 37, 40, 41, 45, 219n, 221n, 227n

battlefields, HW re-visits 1925, 192–5; 1927, 197–8; 1964, 242n

battle rehearsals, 74

Beach Thomas, 144

Beaucourt, 93, 193

Beaumont, C.W. (publisher), 204

Beaumont Hamel (Hamel), 62, 91, 92, 93, 96, 97, 98, 153; *and see* plate 24b

Bedfordshire & Hertfordshire Regimental Association, 189, 197

Bedfordshire Regiment:

HW applies to join, 62–3, 64; ch. 6 (pp 165–187) pervasive; 2 Battln, 178–80, 237n, 238n; 3 Battln, 168, 172, 173–4, 176, 4 Battln, 179; 7 Battln, 238; 8 Battln, 177; consolidating of battalions 1918, 178, 238n; losses at St. Quentin 1918, 179; HW joins the Regimental Association 1920, 189; Colours presented at St Albans Catholic Cathedral, 192; reunion dinners, 197; description of badge, 227n

Beer, Dvr. (208 MGC), 136

BEF, *see* British Expeditionary Force

Belgium and Belgian Army, 10–11, 28, 30, 33, 35, 40, 43, German airship bases in, 77, situation in, 224–5n

Bell, Capt. Douglas H., MC (LRB Cameroons), wounded at Loos, 71–2, 196; HW helps get book published, 204

Belton Park Camp, *see* Grantham

Belton Park Camp (at the Front), 97, 98

Bennett, Arnold, 205

Beresford, J.D., 242n

Bevan, Dvr. (208 MGC), 107, 128, 135, 137, 139, 142, 148, 158

Bihucourt (V Army Corps HQ, May 1917), 154

187 Brigade to, 156, 157

Billjohn, HW's dog, 181

Birdcage, the (Ploegsteert Wood), 45

Bishop of London, 26

Bisley Camp, 2, 12, 13, 15, 22

Blackheath, 181

Bloody Sunday (Trafalgar Square, Nov. 1887), 61, 225n

Blunden, L/Cpl. A.E., 196, 243n

Bocker, Kapitanleutnant (Zepp. pilot), 77

Bolsheviks, inciting revolution, 90

Bolton, L/Cpl. (208 MGC), 96, 117, 128, 136

Bond, Mrs Muriel, 103, 105, 147

Boon, Henry, 155

Boon, Charlie, 3, 17, 62, 65, 88, HW mentions death of, 62, 126, 142

Boone, Marjorie, 3

Bouchoir, 179

Boulogne, 177

Bourlon Wood, 169, 171, 176

Bouzincourt, 179

Bow (and Bromley-by-Bow), Zeppelin raid on, 77

Bowes, Maj., George Bromley, 66, 227n

Boyes, Lt. Col., 8

Boy General, The (Brig. Gen. Bradford), 169, 170, 171, 237n

Bradford, Brig. Gen. Roland Boyes, (The Boy General) 169, 170, 171, 237n

Braithwaite, Maj. Gen. W.P. (62 Div.), 88, 169, 170, 234n

Brandon, 2/Lt. A. de B. (RFC), 77

Braunton Burrows (Devon), 3, 4

Brazil, 122, 146

Bresle, 180, 238–9n

Brett, 2/Lt. J.V., 121, 196

brigades, *see* British Army

Britannia, 203
British Army: BEF, see British
    Expeditionary Force; First,
    capture of Vimy Ridge, 117;
    Second, 161, 180; First and
    Third attack at Arras 1917,
    112; Third, 154, 169, 172,
    178; Fourth, 75, 89, 119, Fifth,
    89, 123, 154, 166, 167, 178;
    Corps: (I) 36, (III) 74; (IV)
    170, (V) 88, (VII) 118, (XVII)
    118; Cavalry, 36; Divisions: (2)
    172, 176; (4) 39, 56; (7) 116,
    138, 140; (8) 74 (30) 178,
    179, 180; (34) 75, (36) 180,
    (40) 171; (47) 171; (51) 170
    (62) 72, 88, 90, 140, 169,
    170, 171, 234n, (63) 90, 179,
    (Scottish) 180; Brigades
    (Infantry): (11) 39, 45, 56,
    (23) 74, 75; (89) (90) 178,
    179; (91) 148; (119, 120,
    121) 171; (185) 170; (186)
    170, 171, 172; (187) 72, 88,
    138, 143, 156, 170; (21
    Composite) 180; Role of in
    1917, 89; desperate for
    reinforcements 1918, 178;
    memorial in Amiens Cathedral
    1925, 193; cemetery at La
    Targette, 1925, 194. For
    regiments see individual entries
British Birds, Richard and Cherry
    Kearton, 4
British Expeditionary Force (BEF), 19,
    24, 33, 35, 43, 56, 124, 163;
    landing in France Aug. 1914,
    33; retreat from Mons, 33–4;
    prestige of, 65; Haig as Field
    Marshal, 89
British Union, xii, 191, 217n
Brockley, (HW born at, xv, 176
Brockton Camp, Staffordshire, 186
Bryant, Jack, 26
Bryers, Rupert, 2, 18, 220n
Buchan, John, witnesses final moment
    of war, 184
Bullecourt, 116, 117, 129, 138, 148,

149, 152, 234n taken by
    2/Gordons, 143, HW gassed
    at, 161, 163; in 1925, 194
Bulow, Gen. von, 34
Bulter, Maj. Gen. R.H.K. (Deputy CGS
    1917), 171
Bunbury, Lt. Col. C.H. de St P., 237–8n
Bunhill Row (HQ, LRB), 8, 62, in
    'Plug Street,' 41
Bunyan, John, 205
Burkit (a friend from home area), 18
Burnell, Maj. (LRB), 41
Burns, John, socialist agitator, 226n
Busby, William, 198
Buvenchy, 179
Byng, Gen. (Commanding Third
    Army) 172, 178, 236n

Cairns, Earl (Col., LRB), 62, 221n,
    227n
Cambrai, 99; Battle of Nov. 1917,
    169–172, 236n
Booklet Precis of Lessons learnt at, 176, in
    1918, 179
Cambridge, HRH The Duke of, (LRB)
    8
Cambridgeshire Daily News, 66
Cambridgeshire Regt, HW attached to
    at Newmarket, 1915, 66–8
Cameroon Highlanders, Douglas Bell
    in, 72, 196
Camp Hill Camp, Crowborough: 1st
    Battn LRB (and HW) training
    at, 12, 20, 23, 29 and see Plate 5;
    HW's letters home from,
    23–32; 2nd Battn training at,
    62
Canadian troops, 93; capture of Vimy
    Ridge, 120, of Passchendaele,
    167; memorial in Amiens
    Cathedral, 193
Canal du Nord (Battle of Cambrai,
    1917), 170, 172, 179, 183
Cannock Chase, (Staffordshire) 186
Carr (HW's Army tailor), 150, 154,
    165
Case, Pte (208 MGC) (HW's batman),
    116, 128, 143

casualty numbers: London Scottish at Messines Ridge, 36; at Neuve Chapelle, 1915, 65; in 2 Beds at Loos, 71; at Somme, 75; in 63 Div., 90; at Cambrai, 169; in 2 Beds spring 1918, 179; from air raids, 231n; at Bullecourt, 235n; the LRB at Ploegsteert, 242n

Casualty Clearing Stations: at Heilly, 76; at Colincamps, 161; at Warloi, 162

Cavalry, 36, 114; 2/4 Duke of Wellington's, 170; 1st Cavalry Brigade, 170

cemeteries: British, at Hermes, German at St Ledger, 194, 195; at La Maison Blanche, 194; English and French at La Targette, 194; LRB at Ploegsteert, 198

Central Foundation School, LRB at, 12 13

Champagne, 175

Chapman, Mrs, 20

Chappell, H.J. (and brother) (LRB), 196

Charterhouse School, LRB at, 12, 13

Cheriton Otter Hunt, 192

Cholmondeley, Col. H.C., (LRB) 62

Christ, 199

Christmas Truce 1914, 47–49; HW's letter about, 47–8 and see plate 7; influence on HW throughout life, 49, 209, 211

Churchill, Winston, 28

church tower, Georgeham: symbolic significance of in The Wet Flanders Plain, 199

Chyebassa, troopship: 32, 33; reunion of LRB survivors, 196–7, 198; History of, 220–1

Cite St Pierre, 70

City Imperial Volunteers (CIV), 62

City of London Regt, 5 Battn, 7

Cole, Peter (HWS member), vii, 231n, 232n

Colfensia, 58–60

Colfe's Grammar School, Lewisham, xv, 1, 7, 21; names of ex-pupils serving in war, 22

Colgate, Capt. Roy (MGC), 232n

Colincamps, 84; 44CCS at, 161

Collings-Wells, Lt. Col. J.S., DSO VC (Beds), 179

communism, HW and, 190–1

corduroy paths, 41

Cornwall, HW convalescent 1917, 165–8

corps, see British Army

Coulson, A.V. (LRB), 196

Croisilles, 107, 112, 193

Crowborough Camp, Sussex (training 1914); 12, 20, 23–31 passim, 196 and see plates 4, 5 and 6a

Crystal Palace (demobilization centre), 187

Cunninghame—Graham, R.B., 225–8n

Cuthbert (MGC), 85

Daily Express: HW's 'Christmas Truce' letter printed in, 48, 50; 1927 war articles printed in, 198; essay 'I Believe in the Men Who Died' printed in, 199, 201, 242n; 'The Last 100 Days' series 1928, 202;

Daily Mail: headlines on outbreak of war, 9–11 available to soldiers, 38, 40 HW asks for, 46; article mentioned, 48; HW mentions in letter, 50, 153, 219n

Daily Mirror, 'Ten Years . . . (II Nov 1928) 203, 243n

Daily Telegraph, 199

Davy, Dvr. (208 MGC), 94, 98, 128, 135, 142

Defence League, HW's letter to father about, 51–2

de la Mare, Richard, 204

Denny, Alfred Champion, MC (Colfe's, Sgt/LRB, Lt./Middlesex, Capt./MGC), 22

Demicourt, 171

Derby, Dowager Lady Constance,

D'Esperey, Gen. (Fr. Army), 34

Devon, *see* Georgeham

Devonport Military Hospital, 168

Devonshire Regt, (re attach, May 1917) 141

'Diehards' (Middlesex Regt), 72

Diplock, Cpl. T.L. (LRB), 197

divisions, *see* British Army

Dolan, Brian (HWS member, researcher), vii, and *passim* in Notes

donkeys, care of, *see* mules and donkeys

Don Quixote, 209, 210

Douai, 120

Drocourt, 150

Duffield, Christine, (2nd wife) xvi

Duke of Wellington's Cavalry, 170

Duncan, Leland, 18, 21, 58, 220n; letter to HW, 22

Dunkerque, 35

Dunstall Priory, 1

Duval, L/Cpl. (208 MGC), 112, 124, 136

Eakring, (re horse training) 85

Eastern Front, (Situation early 1917) 90

Eastern Road, No. 11, Brockley, Lewisham, xiv, 1, 12, 57, 176 *and see* plate 31a; all letters from HW to his parents addressed here inherent in text; No. 18 (the 'Turret House'), 63

East Lancashire Regt, 40

East Yorkshire Regt, (re Colin Traill) 236n

Ecoust, 107, 156

Edmonds, Brig. Gen. (compiler *Official History*), viii, 39. See also *Official History*

Edward, HRH The Prince of Wales, 41

Efford, Thomas, 21, 31, 43, 48, 50, 137, 155

Engelbelmer, 93, 96, 97, 98

Ervillers, (HW at) 130–156 *passim; and see* plate 23

Etaples, English Mutiny at, 168, 206, 236n; IBD at 1918, 177

Extracts from *General Routine Orders issued to the British Armies in France*, F.M. Sir Haig (Army booklet), 175

Fabian Society, 226n

Falmouth Military Hospital, 167

Falmouth, HW convalescent at, 165

Fanshawe, Lt. Gen. (V Corps), 89

fascines, 169, 236–7n

fascism, 191, 199, 217n, 237n

Felixstowe, HW stationed at, 168, 172–185

passim, 197 *see also* Landguard

Field Message Book, HW's, 1917 84–161 *passim*

Finch, Pte (208 MGC), 128, 134, 142

First World War: pervasive throughout text; Declaration of, 9–11; Armistice, xi, 183–4; 10th Anniversary of, 199–204

First World War, The, Martin Gilbert, 183, 184

Flanders Plain, 35, 58, 161, 175, 180, 200

Flesquières, 171

Fletcher, Alan (Haig's ADC), 70

Flynn, L/Cpl. (208 MGC), 114, 124, 128, 137, 142

Foch, Marechel, 34, 180, 182

Folkestone, No. 3 Rest Camp, 185

Fontaine, 130

forage, for mules and horses, 82, 144

Forceville, 88

Formby, Lt. Thomas Hope, 66, 67, 227–8n

Fox, Dvr. G. (208 MGC), 128, 142, 157

Foulkes, Maj., 69

France, mobilization in, 10

Franklin, Pte (Groom, 208 MGC), 128, 135, 142

French Army: in 19th century, 7; mobilization, 10; dispositions Aug. 1914, 33–4, Sixth and Fifth at Battle of the Marne 1914, 34; Tenth, 35; 40 Division, 119; Bed. Regt. relieved by, March 1918, 179;

memorial in Amiens Cathedral 1925, 193, cemetery at La Targette, 194

French, Field Marshal Sir John, 33, 35, 45; concerning trench foot, 57; criticized for behaviour at Battle of Loos, 71; Pres. of Ypres League, 189; mentioned in Notes, 222n, 228n

Frith, Pte (farrier, 208 MGC) 128, 135, 142

Fursdon, 2/Lt. G.E.S., later capt., (LRB), countersignature on HW's letters, 39–45, 223n; at *Chyebassa* reunion 1926, 196, 197

Galsworthy, John, xv, 186, 218n

gas: first use by Germans, 65; by British at Battle of Loos, 69; Haig's concern about, 70–1; gas shell bombardments, 94, 95; gas attacks 1917, 115, 116, 145, 149, 160, 161, 162, 163; at Bullecourt, 234n

gasmasks, home-made, 227n

Gauche Wood, 171

Gentlemen & Officers, K.W. Mitchinson, 7, 9, 32, 38, 220–1n

George V, His Majesty King, 11, 41

Georgeham (Devon), xv, 3–6, 76, 186, 199

German Air Raids on Great Britain 1914–18, Capt. Joseph Morris, 76–9

German Army: xiii; Declaration of war, 10; invasion of Belgium, HW;s early opinion of tactics, 19–20; initial advances, 33–6; dispositions Aug. 1914, 33; BEF sent to oppose Sixth, 35; description of early attacks by, 43–4; soldiers in Christmas Truce 1914, 47–9; fine boots of, 50; first use of gas, 65; Battle of Somme, 74–5; Somme Battle plans known to, 75; withdrawal to Hindenburg Line, 89, 100, withdrawal from

Ancre Valley, 90, HW describes finding dead soldiers, 108–9; number of prisoners Apr. 1917, 117; strength of army, 150; HW notes signs of collapse of, 163; counter offensive at Cambrai, 169; 200 infantry captured, 170; attack on Gonnelieu and Gouzancourt Nov. 1917, 171; spring offensive 1918, 175, 177–180; Ludendorff's intention to destroy British Army, 178; take Hill 63, 180; retreating, 182; forces in chaos, 183; Government accept terms of Armistice, 183; submarines enter Harwich Harbour, 184; graves at St Leger 1925, 194; German cemetery at La Maison Blanche, 194–195; letter from ex-soldier, 202–3

German church Forest Hill raided, 30

German House (Ploegsteert Wood), 45

Gibb (208 MGC), 85

Gibbo, 168, *and see* plate 28c

Gibbs, Phillip, 144

Gilbert, Martin, 183, 184

goat-skin coats, army issue, 46, 224n

Godolphin House, Newmarket, 66

Gold, Capt. E. (meteorologist at Loos), 70

Golding, Misses 'Queenie' and Eileen, 68

Gomiecourt, 103, 113, 115; *and see* plate 24

Gommecourt, 89

Gonnelieu, 171

Gordon, Gen., inspects 208 MGC, 86

Gordons (2nd), take Bullecourt, 143

Gorringe, Gen. Sir Hubert (Commanding Fifth Army), 89, 140, 167, 178

Gouzancourt, 170

Granimont (Front Line 11 Nov. 1918), 182

Grantham, MGC Training Centre, 72, 85, 87, 163

Great Britain: declares war on Germany, 10; bells rung to celebrate Battle of Cambrai, 171

Great Yarmouth, re airship raids, 77

Gregg, Mrs M., see Williamson, Maude

Grenfell, Julian, 229n, 230n

Grey Towers (Hornchurch), 228–9n

Gricoust, 119

Guard's Brigade (1st), 171

gun limber organization, re attack, 114–5

guns: 13 pounder, 33; Howitzers, 46, 65, 94, 118, Lewis Guns, 72, 176; gun defences in London, 77; 8in naval guns etc., 156; machine guns at Cambrai, 170, 176; Stokes' Mortars, 176

Haig, Gen. Sir Douglas GCB, GCVO, KCIE, xiii, 33, 38, 65, 70–1, as Field Marshal, 89, 124, 167, 169, 171, 174, 175, 178, 180, 189, 218n, 235n, 237n, 239n

Hainault Farm (RFC base, Essex), 77

Haldane, Lord, 8, 11, 28

Ham (France) 1918, 177, 179

Hall-Walkers Hospital: HW in 1918, 180, 239n

Hamel 97, 98

Hamilton (208 MGC), acting TO in HW's absence, 154

Hammond, L.E., (LRB) 17

Hampshire Regt, 40

Hands, Sgt. Cook 'Tootsie', 220n

Harding, (LRB) also Sun Fire Ins. Office, 221n

Harris, L/Cpl. (208 MGC), 140, 152

Harwich Command, 173

Harwich Harbour, (German U Boats surrender) 184

Havrincourt Wood, 170

Hawthornden Prize for Literature, XV, 198

Hayes, Pte (208 MGC), 115

Hazebrouck, 40, in 1927, 198

Heilly, CCS at, 76, 230n

Helfaut, gas training at, 69

Henry Williamson Society, vii, xvii; contact addresses, xvii, 245

Henshaw, Sgt. S.T.W. 'Granny' (LRB), 197

Hermes, British cemetery at, 171

Hesdin Court of Enquiry, (into Cambrai) 237n

Heycock, Col. C.T. (Cambs Regt), 66, 227n

Hibbert, Ida Loetitia, xv, 192

Hildersheim, see Eastern Road

Hill 63, 180, 239n

Hilly Fields (The Hill) Lewisham 1, 16, 17, 61, 73, 77, 78, 230n

Hindenburg Line, 89, 100, 106, 108, 112, 113, 114, 115, 117, 120, 140, 144, 166, 193, 194

Hinman, C.P., later Lt. Col., DSO, MC (LRB), 197

History of the Great War Based on Offiicial Documents – Military Operations, Belgium and France 1914–18, see Official History

Hither Green, 61–2

Hitler, Adolf, 191, 199

Hoare, Capt. C.H. (Brig. Maj., 187 Brigade), 90

Holland, (Kaiser fled to 1918) 183

Hollis, E.C. (LRB), 196

Holt & Co (Army Agent Bankers), 63, 183, 188

Holwood Park, Keston, 1, 16, 132

Home Defence Squadrons (RFC), 77

Honourable Artillery Coy (HAC) 40, 141

Hooton, Mr (Sun Fire Ins. Office), 43, 45, 104, 121

Hore Ruthven, Hon A.G.A., 233n

Hornchurch, 26 Middlesex at, 72, 229n

Horseley, 2/Lt. (208 MGC) 87, 96, 116, 148, 154; and see plate 22b

horses: LRB procurement of, 12, 220n; care of 80–83; transportation to France, 85–7; touble with MMP over

watering, 133–4; 88–160 *passim; see also* mules and donkeys
Hose, Horace, school friend, 2, 17
hospitals, HW attends at: No. 1 General Hospital, 56; Ancoats Military Hospital, Manchester, 56, 57; No. 9 General Hosp at Rouen, 76, 230, No. 8 ditto, 163; Sussex Lodge (London), 64; Falmouth Military Hosp, 165; Devonport Military Hosp, 168; Hall-Walkers Hosp, Regent's Park, 180, 239n
Howell, Maj. A., 66, 227n
Howitzers, 46, 65, 94, 118
Hughes, Ted (Poet Laureate), xvi
Hunter-Weston, Brig. Gen., 41, 224n
Husey, Capt., 8–9, 219n, 220n
Hussars (11th), 170
Hutchings, Cpl. (208 MGC), 140

Imperialism, the Last Stage of Capitalism, Lenin, 190–1
Imperial War Museum, viii; HW made tape for, 45
Indian Army, HW's proposed transfer, 1918, 182–3,
Indian troops, xiii
Infantry Brigade, 11th, 40, 45
Irles, 94, 95

Jefferies, Richard, 185–6, 192, 209, 242n
Jennings (201 MGC, believe TO), 112, 117
Joffre, Gen. (Commanding French Army), 34, 35, 89
Johnston, H.L. (LRB), 197
Jonas, Capt. F.C., 67, 69, 228n
Jones, Sgt. (208 MGC), 141
Joy, L/Cpl. (208 MGC), 115, 128, 134, 139, 148
Joyce Green, (re Home Defence Squadrons) 77

Kaiser, The, 10, 89, 183, 219n
Kentish Mercury, 126, 150, 153, 155

Kermode, William, 205, 206
Keston, (childhood haunt) 1
Kiggell, Lt. Gen. Sir Launcelot CGS, 174, 287n
KING ALBERT'S BOOK, 56, 224–5n
King, Capt. Cecil Redmony (CO, 208 MGC):
HW's field messages to, ch. 5 *passim;* particular mentions, 85, 89, 93, 106, 115, 139, 146–7, 154; goes on leave end May 1917, 156; HW writes note about 1957, 166
King Edward's Horse Cavalry, 170
King, Maj. Norman C., later Lt. Col. (LRB), 62, 219n, 227n
King's Royal Rifles, 30
Kitchener, Lord, 11, 71, 222n
Kluck, Gen. von, 34, 222n
Knight, Capt. R.B. (3rd Beds), 173
Kolle, Kapitanleutnant Waldemar (Zeppelin pilot), 78–9
Kodak camera, HW asks for, 137, 153, 156
Kut, recapture of Feb. 1917, 87, 88, 232n

La Boiselle, (German listening post), 75
Ladywell Cemetery, 79
Landguard Fort, HW stationed at, 168, 173, *see also* Felixstowe
Lancers (17th), 114
landsturmers, (mentioned in Xmas 1914 letter), 48
Laon, re 1918 spring attack), 175
La Targette, English and French cemeteries at 1925, 194
Laubernburgh, Lt. (22 MGC), 141
Lawrence, T.E., xii, 206, 241n
Leaver, Hugh, HW's uncle, 17
Leaver, Thomas William (maternal grandfather), 15, 16, 17, 21, 27, 40, 41, 223n
Le Cateau, 34, 222n
Le Condé Canal, 33
Leefe-Robinson, Lt. W. (RFC), 76
Le Feu (Under Fire), Henri Barbusse,

167, 191–2, 207–09, 235n, 241n

L'Enfer (Inferno), Henri Barbusse, 191

Le Gheer, 195

Le Havre, 32, 36, 43, 87

Lenin, Vladimir, 190–1

Lens, 112

Le Quennet farm, 171

'Les Autres Boches,' 74

Lesboeufs, 89

Lewis guns, 72, 176

Lewisham, xx, 1, 21, 22, 27, 61

Leytonstone Crowd (LRB), 196

Liddell Hart, Capt. Sir Basil, XI, XII, 217n

Liddell Hart Centre for Military Archives, viii

Liege, fall of, 33

limbers, pervasive through ch. 5; organization for guns, 115

Linden Day (1 August) (re Beds Regt), 182, 240n

Lloyd George, David, re Somme 75; 87

Lochnagar (mine crater), 74

London: HW's letter about possible invasion by Germans, 51: Zeppelin raids on, 76–9 defences in, 76–7 civilian life in, 126

London Gazette, 80

London Regt, 7

London Rifle Brigade, The (LRB): pervasive through chs 2 and 3; structure of, 7–8; numbers in at outbreak of war, 9 winners of half-marathon 1913 and Brighton march 1914, 8–9 for home defence only, 9; annual training camp, Aug. 1914, 7, 9, 13 mobilization of, 11–12 commandeering horses, 12, 220n conditions in training camps 13ff going abroad, 15–6 mentioned in letter from Leland Duncan, 22; at Camp Hill Camp, 23ff to fight in France, 24; German officer in,

30; leaves for France, 32 list of officers embarked on Chyebassa, 33, 221–2; arrival at Le Havre, 36; proceeds to Front, 37–40, reorganization of Coys, 41; at Ploegsteert, 41ff; in attack 19 Dec. 1914, 45; Christmas Truce, 47–8; article on 'Plug-Street', 53; mentioned in Colfensia, 1915, 58–60, colonel against men applying for commissions, 62; 2 Battn training Crowborough, 62; 3 Bath at London HQ, 62; Douglas Bell in, 72; mentioned in HW letter, 88; HW sees 2 Battn in Front Line, 1917, 112; sergeant wounded, 114; reunions post-war, 196–7; cemetery at Ploegsteert 1927, 198, Douglas Bell writes about life in, 204, 2 Battalion take the 'Red Patch' at Battle of Bullecourt, 235; and see plate 2

London Scottish, The, 8, 24, 27, 28, 36, 39, 46, 58, defective rifles in, 36

London Rifle Volunteers, 7, 8

London to Brighton march, pre-war, 8–9

Lone Tree, 71

Loos, Battle of, 69–72

Lucas, F.W. (Headmaster, Colfe's 'Old Bird'), 8, 21, 220n letter to HW, 21

Lucifer, (metaphor for Hitler) 199

Ludendorff, Maj. Gen. Erich, 178

Luxemburg, German troops invade, 10

Lyman, Pte (208 MGC), 128, 135, 132, 142

Lynton (Devon), 76, 230n

Lys Offensive 1918, 180

McClane, 2/Lt. A.P. (208 MGC), 128, 139, 161, and see plates 22b and 24a

McCleave, 2/Lt. A.P., 130

McConnel, 2/Lt. (208 MGC), 117, 124, 143, 153 and see plates 22b and 24a

McKelvey, Lt. (208 MGC), 117, 128, 136

Machine Gun Company (208) (208 MGC): pervasive through ch. 5; 72, 80, 84, 231–2n; HW training as Transport Officer for, 80–3; HW as Transport Officer, 84–161; list of drivers (mules etc.), 86 and see plate 22a; HW's 'Orders for Entraining', 86–7; move to Front Line area, 88; attached to 62 Div, 187 Inf Brig, 88, role of, 89; HW organizing billets for, 97–8 preparations for battle, 113ff, Transport Section organization, 127, Nominal Roll TS, 128 and see plate 26a; further list of names, 134, decimated in attack 3 May 1917, 138; Coy HQ at Morthomme, 139; TS Roll, 142–3; medals awarded to men, 143, 155; King on leave, new CO arrives, 156; see also Transport Section

Machine Gun Company (34), 93, 97; (201), 112, 118; (206), 156; (213), 97, 170

machine gunners, considered undisciplined, 172

McKonnel, Maj., (208 MGC) 85

Macolm, Lt. Col. G.A., (London Scottish) 36

Marchand, La Veuve, (1925) 195

Maristany, Eugene (Stany), 85, 102, 118, 119, 122, 126, 133, 146, 148, 152, 155, 161, 164, 165, 176, 177, 182, 232n, 240n, and see plate 16b

Marne, Battle of the, 34–5

MARS attack, (1918) 238n

Martin, Pte (Dvr., 208 MGC), 128, 135

Martinsaut, 97, 98

Mary, HRH Princess, 47, 48 and see plates 8 and 9

Mash Valley, (1 July 1916) 74–5

Mathy, Kapitanleutnant (Zeppelin pilot), 77

Maunoury, Gen., (Fr. VIth Army) 34

Mazingarbe, 72

Medical Boards, HW attends, 57, 73, 76, 80, 167, 168, 177, 180, 181, 182

Mendes, Catulle, (re Barbusse) 191

Messines Ridge, 36, 38; 1917, 161, 163; Battle of, 1918, 180; in 1925, 195

MICHAEL attack, 238n

Middlesex Regt: 25 (Reserve) Battn, 72, 228–9n; 2 Battn, 74, losses at Battle of the Somme, 75

Milgate, Lily and family ('Lily Cornford'), 76, 79, 168

Milland (208 MGC), 85

Millbank Military Hospital, HW admitted to, 73

Milling (Beds Regt), re tennis 182 and see plate 30c

Milo, D., 31

mines and mine tunnels, 74

Miraumont, 92, 93, 94, 102, 103, 108–9

Mitchell, Sgt. (TSgt., 208 MGC): HW's messages to, pervasive through 96–159; temp injured, 141, trouble over L/Cpl. Nolan, 146–7 problems over supplies, 143–4, 150–1, 152, HW comments on, 166

Mitchinson, K.W. (Gentlemen & Officers), (LRB) 7, 9, 32, 38, 45, 48, 62, 219 (n 3, 9) 220–1 (n 16, 19, 20)

MMP, see Mounted Military Police

Mobbs, Pte (208 MGC), 128, 135, 142

mobilization, 9–11

Moeuvres, (Cambrai, 2 Div.) 176

Montford, 2/Lt. A.C. (208 MGC), 85, 98 killed in attack, 138, 166 HW notes home address, 141

Monquet Farm, 74

Mons, Battle of, August 1914, 33; returns to Allied Forces 1918, 182

Morthomme, 139

Mory, tanks at 110, 234n;208 NGC at 1917, 112–130 passim; 137

Mosley, Sir Oswald, 191

Motor Cycle, 95, 105, 107, 122, 150, 155

Motor Cycling, 74, 95, 105, 107, 122, 150, 155, 156

Mounted Military Police (MMP), 134, 149

Mounted Officer's Book of Horses & Mules for Transport, 2/Lt. R.J. Day, 80–3

mules and donkeys: pervase through ch. 5; care of, 80–3 transportation of, 86–7 injuries to, refs passim; numbers of in HW's section Apr. 1917, 114; to be ready for battle, 116–7; galls on, 128; injured animals, 130; routine for, 133; being overworked, 136; routine of section, 143 forage for, 144–5 mule races, 151–2 Tommy kicks HW, 157; see also horses

Mullens, Maj. Gen. R.L., 171

Musker, Mr J.: presentation of KING ALBERT'S BOOK, 56

mutiny at Etaples, 168, 236n

Navvies Battln, 72, 228–29n

Neuve Chapelle, Battle of, 65

Neuville St Vlaast 1925, 194

Nevinson, C.R.W. Frontispiece, VII, 204, 243n

Newark, (training as at MGC T.O.) 85

Newfoundland troops, memorial in Amiens Cathedral, 193

Newhaven, invasion defence 1914, 24

Newman, Lt. Col. C.R., 169

Newmarket, garrison at, 66–8

Newmarket Journal, 67, 68

Newne, Sir George, 76

New Zealand troops, 85, at Passchendaele, 167

memorial in Amiens Cathedral, 193

Nicholson, Cuthbert, 163

Nicholson, Doris ('Helena Rolls'), 63, 106, 111, 145, 176, 177, 181, 182, 183, 185

Nicholson, Mrs, 85, 90, 105, 109, 111, 137, 146, 152, 155, 165, 181, 182

Nicholson, Roy, 152, 155, 165

Nivelle, Gen. (French Army), 89

Nolan, L/Cpl. (208 MGC), 112, 116, 128, 134, 136, 139, 142, 146–7, 147, 155

Norman, Squire, 1

Northampton, garrison at, 72

Norton Motorcycle, 63, 74, Brooklands Road Special, 185, 186

Notes from the Front 1915 (Staff Booklet), 64

Notes on Pack Transport, Army Staff, 80

Officers' Instruction course, HW attends 1915, 63–4, and see plate 13

Official History (History of the Great War . . .), viii, 35, 36, 39, 41, 49, 65, 70, 71, 74, 75, 169, 170, 171, 172, 178–9, 179, 211, and passim through Notes

Oise, 1918, 177

Oh What a Lovely War!, 218n

Old Bird, see Lucas, F.W.

Old Hall Farm, xv

Onslow, Lt. Col. C.C. (CO 2/Beds Regt), 71

Orlebar, R.R.B., 189

Orvillers, 74

Orwell estuary, 184

Ostend, (Belgians retreat to 1914) 35

Ox's Cross (Devon), xv, 3

Paget, (re IV Army 1917) 119

Parkinson, Pte (208 MGC), 135

Passchendaele (3rd Battle Ypres), 167; Passchendaele-Broodseinde Ridge, 167, 1918, 179

Peronne, 1917, 101; 1918, 177

Perry's Mill, 1

Peter, Saint, 195

Peterson, Kapitanleutnant (Zeppelin pilot), 77

Petrograd (St Petersburg) riots in 1917, 90

philosophical beliefs, HW's, post-war, ch. 7 passim

Picardy, 175, 179, 238n

Pilgrim's Progress, A, John Bunyan, 205

Pleuresses, Henri Barbusse, 191

Ploegsteert (Plug Street): HW's experiences in 1914–15, 41–55, LRB attack 19 Dec. 1914, 45 article about life in, 53 sketch map of in 1925, 197, 242n; LRB cemetery at, 1927, 198 242n; HW visit 1964, 242n

Plumer, Field Marshal Lord, of Messines, 189

Plymouth, HW convalescent at 1917, 168

Poelcapelle, 180

Policy of Reconstruction, HW's, post-war, 190

Pollack, Capt. (regt not stated), 117

Poperinghe, 198

Portuguese Expeditionary Force, xiii, 89

Post Office Rifle Brigade, 8

Pothecary, Maj. W.F., DCM, 197

Pozieres, 74, 75

Poyntz, Lt. Col. H.S. (Beds Regt), 178, 189

Principles of War, The (1914–15) (Staff Booklet), 64

Pritchard, Lt. T.B. (RFC), 79

Prix Goncourt, (re Barbusse) 191

Pryor, Capt. G.D., (2/1st Cambs), 66, 227n

Putsborough Sands (Devon), 76

Radio Times, 202

Ravensbourne, River, 1, 42

Rawlinson, Gen. Sir Henry (Commanding Fourth Army), 75, 89

Red Patch, the (Bullecourt, 1917) 234–5n

regiments, see individual entries under regimental name

rehearsals for battles, (1916) 74

Rendle, Gwendoline, 185

Rifle Brigade, The, 39, 45

Rifle Volunteer Force, 7

Ritter, Hauptmann, (Lone Tree' 1915), 71

Rochincourt, (HW visit 1925) 195

Romantic Movement, French, (barbusse) 191

Romarin, (1914) 40, 223n

Rose, Lt. Clarence (Adjutant, 208 MGC), 85, 88, 89, 93, 98, 103, 109, 116, 117, 141, 152, 154, 158

Ross, Kathleen Ailsa, (Lt. Formby's bride) 66

Rouen: No. 9 General Hosp at, 76, 230n; No. 8 General Hosp at, 163

Royal Academy, (HW visit 1918), 181

Royal Engineers, 69, 159; '179' Tunnelling Coy, 74

Royal Flying Corps, 26; No. 39 Squadron (attacking Zeppelins over London), 76–9; at Front 1917, 111, 131, 132

Royal Marine Infantry Troops, 35

Royal Naval Air Service (Harwich) 173

rum issue, 106–7, 110

Rupprecht, Crown Prince, 75

Russian Army, xiii, soldiers not landing in Scotland, 15; revolution mentioned in letter, 150; effect of removal from theatre of war, 177–8

St Cyrpian Church, Lewisham, 176

ST GEORGE attacks, 180, 239n

St Julien, attack on (1917) 168

St Leger, (1917) 106, 118; (1925) 194

St-Omer, (1914) 35, 38, 43

St Quentin, (spring 1918) 177, 179

Salmond, Lady Monica, 230n
Sapignes, (CHQ RE 461 Cmp, 1917) 159
Sapogny, 159
Scarborough, bombardment of Dec. 1914, 46
Scarpe, River 1918, 177, 178
Schlieffen Plan, 35, 222n
School of Arms, LRB, 7 and see plate 2
Schwaben Redoubt, 74
Scottish Division, (re HW, 1918) 180
Second World War, xi
Selby, (Terence Tetley at, 1918) 182
Seven Fields of Shrofften, 1
Sevenoaks, (HW on Officers Instruction Course, 1915) 63
Shakespeare, William, 186
Shallowford (Devon) (HW living, 1930s) xv
Sharman, Martin (LRB), 196
Shaw, George Bernard, 225n, 226n
Shelley, Percy Bysse, 186
Sheppard, Robert (Colfe's, Royal Navy), 15, 17
Shooting Common, 1
Shorncliffe, HW stationed at 1919, 185
Siegfried Stellung, see Hindenburg Line
Simpson, Gerald (HW's cousin Jerry) brief mentions in HW's letters home, 87, 88, 91, 93, 102, 104, 119, 126, 148, 150, 155, 233n
Simpson, Hubert, (Jerry's older brother) 233n
Simpson, Sidney St Paul and Maude, 233n
Sisteron, (re Kolle & Zepp. raids) 79
Sivry (Front Line 11 No. 1918), 182
Skindles Hotel (Poperingle) 198
Smith, Dvr. (208 MGC), 136
Smith-Dorrien, Gen. Sir Horace, stand at Le Cateau, 33–4, 222n
Snail's Hall Farm, Zeppelin brought down at, 77
socialist unrest 1887, 61, 225–6n
Soldier's Diary of the Great War, A, Douglas Bell, 72, 204, 228n

Solents, (2 Beds Spring 1918) 179
Somerset Light Infantry, (Ploegstreert wood, 1914) 40, 45
Somers-Smith, J.R. (officer, LRB), 38
Somme: Battle of the, 74–5, 84, 124, in 1917, 166, in 1918, 179; in 1925, 193; HW's thoughts about, 1928, 200
South African Brigade (re John Buchan, end of war) 184
Southampton, embarkation from, 1914, 26; 1917, 87, 164
Southend, training at 1915, 68–9
Southend Pond, 1
Southend Standard, 68–9
Sowrey, 2/Lt. F. (RFC), re-Zepp. raid, 77
Special Constabulary, W.L. Williamson in, 51, 61–2, 225, 226n; and see plate 18
Spire, The, William Golding, 199
Spraecombe (Devon), 3, 5
Squerryes Park, 1
Squire, Sir John C., (Jack) 204
stellenbosch, 174, 237n
Stiffkey (HW's farm in Norfolk), xv
Stirling, L/Cpl. (208 MGC), 87, 127, 128, 142
Story of My Heart, The, Richard Jefferies, influence on HW, 185, 209
Strand Magazine, The, 186
Sun Fire Insurance Office, xx, 3, 7, 103, 104, 196
Sutton's Farm (RFC Base), 76, 77
Sydenham, 188

tanks, 88, 110, 114, 169, 170, 234n
Taube aeroplanes, 40, 44, 55
Taylor, Brig. Gen. (187 Brigade), 88
'Teddy Bears', 180n
Tempest, 2/Lt. W. (RFC), 78
Territorial Force, (The Terriers) 7, 8, 24, 28–9
Territorial Rifle Brigade, 7, 8
Tetley, Terence, mainly mentions in letters, 2, 15, 16, 17, 18, 21, 24, 25, 27, 29, 31, 38, 43, 73, 76, 102, 126, 137, 148, 161,

175, 177, 180, 181, 182–3,
    184, 185, 230n, 240n; and see
    plate 16
Thildonck, 17, 223n
Thomas, Dvr. (208 MGC), 136, 142
Thomas, Edward, (writer) 112
Thompson, Francis, (poet) 242n
Toc H chapel at Poperinghe, 198
Tolstoy, Leo, War and Peace, 208, 210,
    212, 243n
Trafalgar Square, social disturbance in
    1887 ('Bloody Sunday'), 61,
    225–6n
Traill, Maj. Colin, MC, 236n; and see
    plate 28a
Transport Officer, 208 MGC: HW
    training for, 80–83 role of, 89,
    HW as, 84–164
Transport Sergeant, 208 MGC: HW's
    messages to, pervasive through
    96–159, for particular
    mentions see Mitchell, Sgt.
Transport Section, 208 MGC:
    pervasive through ch. 5; List of
    Feb 1917, see Plate 22a,
    Nominal Roll 20 Apr. 1917,
    128; further list of names,
    134–5, rough list of men
    present after battle, 141 Roll,
    142–3; daily routine, 143;
    routine and harness cleaning,
    147–8; list of requirements for,
    158
Trefusis, Auxiliary Hospital for
    Officers: HW convalescent at,
    165, 168; 235n; and see plates
    27 and 28
Tremlett, Lt. (208 MGC), awarded
    DSO, 143; killed 155, 166; and
    see plate 24b
trenches, specific mentions, 41, 42,
    44–5, HW describes life in,
    58–60
trench foot, 43, 45, 57–8
trench maps, 89; and see plate 20c
Tsar, abdicated Feb. (Mar.) 1917, 90
Tuson, Brig. Gen. H.D., (23 Bde, 1 July
    1916) 75

Tyler, L/Cpl. (208 MGC), 141

Under Fire (Le Feu), Henri Barbusse, viii,
    167, 191–2, 204, 207–9,
    235n, 241n
United States of America: enter war
    April 1917, 89, 112,
    involvement of troops 1918,
    178

vaccination, 15, 18, 24
VALKYRIE attack, 1918, 239n
Verdun, re Spring 1918 offensive,
    175, 195
Verlaines, (1918) 179
Veterinary Services (AVC) at Front
    1917, 119, 130, 134, 142
Vimy Ridge: capture by 1st Army, 117,
    120–1 in 1925, 194
Vincent, Brig. Gen. ('Vincent's Force'),
    171

War and Peace, Leo Tolstoy, 208, 210,
    212, 242n
war bonds, 183, 194
Ward, Col. John (Navvies Battn,
    Middlesex Regt.), 72, 228–9n
Warloi, 180
War Office, Whitehall, 62, 154
Warwickshire Regt, 141
Wasp, The, (Beds. Regt. post-war mag.)
    189
Waterton, 2/Lt. Joseph, 68
Watson, 'Bony', 2
Weekly Despatch, xv, 26
Welch Fusiliers, 39
Welch, Horace F., (fict. 'Sailor'
    Jenkins) 226n
Welch Regt. 71, 141
Wespelaer, (re family visit 1912) 26;
    see also Thildonck
West Australian (hospital ship), 164
Western Front, pervasive throughout;
    174–5
West Riding Regt (2), 88, 169, 233n
Westy, HW notes death of, 181, 239;
    see also 40n
West, Capt. 'Spectre' under works by

HW, fictional character/events in

Whitby, bombardment of Dec. 1914, 46

Whitfield, Capt. C.O. (Beds Regt), 197

Williamson, Doris (Biddy) (younger sister), 1, goes into attack 3 May 1917, 138; letter asking her to write to Dvr. Bevan, 148; and not to write to him further, 158, married to William Busby, 198; and see plate 31a

Williamson, Gertrude (mother), 1, 12, 165, 196, 223n; HW's letters to while training 1914, 13–32 and see plate 4b; from Front, 1914–1915, 37–56 and see plate 7; from Front, 1917, 90–163 passim

Williamson, Henry William: effects of First World War, xi boyhood character, xii; vilification by the media, xiv; a patriot, xiv; key dates in the life of, xv–xvi 'a dreaming youth' aged 18, summer 1914, 1; education at Colfe's Grammar School, 1; boyhood pursuits, 1–2; early interest in nature, 2, starts work in Sun Fire Ins. Office, 3, cousins at Aspley Guise, 3, first visit to Georgeham, Devon, May 1914, 3–6; enlists in Territorial Rifle Brigade, LRB, 7; LRB annual training camp, 7, 9; mobilization at outbreak of war, 10–12; early grasp of what war would entail, 13, 14, 15, 17; irritation with mother, 13; letters home while training, 1914, 13–32 and see plates 3 and 4; volunteering foreign service, 13; conditions in training camp, 13; opinion about Germans and war tactics, 17, 18; arrival at Camp Hill Camp, Crowborough, 23–4, and

see 5 and 6a; orders to embark, Nov. 1914, 31; arrival in France, Nov. 1914, 36–7; proceeds to Front Line, 41 at Ploegsteert, 41–55; description of trench warfare, Dec. 1914, 42–47; Christmas Truce 1914, 47–9 and see plate 7; its lasting effect on HW, 49; becomes ill, Jan. 1915, 50, 56 and see plate 9b; letter to father about possible invasion of London, 51 and life at Front, 53–5; suffering from dysentery and trench foot, 56; returns sick to England, Jan. 1915, 56 and see plate 1; convalescence, 57 and see plate 10; articles about experiences printed in Colfensia, 58–60; applies for and obtains commission, 62 and see plates 11, 12 and 14; buys first Norton motorcycle, 63; Initial Officers' Instruction course, 1915, 63–4 and see plate 13; gaucheness as officer, 63–4; attached to 2/1st Cambs Regt at Newmarket, 66; fined for speeding, 68; description of use of gas at Battle of Loos, 69–70; transfer to 25 Battn Middlesex Regt at Hornchurch, 72–3; training with 208 MGC, 72–3; sickness and convalescence summer 1916, 73; behaving wildly with Terence Tetley, summer 1916, 73; did not take part in Battle of the Somme, 74–5; convalescent boliday in Devon, Aug. 1916, 76; still suffering effects of dysentery, Aug. 1916, 76; background to 'Lily Cornford', 76–9; loud as Zepp. raids, 76–9; promoted to full Lieutenant, 80p training for Transport Officer, 80–3; anguish at Christmas throughout life, 84, 232n; Transport Officer 208 MGC, 84–164 and see plate 17; Orders for entraining, 86–7; 208 MGC embark for France, Feb. 1917, 87, at the Front, 88–164; conditions in trenches, 91–2; bad report from Capt. King, 93; anguish at death of mules from shelling and mud, 93, 94; writes poems, 95, 96; organization of billets, 97–8; description of routine, 104; gets lost in Hindenburg Line, 108; gets German relics, 108 and see plate 25; preparatory organization for battle, 113–117; Mory shelled by Germans, 119, 120, thoughts on progress of war (Arras attack), 120–2; justification of himself over bad report, 121; nostalgic for home, 126, 132; trouble with MMP over watering horses, 133–4; feels lucky not to have been killed or injured, 140; thoughts about the attack, 144, 145; trouble between St. Mitchell and L/Cpl. Nolan, 146–7; programme for mule races, 151–2; sent on special duty to the WO, 154; sent on signalling course at Bihucourt, 154; sent back with adverse report, 155; applies for transfer, 156; kicked by mule, 157; feeling ill, 158–164; caught in gas attack, 153, 161; to 44 CCS at Colincamps, 162 and see plate 26b; to Sussex Lodge Hosp, London, 164 to Trefusis Convalescent Hosp, Cornwall, 165, 167 and see plates 27 and 28; starts to write July 1917, 165, 167; sums up adverse report, 166; possibly suffering from nervous breakdown, 167; given 3 months' convalescent leave, 167; joins 3rd Battn Beds Regt, 168 and see plate 29; stationed at Landguard Fort, Felixstowe, 168; Assistant Adjutant at Landguard, 173; attends musketry course, 176; evidence of writing activity, 177; switches name from Home Service to Overseas, 177; embarks for front at Etaples, 27 Mar. 1918, 177, 179, 238n; Hall-Walkers Hosp, 180, 239n; returns to duties at Felixstowe, 181; writing book, 181 finishes with Doris Nicholson, 182; transfer to Indian Army notified and then cancelled, 183; recalled to Felixstowe 8 Nov. 1918, 183; Armistice, 183–4; witnesses German submarines entering Harwich Harbour, 184; transferred to Folkestone, 185; discovers Richard Jeffries, The Story of My Heart, 185; transferred to Cannock Chase, 186; demobilized, 186–7; thoughts after demob., 188–9; goes to live in Devon, 189; 'Policy of Reconstruction', 190; leanings towrds communism in 1920s, 190, influence of Henri Barbusse and Richard Jeffries, 191–2 marries Ida Loetitia Hibbert, 192; return to visit to battlefields, May 1925 (honeymoon), 192–5 and see plate 32; Chyebassa reunion dinners, 196 second visit to battlefields 1927, 197–8, writes First World War articles, 1927, 198, awarded Hawthornden Prize for Literature 1928 for Tarka the Otter, 198; religious and philosophical beliefs, 200–03; Tenth Anniversary of Armistice

1928, 203–4; writing of *The Wet Flanders Plain*, 199–203; writing *The Patriot's Progress*, 204f; the 'Christmas Truce' influence on life, 209, 211; source of 'ancient sunlight' theme, 209; writing *A Chronicle of Ancient Sunlight*, 210f; seeking a fourth dimension 'beyond reality', 212, books as vital memorial to all who took part in the First World War, 212

works by HW, mentioned in the text

'And this was Ypres' ('Vlamertinghe', 'Goldfish Chateaux Mystery', 'How Troop Trains arrived at "Pop"', 'Hotel Skindles'), 198
'Apologia pro vita mea', 199
The Beautiful Years (Vol. 1, Flax), xv, 189, 241n
'A Boy's Nature Diary', 2
'The Christmas Truce', 241n
A Chronicle of Ancient Sunlight, xi, xiv, xvi, 61, 69, 168, 174, 199, 206, 207, 210, 217n, 240n
Dandelion Days (Vol. 2. Flax), 2, 218n
The Flax of Dream, xiv, 189, 198, 210, 241n
A Fox Under My Cloak (Vol. 5, Chronicle), 42, 45–6, 49, 60–72 passim, 217n, 228n
The Golden Virgin (Vol. 6, Chronicle), 72, 74, 75–6, 76, 78, 217n, 229n, 230n, 245
Goodbye West Country, xviii, 190, 245, 219n, 220n,
How Dear is Life (Vol. 4, Chronicle), 7, 9, 11–12, 13, 36, 37, 217, 218n, 219n, 220n, 221n, 245.
'I Believe in the Men Who Died' (later entitled 'Apologia pro vita mea'), 198, 242n
The Labouring Life, essay 'Surview and Farewell', 199
'The Last 100 Days', 202

'The Last Summer', 1, 4–5, 6, 218n
The Lone Swallows, 2, 218n
Love and the Loveless (Vol. 7, Chronicle), 84, 89, 166, 168, 169, 170, 171, 172, 217n, 235–6n, 237n, 245
Lucifer Before Sunrise (Vol. 14, Chronicle), 211, 212
'Money Moon', 181
The Pathway (Vol. 4, Flax), 190, 198
The Patriot's Progress, xi, xiv, 205–7, 217n, 240, 245
'Reality in War Literature' (in *The Linhay on the Downs*), 208, 210, 243n
'Reflections on the Death of a Field Marshal', xiii, 217n
'Return to Hell' (series articles *Evening Stanard*, 1964) including visit to the Plugstreet Wood, 242n
Salar the Salmon, xv
The Scandaroon, xvi,
'The Somme - just Fifty Years After', 241n
'Surview and Farewell' (in *The Labouring Life*), 199
Tarka the Otter, xi, xv, 192, 197, 198
'Ten Years' Remembrance' (Vol. 8, Chronicle), 173, 174–5, 177, 179, 180, 206, 217n, 238–9n
'To An Unknown Soldier', xviii
'The Valley', 203
The Wet Flanders Plain, xi, 198, 199, 200–01, 203, 204, 207, 217n, 240n, 245
'What we should Remember and What Forget', 202, 242–3n
'When I was Demobilised', 186, 188–9, 240n, 241n

fictional characters/events in works by HW

Baldwin, E.W. (London Highlanders – was real name), 11, 220n

Cakebread, Bertie, 233n
Cakebread, Gerry, 233n
Cornford, Lily, 76, 78, 79
Cundall, Tom, 226–7n, 231n
Douglas, Capt., 71
Fairfax, Eve D'Arcy, 185
Forbes, Capt., 11, 219n, 220n
Hobart, Jack, 232n
Gaultshire Regt, 71, 173, 180,
    240n
John Bullock, xiv, 205, 243
Kidd, Maj. Bill, 239n
Kingsman, Capt., 229n
London Highlanders, 36, 37, 42,
    45–6, 219n, 223n
Machine Gun Coy, (286), 84, 168,
    231n
Maddison, Phillip, xiv, 11, 60, 64,
    65, 67, 69, 70, 71, 74, 76, 79,
    84, 168, 171, 172, 173, 175,
    177, 180, 196, 210, 211,
    219n, 238n
Maddison, Richard, 9, 219n, 225n,
    230n
Maddison, Willie, 2, 76, 190, 210
Maddison family home at Colham,
    235n
Minden Day (1 Aug.), 240n
Mortimore, L/Cpl., 11, 12
Neville, Desmond, 78
Pinnegar, Teddy, 232n
'Sailor' Jenkins, 226n
Satchville, Lord, 174
Trident, The, 9
Waterpark, Lt., 68
West, Capt. 'Spectre', 71, 74, 239n,
    240n

Williamson, Henry William (paternal
    grandfather), 40, 223–4n
Williamson, Kathleen (sister), 1, 16,
    17, 28; postcard to, 29 and see
    plate 5; 30, 31, 57, 102, 126,
    165, 223n; and see plate 31a

Williamson, Mary Leopoldina (aunt),
    3, 24–26, 39, 41, 242n
Williamson, Maude (Mrs M. Gregg)
    (aunt), 63, 163
Williamson, Richard (son), viii, 66
Williamson, William Leopold (father),
    xii, xv, 1, 12, 17, 19, 43, 48,
    51, 54, 63, 101, 118, 119,
    137, 144, 147, 160, 165,
    231n; as Special Constable,
    61–2, and see plates 18 and 31a
Willis, Pte (208 MGC), 135, 142
Wilson, President, USA, 89
Wiper's Times, The, 241n
Wishart, Dvr. (208 MGC), 106, 128,
    142
Wisques, Convent at, 38, 40
Woburn (Bedford), 3
Wordsworth, William, 2, 218n
Wright, 2/Lt. (208 MGC), 136, 139,
    141, 161, 166, 235n; and see
    plate 22b
Wrighton, Cpl. (208 MGC), 98
Wynne, Maj. (later Lt. Col.) R.O., DSO
    (Beds Regt), 178, 189, 238n
Wytschaete, in 1914, 36; in 1918,
    180; in 1925, 195

Yeates, Victor, 2, 227n, 231n, 240n
YMCA, 15, 24, for letter headings see
    plate 4
Ypres, First Battle of 35, 39, 45, 124;
    trench foot at (inc. HW) 57;
    Second Battle of, 65, 69; Third
    Battle of, 167, 178; in 1918,
    179
Ypres-Commines Canal, 180
Ypres Times, The, 189
Y Ravine, 91; in 1925, 193
Y Sap, 74

Zeppelin raids, 46, 61, 76–80, 231n;
    and see plate 18c